THE GREENWOOD ENCYCLOPEDIA OF

African American Literature

THE GREENWOOD ENCYCLOPEDIA OF
African American Literature

VOLUME V

U–Z

Edited by

Hans Ostrom and J. David Macey, Jr.

GREENWOOD PRESS
Westport, Connecticut • London

Library of Congress Cataloging-in-Publication Data

The Greenwood encyclopedia of African American literature / edited by Hans Ostrom and J. David Macey, Jr.

    p. cm.

    Includes bibliographical references.

    ISBN 0–313–32972–9 (set : alk. paper)—ISBN 0–313–32973–7 (v. 1 : alk. paper)—
ISBN 0–313–32974–5 (v. 2 : alk. paper)—ISBN 0–313–32975–3 (v. 3 : alk. paper)—
ISBN 0–313–32976–1 (v. 4 : alk. paper)—ISBN 0–313–32977–X (v. 5 : alk. paper) 1. American
literature—African American authors—Encyclopedias. 2. African Americans—Intellectual life—
Encyclopedias. 3. African Americans in literature—Encyclopedias. I. Ostrom, Hans A.
II. Macey, J. David.

    PS153.N5G73   2005

    810.9'896073—dc22   2005013679

British Library Cataloguing in Publication Data is available.

This book is included in the *African American Experience* database from Greenwood Electronic Media.
For more information, visit www.africanamericanexperience.com.

Library of Congress Catalog Card Number: 2005013679

ISBN: 0–313–32972–9 (set)

       0–313–32973–7 (vol. I)

       0–313–32974–5 (vol. II)

       0–313–32975–3 (vol. III)

       0–313–32976–1 (vol. IV)

       0–313–32977–X (vol. V)

First published in 2005

Greenwood Press, 88 Post Road West, Westport, CT 06881
An imprint of Greenwood Publishing Group, Inc.
www.greenwood.com

Printed in the United States of America

The paper used in this book complies with the
Permanent Paper Standard issued by the National
Information Standards Organization (Z39.48–1984).

10 9 8 7 6 5 4 3 2 1

CONTENTS

LIST OF ENTRIES

TOPICAL LIST OF ENTRIES

The following list of entries, organized according to topical categories, includes a complete list of author entries and provides a comprehensive overview of the *Encyclopdedia*'s coverage of the literary, critical, historical, cultural, and regional contexts of African American literature. Please consult the Index for assistance in locating discussions of specific literary texts and other topics.

Athletes and Sports

Ali, Muhammad (born 1942)

Basketball

Campanella, Roy (1921–1993)

Carter, Rubin "Hurricane" (born 1937)

Johnson, Jack (1878–1946)

Jordan, Michael Jeffrey (born 1963)

Louis, Joe (1914–1981)

Mays, Willie Howard, Jr. (born 1931)

Robinson, Jackie [Jack Roosevelt] (1919–1972)

Authors

Abernathy, Ralph David (1926–1990)

Adams, Jenoyne (born 1972)

Adoff, Arnold (born 1935)

Ai (born 1947)

Albert, Octavia Victoria Rogers (1853–1889)

Aldridge, Ira (1807–1867)

Alers, Rochelle (born 1943)

Alexander, Elizabeth (born 1962)

Alexander, Lewis (1900–1945)

Allen, Jeffrey Renard (born 1962)

Allen, Richard (1760–1831)

Allen, Samuel Washington (born 1917)

Allison, Hughes (1908–c. 1974)

Als, Hilton (born 1961)

Amos, Robyn (born 1971)

Anderson, Garland (1886–1939)

Anderson, Mignon Holland (born 1945)

OyamO (born 1943)

Oyewole, Abiodun (born c. 1946)

Packer, ZZ (born 1973)

Parker, Pat (1944–1989)

Parks, Gordon (born 1912)

Parks, Suzan-Lori (born 1963)

Pate, Alexs D. (born 1950)

Patterson, Raymond R. (1929–2001)

Pennington, James William Charles (1807–1870)

Penny, Rob[ert] Lee (1941–2003)

Perdomo, Willie (born 1967)

Perkins, Useni Eugene (born 1932)

Perrin, Kayla (born 1969)

Perry, Charles (1924–1969)

Perry, Phyllis Alesia (born 1961)

Petry, Ann Lane (1908–1997)

Pharr, Robert Deane (1916–1989)

Phillips, Carl (born 1959)

Phillips, Gary (born 1955)

Pinckney, Darryl (born 1953)

Pinkney, Sandra (born 1971) and Myles Pinkney (born 1971)

Plato, Ann (c. 1820–?)

Plumpp, Sterling D. (born 1940)

Polite, Carlene Hatcher (born 1932)

Popel [Shaw], Esther A. B. (1896–1958)

Porter, Connie Rose (born 1959)

Powell, Kevin (born 1969)

Ra, Sun (1914–1993)

Rahman, Aishah (born 1936)

Randall, Dudley Felker (1914–2000)

Randolph, Asa Philip (1889–1979)

Ray, Henrietta Cordelia (c. 1852–1916)

Raymond, Linda (born 1952)

Reed, Ishmael (born 1938)

Reid-Pharr, Robert F. (born 1965)

Remond, Charles Lenox (1810–1873)

Remond, Sarah Parker (1824–1894)

Rhodes, Jewell Parker (born 1954)

Rice, Patty (born c. 1976)

Richardson, Willis (1889–1977)

Ridley, John (born 1965)

Riley, Len

Ringgold, Faith (born 1930)

Rivers, Conrad Kent (1933–1968)

Robinson, C. Kelly (born 1970)

Robotham, Rosemarie Angela (born 1957)

Roby, Kimberla Lawson (born 1965)

Rodgers, Carolyn M[arie] (born c. 1945)

Rose, Tricia (born 1962)

Rowe, George Clinton (1853–1903)

Roy, Lucinda (born 1955)

Rushin, [Donna K.] Kate (born 1951)

Rux, Carl Hancock (born c. 1968)

Salaam, Kalamu ya (born 1947)

Sanchez, Sonia (born 1934)

Sanders, Dori (born 1930)

Sapphire [Lofton, Ramona] (born 1950)

Scarborough, William Sanders (1852–1926)

Schuyler, George Samuel (1895–1977)

Scott-Heron, Gil (born 1949)

Scruggs, Afi-Odelia E. (born 1954)

Seacole, Mary (1805–1881)

Séjour, Victor (1817–1874)

Senna, Danzy (born 1970)

Shackelford, Theodore Henry (1888–1923)

Shaik, Fatima (born 1952)

Shakur, Tupac (1971–1996)

Shange, Ntozake (born 1948)

Shannon, Angela (born 1964)

Historical and Cultural Figures

U

Ulen, Eisa Nefertari (born 1968). Nonfiction writer and novelist. Ulen has contributed essays, articles, and reviews to several publications, including the *Washington Post*, *Ms.*, and *Black Issues Book Review*. She contributed "Letter to Angela Davis" to *Letters of Intent: Women Cross the Generations to Talk About Family, Work, Sex, Love, and the Future of Feminism*. The "Letter" was reprinted in *Step into a World: A Global Anthology of the New Black Literature*, edited by **Kevin Powell**. With Tara Roberts, Ulen wrote "Sisters Spin Talk on Hip Hop" for *Ms.* magazine. For an online publication, *Horizon*, she wrote "Mothers of the Slain," which examines the lives of three women, each of whom had a son who was killed by the police in New York City.

Ulen, a native of **Philadelphia, Pennsylvania**, earned an M.A. at Columbia University, and at this writing is an adjunct lecturer at Hunter College of the City University of New York. In her writing, she is especially interested in "exploring **race**, class, sex, religion, and popular culture" ("Homepage"). In 1999 Ulen was awarded a residency scholarship by the Provincetown Fine Arts Work Center. At this writing, she is at work on a novel tentatively titled *Spirit's Returning Eye*.

Resources: Eisa Nefertari Ulen: Home page, Department of English, Hunter College, http://www.hunter.cuny.edu/~english/adjunct/ulen.shtml; "Letter to Angela Davis," in *Letters of Intent: Women Cross the Generations to Talk About Family, Work, Sex, Love, and the Future of Feminism*, ed. Anna Bondoc and Meg Daly (New York: Free Press, 1999), repr. in *Step into a World: A Global Anthology of the New Black Literature*, ed. Kevin Powell (New York: Wiley, 2000); "Mothers of the Slain," *Horizon*, http://www.horizonmag.com/6/mothers-of-the-slain.asp (1999); Eisa

Nefertari Ulen and Tara Roberts, "Sisters Spin Talk on Hip Hop," Ms., Feb./Mar. 2000, 69–74.

Hans Ostrom

Umbra Workshop (1962–1963). The Umbra Workshop was a collective of Black artists, mostly writers, which existed during the early 1960s on New York City's Lower East Side. The poets **Thomas Covington Dent, David Henderson**, and **Calvin Coolidge Hernton** are generally recognized as having started the group in 1962. Despite the tolerant reputation of the Lower East Side and the various artistic groups emerging from the area, many Black writers felt ignored. The primarily White collectives did not generally address issues that Black writers felt were important. On a larger scale, many also felt that the White literary establishment made it difficult for more than one Black writer to receive recognition at a time. Dent recalls that he and other writers "felt it imperative that we have a device that could deal with **race**, that could serve to bring us together, that could be a vehicle for the expression of the bitterness and the beauties of being Afro-American (as we called ourselves at the time) in this plastic land" (Dent, 106).

Initially, the weekly workshops were held at Dent's apartment and focused on reading and critiquing poetry. Writers who regularly attended included Lloyd Addison, Joe Johnson, **Askia Muhammad Touré** (then Rolland Snellings), Charles and William Patterson, **Lorenzo Thomas**, and **Ishmael Reed**. Visual artists and musicians such as Archie Shepp also participated in the workshops. Although dominated by men, the group did include women, such as Ann Guilfoyle and Brenda Walcott; the latter recalls that in general, the women did not read their poetry, but "were there to serve or observe. It was a very macho group" (Oren, 193). There were also a few white members, including Art Berger and Nora Hicks.

Shortly after they began meeting, the members decided to publish their own literary magazine, choosing the name *Umbra* from a line in one of Addison's poems. Dent, Henderson, and Hernton served as editors. The first issue was published in March 1963 and included a foreword expressing the racial and literary orientation of the magazine. The Black American experience was the basis for the publication, and regardless of what issue was being addressed, all material had to meet a standard of artistic excellence and integrity.

Apart from their commitment to artistic excellence, the group had no specific direction or philosophy. Many of the writers shared feelings of disenchantment with White America and were influenced by the **Civil Rights Movement**. "The young black writers in those years approached their work with a sense of outrage and with a missionary zeal borrowed from the Southern Civil Rights struggle and heightened by an urgency bred by their urban surroundings" (Thomas 1978, 54). The workshops and magazine provided not only an opportunity for these writers to develop their craft, but also a space for expressing feelings of injustice or disillusionment, and to explore notions of **Black Nationalism**. In this sense, Umbra was a predecessor of the **Black Arts**

Movement and helped build a foundation for the artists and aesthetic that emerged later in the decade.

Like some of the other collectives that preceded it, including the Harlem Writers Guild and On Guard for Freedom, Umbra soon experienced the pull of members wanting to take the group in different directions. The magazine editors felt that the literary emphasis should continue, while others, including the Patterson brothers and Touré, felt that a stronger activist and nationalist stance should be taken. There was also jealousy among members who felt that Dent, Henderson, and Hernton often received more attention than the rest of the collective.

By the time the second issue of *Umbra* appeared in December 1963, the group had essentially split apart. It is impossible to single out one particular cause for the split, but the controversy surrounding the refusal to publish a poem by Ray Durem played a large role. In the poem Durem was critical of President Kennedy but, despite some apprehension, the editors agreed to publish it in the second issue. Days later Kennedy was assassinated, and the editors did not publish the poem.

The editors' reversal was especially unpopular among the nationalist members and only added to the existing conflict and tension. The events that followed are unclear. Some claim that the nationalist faction kidnapped a group member and demanded the Umbra bankbook in order to keep the second issue from going to press. Others have denied that any kidnapping took place. What is clear is that the collective could not accommodate so many competing interests, and Umbra ended a little more than a year after its inception.

After the split, Henderson became sole editor of *Umbra* and published three more issues, the final one appearing in 1974. Despite the brief existence of the Umbra Workshop, its impact still resonates in the writers it helped to produce.

Resources: Tom Dent, "Umbra Days," *Black American Literature Forum* 14, no. 3 (Autumn 1980), 105–108; Calvin Hernton, "Umbra: A Personal Recounting," *African American Review* 27, no. 4 (Winter 1993), 579–584; Rashidah Ismaili-Abu-Bakr, "Slightly Autobiographical: The 1960s on the Lower East Side," *African American Review* 27, no. 4 (Winter 1993), 585–592; Daniel Kane, *All Poets Welcome: The Lower East Side Poetry Scene in the 1960s* (Berkeley: University of California Press, 2003); Aldon Lynn Nielsen, *Black Chant: Languages of African-American Postmodernism* (New York: Cambridge University Press, 1997); Michael Oren, "The Umbra Poets' Workshop, 1962–1965: Some Socio-Literary Puzzles," in *Belief vs. Theory in Black American Literary Criticism*, ed. Joseph Weixlmann and Chester J. Fontenot (Greenwood, FL: Penkevill, 1986), 177–223; Eugene Redmond, *Drumvoices: The Mission of Afro-American Poetry* (Garden City, NY: Anchor Books, 1976); Lorenzo Thomas: "Alea's Children: The Avant-garde on the Lower East Side, 1960–1970," *African American Review* 27, no. 4 (Winter 1993), 573–578; "The Shadow World: New York's Umbra Workshop and Origins of the Black Arts Movement," *Callaloo* 4 (Oct. 1978), 53–72.

Raquel Rodriguez

Uncle Tom. Literary character and epithet. The literary character of Uncle Tom first appeared in **Harriet Beecher Stowe**'s 1852 antislavery novel *Uncle Tom's Cabin*. In the book, Uncle Tom is strong, noble, wise, and kind-hearted; he is also a messianic figure who ultimately gives his life in order to save the lives and souls of those around him, both White and Black. Regardless of whether Uncle Tom is interacting with his fellow man or woman in bondage or with a demonic and undeserving character such as the brutal Simon Legree, he appears to have a consistent view of how to behave toward people. Ironically, however, in cheap theater productions and minstrel show adaptations of the book in the late nineteenth and early twentieth centuries, Uncle Tom lost the original Christlike qualities and, through lazy and inaccurate interpretation of the character in the book, took on the negative characteristics of a cowardly and sycophantic Black slave who never contradicted or opposed White "owners," and who went out of his way to acquiesce to the wishes and whims of White individuals in society.

While this interpretation of Uncle Tom is not consistent with an original reading of *Uncle Tom's Cabin*, the negative connotations from the interpretations of the book in the late nineteenth and early twentieth centuries have largely persisted through today. As Alfred Kazin has noted, this negative meaning is not based upon the book *Uncle Tom's Cabin*, but rather upon "the garish dramatizations of Uncle Tom that flourished for decades after the Civil War" (Kazin, vii). In fact, according to Kazin, "Uncle Tom . . . [became] such [a] worn-out symbol that without knowing the book," people use the term Uncle Tom in a derogatory fashion, "without altogether remembering that they have, in fact, never read *Uncle Tom's Cabin*" (vii). Today, the term "Uncle Tom" is used by many in a derogatory fashion to connote an African American who is subservient or servile to White interests. Indeed, the term "Uncle Tom" has even been used to describe Black critics of such programs as **affirmative action** and those who refuse to challenge and/or criticize the current political power structure.

Stowe's passionate attack on **slavery** in *Uncle Tom's Cabin* took the form of a fictional narrative in which the lives of slaves were juxtaposed against the barbarous institution of slavery. The main purpose of Stowe's book was to illustrate the cruelty, barbarity, and deleterious impact of the institution of slavery upon the country as a whole, and upon the lives and suffering of the Black slaves in particular. Uncle Tom, the key character in Stowe's book, suffers a host of trials and tribulations thrust upon him as a consequence of being born into the heinous institution of slavery. Uncle Tom's journey in the book begins with his being sold by his owner, Mr. Shelby, in Kentucky, to satisfy Shelby's gambling debts and poor business decisions. Mr. Shelby sells Uncle Tom despite the facts that Uncle Tom had reared Mr. Shelby since birth, that Uncle Tom was the most valuable and trusted slave on the Shelby property, and that Shelby had promised Uncle Tom his freedom. After being sold to a slave broker, he is bought by Augustine St. Clare as a gift and companion to his daughter Eva. After the death of both Eva and Augustine

St. Clare, Uncle Tom is sold again, this time to the evil Simon Legree, who ultimately murders Uncle Tom by beating him a fit of rage.

Uncle Tom is described in the most glowing and flattering ways throughout the book, and comes across as its strongest and most noble figure, which has caused some twentieth-century writers to describe Uncle Tom as the first Black hero of American literature. He is a physically powerful character; he is not weak. The first physical description of Uncle Tom appears in chapter 4 of the book, where he is described as "a large, broad-chested, powerfully-made man of a full glossy black, and a face whose truly African features were characterized by an expression of grave and steady good sense, united with much kindliness and benevolence" (Stowe, 21). He is also described later in chapter 4 as "a sort of patriarch in religious matters . . . [h]aving, naturally, an organization in which the morale was strongly predominant, together with a greater breadth and cultivation of mind than obtained among his companions" (Stowe, 29).

Several passages in the book make clear that his character was intended to be a Christlike messianic figure. Early in the book, Uncle Tom is told by another slave that she overheard that he is to be sold by Mr. Shelby the next morning. Uncle Tom specifically rejects the possibility of fleeing, saying that it would be better that he be sacrificed, so that no other Black lives would be adversely impacted on the Shelby property. In chapter 5, the evening before being sold by Shelby, Uncle Tom states that "[i]f I must be sold, or all the people on the place, and everything go to rack, why, let me be sold. I s'pose I can b'ar it as well as any on 'em" (Stowe, 37). Much later in the book, Uncle Tom has an opportunity to kill the evil Simon Legree, or to run away. He refuses to kill any human being and also refuses to run away. In describing why he will not flee with another slave, Uncle Tom states that "the Lord's given me a work among these yer poor souls, and I'll stay with 'em and *bear my cross* with 'em till the end" (Stowe, 395; emphasis added). Last, in the passage in involving Uncle Tom's murder by Simon Legree, the Christ comparison is clear. Uncle Tom is suspended off the ground in some fashion and beaten by Legree and his two Black overseers. At the end of his beating, in words reminiscent of Christ on the cross, Uncle Tom utters words of forgiveness to his attackers and says, "Ye poor miserable critter . . . there an't no more ye can do! I forgive ye, with all my soul" (Stowe, 411). After Simon Legree leaves, the two Black attackers feel compunction and remorse, "took him down," and "washed his wounds" (Stowe, 412).

Finally, those who have argued that Uncle Tom represents a sycophantic Black usually do not take into account the last portion of *Uncle Tom's Cabin*, where Uncle Tom is savagely beaten and ultimately murdered because he did not follow Simon Legree's inhuman edicts. Simon Legree originally purchases Uncle Tom to have Uncle Tom serve as a general manager and overseer of the slaves on Legree's plantation. However, Uncle Tom refuses to treat any slave with harshness, and "in a various ways manifested a tenderness of feeling, a commiseration for his fellow-sufferers" (Stowe, 349), knowing that he will probably suffer severe punishment. For example, he refuses to whip a slave when ordered to do so by Legree. This type of behavior is confounding to Legree, who is used to getting his way through his brutal and liberal use of beatings and deprivations. Indeed, Uncle Tom suffers terrible beatings precisely because he refuses to follow Simon Legree's inhuman orders. Shortly before the murder of Uncle Tom, Legree fumes that "I've made up my mind, and counted the cost. *You've always stood it out agin' me: now, I'll conquer ye, or kill ye!*—one or t'other. I'll count every drop of blood there is in you, and take 'em, one by one, *till ye give up!*" (Stowe, 410; emphasis added). Legree murders Uncle Tom in large part because Uncle Tom refuses to reveal the hiding place of two slaves.

The book was very popular, selling over 300,000 copies the first year, and significantly caused many individuals to join the **abolitionist movement** in seeking the eradication of slavery within the United States. It has been said that *Uncle Tom's Cabin* "hastened that dawn of a better day for the Negro. It did not cause the Civil War but it did, more than any other single factor, rally northern opinion against slavery and the South" (Commager, 98). Abraham Lincoln said it best in 1863, when meeting Harriet Beecher Stowe, he exclaimed "so you're the little woman who wrote the book that made this great war" (Commager, 98). Even harsh critics of the novel regard it as a kind of touchstone; for example, in his essay "Everybody's Protest Novel" (1949), **James Baldwin** describes the book as "a very bad novel, having, in its self-righteous, virtuous sentimentality, much in common with *Little Women*" (11–12). Nevertheless, Baldwin uses Stowe's novel as a key reference in his critique of a novel by his contemporary **Richard Wright**, *Native Son*.

Resources: James Baldwin, "Everybody's Protest Novel," in his *Collected Essays* (New York: Library of America, 1998), 11–19; Evan Brandstadter, "Uncle Tom and Archy Moore: The Antislavery Novel as Ideological Symbol," *American Quarterly* 26, no. 2 (1974), 160–175; Henry Steele Commager, *Illustrated History of the Civil War* (New York: Promontory Press, 1976); Alfred Kazin, "Introduction to Uncle Tom's Cabin," in *Uncle Tom's Cabin*, by Harriet Beecher Stowe (New York: Bantam Books, 1981); Harriet Beecher Stowe, *Uncle Tom's Cabin* (1852; repr. New York: Bantam Books, 1981); Mfanya D. Tryman, "Uncle Tom," in *Affirmative Action, An Encyclopedia*, vol. 2, ed. James A. Beckman (Westport, CT: Greenwood Press, 2004).

James A. Beckman

Underground Railroad. The Underground Railroad was a network of people, houses, and communication links by which escaped slaves could first remain in hiding and then flee to the North, to Canada, or to Mexico. Members of the Underground Railroad included free Blacks, former slaves, and White abolitionists, including Quakers, Mennonites, and pastors from other denominations. Before the 1840s, the system of resistance and aid was called the Underground Road. It is estimated that between the Revolutionary War and the **Civil War**, 100,000 people escaped **slavery**; many of them received aid from the Underground Railroad, which became more organized between 1831 and 1865. The dangerous nature of the road to freedom necessitated secrecy to ensure the safety of the helper and the fugitive; therefore, documentation is not readily available with regard to many aspects of the operation. "Conductors" on the Railroad included **Josiah Henson** and **Harriet Tubman** (nicknamed Moses because she led her people to freedom), who were former slaves. Some conductors also lectured, wrote, and shared experiences by interview. For example, Henson, who met **Harriet Beecher Stowe**, provided her with a model for a character in the antislavery novel *Uncle Tom's Cabin* (1852). Henson's **autobiography**, *The Life of Josiah Henson...As Narrated by Himself*, a **slave narrative**, was published in 1849. Approximately seventy slave narratives were published from 1760 onward, and the link between this genre of literature and the Underground Railroad is considerable. Frequently, the **Abolitionist Movement** funded the publication of slave narratives, which have influenced novels by African Americans up to the present time as well as novels written by Whites, including *The Adventures of Huckleberry Finn* (1884), by **Mark Twain**. Some of the most recognizable slave narratives are Frederick Douglass's *Narrative of the Life of Frederick Douglass* (1845), **Henry "Box" Brown**'s *Narrative of the Life of Henry Box Brown, Written by Himself* (1851), **Harriet Ann Jacobs**'s *Incidents in the Life of a Slave Girl* (1861), and **Booker T. Washington**'s *Up from Slavery* (1901). Patterns and themes from slave narratives, a literature of resistance, can be found in **Alex Haley**'s *The Autobiography of Malcolm X* (1965), **Toni Morrison**'s *Beloved* (1987), and **Charles Johnson**'s *Middle Passage* (1990), to name a few.

Other Underground Railroad activists, such as **Sojourner Truth**, took to the podium to promote equal rights; she also helped escaped slaves find shelter. **John Brown**, a White man, took up arms. Harriet Tubman aided John Brown in recruitment for his raid on Harper's Ferry. Three of the African Americans who participated in the raid were from Oberlin College, Ohio, a center for abolitionist planning. Brown had conceived of securing Harper's Ferry as a way station for escapees en route to Pennsylvania. He and his coconspirators were hanged for the attempt.

Candles in the window, quilts, and songs were used to direct slaves to freedom. Rev. John Rankin of Ripley, Ohio, kept a candle in the window of his house to indicate a safe haven. Quilts were used as maps, and songs encoded plans. No bridges existed across the Ohio River before the Civil War, but John Parker, an African American, would guide people across the river to Rankin's. He and Rankin are credited with conducting thousands to safety. A fugitive, Eliza Harris, accompanied by her two-year-old son, is immortalized in Stowe's *Uncle Tom's Cabin*.

Another type of station was a community of free Blacks, one of which existed in Cincinnati. Morrison depicts this community in *Beloved*. Other such communities existed in Florida, where **Zora Neale Hurston**, an author and anthropologist, and Alan Lomax, a Caucasian ethnographer, stayed in 1935 to collect songs, **folklore**, and personal histories from former slaves. Also, in the 1930s the Works Progress Administration collected stories from

An undated watercolor of slaves fleeing to the North. Courtesy of the Library of Congress.

former slaves that are preserved at the Library of Congress. Cincinnati, referred to as the Grand Central Station of the Underground Railroad, will house the National Underground Freedom Center.

People of both races, many nameless and faceless, broke the law in the name of justice, especially after the Fugitive Slave Law of 1850, but the slaves themselves primarily engineered the Underground Railroad; they kept it on track until it was no longer needed.

Resources: *The African American Almanac*, 8th ed., ed. Jessie Carney Smith and Joseph Palmisano (Detroit: Gale, 2000); William Andrews, "Narrating Slavery," in *Teaching African American Literature: Theory and Practice*, ed. Marianna Davis et al. (New York: Routledge, 1998); Henry "Box" Brown, *Narrative of the Life of Henry Box Brown, Written by Himself* (1851; repr. New York: Oxford University Press, 2002); Frederick Douglass, *Life and Times of Frederick Douglass, Written by Himself* (Hartford, CT: Park, 1882); Henry Louis Gates, Jr., "Introduction," in *The Bondswoman's Narrative*, by Hannah Crafts (ca. 1850; repr. New York: Warner Books, 2002); J. Blaine Hudson, *Fugitive Slaves and the Underground Railroad in the Kentucky Borderland* (Jefferson, NC: McFarland, 2002); Harriet A. Jacobs, *Incidents in the Life of a Slave Girl* (1861; repr. New York: Signet Classics, 2000); Robin Kelley and Earl Lewis, eds., *To Make Our World Anew: A History of African Americans* (New York: Oxford University Press, 2000); Lawrence W. Levine, *Black Culture and Black Consciousness: Afro-American Folk Thought from Slavery to Freedom* (New York: Oxford University Press, 1977); National Parks Service, *Underground Railroad: Special Resource Guide*, http://www.nps.gov/undergroundrr/contents.htm; National Underground Railroad Freedom Center, http://www.undergroundrailroad.org; Wilbur H. Siebert, *The Underground Railroad from Slavery to Freedom* (1898; repr. New York: Russell & Russell,

1967); Harriet Beecher Stowe, *Uncle Tom's Cabin* (1852; repr. New York: Modern Library, 1985); Mark Twain, *The Adventures of Huckleberry Finn* (1884; repr. New York: Book-of-the-Month Club, 1992); Booker T. Washington, *Up from Slavery* (1901; repr. New York: New York Limited Editions Club, 1970).

Claudia Matherly Stolz

Utopian Literature. The word "utopia" originates from the Greek words *outopia* (no place) and *eutopia* (good place) and usually signifies a nonexistent, ideal place. Because the word *utopia* can mean both "no place" and "good place," it has a variety of connotations. We can view utopian texts as presenting a nonexistent but ideal arrangement of possibilities that we should strive for. Or, to borrow Ernst Bloch's definition, we can approach utopian narratives as presenting the "Not-Yet-Conscious" but "real and concrete final state which can be achieved politically" (Suksang, 130). Of course, utopias can also be taken as flights of fancy aimed at entertaining the reader. Whichever view of utopian literature is emphasized, it is certain that utopias, especially works of utopian literature, have the power to "defamiliarize us with our own society, allowing us to see clearly its failings" (Jones, 119).

Utopia (1516), by the English writer Sir Thomas More, gave its name to the literary genre. In this tract written in Latin, More named his imaginary republic Utopia, perhaps creating "an ambiguous midterm" between the words *outopia* and *eutopia* (Mumford, 8). The work contrasts the laws, social order, and customs of Utopia with those in sixteenth-century England. More's is certainly not the oldest utopia ever written, however. We can find a description of an earthly paradise in the epic *Gilgamesh*, written sometime in the second millennium B.C.E. Plato, in his *Republic* (360 B.C.E.), provided an outline of an ideal society ruled by a philosopher-king. *The City of God* (413), by St. Augustine, developed the notion of an attainable paradise even though for Augustine it was a heavenly rather than an earthly city. Christine de Pisan wrote *The Book of the City of Ladies* (1404–1405), in which Christine, with Reason, Rectitude, and Justice, builds a city whose goal is to provide "a refuge and defense" to "ladies and all valiant women" (10). And there are, of course, the many legends and stories of "the land of plenty" where people do not have to work, food is plentiful, and a general feeling of pleasure, ease, and luxury prevails. Many writers after More have presented their literary visions of utopia: Tommaso Campanella, in *City of the Sun* (1602); Margaret Cavendish, in *The Description of a New World, Called the Blazing World* (1666); Francis Bacon, in *New Atlantis* (1626); Samuel Johnson, in *Rasselas* (1759); Samuel Butler, in *Erewhon* (1872) (Erewhon is Nowhere spelled backward); William Morris, in *News from Nowhere* (1890); H. G. Wells, in *A Modern Utopia* (1904); and B. F. Skinner, in *Walden Two* (1948).

The second half of the nineteenth century saw a proliferation of utopian literature in the United States. According to Kenneth Roemer, more than 150 utopian works were published between 1888 and 1900 (8). Optimistic about the industrial development and excited about the possible social progress of the country, some utopian writers reflected in their works their faith in the bright future but also, through comparison with their utopian worlds, pointed out the appalling conditions in which many people lived in contemporary society. The most popular utopia of the nineteenth century, and probably the most successful and widely read American utopia ever, is *Looking Backward, 2000–1887* (1888), by Edward Bellamy. In Bellamy's novel, Julian West wakes up after more than a century-long sleep in Boston in the year 2000. The family of Dr. Leete familiarizes him with new inventions and explains to him the changes in society that have led to the dramatic metamorphosis of the whole country. Bellamy's novel, as a call for social reform, presents America in the year 2000 as the place where people do not lack anything and live in harmony. The portrayal of women in the twentieth century America is, however, one of the novel's shortcomings; their conditions and behavior adhere to Victorian values and concepts. It is also important to note that even though utopian works usually strive to present ideal worlds, the issue of **race** seems irrelevant to the majority of these visions published before the second half of the twentieth century. These utopias are either openly racist or, at best, ignore the racial question.

The utopian genre has served as a vehicle for drawing attention to social, economic, and political problems in general, but it has also proved to be an excellent means of expression for women and their issues. In her novel *Mizora: A World of Women* (1890), Mary Bradley Lane presents a portrait of an all-female and self-sufficient society. The society of women abounds with scientific inventions and focuses on health, education, and fulfillment of the female citizens. Charlotte Perkins Gilman, widely known for her short story "The Yellow Wallpaper" (1892), wrote several utopias, of which *Herland* (1915) is certainly the most renowned. Like Lane, Gilman comments on the relationship between men and women and stresses that the development of females and, consequently, society as a whole has been hindered by social and cultural constraints placed upon women. In the 1970s, the feminist movement rediscovered the utopian genre and caused its second boom in the United States, focusing on the criticism of the patriarchal norms and values and on the subjects of **gender**, women's roles, community, and ecology. *The Female Man* (1975), by Joanna Russ; *The Dispossessed: An Ambiguous Utopia* (1974), by Ursula K. Le Guin; *Woman on the Edge of Time* (1976), by Marge Piercy; *Motherlines* (1978), by Suzy McKee Charnas; and *The Shore of Women* (1986), by Pamela Sargent, are some of the numerous feminist utopias written in the 1970s and 1980s.

Although they were not numerous, some African American writers at the turn of the twentieth century utilized the utopian genre to address sociopolitical problems specific to African Americans. While these writers followed the conventions of the genre, they also made it distinctively African American. The majority of utopian societies in the works of European and White American writers are usually separated in time or space from the contemporary society, but the utopias by African American writers often use what

M. Giulia Fabi calls "race travel as the distinctive device that structures these texts" and present American society "from the displaced, marginalized perspective of segregated black Americans" (46). Examples of such works include **Frances Ellen Watkins Harper**'s *Iola Leroy* (1892), **Sutton E. Griggs**'s *Imperium in Imperio* (1899), **Pauline Elizabeth Hopkins**'s *Of One Blood* (1902–1903), Edward A. Johnson's *Light Ahead for the Negro* (1904), and Lilian Jones's *Five Generations Hence* (1916). Later in the twentieth century, more utopias by African American writers appeared. In **Samuel R. Delany**'s *Trouble on Triton: An Ambiguous Heterotopia* (1976), an interplanetary war is waged between a utopian society and the planet Earth. **Octavia E. Butler**'s Xenogenesis trilogy—*Dawn* (1987), *Adulthood Rites* (1988), and *Imago* (1989)—also has some utopian elements. The trilogy starts 250 years after the planet Earth was destroyed by a nuclear war and ends with a new human colony on Mars. Finally, one could argue that **Toni Morrison**'s *Paradise* (1998) is a utopian work that juxtaposes two attempts for an ideal community: Ruby, an all-black town run by men, and the all-female Convent. These gendered alternatives of paradise fail, however, when one turns against the other.

Resources: Ernst Bloch, *The Utopian Function of Art and Literature: Selected Essays* (Cambridge, MA: MIT Press, 1988); Christine de Pisan, *The Book of the City of Ladies*, trans. Earl Jeffrey Richards (New York: Persea Books, 1998); Robert C. Elliott, *The Shape of Utopia: Studies in a Literary Genre* (Chicago: University of Chicago Press, 1970); M. Giulia Fabi, "Race Travel in Turn-of-the-Century African American Utopian Fiction," in her *Passing and the Rise of the African American Novel* (Urbana: University of Illinois Press, 2001), 44–71; Edward A. Johnson, *Light Ahead for the Negro* (1904; repr. New York: AMS, 1975); Libby Falk Jones, "Gilman, Bradley, Piercy, and the Evolving Rhetoric of Feminist Utopias," in *Feminism, Utopia, and Narrative*, ed. Libby Falk Jones and Sarah Webster Goodwin (Knoxville: University of Tennessee Press, 1990), 116–129; Lillian Jones, *Five Generations Hence* (Fort Worth, TX: Dotson-Jones, 1916); Frank E. Manuel and Fritzie P. Manuel, *Utopian Thought in the Western World* (Cambridge, MA: Belknap Press, 1979); Tom Moylan, *Demand the Impossible: Science Fiction and the Utopian Imagination* (New York: Methuen, 1986); Lewis Mumford, "Utopia, the City and the Machine," in *Utopias and Utopian Thought*, ed. Frank E. Manuel (Boston: Houghton Mifflin, 1966); Kenneth Roemer, *The Obsolete Necessity: America in Utopian Writings, 1888–1900* (Kent, OH: Kent State University Press, 1976); Duangrudi Suksang, "A World of Their Own: The Separatist Utopian Vision of Mary E. Bradley Lane's *Mizora*," in *Redefining the Political Novel: American Women Writers, 1797–1901*, ed. Sharon M. Harris (Knoxville: University of Tennessee Press, 1995), 128–148.

Iva Balic

V

Van Der Zee, James (1886–1983). Photographer. Van Der Zee is well known in part for having photographed notable African Americans, including the writer **Countee Cullen**, and for documenting life in **Harlem, New York**. Born in Lenox, Massachusetts, Van Der Zee moved to New York City in 1905 and permanently settled there in 1910. His first camera, received as payment for selling perfume, failed to work, but Van Der Zee learned the basics of photography from its instructions. He bought another camera and began taking photos while still in Lenox. He had his first job at an inexpensive photography studio in Newark, New Jersey, in 1915. Though he worked in the darkroom, he filled in as photographer when needed, taking the time to pose his subjects for their photographs. Soon Van Der Zee had acquired a clientele of his own. In 1917 he opened the Guarantee Photo Studio, which changed its name to G.G.G. Studio when incorporated (for Gaynella Grenly Greenlee, his second wife, whom he married in 1918).

Van Der Zee is noted for his documentation, mostly through group portraits, of the prime years of Harlem's vibrancy and prosperity. Soft focus and trompe l'oeil backdrops that recall early modern European paintings are among his hallmarks. His oeuvre also encompasses many scenes of African American businesses, including barbershops and shop windows. In the 1920s Van Der Zee was commissioned to photograph New York activities of **Marcus Garvey**'s United Negro Improvement Association, and over his career he photographed many prominent African Americans, including Mamie Smith and Hazel Scott, Daddy Grace, Father Divine, Adam Clayton Powell, Sr. and Jr., the heiress A'Lelia Walker, and the boxers Harry Wills, **Jack Johnson**, and **Joe Louis**. (At the end of his life he again photographed famous subjects such as **Romare Bearden, Muhammad Ali**, Jean-Michel Basquiat, Eubie Blake, and Lou Rawls.) Van Der Zee's studio was located at various times at 109 W. 135th Street (until 1930), at 2070 7th Avenue (until 1943), and finally at the house he bought at 272 Lenox Avenue. There his studio operated until 1969, when the property was repossessed.

In 1969 Van Der Zee was featured in the controversial exhibit "Harlem on My Mind" at the Metropolitan Museum of Art, which brought his photographs to national attention and led to the publication of the first catalog of his work, *The World of James Van Der Zee: A Visual Record of Black Americans* (1969). After this exhibit he was named Honorary Fellow for Life at the Metropolitan Museum of Art and featured in Evelyn Barron's documentary *Uncommon Images: James Van Der Zee* (1979), and he received honorary doctorates (including one from Howard University in 1983) and the U.S. Living Legacy Award (1978). In 1978 a book of his funeral home photographs was published, *The Harlem Book of the Dead*. The photographs are interspersed with poetry by **Owen Dodson** and an extended interview with Van Der Zee about his life and attitudes toward death. **Toni Morrison**, who wrote the book's foreword, used one of these photographs, of a woman shot by her lover, as inspiration for her novel *Jazz* (1992). A family photo from 1926 helped Roland Barthes explain a crucial section of his theory of photography in *Camera Lucida* (1981).

Resources: Roland Barthes, *Camera Lucida: Reflections on Photograhy*, trans. Richard Howard (New York: Hill and Wang, 1981); Kobena Mercer, *James Van Der Zee* (New York: Phaidon, 2003); Toni Morrison, *Jazz* (New York: Knopf, 1992); Deborah Willis Ryan, "James Van Der Zee," in *Harlem Renaissance: Art of Black America*, by David Driskell, David L. Lewis, and Deborah Ryan (New York: Abrams, 1987), 155–167; James Van Der Zee, *The World of James Van Der Zee: A Visual Record of Black Americans*, ed. Reginald McGhee (New York: Grove, 1969); James Van Der Zee, Owen Dodson, and Camille Billops, *The Harlem Book of the Dead* (Dobbs Ferry, NY: Morgan and Morgan, 1978).

Ian W. Wilson

Van Peebles, Melvin (born 1932). Filmmaker, playwright, novelist, memoirist, and nonfiction writer. Although Van Peebles is best known for his filmmaking, he is also the author of plays, screenplays, novels, memoirs, books on finance, and works of nonfiction. Melvin Van Peebles was born August 21, 1932, on the South Side of **Chicago, Illinois**, and grew up in the suburb of Phoenix, Illinois. In 1953, he graduated from Ohio Wesleyan University with a degree in English literature. After college, he served four years in the Air Force as a flight navigator. Unable to find employment in the domestic aviation industry, Van Peebles moved to **San Francisco, California**, where he worked as a cable car operator. In 1959, he published *The Big Heart*, dealing with his employment in San Francisco, and was fired from his cable car job. After experimenting with some low budget films, Van Peebles was frustrated that he could not find employment with a major film studio.

He moved his family to the Netherlands, where he briefly studied at the University of Amsterdam. After breaking up with his wife in 1960, Van Peebles moved to France and continued to explore artistic possibilities on the Continent. Although his French was self-taught, Van Peebles published five novels in France. In 1967, he directed *The Story of a Three Day Pass*, about an affair between a Black American soldier and a young, White French woman.

Favorable reviews of *The Story of a Three Day Pass* led Van Peebles to return to the United States and an assignment from Columbia Pictures to direct *Watermelon Man* (1970), featuring the comedian Godfrey Cambridge. Reviews for *Watermelon Man* were mixed, but the film did make money. Van Peebles used his profits from the film to finance *Sweet Sweetback's Baadasssss Song* (1971). Many film historians credit *Sweetback* as beginning the wave of **blaxploitation** films of the 1970s in which, for better or worse, Hollywood discovered Black audiences. Made on a shoestring budget of $500,000 and shot in only nineteen days, *Sweetback* grossed over $10 million. Van Peebles wrote, directed, and starred in this picture which he credited as featuring the Black community. Essentially, the film tells the story of a Black pimp and sexual performer whose consciousness is aroused when he sees a community activist beaten by the police. Sweetback attacks the police officers and becomes the subject of an intensive manhunt. Through his ingenuity, sexual prowess, and, most important, support from the Black community, Sweetback is able to flee the authorities and escape into Mexico. The film concludes with the caption "A Baadasssss Nigger Is Coming Back to Collect Some Dues."

After his success with *Sweetback*, Van Peebles turned his attention to Broadway, producing *Ain't Supposed to Die a Natural Death* (1971) and *Don't Play Us Cheap* (1972). He also tried his hand at television with *Just an Old Sweet Song* (1976) and the well-regarded 1981 miniseries *The Sophisticated Gents*. His 1982 autobiographical play, *Waltz of the Stork*, was poorly received, but Van Peebles the hustler continued to make money, enjoying success as a floor trader on Wall Street and describing his business success in *Bold Money: A New Way to Play the Options Market*.

His business interests did not distract Van Peebles from pursing his artistic endeavors. In 1986 his teleplay *The Day They Came to Arrest the Book* won an Emmy. In 1990 he directed his son Mario in *Identity Crisis*, and in 1993 the son reciprocated by featuring his father in *Posse*. Their collaboration continued in 1995 with *Panther*, in which Mario directed a film about the origins of the **Black Panther Party** from a novel and script produced by his father. Van Peebles remains a renaissance man pursing his business and artistic concerns.

Resources: Don Bogle, *Blacks in American Films and Television: An Encyclopedia* (New York: Garland, 1988); Anthony Loeb, *Filmmakers in Conversation* (Chicago: Columbia College Press, 1982); Melvin Van Peebles: *Ain't Supposed to Die a Natural Death* (New York: Bantam Books, 1973); *A Bear for the F.B.I.* (New York: Trident, 1968); *Bold Money: A New Way to Play the Options Market* (New York: Warner Books, 1986); *Don't Play Us Cheap: A Harlem Party* (New York: Bantam Books, 1973); *The*

Making of Sweet Sweetback's Baadasssss Song (New York: Lancer Books, 1972); *The True American* (New York: Doubleday, 1976); Melvin Van Peebles, dir., *The Story of a Three-Day Pass* (1968; repr. Los Angeles: Xenon 2, 1996), VHS format; Melvin Van Peebles and Mario Van Peebles, *No Identity Crisis: A Father and Son's Own Story of Working Together* (New York: Simon and Schuster, 1990).

Ron Briley

Van Vechten, Carl (1880–1964). Writer, critic, photographer, patron of the arts, and man of letters. Born in Cedar Rapids, Iowa, Van Vechten graduated from the University of Chicago, where he majored in English and began writing for the *Chicago American*, a Hearst newspaper, during his senior year. He joined the staff of the *New York Times* in 1907 as an assistant music critic. He became the paper's first dance critic, chiefly because his boss did not want the job. During a visit to **Paris, France**, in 1914, Van Vechten met the socialite Mabel Dodge (Luhan), who introduced him to Gertrude Stein. Back in New York, Van Vechten and his wife, the Russian-born actress Fania Marinoff, became regulars at Dodge's salons in her Fifth Avenue apartment. There they met artists, performers, writers, and Bohemian intellectuals. In 1915, Van Vechten published a collection of his music criticism in book form, and followed it with five more books over the next four years. He became one of **Alfred A. Knopf**'s Borzoi writers and had connections to both mainstream and avant-garde publishing houses. During this period, Van Vechten began his practice of championing unknown and aspiring writers and helping them publish their work. Gertrude Stein was among his earliest finds. Later successes included **James Weldon Johnson, Langston Hughes, Zora Neale Hurston**, and Wallace Stevens.

Beginning in 1922, Van Vechten wrote seven novels. Most successful was *Nigger Heaven*, published in 1926. A best-seller that went through twelve printings in ten months, it attempted to capture the essence of Black culture at the height of the **Harlem Renaissance**. *Nigger Heaven* tells the story of a failed romance between an aspiring Black writer trying to break into the largely White world of publishing and an unassuming, proper, well-read middle-class librarian. Van Vechten overloads the novel with lessons on Black history and literature; social issues inside and outside **Harlem, New York**; vignettes of Harlem life, endorsements of Gertrude Stein, Langston Hughes, **Charles Waddell Chesnutt**, and other favorites; and a "Glossary of Negro Words and Phrases." Small wonder that one reviewer called Van Vechten "the Baedeker of the intelligentsia" (Beach, 141). Hughes came to his patron's aid when Van Vechten faced a lawsuit for using bits of copyrighted song lyrics throughout the book. Over a weekend, Hughes wrote replacement lyrics to fit the spaces left when the pirated material was removed. The novel divided critics. **W.E.B. Du Bois** assailed it as "a blow in the face.... An affront... not a true picture of Harlem life" (81–82), while James Weldon Johnson defended it as an accurate depiction of Harlem "from the dregs to the froth" and praised Van Vechten's astonishing "inside knowledge and insight" (316–317, 330). In retrospect, *Nigger Heaven* survives as an important, even essential, cultural artifact for the serious student of the Harlem Renaissance, despite its many artistic failings.

Van Vechten's popular success and a sizable family inheritance ensured a comfortable income for life and allowed him the luxury of pursuing his interests in arts and letters. It also allowed him to throw legendary parties at his Manhattan apartment in the 1920s. His soirées were eclectic mixtures of guests, both Black and White. Socialites, artists, actors, and writers from Manhattan rubbed elbows with Harlem counterparts, many of whose careers Van Vechten hoped to boost into a wider following.

After novel-writing, photography became Van Vechten's primary means of artistic expression. He photographed the famous and near-famous in a make-shift studio in his apartment and showed particular skill at photographing Black subjects, Zora Neale Hurston, **Paul Robeson**, and Langston Hughes among them. Much of Van Vechten's best work was published in the 1993 collection *Generations in Black and White*.

In 1941, Van Vechten established the James Weldon Johnson Memorial Collection of Negro Arts and Letters at Yale University. He founded two special collections at Fisk University: the George Gershwin Memorial Collection of Music and Musical Literature in 1944 and the Stettheimer Memorial Collection of Books About the Fine Arts in 1949. In 1946 he founded the McClendon Memorial Collection of Photographs of Celebrated Negroes at Howard University. That same year he became Gertrude Stein's literary executor upon her death. Fisk awarded him an honorary degree in 1955. In 1961, three years before his death at eighty-one, Carl Van Vechten was named to the National Institute of Arts and Letters.

Van Vechten's life and works help illuminate issues of White patronage in the Harlem Renaissance, a movement that Bruce Kellner convincingly argues "would never have progressed beyond Harlem without the intervention and support of white

Undated drawing of Carl Van Vechten. Yale Collection of American Literature, Beinecke Rare Book and Manuscript Library.

patrons" ("Refined Racism," 93). Additionally, *Nigger Heaven* certainly raises questions about how legitimately and effectively White authors can write about the imagined, rather than lived, experience of being Black. Langston Hughes offered a succinct and straightforward perspective on the patronage issue. Recalling his early association with Van Vechten, he wrote, "What Carl

Van Vechten did for me was to submit my first book of poems to Alfred A. Knopf, put me in contact with the editors of *Vanity Fair* . . . caused me to meet many editors . . . cheered me on in the writing of my first short stories, and otherwise aided in making life for me more profitable and entertaining" (272).

Resources: Joseph Warren Beach, *The Outlook for American Prose* (Chicago: University of Chicago Press, 1926); Emily Bernard, ed., *Remember Me to Harlem: The Letters of Langston Hughes and Carl Van Vechten, 1925–1964* (New York: Knopf, 2001); W.E.B. Du Bois, "Books," *The Crisis* 33 (1926), 81; John Feaster, "The Perils of Multiculturalism: Carl Van Vechten's *Nigger Heaven*," *The Cresset*, Oct. 1993, 5–10; Langston Hughes, *The Big Sea* (New York: Knopf, 1940); James Weldon Johnson, "Romance and Tragedy in Harlem—A Review," *Opportunity* 4 (1926), 316–318; Bruce Kellner: *Carl Van Vechten and the Irreverent Decades* (Norman: University of Oklahoma Press, 1968); "Refined Racism: White Patronage in the Harlem Renaissance," in *The Harlem Renaissance Re-examined*, ed. Victor A. Kramer (New York: AMS, 1987); Edward Lueders, *Carl Van Vechten* (New York: Twayne, 1965).

David M. Owens

Vashon, George Boyer (1824–1878). Educator and poet. Though better known for his teaching and activism, Vashon published a handful of important poems and essays.

Born to the activist John B. Vashon and Anne Smith in Carlisle, Pennsylvania, George Boyer Vashon spent most of his childhood in **Pittsburgh, Pennsylvania**, where his father helped found a school for African Americans. When only fourteen, Vashon helped found the Juvenile Anti-Slavery Society, and his earnest desire to aid fellow African Americans led him to enroll at Oberlin College in 1840. He became Oberlin's first African American graduate in 1844. While attending Oberlin, he taught African American children in the area, including the young **John Mercer Langston**.

Vashon returned home and studied law, but when he applied to the Pennsylvania bar in 1847, he was rejected because of his **race**. He considered emigrating to **Haiti**, was admitted to the New York bar, and then decided that he would, indeed, emigrate. Between 1848 and 1850, Vashon taught in Haiti and sent regular reports to **Frederick Douglass**'s newspaper, *North Star*. Upon returning to New York state, he settled in Syracuse, began practicing law, and became active in African American politics. His interest in literature and his classical education led him to write "Vincent Oge," an **epic poem**, in 1853; what he referred to as "fragments" from the poem appeared in the 1854 *Autographs for Freedom*, which detailed a failed early uprising of Haitian Blacks and functioned in dialogue with several other antebellum African American accounts of Haiti. Such accounts were designed, in part, to recognize the potential for armed slave rebellion.

In 1854, Vashon began teaching at New York Central College; the school's troubled finances led him to leave in 1857 and return to Pittsburgh. He taught in Pittsburgh's African American schools until 1863; in 1859, he married fellow teacher Susan Paul Smith (the granddaughter of the noted abolitionist

Rev. Thomas Paul). They had seven children. One of them, John Boyer Vashon, followed in his parents' footsteps and become an important educator in **St. Louis, Missouri**.

In 1863, Vashon became President of Avery College, and during his four years there, he remained active in agitating for civil rights; he also published a long allegorical poem, "A Life Day." He again attempted to gain admission to the Pennsylvania bar in 1867, but the bar refused to act on his application. Moving to **Washington, D.C.**, he worked in the Solicitor's Office at the Freedmen's Bureau and helped found the night school at Howard University. His time in Washington led to a third, equally brief, engagement with literary work. He contributed a rich range of texts to *The New Era* in 1870 and befriended **Frank J. Webb**, who was also working for the Freedmen's Bureau and publishing in *The New Era*.

Vashon's first love, though, was always teaching, and after holding a variety of minor government positions, he was appointed to Alcorn University in 1873, where he taught until his death from yellow fever.

Resources: Frank R. Levstik, "Vashon, George Boyer," *American National Biography Online*, http://www.anb.org/articles/09/09-00770.html; Joan R. Sherman, *Invisible Poets: Afro-Americans of the Nineteenth Century*, 2nd ed. (Urbana: University of Illinois Press, 1989), 53–61.

Eric Gardner

Verdelle, A. J. (born 1960). Novelist. A. J. Verdelle is an emerging African American writer whose novel, *The Good Negress* (1995), has been highly acclaimed. She has received the American Academy of Arts and Letters Howard D. Vursell Award, the PEN/Faulkner Finalists Award, the Whiting Writers Award, and a Bunting Fellowship from Radcliffe College at Harvard University. Verdelle has studied and worked in political science and statistics, and she currently teaches creative writing at Princeton University.

Though she belongs to the generation of authors inspired by **Toni Morrison** and **Alice Walker**, Verdelle can also be situated in a longer Black literary tradition, one that includes the work of **Harriet Ann Jacobs**, **Countee Cullen**, and **Zora Neale Hurston**. Her first, and as yet only, novel, also published under the title *This Rain Coming*, explores themes of adolescence, family relations, economic disadvantage, and education, and it presents a cultural geography of North and South. Charting Denise Palms's passage into womanhood and self-determination, despite the constraints placed upon her progress, the first-person narrative of *Negress* weaves together an intimate account of the protagonist's past, both distant in rural Virginia and recent, involving her family's struggles in 1960s **Detroit, Michigan**. Questions of hegemonic or dominant discourse versus the use of the Black **vernacular** are raised and complicated in the novel because Denise decides "to write [herself] to a future" (175).

Resources: Arlyn Diamond, "Short Subjects: History Lesson," *Women's Review of Books* 12, no. 10–11 (1995), 33; E. Shelley Reid, "Beyond Morrison and

Walker: Looking Good and Looking Forward in Contemporary Black Women's Stories," *African American Review* 34, no. 2 (2000), 313–328; Jill Rendelstein, "The Language of Identity: A Profile of A. J. Verdelle," July 2001, www.worldandihomeschool.com/public_articles/2001/july/wis21370.asp; A. J. Verdelle: "Classroom Rap," *The Nation* 264, no. 3 (1997), 5–6; "Foreword," in *Scarlet Sister Mary*, by Julia Peterkin (Athens: University of Georgia Press, 1998); "Gibraltar Jones," *Critical Quarterly* 39, no. 2 (1997), 60–74; *The Good Negress* (Chapel Hill, NC: Algonquin, 1995); "Preface," in *Imperium in Imperio*, by Sutton Griggs (New York: Modern Library, 2003); *This Rain Coming* (London: Women's Press, 1996); "The Truth of the Picnic: Writing About American Slavery," *Representing Slavery: A Roundtable Discussion*, July 2001, www.common-place.org.

Jennifer Terry

Vernacular. The vernacular is the language people use most comfortably, when very little attention is paid to conventional correctness of speech. It is the language used when people are not concerned about how they sound to a listener or how "correct" or "proper" they seem. It is also, therefore, a language that literary writers attempt to represent. Linguists, those who study language structure and language use, believe that the vernacular is used mostly in the home with close family members. Speakers of all types of English (American English, British English, Australian English, etc.)—or any other language, for that matter—have a vernacular and many other varieties of a language from which to choose. Everyone has numerous of ways of speaking, depending on the context of the interaction, and everyone has a vernacular language. Linguists call these different ways of speaking "variations in language use" or "varieties" of a person's language. People use different varieties for particular purposes and in different environments. Any person can have numerous ways of speaking that may range from very formal varieties to less formal ones. A variety used with family or friends may be different from one used in a job interview or during a formal presentation. All of these various ways of speaking are viable, systematic forms of language, governed by certain rules and conventions, and appropriate or inappropriate, depending upon the social or rhetorical situation.

Despite the concept and belief that the vernacular exists, it is almost impossible to define it or locate it scientifically. Linguistically, it is more of a **myth** than anything concrete because it is difficult to capture. We know it exists because we hear it and use it on a regular basis, but linguists are not convinced that it can be captured and analyzed, and therefore the vernacular remains something of a mystery to the academic community. Any attempts to capture the vernacular by way of recording change the use of language because when someone knows he or she is being recorded, his or her language changes—usually away from the vernacular. Moreover, the presence of an interviewer or someone unfamiliar attempting to capture the vernacular of a person automatically alters the language a person uses. That change is often unconscious.

For African American communities, the term "vernacular" usually refers to the language used by many African Americans in a comfortable setting. This variety of language is often called African American Vernacular English (AAVE), Black English (BE), Ebonics, or Non-standard English. Although in some contexts these terms are synonymous, the more accepted terms are AAVE and BE. The term "Ebonics," linguistically, does not necessarily mean the English spoken by African Americans—although in recent years the general population has made that association. It was coined by Robert Williams and a group of other Black linguists in 1973 at a conference on language development in Black children, and refers to the similarity in the way languages of the African **diaspora** sound. (The African diaspora is the term used for the scattering of Black people throughout the world as a result of the slave trade.) Although the slaves taken from Africa did not all speak the same language, the sound systems of their languages were similar, influencing the language used by descendants of African slaves, to which the name Ebonics refers—Ebony + phonics.

The use of "Ebonics" became popularly recognizable in 1996 when the Oakland, California, School Board attempted to pass the Ebonics Resolution, which addressed language-variation issues and their impact on the learning environment. Since then, the terms AAVE and Ebonics have become almost synonymous; however, their meanings are strikingly different linguistically. To a general audience, Ebonics carries a more negative connotation, language that is looked down upon or language of an uneducated group of people. The use of the term often connotes a negative image of Black people incapable of speaking Standard English. AAVE, on the other hand, does not always conjure up such negative feelings in the general population. Linguistically, however, neither of these terms has negative implications; they are just terms used to help describe variations in language use.

Vernacular, AAVE or BE is neither slang nor incorrect language. Linguistically speaking, there is no such thing as incorrect language, because as long as someone is talking and is being understood by the person listening, communication occurs between speaker and listener—making language neither wrong nor right. Standardized rules that seem to govern language (e.g., do not use double negatives) are only prescriptive, meaning that someone at some time decided to add this rule to language. However, it is not a rule at all, but a way of evaluating language, for a rule of language is a feature that, if violated, renders the language unable to be understood. Avoiding double negatives is not a rule for English. For example, the use of double or even multiple negatives does not make the sentence positive, but instead makes it even more negative. Consider for a moment the sentence "There is no tea." This clearly means no tea is available, which is obvious by the one negative in the sentence. Now consider the sentence "We don't have no tea." The use of two negatives in this sentence does not make it positive. There is still no tea. However, the second sentence seems to show more of a negative sentiment. The use of a double negative does not make the sentence less understandable, but it does place the sentence in a different variety of language, one that might be called the vernacular.

Many would consider the use of double negatives as incorrect grammar or as **slang**. It is not incorrect grammar, but a grammatical construction that is not considered *standard*. Because it is still understandable, it is not grammatically incorrect. For something to be grammatically incorrect, it cannot be understood by listeners. Slang is not the use of incorrect grammar and is not a variety of English on its own; slang words or phrases can be used within any variety that is spoken. Therefore, one could use slang with a more formal variety of language or more commonly in a casual setting when the vernacular is being used.

Most linguists suggest that African Americans, in a broad sense, speak differently from White Americans, even if this difference is noticeable only in the vernacular. Not all African Americans speak AAVE, however. Moreover, not all speakers of AAVE are African American. People can often tell a person's ethnicity by the way he or she speaks without even seeing the person. That recognition of ethnicity or culture without visual representation is not insulting, but it does acknowledge that there are variations in language based on race or culture. Rickford and Rickford state emphatically, "The fact is that most African Americans *do* talk differently from whites and Americans of other ethnic groups, or at least most of us [African Americans] can when we want to. And the fact is that most Americans, Black and white, know this to be true" (4). The question, therefore, becomes what distinguishes African American speech from that of White Americans. In other words, what is AAVE? The descriptions of AAVE are not always positive. H. L. Menken declared that AAVE "may be called the worst English in the world" (cited in Smitherman, 74). Other early critics of AAVE have called it "baby talk," "infantile English," and "slovenly and careless" (75). Although most current descriptions are less caustic, negative attitudes toward AAVE still exist. The effort to recognize the language of African Americans as something other than deficient and substandard has resulted in countless studies that have deconstructed AAVE into its most salient features. Still, supporters of the language have found it difficult to define exactly what AAVE is, though it is clear why people use this form of vernacular.

People of any culture use their vernacular variety for a number of reasons. First, people tend to use the vernacular because it is the language they learned at home. It is the language their family and friends use when they are at ease with each other. It is a language that people do not have to worry about "getting right" because it is their first language, so it comes naturally. A vernacular "retains the associations of warmth and closeness for the many . . . who first learn it from their mothers and fathers and other family members; it expresses camaraderie and solidarity among friends" (Rickford and Rickford, 10).

Therefore, it is not surprising that some writers of African American literature would use the vernacular in the development of characters. The use of vernacular in literature is a stylistic choice. Vernacular has been used in fiction by many, from early African American writers to contemporary ones. The use of the vernacular in writing has many purposes. It can connect a character to a social group or location, without the author having to explicitly give the reader the information. Using the vernacular helps authors make their characters more real and believable, and therefore is used often. However, the use of vernacular in writing is not a formalized or standardized process. Often, writers attempt to represent the speech of the characters they create in inventive and individual ways. They use variations of English spelling because vernacular is difficult to represent with standardized English spelling, and take liberties with how they present the vernacular. Therefore, the representation of the vernacular varies by text and by author.

Arna Bontemps, born into a **Creole** community in Alexandria, Louisiana, included the Creole vernacular in much of his writing. Although the vernacular used is Louisiana Creole, in print it is difficult to distinguish from AAVE. In the following excerpt from "Summer Tragedy" (*African American Literature: An Anthology of Nonfiction, Fiction, Poetry, and Drama*, 1993), Bontemps presents his characters through the use of the local vernacular. In the following selection, the main character, Jeff Patton, is talking to his wife Jennie.

"You oughta could do a heap mo' wid a thing like that'n me—beingst as you got yo' good sight" [says Jennie].

"Looks like I oughta could," he admitted. "But my fingers is gone democrat on me. I get all mixed up in the looking glass an' can't tell wicha way to twist the devilish thing." (41)

Notice the use of both vernacular and slang in this exchange between Jeff and his wife. *Oughta* clearly represents *ought to*, but the typing of those words as one word shows how they sound when spoken together in a casual setting, as between a man and his wife; hence the vernacular. Additionally, the use of the phrase *gone democrat* (being disorderly) shows the slang of the time incorporated in the everyday language of the people. The conversation between Jennie and Jeff illustrates not only their closeness, but also the Creole culture they share.

In "The Steel Drivin' Man," by **A. Philip Randolph** and Chandler Owen, the characters are given depth with the use of the vernacular in contrast with characters who do not use African American Vernacular English. The following is an exchange between the main character, John, and his employer, who have worked together for a significant period of time.

"John, John, come here John. John I bet that fool Yankee that you and your hammer can beat that steam contraption he's got. Think you can John?"

"Yessah Cap'n, yessah, yassah."

"Well, John, we'll have the race tomorrow and you do it. You beat him and I'll give you—ah—I'll give you fifty dollars." (75)

In this exchange, the Captain is clearly speaking a more standardized variety, while John speaks a more vernacular variety, which is obvious even from the few words that John speaks. The use of the vernacular here gives detail about the characters without the author having to explain their backgrounds. It is clear that the Captain is the one in charge or in control because John refers to him as "Cap'n" and also uses "yessah." Additionally, this conversation conveys the social structure at that time. With this short passage the reader can ascertain that the Captain is most likely White, while John is most likely African American because of his use of the vernacular. The use of vernacular sets up the dynamic between the characters without the author having to describe it explicitly.

In a novel by **Ernest James Gaines**, *A Lesson Before Dying* (1993), the main character, Grant Wiggins, has returned to his Cajun hometown after college to teach school. He befriends and mentors Jefferson, a young convict who is on death row. During their time together, they become close. The language they use, the vernacular and the more standard variety, illustrates the experiences of both, as shown in the following exchange.

> "Now all y'all want me to be better than ever'body else. How, Mr. Wiggins? You tell me."
> "I don't know, Jefferson."
> "What I got left, Mr. Wiggins—two weeks?"
> "I think it's something like that—if nothing happens."
> "Nothing go'n happen, Mr. Wiggins." (89)

In this exchange the reader can see the difference in Wiggins's and Jefferson's experiences. Wiggins had been away to school, as evidenced by his use of a more standard variety. On the other hand, Jefferson has not. He has lived in the same town all his life and in fact will die there. The author uses the vernacular in the speech of Jefferson to illustrate this.

The vernacular can help give characters qualities that only language can—for example, where a person is from. In **Zora Neale Hurston**'s study of Black folklore in her hometown of Eatonville, Florida, her characters' speech easily identifies them as Southerners. In the following passage, Zora has returned home and has just seen some old friends.

> "You gointer stay awhile, Zora?"
> "Yep. Several months."
> "Where you gointer stay, Zora?"
> "With Mett and Ellis, I reckon." (52)

This exchange between Hurston and her characters shows their Southern identity. Although Zora has lived outside of **the South** for many years, her use of the vernacular shows her connection with the South and her identity as a Southerner. Hurston deployed the vernacular in her fiction as well.

The vernacular is also used in poetry and **drama**. The poets **Paul Laurence Dunbar, Sterling A. Brown**, and **Langston Hughes**, for example, drew on the vernacular in some of their poetry, and Dunbar in particular has been characterized as writing "dialect" poetry. **Ntozake Shange**'s play *for colored girls who have considered suicide/when the rainbow is enuf* uses the vernacular to give dimensions to characters. A stanza spoken by the "lady in blue" illustrates this. She says, "i got sorry greetin me at my front door," for example, and "didnt nobody stop usin my tears to wash cars" (155). The lady in blue uses the vernacular in her speech, and obviously she is talking to people who understand her and her situation, perhaps girlfriends who can identify with her.

The vernacular is used in many ways and for many purposes. It can help give characters personality beyond what the author describes. It can also help readers connect and identify with characters. When authors incorporate the vernacular in their texts, they are doing so purposefully. On the other hand, the use of the vernacular in everyday life may not always be so intentional. People use the vernacular when they are in comfortable settings and know their language is not being judged. This switch is often not noticeable; sometimes, however, it can be very intentional. People often switch their language to the vernacular to show solidarity with other speakers or to make it obvious to others where they come from, what their experiences have been, and with whom they identify. Despite the reasons for using the vernacular, one thing is clear: the vernacular of everyday people is a true and correct language, and is worthy of recognition. (*See* **Dialect Poetry; Folklore; Performance Poetry; Signifying**.)

Resources: Arna Bontemps, "A Summer Tragedy," in *African American Literature: An Anthology of Nonfiction, Fiction, Poetry, and Drama*, ed. D. A. Worley and Jesse Perry (Lincolnwood, IL: National Textbook Company, 1993), 40–49; Ernest J. Gaines, *A Lesson Before Dying* (New York: Knopf, 1993); Zora Neale Hurston, *Mules and Men* (1935; repr. Bloomington: Indiana University Press, 1978); Hans Ostrom, *A Langston Hughes Encyclopedia* (Westport, CT: Greenwood Press, 2002); A. Philip Randolph and Chandler Owen, "The Steel Drivin' Man," in *African American Literature: An Anthology of Nonfiction, Fiction, Poetry, and Drama*, ed. D. A. Worley and Jesse Perry (Lincolnwood, IL: National Textbook Company, 1993), 72–77; J. R. Rickford and R. J. Rickford, *Spoken Soul: The Story of Black English* (New York: Wiley, 2000); Ntozake Shange, "one thing i dont need," in *African American Literature: An Anthology of Nonfiction, Fiction, Poetry, and Drama*, ed. D. A. Worley and Jesse Perry (Lincolnton, IL: National Textbook Company, 1993), 154–157; G. Smitherman, *Talkin' That Talk: Language, Culture, and Education in African America* (New York: Routledge, 2000).

Iyabo F. Osiapem

Vernon, Olympia (born 1973). Novelist. Vernon has published two critically acclaimed novels, *Eden* and *Logic*. The main character of *Eden* is a fourteen-year-old African American girl named Maddy Dangerfield; much of the narrative involves her difficulty in having to care for a dying aunt, her conflict with her mother, and her growing sexual awareness. The novel is set in fictional Valsin County in rural Mississippi. *Logic* concerns the plight of a brain-damaged young African American woman named Logic, and is also set in Valsin County. One reviewer found *Logic* to be heavy with symbolism and "bewildering and bewitching," and suggested that "[t]he novel's ending turns the concept of Christian mercy on its head in a way few readers could possibly anticipate" (Howard). Vernon's writing has been compared to that of **Alice Walker** and **Toni Morrison**. Vernon grew up in Mt. Hermon and Osyka, Mississippi, and attended Southeastern Louisiana State University. She has expressed gratitude to two professors there, William Dowie and Carole McAllister, for encouraging her to write, and has indicated that without such encouragement, she might have pursued a career in law enforcement instead of one in writing ("Women's History Month"). (*See* **Coming-of-Age Fiction**.)

Resources: Rachel Howard, "Review of *Logic*," *San Francisco Chronicle*, June 13, 2004, p. M4; Olympia Vernon: *Eden* (New York: Grove, 2003); *Logic* (New York: Grove, 2004); "Women's History Month Concludes with Lectures, Author," *Bylion: Faculty Staff Newsletter*, Southeastern Louisiana State University, http://www.selu.edu/NewsEvents/PublicInfoOffice//bl3-24-03.html.

Hans Ostrom

Vietnam War (1961–1975). Vietnam veterans and war resisters are among the best chroniclers of the African American Vietnam experience through their novels, poetry, plays, and memoirs. The Vietnam War was waged by America's first fully integrated armed forces, and it was also America's longest and most bitterly protested war. Black soldiers had the unique experience of risking their lives fighting for democracy in a foreign country while the battle for their civil rights was being waged at home. For many soldiers, protesters, and ordinary citizens, Vietnam left a confused legacy of pride, anger, pain, and guilt. This legacy, coupled with the quest for healing, is a recurrent them in the literature of the war.

In the early 1960s Black men enlisted in the military from a sense of patriotic duty as well as for the better opportunities afforded. As the war escalated, Blacks were drafted at a higher rate than Whites because many failed to qualify for deferments and there was virtually no Black representation on draft boards. Once drafted, they were disproportionately assigned to combat duty, and at one point accounted for more than 20 percent of all casualties though just 10 percent of all troops. In the war's later years new military policies reduced this percentage, but the belief by some African American leaders that Blacks were being used as cannon fodder for the White man's war remained. **Malcolm X** spoke against the war from the beginning, and by 1966 both the Student Nonviolent Coordinating Committee, led by **Stokely Carmichael**, and the Southern Christian Leadership Conference had come out against the war. In 1967, **Martin Luther King, Jr.**, condemned the war in his speech "A Time to Break the Silence," and **Muhammad Ali** refused military induction.

After the heavy American casualties of the Tet Offensive in 1968, the murder of Martin Luther King later that year, and the influx of new recruits infused with **Black Power** ideology, Black soldiers became increasingly militant in a system they saw as oppressive. Racial separation and strife outside the combat zone became more common. For a few Black soldiers the Viet Cong became less the enemy than fellow people of color. Black veterans returning home grew disillusioned and angry as they confronted further discrimination and joblessness. They had fought, had been wounded, and had watched friends die beside them, only to find that their country did not honor their service.

Two novels by Black Vietnam veterans are *Coming Home* (1971), by George Davis, and *De Mojo Blues* (1985), by **Arthur Rickydoc Flowers**. *Coming Home* is written from the perspective of three air force pilots, two Black and one White, stationed in Thailand. The war seems unreal to them because they drop bombs on an enemy they can't see. Racism is casual and pervasive, and one of the pilots speaks of identifying with the Vietnamese struggle to be free of foreign dominance. *De Mojo Blues* (1985) is the story of three soldiers dishonorably discharged for alleged fragging (killing a superior). Inspired by the gift of bones given him by a dying friend in Vietnam, the protagonist, Tucept HighJohn, finds self-empowerment by training with a hoodoo master (*see* **John the Conqueror**).

The novelists **John A. Williams** and **Clarence Major** both served in the military before Vietnam. Williams wrote *Captain Blackman* (1972), in which Abraham Blackman is wounded in Vietnam and experiences a surreal journey into history, fighting as a Black soldier in every American war from the Revolution to Vietnam. Williams quotes historical documents from each war to reflect both the bravery of Black troops and the racism of the military. The book concludes with a future war in which the Black soldier, using skill and knowledge honed over centuries, finally triumphs. Clarence Major's *All-Night Visitors* (1969) follows the odyssey of a psychologically scarred veteran who struggles to reclaim his identity. Major also wrote the short story "Dossy O" (1972), a soldier's cocaine-fueled rap on surviving the carnage, as well as several war poems. In S. E. Anderson's short story "Soldier Boy" (1970), the soldier narrator shares a brief, human moment with a Viet Cong as the war rages around them. Like his character Melvin Ellington in *Tragic Magic* (1978), Wesley Brown was jailed as a conscientious objector during the Vietnam War. Brown's protagonist endures society's violence toward the Black man, and recalls demonstrations and beatings. Just out of prison, he finds that he is unable to escape the brutality around him, and himself becomes a killer.

Two novels for young people are *Fallen Angels* (1989), by **Walter Dean Myers**, and *Mote* (1988), by Chap Reaver. *Fallen Angels*, which won the Coretta Scott King Award, describes the tight bonds of friendship that form in an integrated combat squad. Reaver's *Mote* is a Vietnam veteran who is still struggling, twenty years later, to come to terms with a wartime killing he committed to survive.

Among the most important poets of the Vietnam War is **Yusef Komu-nyakaa**, who published *Dien Cai Dau* (a Vietnamese phrase, meaning "crazy," used to describe American soldiers) in 1988 and who won the Pulitzer Prize for *Neon Vernacular* (1993). From the distance of time Kommunyakaa intertwines images of war and the Vietnamese people and landscape, evoking the fear and confusion of the soldiers and the beauty of the countryside. Fellow veteran Horace Coleman's war poems are laced with anger and bitter humor in his books *A Rock & a Hard Place* (1977) and *In the Grass* (1995). Lamont Steptoe, another veteran, wrote two books of Vietnam poetry, *Mad Minute* and *Uncle's South China Sea Blue Nightmare* (1994). **Michael S. Harper** alternates verse and prose in *Debridement* (1973), his portrayal of a Black Medal of Honor winner who returns from Vietnam only to die on the streets. Though Harper's work is fiction, it has roots in the true story of Dwight H. Johnson, a Medal of Honor winner who returned as a hero from Vietnam only to sink into despair and die tragically in **Detroit, Michigan**.

Samm-Art Williams's play *Home* (1978) uses poetry, prose, song, and **humor** to tell the story of Cephus Miles, a simple Southern farmer who follows the commandment "thou shalt not kill." While imprisoned for resisting the draft, he loses his land and the woman he loves, but in a twist regains them at the end. Keusi, a Vietnam veteran, is one of the leaders of a revolutionary group in *Black Terror* (1971), by Richard Wesley. As his fellow radicals urge killing moderate Blacks, Keushi responds that he's seen enough death. He argues that activists should fight for Black unity, but his words go unheeded. Wesley also wrote the play *Strike Heaven in the Face* (unpublished), based on the Dwight Johnson story.

Oral history and memoirs have an important place in the Black literature of Vietnam, telling stories of soldiers who fought the war and of men who refused to fight. Wallace Terry's *Bloods* profiles twenty soldiers, using their own words. They recall the adrenaline and fear of combat, the pride of fighting well, the trauma of being wounded and seeing friends die, the horror of witnessing atrocities committed by both sides, and their anger against institutionalized discrimination. Many express bitterness toward the government for waging a limited war, and disillusionment at returning home to an uncaring country. *Brothers: Black Soldiers in the Nam* (1982), by Stanley Goff and Robert Sanders, provides detailed accounts of their frontline combat.

David Parks's *GI Diary* (1968) is a memoir of his year in Vietnam and includes his photographs. In *The Courageous and the Proud* (1970), Samuel Vance, a sergeant and troop leader in Vietnam, tells his story as a Black man in a White man's army. Albert French speaks as a wounded Vietnam veteran who struggles to find peace after his return to civilian life in *Patches of Fire* (1997). *Memphis, Nam, Sweden* (1971), by the decorated soldier Terry Whitmore, describes his desertion from the Marines and his flight to Sweden to start a new life. *A Hero's Welcome* (1975; republished as *Black Prisoner of War*, 2000) relates the story of James A. Daly, a Jehovah's Witness who is denied conscientious objector status. When told he will be an Army cook, Daly enlists but is sent into combat. Captured and imprisoned for more than five years, he speaks out against the war while a POW. The Army charged him with collaboration with the enemy but eventually dropped the charges.

Resources: Primary Sources: S. E. Anderson, "Soldier Boy," *Black World* 19, no. 8 (1970), 88–92; Wesley Brown, *Tragic Magic* (New York: Random House, 1978); Horace Coleman: *Between a Rock and a Hard Place* (Kansas City, MO: BkMk Press, 1977); *In the Grass* (Woodbridge, CT: Viet Nam Generation & Burning Cities, 1995); James A. Daly and Lee Bergman, *A Hero's Welcome* (Indianapolis: Bobbs-Merrill, 1975); George Davis, *Coming Home* (New York: Random House, 1971); Arthur R. Flowers, *De Mojo Blues* (New York: Dutton, 1985); Albert French, *Patches of Fire* (New York: Anchor, 1997); Stanley Goff, Robert Sanders, and Clark Smith, *Brothers: Black Soldiers in the Nam* (Novato, CA: Presidio, 1982); Michael S. Harper, *Debridement* (Garden City, NY: Doubleday, 1973); Yusef Komunyakaa: *Dien Cai Dau* (Middletown, CT: Wesleyan University Press, 1988); *Neon Vernacular* (Middletown, CT: Wesleyan University Press, 1993); Clarence Major: *All-Night Visitors* (New York: Olympia, 1969); "Dossy O," *Black Creation* 3–4 (1972), 4–5; David Parks, *GI Diary* (New York: Harper & Row, 1968); Lamont Steptoe: *Mad Minute* (Camden, NJ: Whirlwind, 1990); *Uncle's South China Sea Blue Nightmare* (York, PA: Yardbird, 1994); Wallace Terry, *Bloods* (New York: Ballantine, 1985); Samuel Vance, *The Courageous and the Proud* (New York: Norton, 1970); Richard Wesley, "Black Terror," in *New Lafayette Theatre Presents*, ed. Ed Bullins (Garden City, NY: Anchor, 1974), 219–301; Terry Whitmore, *Memphis, Nam, Sweden* (Garden City, NY: Doubleday, 1971); John A. Williams, *Captain Blackman* (Garden City, NY: Doubleday, 1972); Samm-Art Williams, *Home* (Garden City, NY: Doubleday, 1978). **Secondary Sources:** Milton J. Bates, *The Wars We Took to Vietnam* (Berkeley: University of California Press, 1996); Michael Bibby, *Hearts and Minds* (New Brunswick, NJ: Rutgers University Press, 1996); Kevin Bowen and Bruce Weigl, eds., *Writing Between the Lines* (Amherst: University of Massachusetts Press, 1997); David J. Soldados Razos DeRose, "Issues of Race in Vietnam War Drama," *Viet Nam Generation Journal* 1, no. 2 (1989), 38–55; W. D. Ehrhart, ed., *Carrying the Darkness* (New York: Avon, 1985); Vince Gotera, *Radical Visions* (Athens: University of Georgia Press, 1994); Norman Harris, *Connecting Times* (Jackson: University Press of Mississippi, 1988); Trudier Harris-Lopez, ed., *Afro-American Writers After 1955* (Detroit: Gale, 1985); Jeff Loeb, "MIA: African American Autobiography of the Vietnam War," *African American Review* 31 (1997), 105–123; JSTOR, Oregon State University Library, http://www.jstor.org; Robert W. Mullen, *Blacks in America's Wars* (New York: Monad, 1973); Ernest M. B. Obdele-Starks and Amilcar Shabazz, "Blacks and the Vietnam War," in *The Vietnam War: Handbook of Literature and Research*, ed. James S. Olsen (Westport, CT.: Greenwood Press, 1993); Heike Raphael-Hernandez, "'The First Animal I Ever Killed Was a Gook,'" in *Literature on the Move*, ed. Dominque Marçais et al. (Heidelberg: Universitätsverlag C. Winter, 2002), 131–146; Clyde Taylor, ed., *Vietnam and Black America* (Garden City, NY: Anchor, 1973).

Maureen A. Kelly

Villanelle. The villanelle is a poetic form of nineteen lines that both rhymes and repeats whole lines in a predetermined manner as a refrain, which can create the effect of incantation, but can also emphasize images and ideas. Five stanzas of three lines each are followed by a quatrain. The pattern of repetition is rather complicated. The first and third lines of the first stanza are repeated in a prescribed order as the last lines of the remaining tercets (three line stanzas), then as the last two lines of the final quatrain. The rhyme scheme is AbA, abA, abA, abA, abA, abAA.

The French term *villanelle* was derived from the Italian word *villanorustic*, which referred to a rustic song. The modern form evolved from French poetry in the late sixteenth century, and later poets patterned their villanelles on the arrangement popularized by Jean Passeret, who established the seven-syllable lines using two rhymes, distributed typically in five tercets and a final quatrain, with line repetitions similar to those described above (Baldick).

Although it is a complicated, predetermined form, the villanelle can give a pleasant impression of simple spontaneity, as in Edwin Arlington Robinson's poem "The House on the Hill." The British poets W. H. Auden, William Empson, and Derek Mahon adopted the form, but the best-known villanelle in English is Dylan Thomas's "Do Not Go Gentle into That Good Night" (1952). The American poets Theodore Roethke, Carolyn Kizer, and Elizabeth Bishop have also used the form. Roethke's villanelle "The Waking" is often anthologized.

In African American literature, the villanelle has been used to juxtapose form with function and with meaning. **Rita Dove**'s poem "Parsley," included in her collection *Museum*, illustrates this approach. Dove's poem is constructed in two parts. The first, a villanelle, presents the **drama** of a dictator, Rafael Trujillo, who orders the annihilation of 20,000 Blacks in the Dominican Republic because they cannot pronounce the letter "r." The story is all the more terrifying because the facts smash against the stark and beautiful vehicle of the villanelle form itself. In the second part of the poem, a third-person narrator examines the dictator's relationship to his mother, who can "roll her 'r's' like a queen." Other poets, such as **Sonia Sanchez** and **Quincy Thomas Troupe, Jr.**, have taken liberty with the form. Troupe's villanelle "Poem for Michael Jordan" is intended to play on the sound qualities of this poetic form. (*See* **Formal Verse; Sonnet.**)

Resources: Christopher Baldick, *The Concise Oxford Dictionary of Literary Terms* (New York: Oxford University Press, 1990); Allan Burns, *Thematic Guide to American Poetry* (Westport, CT: Greewood Press, 2002); Rita Dove, *Museum* (Pittsburgh, PA: Carnegie-Mellon University Press, 1983); Sonia Sanchez, *Shake Loose My Skin* (Boston: Beacon, 1999); Paul Q. Tilden, ed., *African-American Literature: Overview and Bibliography* (New York: Nova Science Publishers, 2003); Quincy Troupe, *Choruses: Poems* (Berkeley: University of California Press, 2000); Helen Vendler, *Soul Says: On Recent Poetry* (Cambridge, MA: Belknap Press of Harvard University Press, 1995).

Carol Elizabeth Dietrich

Voice of the Negro, The (1904–1907). Journal. *The Voice of the Negro* was first published in 1904 in **Atlanta, Georgia**. The journal was created by Austin N. Jenkins, a **White** publisher and vice president of the publishing firm J. L. Nichols. John Wesley Edward Bowen was appointed editor of *The Voice of the Negro* in October 1903. In November 1903, J. Max Barber was named managing editor (Harlan). Politically, Barber was relatively radical, more interested in pressing for fundamental political and social change for African Americans than were **Booker T. Washington** and his followers, who were often labeled as "accomodationist." Washington's private secretary, Emmett Jay Scott, was the journal's associate editor, giving Washington an inside view of its workings. *The Voice of the Negro* was the first magazine in **the South** to be edited by African Americans.

In an effort to unite the **Negro** population, the journal attempted to reach a compromise between accomodationists, those influenced by Washington's views, and radicals, who might align themselves with the views of **W.E.B. Du Bois**. Hence, the first issue of *The Voice of the Negro*, published in January 1904, included writings by both Washington and Barber. However, the publishing firm discovered that Washington jointly owned a rival journal, and in August 1904, amid controversy, Scott resigned his position as associate editor, citing personality conflicts with Barber.

Once the influence of Washington was gone, Barber began journalistic warfare by publishing satirical articles concerning Washington. Scott retaliated by urging the Afro-American Realty Company in **Harlem, New York**, to cease advertising in *The Voice of the Negro*. The continued hostility between the two political groups was increased by Barber's participation in the Niagara Movement, which Washington considered a conspiracy. Amid the ensuing chaos, Du Bois replaced Washington "as the official hero of the journal" in 1905 (Harlan, 54). However, the bad blood continued between Washington and Scott, and Barber and *The Voice of the Negro*.

Following an anonymous letter written by Barber pertaining to the September 1906 Atlanta **race riot** in which Barber addressed the alleged assaults of White females by Black males, Barber was confronted by city officials. Given the choice of serving time in jail or leaving town, Barber moved himself and *The Voice of the Negro* to **Chicago, Illinois**. Barber shortened the name of the journal to *The Voice* in an effort to start anew, but the race riot controversy had been a fatal blow. *The Voice of the Negro* ceased publication in 1907.

During publication, *The Voice of the Negro* addressed many social and political issues, such as voting rights, race relations in America, African American education, and the **labor** movement. *The Voice of the Negro* also published works by many respected African American authors such as **Mary Church Terrell**, William Pickins, Du Bois, Washington, and John Hope (Harlan; Johnson). (*See* **NAACP.**)

Resources: Louis R. Harlan, "Booker T. Washington and the *Voice of the Negro, 1904–1907*," *Journal of Southern History* 45 (Feb. 1979), 45–62; Charles S. Johnson,

"The Rise of the Negro Magazine," *Journal of Negro History* 13, no. 1 (Jan. 1928), 7–21.

DaNean Pound

Voodoo/Vodoun. "Voodoo" is a well-known term in American culture, and there are countless references to "voodoo" in books, films, and music. However, the origin, practice, symbolism, and draw of vodoun (the preferred term for scholars if not the general public) remain a mystery to many. The term "voodoo" gained popularity during the U.S. occupation of **Haiti** from 1915 to 1934. "Voodoo" continues to be depicted as a primitive and "uncivilized" religion based on witchcraft and superstition, so many users have moved to the spelling "vodoun" (also "vodou" and "vodun") to distinguish the religion and culture from the mainly negative stereotypes associated with "voodoo." Vodoun is linked to, but is not the same as, other African-based **diaspora** religions such as *condomblé* in Brazil, Santería in Cuba, and hoodoo in the Southeastern United States.

Vodoun is a syncretic practice derived from a number of regional and cultural sources. First and foremost, it draws from West Africa, primarily the Fon traditions (*vodun* is the Fon word for "God" or "mysteries") of the kingdom of Dahomey (roughly modern-day Benin) and the Bantu-speaking people of the Kongo basin. Vodoun also has elements of Native American cultures, including those of the original inhabitants of the Caribbean islands, the Arawak/Taino people. There are also European influences on vodoun, such as Catholicism and the mysticism of French gypsies.

Vodoun had a marked influx into North America in the eighteenth century with the importation of French West Indian slaves to Louisiana. Vodoun was suppressed by the elite because it often operated outside of White plantation control; during this period it began to be redeveloped and known as "hoodoo" by slaves. During the last phases of the United States occupation of Haiti, however, vodoun began to capture the global imagination through stories told both by U.S. Marines, who served as administrators, and by Haitians, as a nationalist way to reclaim their culture. William Seabrook's *The Magic Island* (1929) excited widespread curiosity about this land within the American empire. With the onset of the **New Negro** movement, or **Harlem Renaissance**, in the United States, and the **Négritude** movement in France, an increased Pan-African consciousness led to the reinvestigation of vodoun during the 1920s and 1930s. As literary and intellectual movements sought to reclaim and celebrate Black culture, vodoun was recognized and studied as a vehicle for cultural survival.

The subject and symbols of vodou were, and continue to be, central to African American literature. **Paul Robeson**'s first professional role was as a lead in the 1922 Broadway play *Taboo* (later retitled *Voodoo*), in which his character, a wandering minstrel in the antebellum South, at one point becomes a "voodoo king" (Lewis). No one, however, deserves more credit for the early investigation and validation of vodou than Harlem Renaissance author **Zora Neale Hurston**. Her study of "conjure lore" brought her to the American

Southeast, where she was enthralled by hoodoo and ultimately initiated as a priestess. From 1936 to 1937 she traveled to Jamaica and Haiti, doing ethnographic research and collecting **folktales**, and published her findings in *Tell My Horse* (1938):

> Particularly in Hoodoo, the North American offshoot of vodoun, power was often used by women over men, or by blacks against white racial injustice, constituting an alternative system of power and authority. Because the idea of "deep secrets" is central to vodoun, it can function and give meaning as a cultural system within a larger cultural frame from which people feel excluded. Vodoun exemplifies both blackness and femaleness unleashed, and as such it posed a threat to white male-dominated American culture. (35)

Ishmael Reed is another preeminent author who has explored and exalted vodoun culture. Deeply influenced by Hurston's 1939 novel *Moses, Man of the Mountain*,

Zora Neale Hurston participating in a voodoo ceremony, probably in Haiti, 1937. Courtesy of the Library of Congress.

which blends the stories of the Moses of the Bible and the Moses of Black **folklore**, who becomes a vodoun magician, Reed published *Mumbo Jumbo* in 1972. The use of vodoun in literature not only provides a setting in which to invert and reexamine power structures, but also shapes a more philosophical realm. Reed created a literary theory he calls Neo-Hoodoo Aesthetics, articulating what he believes to be the "true Afro-American aesthetic," one that is a hybrid of cultures (Martin). He views vodoun culture as a model for multicultural syncretism. Far from its stereotype of evil witchcraft, vodoun culture, largely through works of literature, has been rehabilitated and has come to be viewed not only as a legitimate religion but also as an alternative way to view power relations and African American experience. (*See* **Conjuring.**)

Resources: Kwame Anthony Appiah, *In My Father's House: Africa in the Philosophy of Culture* (New York: Oxford University Press, 1992); Valerie Boyd, *Wrapped in Rainbows: The Life of Zora Neale Hurston* (New York: Scribner's, 2003); Donald J. Cosentino, ed., *The Sacred Arts of Haitian Vodou* (Los Angeles: UCLA Fowler Museum of Cultural History, 1995); Joan Dayan, *Haiti, History, and the Gods* (Berkeley: University of California Press, 1995); Maya Deren, *Divine Horsemen: The Living Gods of Haiti* (New York: Thames and Hudson, 1953); Joseph E. Holloway, ed., *Africanisms in American Culture* (Bloomington: Indiana University Press, 1990); Zora Neale

Hurston: *Moses, Man of the Mountain* (Philadelphia: Lippincott, 1939; repr. New York: HarperPerennial, 1991); *Mules and Men* (1935; repr. New York: HarperPerennial, 1990); *Tell My Horse* (1938; repr. New York: HarperPerennial, 1990); David Levering Lewis, *When Harlem Was in Vogue* (New York: Knopf, 1981), 109; Reginald Martin, "An Interview with Ishmael Reed" (Emeryville, CA, July 1983), http://www.centerforbookculture.org/interviews/interview_reed.html; Ishmael Reed: *Mumbo Jumbo* (Garden City, NY: Doubleday, 1972); "Neo-HooDoo Manifesto," *Los Angeles Free Press*, Sept. 18–24, 1969, p. 42; Mary A. Renda, *Taking Haiti: Military Occupation and the Culture of U.S. Imperialism, 1915–1940* (Chapel Hill: University of North Carolina Press, 2001); William B. Seabrook, *The Magic Island* (New York: Harcourt, Brace, 1929); Robert Tallant, *Voodoo in New Orleans* (Gretna, LA: Pelican Press, 1945); Robert Farris Thompson, *Flash of the Spirit: African and Afro-American Art and Philosophy* (New York: Random House, 1983).

Emily McTighe Musil

Vroman, Mary Elizabeth (1923–1967). Novelist. Born in Buffalo, New York, Vroman completed a B.A. at the Alabama State Teachers College. For the next two decades, she taught at the Camden Academy in Camden, Alabama, and then at several other high school in Alabama, **Chicago, Illinois**, and New York City. In 1967, she died from complications following surgery.

Vroman's abbreviated writing career had three main high points. In 1952, her short story "See How They Run" was published in *Ladies Home Journal*, received additional attention when it received a Christopher Award for most inspirational magazine story, and was adapted as the film *Bright Road* (1953). The film starred Dorothy Dandridge and Harry Belafonte, and for her work on the screenplay, Vroman became the first African American woman to hold membership in the Screenwriters Guild. Drawn broadly from Vroman's own life, the story relates the experiences of an earnest, well-intentioned schoolteacher from the North who grapples with the deficiencies of the schools for African American children in the segregated South.

A decade passed before the publication of Vroman's first novel. In *Esther* (1963), she focuses on the interconnected stories of two African American women, a midwife named Lydia Jones and her granddaughter, Esther Kennedy. The novel chronicles the obstacles that Lydia overcomes in her determination to support financially Esther's ambition to become a registered nurse. The story is given added dimension through its treatment of the obstacles that Esther herself must overcome. In the end, although Esther does become a nurse, the effort that has been required to surmount the barriers posed by poverty and racism reflects well on the main characters but very badly on the society that would compound the difficulties in achieving personal goals that collectively define social progress.

Vroman's last published work was a novel for young adults, *Harlem Summer* (1967), which describes an Alabama teenager's decision to take a summer job in **Harlem, New York**. The novel vividly conveys the "culture shock" that the protagonist experiences as he leaves a closely knit rural community for what is certainly one of the most dynamic and volatile urban districts with a predominantly African American population.

Resources: Saul Bachner: "Black Literature: The Junior Novel in the Classroom—*Harlem Summer*," *Negro American Literature Forum* 7 (Spring 1973), 26–27; "Writing School Marm: Alabama Teacher Finds Literary, Movie Success with First Short Story," *Ebony*, July 1952, 23–28; Mary Elizabeth Vroman: *Esther* (New York: Bantam, 1963); *Harlem Summer* (New York: Putnam, 1967).

Martin Kich

W

Wade-Gayles, Gloria Jean (born 1938). Essayist, autobiographer, educator, editor, poet, and activist.

Gloria Wade-Gayles's presence in African American literature is marked by her commitment to writing about her community, personal experiences that have helped shape her identity and vision, and social injustice. Her memoir *Pushed Back to Strength* (1993) details her experiences growing up in a housing project in segregated **Memphis, Tennessee**; serving as an activist for civil rights; and confronting a society that often attempted to deny her and other African Americans full personhood. The memoir shows how she was able to find self-affirmation in the vision of strength she received from the maternal line of her family. In the book, Wade-Gayles also discusses the strength that, in her view, resulted from "total immersion in a black community grounded in values that translated into a sense of self"(6).

This sense of self-love and love for her ancestors, heritage, and family is also conveyed in her poetry collection *Anointed to Fly* (1991), as well as in collections that she has edited, including *My Soul Is a Witness: African-American Women's Spirituality* (1995) and *Father Songs: Testimonies by African-American Sons and Daughters* (1997). It also resounds through her collection of personal essays *Rooted Against the Wind* (1996), written on such issues as African American women and aging, sexuality, and violence against women. Always invested in exposing the impact that interlocking systems of **race**, class, and **gender** have on the lives of African American women, she wrote the interdisciplinary study *No Crystal Stair: Visions of Race and Gender in Black Women's Fiction* (1984; 2nd ed., 1997), one of the first book-length examinations of African American women's literary productions. It continues to stand, like her other work, as an important contribution to African American literature and feminist studies.

Wade-Gayles earned her Ph.D. in American studies from Emory in 1981. Known as an engaging, illuminating, and challenging professor, she has taught at historically Black colleges for more than three decades and holds the Eminent Scholar's Chair at Spelman College. In 2003 she edited an anthology of essays titled *In Praise of Our Teachers: A Multicultural Tribute to Those Who Inspired Us*. (*See* **Feminism/Black Feminism.**)

Resources: Gloria Wade-Gayles: *Anointed to Fly* (New York: Writers & Readers, 1991); *No Crystal Stair: Visions of Race and Gender in Black Women's Fiction*, 2nd ed. (Cleveland: Pilgrim Press, 1997); *Pushed Back to Strength: A Black Woman's Journey Home* (Boston: Beacon, 1993); *Rooted Against the Wind: Personal Essays* (Boston: Beacon, 1996); Gloria Wade-Gayles, ed.: *Conversations with Gwendolyn Brooks* (Jackson: University Press of Mississippi, 2003); *Father Songs: Testimonies by African American Sons and Daughters* (Boston: Beacon, 1997); *In Praise of Our Teachers: A Multicultural Tribute to Those Who Inspired Us* (Boston: Beacon, 2003); *My Soul Is a Witness: African-American Women's Spirituality* (Boston: Beacon, 1995).

Amanda Davis

Walker, Alice (born 1944). Novelist, essayist, poet, literary critic, and activist. Born in Eatonton, Georgia, Alice Malsenior Walker was the youngest of eight children born to sharecroppers Willie Lee and Minnie Grant Walker. As a young child, Walker was blinded in one eye when one of her brothers shot her with a BB gun. After this incident, her exuberance was replaced with a quiet retreat into literature and writing. Early on, Walker was greatly influenced by Russian novelists such as Dostoyevsky, Gogol, and Tolstoy. She read them as if "they were a delicious cake" (Gentry, 33). Walker studied at Spelman College for her first two years of undergraduate school (1961–1963). However, she knew that her need to react politically to the mistreatment of Blacks was at odds with the aims of Spelman. Consequently, she transferred to Sarah Lawrence College in Bronxville, New York, where she earned a bachelor's degree in 1965. Her first book of poems, *Once* (1968), was written during her senior year at Sarah Lawrence after she had experienced thoughts of suicide and undergone an abortion. Walker's mentor, the poet and professor Muriel Rukeyser, helped Walker publish her first volume of poetry.

Walker was active in the **Civil Rights Movement** of the 1960s, and in 1967 she married civil rights attorney Mel Leventhal. Soon thereafter, the couple moved to Mississippi to volunteer with the voter-registration drives. They were the only interracial married couple in their community. That same year, Walker received a McDowell Fellowship, which allowed her to complete her first novel, *The Third Life of Grange Copeland* (1970). From 1968 to 1972, she was a writer-in-residence and professor of women's studies at Jackson State University, Tougaloo College, and Wellesley College. Later, Walker published a collection of short stories, *In Love and Trouble* (1973). She published a children's book titled *Langston Hughes: American Poet* (1974), a biography of the **Harlem Renaissance** poet, whom she had met during her college years. Hughes also helped Walker publish her first short story, "To Hell with Dying."

Walker was instrumental in recovering the lost works of another crucial participant in the Harlem Renaissance, **Zora Neale Hurston**. At Wellesley, Walker began to notice certain Black women writers who were shrouded in obscurity. She was particularly taken with Hurston's use of **the vernacular**. In spite of her success as a writer, Hurston had died poor and was buried in an unmarked grave in the Garden of Heavenly Peace Cemetery in Florida. In 1973, Walker journeyed to the gravesite and placed a marker on what she believed was Hurston's grave in Fort Pierce, Florida. The marker lauded Hurston a "genius of **the south**." Walker published an essay in *Ms.* magazine entitled "In Search of Zora Neale Hurston," (1974), detailing her experiences resurrecting Hurston's lost works. Today, Hurston's major works all are again in print, due largely to the efforts of Alice Walker. Walker published another novel, *Meridian* (1976), that dealt with the Civil Rights Movement. Several years later she edited a Zora Neal Hurston reader titled *I Love Myself When I Am Laughing . . . and Then Again When I Am Looking Mean & Impressive* (1979). Walker published a book of short stories, *You Can't Keep a Good Woman Down*, in 1981.

While these works received good critical notices, it was Walker's third novel, *The Color Purple* (1982), that made her a widely acclaimed, internationally known writer. The novel was nominated for the National Book Critics Circle Award, won the American Book Award, and won the Pulitzer Prize for fiction. *The Color Purple* is told in a series of letters written by Celie, the novel's heroine, to God and to her younger sister Nettie. In the novel, Celie is a poor Black woman who is raped by her father and beaten by her husband. However, despite these hardships, Celie prevails in the end by finding both her own independent voice and strength in other female characters in the novel, Sophia and Shug Avery. By the end of the novel, the men in the story are transformed, and healing begins for Celie. Despite the popularity of this work, Walker received some harsh criticism. The harshest came from critics who focused on the allegedly stereotypical manner in which Black men are portrayed in the work (Early; Harris). Critics chided Walker for her portrayal of men as overly aggressive and violent. Others focused on what they perceived to be Walker's failure to produce a historically accurate novel (Early).

Trudier Harris, in "On *The Color Purple*, Stereotypes, and Silence," heavily criticizes Walker's depiction of Mr. _____ and Celie's stepfather. Harris suggests that Celie's hardships and subsequent complacency are hard to believe, and laments that she was not able to defend herself. She compares Celie to a slave and Mr. _____ to a slaveholder. Harris characterizes the love affair between Celie and Shug as "the height of silly romanticism" (157). **Gerald Lyn Early**'s assessment is also harsh: "*The Color Purple*, by black feminist writer Alice Walker, is not a good novel" (261). Early suggests that the novel is a trivial production of popular culture. He says, "*The Color Purple* is guilty of

Author Alice Walker reading from *The Color Purple*, 1985. © Bettmann/Corbis.

being nothing more than a blatant 'feel-good' novel, just the sort of book that is promoted among the nonliterary" (271). He calls the book a fantasy that has about as much historical fact as *Cinderella*. Margaret Walsh also discusses the idea of fantasy in "The Enchanted World of *The Color Purple*"; however, she suggests that the novel does not present itself as a work of history and that its richness lies elsewhere. **Gloria Wade-Gayles** applauds Walker as both a Southern writer and a woman writer. She discusses Walker's use of the term "womanist" and how it differs from the term "feminist." She says, "[S]he [Walker] is a womanist who is to feminist as 'purple is to lavender'" (302). Walker, in the nonfiction book *In Search of Our Mothers' Gardens* (1983), herself coined the term "womanist" to describe Black feminists and other feminists of color. Walker emphasizes that sexism is not the only concern for women of color and argues that womanists may delve into other issues of class and race instead of just considering sexism as the main issue crippling women.

The Color Purple was adapted into a film by Steven Spielberg and released in 1985. It received eleven Academy Award nominations, including a best picture nomination; a supporting actress nomination for **Oprah Winfrey** in her role as Sophia; and a Best Actress nomination for **Whoopi Goldberg** for her role as Celie. About ten years after the release of the film version, Walker wrote *The Same River Twice: Honoring the Difficult* (1996). Here she details some of her disappointment with the critics' reception of the novel and film, and she explains how her own screenplay adaptation of the novel was not accepted by Spielberg.

Walker later published *Living by the Word: Selected Writings, 1973–1977* (1988), a collection of essays, and *The Temple of My Familiar* (1989), a romantic novel. Her other novel, *Possessing the Secret of Joy* (1992), underscores Walker's activism with woman's issues, namely, the brutality of female genital mutilation practices, particularly in Africa. Walker published a second book on this subject, *Warrior Marks: Female Genital Mutilation Practices and the Sexual Blinding of Women* (1993). Walker's other works include *By the Light of My Father's Smile* (1998), *The Way Forward Is with a Broken Heart* (2000), and *Sent by Earth: A Message from the Grandmother Spirit after the Bombing of the World Trade Center and the Pentagon* (2001).

Among Walker's many awards, in addition to the Pulitzer Prize, are the Lillian Smith Award from the National Endowment for the Arts, the Rosenthal Award from the National Institute of Arts and Letters, a nomination for the National Book Award, a Radcliffe Institute Fellowship, a Merrill Fellowship, a Guggenheim Fellowship, a Townsend Prize, a Lynhurst Prize, and the Front Page Award for best magazine criticism from the Newswoman's Club of New York. (*See* **Epistolary Novel; Feminism.**)

Resources: Primary Sources: Alice Walker: *By the Light of My Father's Smile* (New York: Random House, 1998); *The Color Purple* (New York: Harcourt Brace Jovanovich, 1982); *In Love and Trouble* (New York: Harcourt Brace Jovanovich, 1973); *In Search of Our Mothers' Gardens* (San Diego: Harcourt Brace Jovanovich, 1983); "In Search of Zora Neale Hurston," *Ms.* 3 (Mar. 1975), 74–90; *Langston Hughes: Poet* (New York: Crowell, 1974); *Living by the Word: Selected Writings, 1973–1977* (San Diego: Harcourt Brace Jovanovich, 1988); *Meridian* (New York: Harcourt Brace Jovanovich, 1976); *Once* (New York: Harcourt, Brace, and World, 1968); *Possessing the Secret of Joy* (New York: Harcourt Brace Jovanovich, 1992); *The Same River Twice: Honoring the Difficult* (New York: Scribner's, 1996); *Sent by Earth: A Message from the Grandmother Spirit after the Bombing of the World Trade Center and the Pentagon* (New York: Seven Stories Press, 2001); *The Temple of My Familiar* (San Diego: Harcourt Brace Jovanovich, 1989); *The Third Life of Grange Copeland* (New York: Harcourt Brace Jovanovich, 1970); *Warrior Marks: Female Genital Mutilation Practices and the Sexual Blinding of Women* (New York: Harcourt Brace, 1993); *The Way Forward Is with a Broken Heart* (New York: Random House, 2000); *You Can't Keep a Good Woman Down* (New York: Harcourt Brace Jovanovich, 1981); Alice Walker, ed., *I Love Myself When I Am Laughing . . . and Then Again When I Am Looking Mean and Impressive* (Old Westbury, NY: Feminist Press, 1979). **Secondary Sources:** Gerald Early, "*The Color Purple* as Everybody's Protest Art," *Antioch Review* 44, no. 3 (Summer 1986), 261–275; Tony Gentry, *Alice Walker* (New York: Chelsea House, 1993); Trudier Harris, "On *The Color Purple*, Stereotypes, and Silence," *Black American Literature Forum* 18, no. 4 (Winter 1994), 155–161; Evette Porter, "Absolute Alice," *Black Issues Book Review*, Mar./Apr. 2003, 34–38; Gloria Wade-Gayles, "Black, Southern, Womanist: The Genius of Alice Walker," in *Southern Women Writers: The New Generation*, ed. Tonette Bond Inge (Tuscaloosa: University of Alabama Press, 1990); Margaret Walsh, "The Enchanted World of *The Color Purple*," *Southern Quarterly* 25, no. 2 (Winter 1987), 89–101.

Gail L. Upchurch

Walker, Blair S. (born 1955). Novelist, journalist, and biographer. Walker's work ranges from business journalism to comic adventure novels to biographies written with prominent African Americans. Born and raised in **Baltimore, Maryland,** Walker showed an early enthusiasm for car racing, and he aspired to be fighter pilot. After training as a military linguist specializing in Korean, he began working as a reporter at *USA Today* in 1980; his frequent contributions included automobile reviews and financial reports. Since then his work has appeared in the *Baltimore Sun*, the Associated Press, *Savoy*, and *African Americans on Wheels*. Walker also worked as an editor at *New York Newsday* and the *Washington Post*, and has taught journalism courses at the University of

Maryland. In 1994 he received a law degree from the University of Maryland and shifted from corporate journalism to writing full-time, completing entrepreneur Reginald F. Lewis's **autobiography**, *Why Should White Guys Have All the Fun? How Reginald Lewis Created a Billion-Dollar Business Empire* (1994). The book was listed as a best-seller in the periodical *Business Week*.

Walker went on to write autobiographies with retired Army General Clara Adams-Ender (*My Rise to the Stars*, 2001) and television personality Judge Greg Mathis (*Inner City Miracle*, 2002). He has written three novels featuring the Baltimore reporter Darryl Billups: *Up Jumped the Devil* (1997), *Hidden in Plain View* (1999), and *Don't Believe Your Lying Eyes* (2002). Of Walker's fiction one reviewer writes, "Billups points out the inequities he and others suffer because of their race with frustration and forthrightness, but never climbs up on a soapbox to do so" (McLarin, 1486). Another notes Walker's particular talent, through the character of Billups, for "opening up to the reader the world of newspapers, the drudgery of beat reporting, the politics of newsrooms, and what it's like to be young, black and middle-class" (McKissack, 9).

Resources: Primary Sources: Reginald F. Lewis and Blair S. Walker, *Why Should White Guys Have All the Fun? How Reginald Lewis Created a Billion-Dollar Business Empire* (New York: Wiley, 1994); Greg Mathis and Blair S. Walker, *Inner City Miracle* (New York: Ballantine/One World, 2002); Blair S. Walker: *Don't Believe Your Lying Eyes* (New York: Ballantine/One World, 2002); *Hidden in Plain View* (New York: Avon, 1999); *Up Jumped the Devil* (New York: Avon, 1997). **Secondary Sources:** Jenna Glatzer, "Interview with Blair Walker," *Absolute Write*, http://www.absolutewrite.com/novels/blair.htm; Fredrick McKissack, Jr., "The Terrorist and the Journalist," review of *Up Jumped the Devil*, *Washington Post*, Feb. 15, 1998, sec. X, p. 9; Jenny McLarin, "Review of *Hidden in Plain View*," *Booklist* 95, no. 16 (Apr. 15, 1999), p. 1486.

Alex Feerst

Walker, David (1785–1830). Antislavery orator and pamphleteer. David Walker was born in Wilmington, North Carolina, to a slave father and a free mother in 1785. At the age of twenty-seven, Walker moved to **Boston, Massachusetts**, where he set up a secondhand clothing business. From hearing his father's remembrances of experiences in **slavery** and because of his marriage to a fugitive slave (1828), Walker developed a keen interest in the history of slavery, in both classical times and in the United States. Walker also served as the Boston agent for the nation's first African American newspaper, *Freedom's Journal*. The *Journal* was the first periodical to publish one of Walker's antislavery speeches (1828). Walker was in demand to speak to meetings of Boston's African American community, urging his listeners to grasp the importance of Black unity and seeking to end complacency among African Americans in the North. His single extended work, *Walker's Appeal*, was first published in September 1829. He subsequently published two additional editions—each more urgent than the last in its denunciation of slavery. These editions appeared in 1829 and 1830.

Walker's *Appeal* appropriates and transforms the rhetoric from the founding of the United States to serve radical revolutionary ends, as is evident in the title: *Appeal, in Four Articles, Together with a Preamble, to the Colored Citizens of the World, but in Particular, and Very Expressly, to Those of the United States of America*. This language reflects the structure of the Constitution: a preamble followed by the articles.

However, Walker insists from the beginning that this is an appeal "to the colored citizens of the world." He points to the economic foundation (which included slavery) of the American nation, calling slavery a "curse to nations" that "will bring other destructions upon them" by splitting and dividing the population. Walker highlights the artificiality of racial distinctions to argue that despite their "improminent noses and wooly heads," African Americans "are men." Combining this premise with the idea that man was made to serve God alone, Walker presents a powerful argument against slavery that is, in part, based upon alleged physical differences. In an interesting, reasonable reversal of the logic supporting slavery, Walker asserts that it is not **nature** that makes slaves violent and rebellious, but "that Slavery is the principal cause [of such violence]." Unable to find a suitable historical reason for slavery's existence, Walker concludes that the Americans continue "to punish us for nothing else, but for enriching them and their country." He then argues that his situation, whereby one's hard-earned **labor** could be taken away, flies in the face of America's promise of equal opportunity and rewards for hard work. Walker's *Appeal* thus demonstrates his adeptness at using familiar American rhetoric to pose a tangible threat to the concept of unity upon which the country was founded. Walker also appropriates rhetoric of the "naturalness" of American independence and self-governance to highlight the serious effects of slavery, which he says has made "the white Americans our natural enemies," although they were not, "from the beginning...natural enemies to each other." According to Walker, slavery was an evil bound to harm the nation as a whole, was not justified because African Americans were men in the eyes of their creator, and ran counter to the nation's promises of equality and rewards for hard work.

Peppered throughout Walker's *Appeal* are allusions to the inevitability of violence if the slave system is not dismantled. Walker never directly threatens White slaveholders. But phrases such as "kill or be killed" and questions such as "Remember, Americans, that we must and shall be free and enlightened as you are, will you wait until we shall, under God, obtain our liberty by the crushing arm of power?" reveal the violence that Walker believed to be inevitable if slavery were not ended.

Responses to the more violent and revolutionary aspects of Walker's *Appeal* were swift and unsurprising. Northern abolitionists such as William Lloyd Garrison and Benjamin Lundy denounced Walker's violent rhetoric, seeing it as a liability to the **Abolitionist Movement**. Southerners, meanwhile, sprang into action to counter the effect of Walker's work. Laws were passed to prohibit the dissemination of "seditious" writings and to make it illegal for

African Americans to learn to read and write. The Virginia legislature met in secret to cope with the emergency prompted by the pamphlet. The Mayor of Savannah asked the Mayor of Boston to arrest Walker. A reward of $1,000 was offered for Walker's death, $10,000 dollars if he was returned alive to **the South**. When Walker died suddenly on June 28, 1830, many suspected foul play by any number of his critics and enemies. Although poison was for a long time considered the cause of Walker's untimely death, more recent research indicates that he probably died of natural causes, and that he may have died of tuberculosis ("David Walker").

Walker's work gave an articulate and militant voice to the plight of American slaves in the antebellum era, and his influence on others is difficult to overestimate. While some saw **Nat Turner**'s 1831 insurrection in Southampton County, Virginia, as an example Walker's words put into action, Walker's actual influence on Turner is unknown. More significant are Walker's contributions to nascent **Black Nationalism** and his influence on writers, antislavery agitators, and advocates for African American equality from **Henry Highland Garnet** to **W.E.B. Du Bois**.

Resources: Herbert Aptheker, *"One Continual Cry": David Walker's Appeal to the Colored Citizens of the World, 1829–1830, Its Setting and Its Meaning* (New York: Humanities Press, 1965); "David Walker," *Black History Daily*, http://www.blackseek .com/bh/2001/26_DavidWalker.htm; Peter P. Hinks, *To Awaken My Afflicted Brethren: David Walker and the Problem of Antebellum Slave Resistance* (University Park: Pennsylvania State University Press, 1997); David Walker, *Walker's Appeal, in Four Articles* [published with] *An Address to the Slaves of the United States of America*, by Henry Highland Garnet (1829; repr. New York: Arno, 1969).

Matthew R. Davis

Walker, Joseph A. (1935–2003). Playwright, actor, choreographer, and professor. Walker is considered an important figure in African American drama during the **Black Arts Movement**. He was born February 23, 1935, in **Washington D.C.**, Walker was the first African American playwright to receive a Tony Award. Like the main character, Johnny, in his award-winning play, *The River Niger*, Walker struggled as a young playwright. Even though he earned a B.A. from Howard University and an M.F.A. from Catholic University, he worked as a door-to-door salesman, taxi driver, postal clerk and English teacher in New York City and Washington, D.C.

Walker's career took a leap forward in 1967, when the Negro Ensemble, cofounded by **Douglas Turner Ward**, offered Walker his first theatrical job as set designer and playwright. By 1969 Walker had become a director, playwright, and choreographer-in-residence at Yale University. From 1968 through 1975, he honed his craft as writer and director with such critically acclaimed productions as *The Believers*, produced at the Garrick Theater in New York City, and *The Harangues* and *Ododo*, both produced at St. Mark's Playhouse in New York City. For the *The River Niger* (1972), also produced at St. Mark's Playhouse, Walker received the Tony Award.

Throughout his academic and theatrical career, Walker sought to explain the enigmatic struggle African Americans inherited from a country that systematically ignored their labor and genius as contributing factors in the development of American democracy. Like his contemporaries LeRoi Jones (**Amiri Baraka**) and **Ed Bullins**, Walker pushed the boundaries of **drama** as he depicted racial conflict.

Resources: Chester J. Fontenot, "Mythic Patterns in *River Niger* and *Ceremonies in Dark Old Men*," *MELUS* 7, no. 1 (Spring 1980), 41–49; Dorothy Lee, "Three Black Plays: Alienation and Paths to Recovery," *Modern Drama* 19 (1976), 397–404; Elizabeth C. Phillips, "'South...Grown Deep': The River Trope in a Recent American Drama," *Interpretations: Studies in Language and Literature* 6 (1974), 64–69; Nefertete S. Rasheed, "A Biographical and Critical Investigation of the Stage Plays of Joseph A. Walker," *Dissertation Abstracts International, Section A: The Humanities and Social Sciences* 58, no. 2 (Aug. 1997), 342–343; Joseph A. Walker, *The River Niger* (New York: Hill and Wang, 1973).

Robert H. Miller

Walker, Margaret Abigail (1915–1998). Poet, novelist, essayist, and educator. Margaret Walker was one of the leading African American women writers of the twentieth century. In a career that spanned six decades, she published ten books, including poems, essays, short stories, and a novel. Among these are her award-winning *For My People* (1942), her acclaimed **historical novel** *Jubilee* (1966), *Ballad of the Free* (1966), *Prophets for a New Day* (1970), and *October Journey* (1973). Her contributions to African American letters are all the more impressive when one considers that she achieved most of them after 1943, when she was a college professor at Jackson State University, a wife, and the mother of four children.

Margaret Abigail Walker was born on July 7, 1915, in Birmingham, Alabama, into a family of storytellers, musicians, ministers, and teachers. Her father, Sigismund C. Walker, was a Methodist minister and educator. Her mother, Marion Dozier Walker, was a music teacher. Margaret was encouraged from an early age to read, listen to music, and express her creativity (Graham, xiii).

The storyteller in the family was Margaret's grandmother, Elvira Ware Dozier. The stories that her grandmother told would eventually become the heart and soul of Walker's novel *Jubilee*. In her essay "How I Wrote *Jubilee*," Walker describes the nurturing role her grandmother played in her life. "Since my grandmother lived with us until I was an adult, it was natural throughout my formative years for me to hear stories of slave life in Georgia" (*How I Wrote "Jubilee,"* 51).

As Walker grew older, she began to realize the importance of her grandmother's stories. She understood, even then, that "I was already conceiving the story of *Jubilee* vaguely, and in my early adolescence, while I was still hearing my grandmother tell old slavery-time stories and incidents from her mother's life, I promised my grandmother that when I grew up I would write her mother's story. I'm sorry she did not live to see the book" (*How I Wrote "Jubilee,"* 51).

It wasn't just Walker's grandmother who inspired and encouraged her. She grew up in a household where the importance of education was stressed and individual talents were nurtured. Margaret started writing poetry when she was eleven. On the Christmas following her twelfth birthday, her father gave Margaret her first writer's journal. By the time she was eighteen, she had filled the journal with 365 poems.

Walker felt that her parents were her first source of poetic inspiration. Her father suggested that she should always include three elements in her poems: pictures or images, music or rhythm, and meaning. And it was her mother's music, vocal and instrumental, that gave Margaret her sense of rhythm. In *This Is My Century*, she writes: "Whether the music was classical—Bach, Beethoven, and Brahms—church hymns, or anthems, folk songs such as spirituals, work songs, blues, or ragtime and popular ballads and jazz, I heard music, my mother's music, as my earliest memory" (xii).

These experiences left lasting impressions. They helped shape Walker's outlook on life and became the inspiration for much of the literature that she created. The images that she used in her poetry and fiction were drawn from the Southern landscape of her early childhood and adolescence. The meaning or philosophy that was central to her writing came from her father, from his books and his sermons. Most of all, it came from reading the Bible (*This Is My Century*, xii).

In 1925, the Walkers moved to **New Orleans, Louisiana**; Margaret's parents taught at New Orleans University (now Dillard University). Walker completed her high school education at Gilbert Academy and enrolled at the university where her parents taught. During her freshman year she came under the influence of sympathetic teachers besides her parents. In particular, she was drawn to Miss Fluke, her freshman composition teacher. It was Miss Fluke who first suggested to Margaret's parents that their daughter should be sent to a school where she would be challenged.

The following year Walker was introduced to the poet **Langston Hughes**, who came to the university to give a poetry reading. He read her poetry, said that she had talent, and supported Miss Fluke's suggestion that Margaret's parents get her out of **the South** so she could develop into a writer. Miss Fluke was a graduate of Northwestern University in Evanston, Illinois. So was Walker's father. "That summer after Mr. Hughes's visit in February, my parents took me, along with my sister Mercedes, a gifted musician and fifteen-year-old high school graduate, to Northwestern" (*This Is My Century*, xii).

At Northwestern, Walker met two men who greatly influenced her life. **W.E.B. Du Bois** published her poetry for the first time in a national magazine, **The Crisis**, when she was eighteen. Professor Edward Buell Hungerford taught Margaret in her senior year. He introduced her to Saul Bellow and John Gardner. More important, she wrote the first 300 pages of *Jubilee* in his class. It was also at Northwestern that Walker first heard of *Poetry, A Magazine of Verse* and the Yale University Younger Poets competition.

Walker graduated from Northwestern in June 1935 with a Bachelor of Arts degree in English. After seven months of looking for a job, she was hired by the WPA Writers' Project in **Chicago, Illinois**, (part of the **Federal Writers' Project**). It was there that she met **Richard Wright**. Shortly after her twenty-second birthday she sat down at her typewriter and wrote all but the last stanza of "For My People." It took her fifteen minutes. In November 1937, "For My People" was published in *Poetry*, followed by "We Have Been Believers" (1938) and "The Struggle Staggers Us" (1939).

Of all the individuals Walker encountered during her tenure at the WPA, it was her friendship with Wright that had the most profound impact on her life. So much so, that she wrote his biography nearly fifty years later: *Richard Wright, Daemonic Genius: A Portrait of the Man, a Critical Look at His Work* (1988). Unfortunately, their friendship came to an abrupt, unexplained termination in the summer of 1939. That same year Walker enrolled in a graduate program to earn a master's degree. She left Chicago for the University of Iowa Writers' Workshop, where she earned a Masters of Arts degree in 1940. During her year in Iowa, Walker completed *For My People*, a volume of poems that she used to satisfy her thesis requirement. Twenty-five years later, in 1965, Walker earned a Ph.D. at the Iowa Writers' Workshop. She used her novel *Jubilee* as her dissertation.

Two years after Walker earned her M.A. from the University of Iowa, her volume of poems *For My People* won the Yale University Younger Poet's Award, making her the first African American to win this prestigious national literary competition. *For My People* was published by Yale University Press in 1942. The twenty-six poems of *For My People*, like the rest of Margaret Walker's creative work, exhibit a pride in the writer's African American heritage and interweave autobiographical elements with larger themes of African American history and culture.

Now that she had completed her master's degree, Walker began a distinguished teaching career that spanned over thirty years. Her first teaching assignment was at Livingston College in North Carolina. She also taught for a year at West Virginia State College. In 1943, she married Firnist James Alexander. They had four children and remained together until his death in 1980.

In 1949, the Alexanders moved to Jackson, Mississippi, where Margaret began an extended teaching career at Jackson State College (now Jackson State University) that lasted until her retirement in 1979. She earned her Ph.D. in 1965, and the following year she published *Jubilee*, a work that had taken her over thirty years to complete. *Jubilee* is an epic novel based on the stories that Elvira Ware Dozier told her granddaughter about slavery time in Georgia. It is considered the first truly historical novel written about slavery by an African American. The novel has enjoyed tremendous success, winning the Houghton Mifflin Literary Award in 1968. *Jubilee* has been translated into seven languages, and has never gone out of print.

After the publication of *Jubilee* and her retirement from Jackson State University, Walker continued her literary career with *Poetic Equation: Conversations with Nikki Giovanni and Margaret Walker* (1974), *This Is My Century: New and Collected Poems* (1989), *How I Wrote "Jubilee" and Other Essays on Life and Literature* (1990), and *On Being Female, Black, and Free: Essays by Margaret Walker, 1932–1992* (1997).

Walker's work is a grand expression of the American poetic voice and a model of the Afro-American classic literary tradition. She exemplified the living continuum of the great revolutionary democratic arts culture that has sustained and inspired Afro-Americans since the **Middle Passage** (Baraka, 32).

Resources: Amiri Baraka, "Margaret Walker Alexander," *The Nation*, Jan. 4, 1999, p. 32; Maryemma Graham, "Introduction," in *How I Wrote "Jubilee" and Other Essays on Life and Literature*, ed. Maryemma Graham (New York: Feminist Press, 1990); R. Baxter Miller, "The 'Etched Flame' of Margaret Walker: Biblical and Literary Re-Creation in Southern History," *Tennessee Studies in Literature* 26 (1981), 158–172, repr. in *Poetry Criticism*, vol. 20 (Detroit: Gale, 1998); Margaret Walker: *For My People* (New Haven, CT: Yale University Press, 1942); *How I Wrote "Jubilee" and Other Essays on Life and Literature*, ed. Maryemma Graham (New York: Feminist Press, 1990); *This Is My Century: New and Collected Poems* (Athens: University of Georgia Press, 1989).

John Greer Hall

Walker, Persia (born 1957). Mystery author. Walker was born and grew up in **Harlem, New York**. She is best known for *Harlem Redux*, a historical murder mystery that vividly captures aspects of the **Harlem Renaissance** and that focuses in part on conflicts between working-class and middle-class African Americans, the latter living on "Strivers' Row" in Harlem. The novel's main character is David McKay, a young African American man who must negotiate class conflict, try to find out how his sister died, and navigate the complexities of White New Yorkers' sudden interest in Harlem and African Americans. Walker attended the High School of Performing Arts in New York City and graduated from Swarthmore College in 1978. She worked as a radio news reporter at local stations before joining the Associated Press. Later she moved to Munich, Germany, to work for Radio Free Europe/Radio Liberty ("Biography"). (*See* **Crime and Mystery Fiction**.)

Resources: Persia Walker: "Biography," *Persia Walker* (2002), http://members.authorsguild.net/persia/disc.htm; *Harlem Redux* (New York: Simon and Schuster, 2002).

Hans Ostrom

Walker, Rebecca (born 1969). Essayist, memoirist, literary and cultural theorist, and political activist. Walker has figured prominently as a leading theorist of third-wave **feminism**. Born in Jackson, Mississippi, she is the self-described civil-rights "movement child" of the writer **Alice Walker** and the attorney Mel Leventhal. With a childhood spent alternating between divorced parents and two racial identities, Walker grew up in Mississippi, **Brooklyn, New York**; **San Francisco, California**; **Washington, D.C.**, and the Bronx and Larchmont, New York. In 1992, she completed a B.A. from Yale University, receiving the Pickens Prize for excellence in African American scholarship, and was named Feminist of the Year by the Fund for the Feminist Majority. Also in 1992, she founded the nonprofit Third Wave Direct Action Corporation. In 1994 Walker was named one of *Time* magazine's fifty future leaders of the United States. Her essay "Lusting for Freedom," in the collection *Listen Up: Voices from the Next Feminist Generation* (1995), and her edited volume *To Be Real: Telling the Truth and Changing the Face of Feminism* (1995), are defining documents of third-generation feminism, which she characterizes as "including more than excluding, exploring more than defining, searching more than arriving...facing and embracing...contradictions and complexities and creating something new and empowering" (*To Be Real*, xxxiii, xxxv).

Walker's memoir, *Black, White, and Jewish: Autobiography of a Shifting Self* (2001), chronicles childhood struggles with identity, showing through anecdote and personal memory the experiences that, as Julie Gozan observes, suggest "how Walker's nuanced and inclusive brand of twenty-first century feminism may have evolved" (30). She has also edited a collection of essays on masculinity, *What Makes a Man: 22 Writers Imagine the Future* (2004) and worked as a contributing editor for *Ms.* magazine. Periodicals featuring her work include *Black Scholar, Essence, Harper's, Mademoiselle*, the *New York Daily News, Sassy, Spin*, and *VIBE*.

Resources: Meri Nana-Ama Danquah, "Keeping the Third Wave Afloat," *Los Angeles Times*, Dec. 6, 1995, p. E1; Jennifer Drake, "Third Wave Feminisms," *Feminist Studies* 23, no. 1 (Spring 1997), 97–108; Emilie Falc, "Review of *To Be Real*," *Women and Language* 21, no. 2 (Fall 1998), 50–52; Stephanie Gilmore, "Looking Back, Thinking Ahead: Third Wave Feminism in the United States," review of *To Be Real*, *Journal of Women's History*, Winter 2001, 215–221; Julie Gozan, "Review of *Black, White, and Jewish: Autobiography of a Shifting Self*," *Lambda Book Report* 10, no. 10 (May 2002), 30; "Rebecca Walker," *Contemporary Authors Online* (Gale Group, 2002), galenet.galegroup.com; Heather Tenzer, "Identity Catharsis," *Moment* 26, no. 2 (Apr. 30, 2001), 41–43; Rebecca Walker, *Black, White, and Jewish: Autobiography of a Shifting Self* (New York: Riverhead, 2001); Rebecca Walker, ed.: *To Be Real: Telling the Truth and Changing the Face of Feminism* (New York: Anchor, 1995); *What Makes a Man: 22 Writers Imagine the Future* (New York: Riverhead, 2004).

Alex Feerst

Wallace, Michele Faith (born 1952). Nonfiction writer, essayist, and reviewer. Wallace is the daughter of **Faith Ringgold**, a writer of literature for children and young adults, and the musician Robert Earl Wallace. She gained international recognition in 1979 with the publication of *Black Macho and the Myth of the Superwoman*, which developed an original feminist analysis of how African American women are portrayed in artistic and popular media. In the book Wallace discusses the extent to which African American women tend to be either invisible in or made exotic by American art, literature, and popular culture. It was reissued with additional material in 1990. In the decades following publication of *Black Macho*, Wallace has contributed essays and reviews to such periodicals as *Essence*, *Ms.*, the *New York Times*, the *Village Voice*, *Black Cinema*, and *Artforum*. Wallace is a professor of English in the Graduate Center at the City University of New York.

Resources: Michele Wallace: *Black Macho and the Myth of the Superwoman* (New York: Dial, 1979); *Invisibility Blues: From Pop to Theory* (New York: Verso, 1990).

Hans Ostrom

Walrond, Eric D[erwent] (1898–1966). Short story writer and essayist. Walrond was one of the great early writers of the West Indian **diaspora**, and like **Claude McKay**, he played a central role in the **Harlem Renaissance** before leaving the United States for Europe. Today he is known chiefly for one collection of ten stories, *Tropic Death* (1926), which with McKay's *Gingertown*, **Jean Toomer**'s *Cane*, and **Langston Hughes**'s *The Ways of White Folks*, constitute the major **short fiction** collections of the Harlem Renaissance. Like the Jamaican native McKay, Walrond was a promoter of racial pride who incorporated primitivist elements in his work. He was not interested in publishing for the **"Talented Tenth"** of the African American community, and like McKay, he did not flinch from presenting topics, such as murder and prostitution, which some Black writers wished to avoid. Walrond, a pioneer in writing in West Indian dialects, used a vivid impressionistic style which carefully incorporated symbolist elements. Although he did write stories on New York City, most notably "Miss Kenny's Marriage" and "City Love," all of the stories of *Tropic Death* are set in the Caribbean: British Guiana, Barbados, the Panama Canal Zone, and on shipboard. The plots are slight, and the characters too briefly described to escape being types. What is remarkable are the style, the creation of atmosphere, and the use of language to capture regional dialects. Walrond is excellent at portraying folk customs and the problems that develop around nationality, language, and **race**. He presents both the positive and the negative aspects of rural Caribbean life, and he never idealizes his Black and **mulatto** characters. He depicts African Americans as often subject to a self-defeating color consciousness, but he shows them holding on in the face of White exploitation as well.

All stories of *Tropic Death* but the last end bleakly with death, and even in this one, death is not far away for the errant father. Six of these works are in the impressionist/realist mode. For example, in "Drought" a desperately poor little girl dies of ingesting marl; in "Panama Gold" a shop owner dies in a suspicious fire; in "The Yellow One" a mother is trampled to death in a fight on a boat; in "The Palm Porch" a woman who runs a brothel in which her daughters serve as bait stabs a drunken customer to death; and in "Subjection" a Black man in the Canal Zone who stands up for one of his fellows is shot by the racist Marine in charge. At the end of "Tropic Death," the wastrel father of the protagonist is severely ill with leprosy and will be transported to a leper colony, but before he leaves, he is partially reconciled to his son. "Subjection" is the only story in the collection that fits into the racial protest story tradition, and it is generally considered the weakest.

In the other four stories of *Tropic Death*, religious magic, obeah, is featured. In "The Wharf Rats," a boy who has been indifferent to his mother's servant's affections is eaten by sharks, and she chalks his death up to her use of obeah in revenge. Tables are turned in the yard wars of "The Black Pin," where a woman turns the deadly, smoky wind on the neighbor woman who tried to kill her. A plantation heir, the only White man with a large part in the stories, fails in "The Vampire Bat" to heed warnings of danger and rescues a Black baby who turns into a vampire bat and kills him. Even more fantastic than the latter two stories is "The White Snake," in which a young mother thinks that she is nursing her baby in her sleep. However, it is apparently a large snake, which is found dead soon after, perhaps killed by the mother after she makes the discovery of the transformation. The one other story, "The Voodoo's Revenge," fits in well with the others of this collection (*see* **Vodoo/Voudon**).

Walrond was born in Georgetown, British Guiana. His father moved to the Canal Zone, deserting his family. Walrond's mother was an evangelical Protestant, and although he respected some elements of this tradition, he was not associated with it in later life. His early years were spent in Barbados, but then he moved with his mother to Panama, where she attempted to find her husband. After he came to the United States in 1918, Walrond was attracted to **Marcus Garvey**'s Universal Negro Improvement Association and was an editor of his publication *The Negro World* from 1921 to 1923. Walrond studied at City College of New York (1922–1924) and at Columbia University (1924–1926), and spent a semester as a Zone Gale fellow at the University of Wisconsin (1928), but he never received a B.A. degree.

Walrond developed quickly as a writer, from short articles to sketches to short stories from 1925 to 1927, and was at the height of his powers in 1926 to 1928, when he left the United States to work on a book on the Panama Canal, which he was never able to complete. He traveled to the Canal Zone and then, after stopping in **Haiti** and the Dominican Republic, went on to France, where he stayed for several years, at one point joining Nancy Cunard's circle, before moving to England in 1932. Walrond lived in London from 1932 to 1939, when he moved to Bradford-on-Avon. From 1936 to 1938 he contributed short pieces to Marcus Garvey's periodical *Black Man*. He died in London of a heart attack in 1966. There is no biography of Walrond. Parascandola summarizes much of what is known about his life in his Introduction to *Winds Can Wake Up the Dead* (11–42).

Resources: Primary Sources: Louis J. Parascandola, ed., *Winds Can Wake Up the Dead: An Eric Walrond Reader* (Detroit: Wayne State University Press, 1998); Eric

Walrond, *Tropic Death* (1926; repr. New York: Collier, 1972); Eric Walrond and Rosey E. Pool, eds., *Black and Unknown Bards: A Collection of Negro Poetry* (Aldington, UK: Hand & Flower Press, 1958, 1971; repr. Ann Arbor, MI: University Microfilms, 1991). **Secondary Sources:** Cora Agatucci, "Eric Walrond," in *African American Authors, 1745–1945: A Bio-Bibliographical Critical Sourcebook*, ed. Emmanuel S. Nelson (Westport, CT: Greenwood Press, 2000), 429–439; Jay Berry, "Eric Walrond," in *Dictionary of Literary Biography*, vol. 51, *Afro-American Writers from the Harlem Renaissance to 1940*, ed. Trudier Harris (Detroit: Gale, 1987), 296–300; Enid E. Bogle, "Eric Walrond," in *Fifty Caribbean Writers: A Bio-Bibliographical Critical Sourcebook*, ed. Daryl Cumber Dance (Westport, CT: Greenwood Press, 1986), 474–482; Tony Martin, "The Defectors—Eric Walrond and Claude McKay," in his *Literary Garveyism* (Dover, MA: Majority Press, 1983), 124–138; Kenneth Ramchand, "The Writer Who Ran Away: Eric Walrond and *Tropic Death*," *Savacou* (Kingston, Jamaica) 2 (Sept. 1970), 67–75; Carl A. Wade, "African-American Aesthetics and the Fiction of Eric Walrond: *Tropic Death* and the Harlem Renaissance," *CLA Journal* 42, no. 4 (June 1999), 403–429.

Peter Glenn Christensen

Walter, Mildred Pitts (born 1922). Children's book author and political activist. Walter was born in the rural town of Sweetville, Louisiana, in 1922. Before embarking on a career as a writer of picture books, novels, and nonfiction books for young people, she attended Southern University, where **Frank Yerby** was one of her teachers. After graduation, Walter moved to **Los Angeles, California**, and became an elementary school teacher and an activist. The first person to graduate from college in her family, she completed requirements for a teaching certificate at California State College and earned an M.Ed. at Antioch College in Yellow Springs, Ohio. In 1947, Walter married Earl Walter, and together the couple became active in the **Civil Rights Movement**. Later, Walter became a member of the board of directors of the American Civil Liberties Union of Southern California and an American delegate to the Second World Black and African Festival of the Arts and Culture in Lagos, Nigeria.

As a teacher, Walter learned firsthand that there were few books about African Americans available to share with her students. After voicing her concerns about this to Dick Lewis, an owner of Ward Ritchie Press, he suggested that Walter begin writing books about African Americans. She had written book reviews for the *Los Angeles Times* in 1965. Accepting Lewis's challenge, she wrote *Lillie of Watts: A Birthday Discovery* (1969). Two years later the sequel, *Lillie of Watts Takes a Giant Step* (1971), was published. For several years after the publication of *Lillie of Watts Takes a Giant Step*, Walter had difficulty publishing her work. As a result, she attended writing workshops and formed alliances with several key people in the publishing industry. After a lengthy hiatus, she published *Ty's One Man Band* (1980). When Darwin L. Henderson and Consuelo W. Harris asked Walter what she hoped children learned as a result of reading her books, she said, "I hope that African

American children who read my books will identify with the characters—see themselves living in the books and become aware of who they are" (185).

Walter is probably best known for her book *Justin and the Best Biscuits in the World* (1986), which won a Coretta Scott King Honor Book Award in 1987. She was unable to attend the award ceremony, however, because she was participating in a peace walk from Leningrad to Moscow. Her first work of nonfiction, *Mississippi Challenge* (1992), was honored with the Christopher Award and the Carter G. Woodson Secondary Book Award (both in 1993). Walter has received other awards: the Parents' Choice Award for *Because We Are* (1983) and *Brother to the Wind* (1985) in 1984 and 1985, respectively; the Coretta Scott King Honor Book Award for *Because We Are* and *Trouble's Child* (1985) in 1984 and 1985, respectively; and the Jane Addams Honor Book Award and the Virginia Library Association Jefferson Cup Worthy of Special Note Award in 1997 for *Second Daughter: The Story of a Slave Girl* (1996). Her second nonfiction book, *Kwanzaa: A Family Affair*, was published in 1995.

Other works by Walter include *Tiger Ride* (1994), *Darkness* (1995), *Suitcase* (1999), and *Ray and the Best Family Reunion Ever* (2002). In 1996, she was inducted into the Colorado Women's Hall of Fame. Walter's books often feature intergenerational relationships, African American history and culture, and the importance of family and community. Harris argues, "Walter's lasting contribution to children's and young adult literature is the creation of accessible characters who symbolize the range of experiences found among African Americans" (755).

Resources: Violet J. Harris, "Walter, Mildred Pitts," in *The Oxford Companion to African American Literature*, ed. William L. Andrews, Frances Smith Foster, and Trudier Harris (New York: Oxford University Press, 1997), 754–755; Darwin L. Henderson and Consuelo W. Harris, "Profile: Choice, Courage, and Change Yield Character: An Interview with Mildred Pitts Walter," *Language Arts* 69, no. 7 (1992), 544–549; "Mildred Pitts Walter," *Children's Literature Review* 61 (2000), 182–195; Mildred Pitts Walter: *Because We Are* (New York: Lothrop, Lee & Shepard, 1983); *Brother to the Wind* (New York: Lothrop, Lee & Shepard, 1985); *Justin and the Best Biscuits in the World* (New York: Lothrop, Lee & Shepard, 1986); *Lillie of Watts: A Birthday Discovery* (Los Angeles: Ward Ritchie Press, 1969); *Lillie of Watts Takes a Giant Step* (Garden City, NY: Doubleday, 1971); *Mississippi Challenge* (New York: Bradbury Press, 1992); *Second Daughter: The Story of a Slave Girl* (New York: Scholastic, 1996); *Trouble's Child* (New York: Lothrop, Lee & Shepard, 1985).

KaaVonia Hinton-Johnson

Walton, Anthony (born 1960). Novelist, essayist, poet, and editor. Anthony Walton grew up in Aurora, Illinois, in a middle-class family. He received his undergraduate degree from Notre Dame and an M.F.A. from Brown University. Walton was the first person in his family to receive a college education. His first publication, edited with his mentor and friend, Prof. **Michael Harper**, *Every Shut Eye Ain't Asleep: An Anthology of Poetry by African Americans Since 1945* (1994), is an anthology of post–**World War II** African American poets that introduces a rich variety of dazzling styles and voices. In 1995 Walton published *Cricket Weather*, a collection of poetry that explores the gentle buoyancy of life framed within the Maine countryside. His widely successful first novel, *Mississippi: An American Journey* (1996), is Walton's personal journey into the heart of American racism as well as a discovery of his own heritage. Though *Mississippi* explores the many horrendous acts of violence and racism against Blacks in Mississippi, his novel is a testimony to the perseverance and resilience of African Americans throughout the country.

Walton's works inexorably intertwine the present with the past, as he explores American racism and the interconnectedness of the histories of both Whites and Blacks in the United States. As Walton explains: "You can't understand the **Civil Rights Movement** until you understand Jim Crow, and you can't understand Jim Crow unless you understand **Reconstruction**; and you can't understand Reconstruction unless you understand **slavery**; and you can't understand slavery until you understand the development of industrialism, the rise of technology, the invention of the cotton gin and the invention of the sail" (Mahdesian). Walton has published numerous essays on all aspects of the African American experience in the *New York Times*, *Harper's* magazine, *Atlantic Monthly*, and many others. His poems appear regularly in *The Kenyon Review*. His other works include *The Vintage Book of African American Poetry* (2000), edited with Michael S. Harper, and *Brothers in Arms: The Epic Story of the 761st Tank Battalion, WWII's Forgotten Heroes* (2004), written with the former professional basketball player Kareem Abdul-Jabbar. Walton lives in Brunswick, Maine, and is writer-in-residence at Bowdoin College.

Resources: Norman Boucher, "From the Green to the Delta and Back," *Brown Alumni Magazine*, Mar. 1996, http://brownalumnimagazine.com/storyDetail.cfm?ID=551; W. Ralph Eubanks, *Ever Is a Long Time: A Journey into Mississippi's Dark Past. A Memoir* (New York: Basic Books, 2003); Linda J. P. Mahdesian, "Author Faces Down Ghosts of the Past," *George Street Journal* 20, no. 27 (1996), http://www.brown.edu/Administration/George_Street_Journal/v20/v20n27/walton.html; Anthony Walton, *Mississippi: An American Journey* (New York: Knopf, 1996); Anthony Walton and Kareem Abdul-Jabbar, *Brothers in Arms: The Epic Story of the 761st Tank Battalion, WWII's Forgotten Heroes* (New York: Broadway Books, 2004); Anthony Walton and Michael S. Harper, eds.: *Every Shut Eye Ain't Asleep: An Anthology of Poetry by African Americans Since 1945* (Boston: Little, Brown, 1994); *The Vintage Book of African American Poetry* (New York: Vintage, 2000).

Debbie Clare Olson

Waniek, Marilyn Nelson. *See* **Nelson, Marilyn**

Ward, Douglas Turner (born 1930). Actor, playwright, and director. In addition to writing several satirical plays about relationships between Blacks and Whites, Ward is most often associated with the Negro Ensemble Company, which he founded and which has produced numerous plays by African American dramatists and for African American audiences. Douglas Turner

Ward was born in Burnside, Louisiana, and moved to **New Orleans, Louisiana**, to live with a relative during his formative years. A precocious youngster, he graduated from high school at the age of twelve. He attended Wilberforce College for a year in 1946, and then transferred to the University of Michigan, where he also stayed for a year (1947–1948). In 1948, Ward moved to New York City, where he became involved in politics and worked as a journalist for the *Daily Worker* from 1948 to 1951.

It was his political involvement that led Ward into the theater. Bored by the discussions at many political meetings, he began to try his hand at writing entertaining skits that encompassed the message and theme argued about during these meetings, and at the age of nineteen, Ward determined to become a dramatist. He honed his skills at the Paul Mann Actor's Workshop, which he attended for over two years. It was here that Ward realized his considerable acting ability as well, and he made his acting debut in an off-Broadway production of Eugene O'Neill's *The Iceman Cometh*. Several other acting roles followed, including the role of Walter Lee Younger in the tour of **Lorraine Hansberry**'s *A Raisin in the Sun*. Ward established his acting career under the name Douglas Turner. In 1965, Ward's one-act satirical plays *Happy Ending* and *Day of Absence* made their off-Broadway debuts and ran for 504 performances, making them among the longest-running off-Broadway plays. Ward received the Vernon Rice/Drama Desk Award for playwriting and an Obie for acting in 1965–1966 for these plays. Other plays by Ward include *The Reckoning* (1969), *Brotherhood* (1970), and *The Redeemer* (1979).

In 1968, after publishing an influential article in the *New York Times* titled "American Theatre: For Whites Only?," which argued that Black playwrights did not have artistic freedom writing for a theater controlled by Whites, Ward was given a Ford Foundation grant to establish the Negro Ensemble Company (NEC). The company was founded by Ward, who served as its artistic director; Robert Hooks, who was managing director; and Gerald Krone, the administrative director. The company produced several works by African American playwrights, including **Lonne Elder**'s *Ceremonies in Dark Old Men*, **John D. Weaver**'s *The Brownsville Raid* (1976), and **Charles H. Fuller, Jr.**'s *A Soldier's Play* (1982), as well as all of Ward's own plays. In addition to his responsibilities as artistic director, Ward acted in and directed several NEC productions. His directorial debut occurred with the production of **Richard Wright**'s *Daddy Goodness* in 1968. He received an Obie for his acting performance in the NEC production of **Joseph Walker**'s *The River Niger*, and a Tony nomination for Best Supporting Actor for the same role in 1973. (*See* **Satire**.)

Resources: Jeanne-Marie A. Miller, "Douglas Turner Ward," in *Encyclopedia of African American Culture and History*, vol. 5, ed. Jack Salzman, David Lionel Smith, and Cornel West (New York: Macmillan Library Reference, 1996); Bernard Peterson, Jr., *Contemporary Black American Playwrights and Their Plays: A Biographical Directory and Dramatic Index* (Westport, CT: Greenwood Press, 1988); Stephen Vallillo, "Douglas Turner Ward," in *Dictionary of Literary Biography*, vol. 38, *Afro-American Writers after 1955: Dramatists and Prose Writers* (Detroit: Gale, 1985); Douglas Turner

Ward: "American Theatre: For Whites Only?" *New York Times*, Aug. 14, 1966, sec. 2, p. 1; *Brotherhood* (New York: Dramatists' Play Service, 1970); *Happy Ending* and *Day of Absence* (New York: Dramatists' Play Service, 1966); *The Reckoning* (New York: Dramatists' Play Service, 1970).

Ama S. Wattley

Ward, Jerry Washington, Jr. (born 1943). Scholar, critic, poet, editor, and professor. For more than thirty years, Ward has educated students in an effort to nurture a community of sensible, responsible literary and cultural critics and writers. He was born in **Washington, D.C.**, on July 31, 1943. A graduate of Tougaloo College, he served there for many years as a member of the faculty and finally as Chair of the Department of English. In 2002, Ward accepted an endowed chair as Distinguished Scholar and Professor of English and African World Studies at Dillard University. He has helped many students to pursue graduate work in literary studies and thereby to gain academic appointments.

Ward's poem "Jazz to Jackson to John" is his best-known, and he authored the introduction for the 1993 edition of **Richard Wright**'s *Black Boy*. He has also published dozens of critical essays and articles, and he has coedited a collection of scholarly essays, *Redefining American Literary History*. With Charles Rowell and **Thomas Covington Dent**, Ward was a founder of *Callaloo*, a journal of African American and African arts and letters, and he has held editorial positions with *Callaloo* and such other journals as *African American Review*, *OBSIDIAN II*, and *Mississippi Quarterly*. Ward edited *Trouble the Water: 250 Years of African American Poetry* (1997), a comprehensive and affordable anthology of African American poetry from the eighteenth century to the late twentieth century.

Resources: Jerry Ward, Jr., "Introduction," in *Black Boy*, by Richard Wright (New York: Perennial Classics, 1998); Jerry Ward, Jr., ed., *Trouble the Water: 250 Years of African American Poetry* (New York: Mentor, 1997); Jerry Ward, Jr., and John Oliver Killens, eds., *Black Southern Voices* (New York: New American Library, 1992); Jerry Ward, Jr., and A. LaVonne Brown Ruoff, eds., *Redefining American Literary History* (New York: Modern Language Association, 1990).

Kysha Brown Robinson

Ward, [James] Theodore (Ted) (1902–1983). Playwright, essayist, poet, and librettist. Best known as the playwright of *Our Lan'*, one of the first plays by an African American to be produced on Broadway, Ward wrote more than thirty plays in his lifetime and dedicated his life to developing a theater created by and for African Americans.

Ward was born in Thibodaux, Louisiana, the eighth of eleven children. His father, a highly religious man, was a schoolteacher and a salesman. At age thirteen, after his mother's death, Ward ran away from home and worked his way through **Chicago, Illinois**, Seattle, Washington, and Salt Lake City, Utah, performing a variety of jobs including barbershop attendant, busboy, and shoe shiner. While in Salt Lake City he attended the University of Utah, where he was awarded a Zona Gale Fellowship for creative writing. He continued his education, writing and performing in plays at the University of Wisconsin, then moved to Chicago to teach **drama** at the Abraham Lincoln Center (Hatch, "Theodore Ward"). While there, he wrote his first full-length play, *Big White Fog* (1937), which was produced the following year by the **Negro Unit** of the Chicago Federal Theatre Project.

Ward then moved to New York City and, with **Langston Hughes, Loften Mitchell, Paul Robeson,** and **Owen Dodson,** founded the Negro Playwrights Company (1940). The company's mission was to create a theater that would both employ African Americans and mirror their lives. *Big White Fog* was chosen as the inaugural production, but the company quickly disbanded due to lack of funding.

Ward's next major play, a historical drama titled *Our Lan'* (1941), details the harsh realities encountered by a group of freed slaves attempting to settle off the coast of Georgia after the **Civil War.** *Our Lan'* became one of the most successful plays written by an African American during the 1940s and one of the earliest plays by an African American to be produced on Broadway (1947). The receipt of a Guggenheim Fellowship (1948) enabled Ward to begin research on the radical abolitionist **John Brown,** who became the subject of Ward's next play, *Of Human Grandeur* (originally *John Brown,* 1949; revised and retitled, 1963).

Interest in Ward's work revived during the **Black Arts Movement** of the 1960s, and several of his more notable plays returned to the stage. Additional works include *The Daubers* (1953), *Candle in the Wind* (1967), and musicals titled *Charity* (1960), *Big Money* (1961), and *The Bell and the Light* (1962).

Resources: James V. Hatch, "Theodore Ward: Black American Playwright," *Freedomways* 15 (Spring 1975), 37–41; "Interview with Playwright Ted Ward," *Afrika Must Unite* 2, no. 15 (1973), 9–11; Theodore Ward: *Big White Fog,* in *Black Theatre U.S.A.: Plays by African Americans 1847 to Today,* rev. and enl. ed., ed. James Vernon Hatch and Ted Shine (New York: Free Press, 1996); *Our Lan',* in *Black Drama in America: An Anthology,* 2nd ed., ed. Darwin T. Turner (Washington, DC: Howard University Press, 1994); "Why Not a Negro Drama for Negroes by Negroes?," *Current Opinion* 72 (1972), 639–640; "Theodore Ward, Special Collection," Hatch-Billops Collection, New York.

Elizabeth A. Osborne

Washington, Booker T. (1856–1915). Autobiographer, orator, human rights advocate, and educator. Owing to his nonconfrontational approach to **race** relations and his belief that vocational training would allow African Americans to succeed in business as in life, Washington became one of the most influential leaders of the late nineteenth century. However, the late twentieth-century scholarly consensus revealed, for example, in his being mentioned in only two passing citations in a *Publications of the Modern Languages Association* special issue on African American literature, casts him as a post-**Reconstruction** puppet who attempted to counteract the radicalism of rival

Black leaders, including, but certainly not limited to, **W.E.B. Du Bois**. But this view of Washington, as Mark Bauerlein has pointed out, overlooks larger historical contexts, including the realities and consequences of Jim Crow laws and other conditions with which African Americans had to contend. The view may also underestimate the extent to which Washington covertly sponsored activism and protest. Much of the information about Washington's life comes from his reflections on what he was able to achieve as a result of his unflagging effort and determination. *The Story of My Life and Work* (1896) was written primarily for Black readers and was sold door-to-door, while *Up from Slavery* (1901), written with the journalist Max Bennett Thrasher, was designed to reach a wider audience. Washington's aim in writing these works was to present his own story as an exemplar for aspiring Blacks, and to encourage the next generation to face the new era of opportunity, after Reconstruction, with pride and courage.

Because Booker Taliaferro Washington was born into **slavery**, the property of James Burroughs of Virginia, the exact date of his birth is not known. Even though his mother was a plantation cook, his childhood was one of privation, and conditions for his family seem only to have worsened after emancipation. His family moved to Malden, West Virginia, where his stepfather had found work packing salt. Washington was expected to work at the salt facility as well, and he recalls the deep impression made on him by the sight of **White** children studying in a schoolroom that he was unable to attend. He managed to get night lessons, and at last his parents allowed him to attend day school, but he was still required to put in several hours at the salt furnace, beginning at sunrise. Later, as he writes in the chapter "The Struggle for Education" (in *Up from Slavery*), while working in the coal mines, he overheard men talking about a school for "colored people" in Virginia, and so, in 1872, at the age of sixteen, he walked approximately 200 miles to enroll in the Hampton Normal and Agricultural Institute. Having arrived without money for tuition or board, he paid his way working as a janitor. The school was founded and run by General Samuel Chapman Armstrong, who profoundly influenced Washington's life and philosophy of education. In addition to learning the value of hard work and good study habits, Washington readily accepted Armstrong's doctrines of self-discipline, self-reliance, morality, and cleanliness. Armstrong was dedicated to showing the world that former slaves could learn menial trades and could become teachers. His vision was one of uplift for Blacks, brought about through a serious and sustained effort to provide general education for anyone with a sincere desire to persevere (*see* **Race Uplift Movement**).

Following graduation from the Hampton Institute, Washington took a teaching job in Tinkersville, West Virginia, near his family home. He left in 1878 to attend Wayland Seminary in **Washington, D.C.**, for six months. The following year Armstrong invited him to return to Hampton as a teacher, and in 1881 recommended him as the principal of a new school called Tuskegee Normal and Industrial Institute in Alabama's Black Belt (named for the rich, heavy soil). When he arrived, the main buildings were a stable and a hen house that the first thirty students, male and female, converted into living space. Classes were held in the African Methodist Episcopal Zion Church. As part of what was to become a hallmark of the Tuskegee educational tradition, the first permanent building, constructed a year later, was designed and built by instructors and students. In addition to pursuing basic academic subjects, students learned skills that were of immediate and practical value: brick-making, woodworking, cooking, farming, animal husbandry, dressmaking, and weaving. They made mattresses, brooms, rugs, shoes, and soap, and eventually sold the surplus to people in the area to bring in extra money. Soon they had their own print shop, and new tools, instruments, and machines were acquired every year.

The first students graduated in 1885. By 1888 the school owned 540 acres of land and had over 400 students. In the next decade Washington hired George Washington Carver to teach agriculture and help the school take advantage of the fertile soil surrounding the campus. His innovative farming research is now legendary, but the early years of Tuskegee were filled with many shortages and setbacks. As his writings make clear, Washington was keenly aware that the success or failure of his enterprise would significantly affect future opportunities for African Americans in **the South**. Consequently, he traveled widely to solicit donations, endorsements, supplies, and publicity. He became a well-known speaker and, because of his warm personality and devotion to his educational mission, he eventually became a welcome guest in the homes of some of the wealthiest men and women in the United States.

Washington was asked to speak at the opening of the 1895 Atlanta Cotton States and International Exposition. No such honor had ever been given to a Southern Black. The impact of that fifteen-minute speech was phenomenal. It was later reprinted and widely circulated, along with letters of congratulation from eminent statesmen and prospective benefactors, and headlines from around the country. Speaking directly to Whites and indirectly to Blacks who shunned manual **labor**, he advocated economic and moral advancement rather than political agitation and legal wrangling as the surest pathway to citizenship.

This willingness to compromise drew criticism from some Black leaders of the day, most notably Du Bois, who, in *The*

Booker T. Washington, 1895. Courtesy of the Library of Congress.

1693

Souls of Black Folk (1903), denounced Washington's gradualism and his stated policy of accommodation; moreover, Du Bois distrusted the beneficence of such wealthy White industrialists as Andrew Carnegie, Collis P. Huntington, and John D. Rockefeller—all of whom regularly gave money to Washington for his work at the Tuskegee Institute. Washington's increasing comfort among powerful White businessmen and politicians, coupled with his wide-ranging knowledge of people and activities concerned with Black advancement, led him to be a frequent, if unofficial, adviser to presidents Cleveland, McKinley, Theodore Roosevelt, and Taft. In fact, at the invitation of Theodore Roosevelt, Washington attended a dinner at the White House in 1901, the first Black to do so. Washington maintained that he helped in a more substantial way "by assisting in the laying of the foundation of the race through a generous education of the hand, head, and heart" (*Up from Slavery*, 41).

In addition to expanding program offerings at Tuskegee, Washington instituted a variety of programs for rural extension work, and in 1900 he helped to establish the National Negro Business League. He received honorary degrees from Harvard University (1896) and Dartmouth College (1901) and wrote more than a dozen books, including *The Future of the American Negro* (1902), *Working with the Hands* (1904), and *My Larger Education* (1911). In all of his writings he frequently comments on the love of labor, not for financial gain alone, but for its own sake and the satisfaction that comes from doing something that needs to be done. His moral essays reiterate the value of good work. Washington had faith that markets and consumers cared more about the products of labor than the skin color of the laborer. This theme emerges often in his autobiographical works and in occasional writings on the benefits of clean living and hard work. Washington served on the boards of trustees of Fisk and Howard universities and directed philanthropic initiatives nationwide.

Despite his high visibility and extensive publication, Washington was a complex, discreet, and private man. We learn almost nothing from his autobiography about what he actually advised powerful politicians to do, and even less about his domestic life. While in New York in 1915, he was admitted to St. Luke's Hospital, suffering from arteriosclerosis. He insisted on returning home to Tuskegee, where, a little more than a week later, on November 14, he died. His funeral was attended by over 8,000 people. In 1940 he was the first American of African descent to appear on a U.S. postage stamp.

Resources: Mark Bauerlein, *Negrophobia: A Race Riot in Atlanta, 1906* (San Francisco: Encounter Books, 2001); Louis R. Harlan: *Booker T. Washington: The Making of a Black Leader, 1856–1901* (New York: Oxford University Press, 1972); *Booker T. Washington: The Wizard of Tuskegee, 1901-1915* (New York: Oxford University Press, 1983); Booker T. Washington: *The Future of the American Negro* (Boston: Small, Maynard, 1902); *My Larger Education* (Garden City, NY: Doubleday, Page & Co., 1911); *Up from Slavery* (1901; New York: Dover, 1995); *Working with the Hands* (New York: Doubleday, Page & Co., 1904).

Bill Engel

Washington, Mary Helen (born 1941). Scholar, literary critic, editor, and professor. Washington is a feminist scholar and literary critic who has edited several significant anthologies of literature written by African American women and has focused critical attention on the substance and importance their works.

Mary Helen Washington was born in Cleveland, Ohio, in 1941 to David C. Washington and Mary Catherine Dalton Washington. She received her B.A. in 1962 from Notre Dame College in Manchester, New Hampshire. She received her M.A. and Ph.D. from the University of Detroit in 1966 and 1976, respectively.

Washington has a long career in teaching and scholarship. She was a high school teacher in the public schools of Cleveland from 1962 to 1964. She was an instructor at St. John's College in Cleveland from 1966 to 1968. Washington was an assistant professor at the University of Detroit (1972 to 1975), where she began serving as the director of the Center for Black Studies in 1975. She was an associate professor of English from 1980 to 1989 at the University of Massachusetts, Boston. Currently she is a professor of English at the University of Maryland, College Park, where she has been since 1989 (*see* **Black Studies**).

Washington helped to develop the Black Studies Department at the University of Detroit in the 1970s when she began to conduct research on African American women's literature. She saw value in this writing and took it seriously—subsequently, she has produced four significant literary anthologies of African American literature: *Black-Eyed Susans* (1975), *Midnight Birds* (1980), *Invented Lives* (1987), and *Memory of Kin* (1991). Writings from the most celebrated African American women writers have appeared in these anthologies. They include works by **Toni Cade Bambara, Gwendolyn Brooks, Frances Ellen Watkins Harper, Pauline Elizabeth Hopkins, Zora Neale Hurston, Harriet Ann Jacobs, Gayl Jones, Louise Meriwether, Toni Morrison, Ann Lane Petry, Ntozake Shange, Alice Walker**, and **Dorothy West**. In her anthologies, Washington has included thoughtful and incisive introductions as well as essays and critical notes about the authors and the social and historical context of their works.

Washington's feminist appraisal of African American women's literature provides insight into the history and originality of their contributions. She argues for the universality of the human experience present in the works of African American women authors although their writing, like much of women's writing, tends to focus on personal experience and the micro scale of interpersonal interactions of the protagonist (e.g., within the family or the community) rather than on the direct engagement of a protagonist and the politics of larger social forces, as is often seen in literature written by African American males. Washington's critical work underlines the recurring themes in African American's women's writing—family, community, and work—and how, within these themes, the wider themes of **race** and **gender** oppression are explored.

Besides anthologies, Washington has written introductions to reissued editions of several important African American women's texts, such as **Anna Julia Haywood Cooper**'s *A Voice from the South*, **Paule Marshall**'s *Brown Girl, Brownstones*, and **Zora Neale Hurston**'s *Their Eyes Were Watching God*.

Washington's current research is devoted to uncovering and analyzing uncanonized texts written by African Americans during the 1950s that served to further the radical and progressive politics of the day.

Resources: Primary Sources: Mary Helen Washington: "Afterword," in *Brown Girl, Brownstones*, by Paule Marshall (New York: Doubleday, 1981); "Foreword," in *Their Eyes Were Watching God*, by Zora Neale Hurston (New York: Perennial Library, 1990); "Foreword," in *A Voice from the South*, by Anna Julia Cooper (New York: Oxford University Press, 1988); "Introduction," in *I Love Myself When I Am Laughing . . . and Then Again When I Am Looking Mean and Impressive*, by Zora Neale Hurston (Old Westbury, NY: Feminist Press, 1979); Mary Helen Washington, ed.: *Black-Eyed Susans: Classic Stories by and about Black Women* (Garden City, NY: Anchor, 1975); *Invented Lives: Narratives of Black Women, 1860–1960* (Garden City, NY: Anchor, 1987); *Memory of Kin: Stories About Family by Black Writers* (New York: Doubleday, 1991); *Midnight Birds: Stories by Contemporary Black Women Writers* (Garden City, NY: Anchor, 1980). **Secondary Sources:** "Mary Helen Washington," in *Black Writers: A Selection of Sketches from Contemporary Authors*, 3rd ed. (Detroit: Gale, 1999); "Mary Helen Washington," in *Contemporary Authors*, new revision series, vol. 51 (Detroit: Gale, 1989); Hans Ostrom, "Families: Minefields and Mysteries" (profile of Washington, review of *Memory of Kin*), *Soundlife* (Sunday supp.), *Morning News Tribune* (Tacoma, WA), Feb. 24, 1991, p. 8.

Kimberly Black-Parker

Washington, Teresa N. (born 1971). Scholar, teacher, and poet. Born in Peoria, Illinois, Washington completed a Ph.D. and taught as an assistant lecturer at Obafemi Awolowo University in Ile-Ife, Nigeria. She has subsequently joined the faculty at Kent State University.

A new voice in African American literary and cultural studies, Washington has written one book and has contributed critical and creative work to a variety of journals. Her first book, *Our Mother, Our Powers, Our Texts: Manifestations of Ajé in Africana Literature*, was in 2005.

Washington's work has appeared in the collections *A Pilgrimage of Color* (2000) and *Step into a World: A Global Anthology of the New Black Literature* (2000). Her contributions to journals and **newspapers** have appeared in *The Literary Griot* (1997, 2001), *Southern Exposure* (1997), and *The Daily Mississippian* (1995), and she has contributed reviews to *African-American Review*.

Washington's poems have appeared in *The Estrella Mountain Community College Literary Review*, *The Griot*, and *Obsidian II*. In addition, she coedited the anthology *A Festival of Poetry: An Anthology of Poems from the First Annual OAU Poetry Festival* (1998).

Resources: Teresa Washington, *Our Mother, Our Powers, Our Texts: Manifestations of Ajé in Africana Literature* (Bloomington: Indiana University Press, 2005); Teresa

Washington and Adebayo Lamikrana, eds., *A Festival of Poetry: An Anthology of Poems from the First Annual OAU Poetry Festival* (Ile-Ife, Nigeria: Obafemi Awolowo University Poet's Press, 1998).

Martin Kich

Washington, D.C. Capital of the United States. Many African American writers were born and raised, attended college, and/or worked in Washington, but the city has often been overlooked as a literary center, seemingly because some writers were residing elsewhere when they first achieved critical acclaim, or because they lived for a longer period of time in another city. Nonetheless, a number of writers who had a significant impact on African American literature spent most of their lives in Washington (sometimes known as the "District"). African Americans with District connections were particularly important in helping shape the writing of three major literary movements: the essays and memoirs from the civil rights struggles of the late nineteenth and early twentieth centuries, the **Harlem Renaissance** of the 1920s; and the Black gay renaissance of the 1980s and early 1990s.

Being the nation's capital and having the country's premier African American school system, Washington attracted many African American political and educational leaders beginning in the mid-nineteenth century. In 1872, **Frederick Douglass** moved his family to the city, where he served as editor and publisher of the *New National Era*. While holding a series of federal appointments over the next two decades, he continued to write and speak regularly on racial issues and women's suffrage, and published his third autobiography, *Life and Times of Frederick Douglass* (1881; rev. 1892).

In the late nineteenth and early twentieth centuries, some of the country's leading Black activists and writers taught at Washington's renowned M Street High School (later known as Dunbar High School). **Anna Julia Haywood Cooper**, who taught there for more than forty years, was one of the foremost orators of her time and a leader in a number of women's organizations, including the Colored Women's YWCA. Her major work, *A Voice from the South* (1892), is considered a groundbreaking articulation of **feminism/Black feminism**. Another M Street teacher, **Mary Church Terrell**, was a charter member and first President of the National Association of Colored Women, one of the few women involved in founding the **NAACP**, and the first Black woman in the United States to be appointed to a school board. The story of her lifelong struggle for **race** and **gender** equality, *A Colored Woman in a White World* (1940), was the first full-length **autobiography** published by an African American woman. The historian **Carter G. Woodson** likewise taught at the school; while there in 1915, he began his long career as a researcher and writer by establishing the Association for the Study of Negro Life and History and publishing his first book, *The Education of the Negro Prior to 1861*. **Langston Hughes** later worked for him briefly.

Along with boasting the nation's leading Black high school, Washington was home to the country's oldest and most prestigious college for African

Americans, Howard University. Its faculty included such eminent scholars and writers as the philosopher and literary critic **Alain Locke**, the sociologists Kelly Miller and **Edward Franklin Frazier**, the historian Rayford Logan, the poet **Sterling A. Brown**, and the political scientist Ralph Bunche.

Alain Locke's contributions to African American literature in the early and mid-twentieth century are particularly significant. After taking a position at Howard University in 1912, Locke consciously cultivated a place for himself as the literary arbiter and leading publicist for a promising new generation of Black writers and artists. He especially sought to assist writers and artists who apparently shared his attraction to men, including **Countee Cullen**, Langston Hughes, **Claude McKay**, **Richard Bruce Nugent**, and Glenn Carrington. He encouraged and critiqued their work, helped them find publishers and sources of funding, sometimes provided money himself, and promoted their writing through essays and reviews in Black periodicals such as *Opportunity* and *Phylon*, and White-edited publications such as *Survey*. Locke edited a special issue of *Survey Graphic* on **Harlem, New York**, that served as the nucleus of his landmark text that helped define the emerging Black renaissance, *The New Negro* (1925).

The proliferation literary and artistic works by African Americans in the 1920s and the deliberate promotion of **"Negro"** art are often referred to as the Harlem Renaissance, but many writers of the period were born and raised outside of Harlem, in places including Washington. Some writers were educated in the District, or, as in the case of Locke, spent a substantial part of their careers in the city. More than a third of the African Americans who had a major book published during the 1920s and nearly half of the contributors to *The New Negro* had connections to Washington, D.C. For example, **Zora Neale Hurston** moved to Washington in 1918 to attend Howard University, where she participated in a student writers group organized by Locke and by Montgomery Gregory, a faculty member in the English and drama departments who had founded the influential Howard Players theater company. Hurston published her first short story, "John Redding Goes to Sea," in *Stylus*, the group's magazine, in 1921.

Some of Langston Hughes's earliest published poems were written while he was in Washington. Although Hughes lived in the District for only a little more than a year in the mid-1920s, his first two collections of poetry, *The Weary Blues* (1926) and *Fine Clothes to the Jew* (1927), reflected his experiences patronizing the Black working-class bars and storefront churches on 7th Street in Northwest Washington. In many of these poems, Hughes drew inspiration from the **blues** and **spirituals** he heard there; the themes and rhythms of the music had a lasting influence on his poetry and prose. **Jean Toomer**, a native Washingtonian, was likewise captivated by Black life on 7th Street, and most of the prose sketches and poems in the second section of *Cane* (1923) are set in this "crude-boned, soft-skinned wedge of [Black] life" (Toomer, 41).

Other important Harlem Renaissance writers who spent time in Washington include **Jessie Redmon Fauset**, **Angelina Weld Grimké**, **Rudolph John Chauncey Fisher**, and **Richard Bruce Nugent**. Fauset and Grimké both taught for many years at the city's M Street High School; Fisher and Nugent were both born in the District and briefly lived there as young adults before joining the growing exodus of writers to Harlem.

Although some Washington writers had migrated to what Nathan Huggins calls the "capital of the Black world" (1971, 13)—Harlem—by the mid-1920s, a significant number remained in the nation's capital. Many of these local writers attended the Saturday night literary salons that the poet and playwright **Georgia Douglas Johnson** hosted in her home on S Street from 1925 through the mid-1930s. These gatherings were renowned for bringing together the brightest local talent, including the playwrights **Marita Bonner, May Miller, Mary Powell Burrill**, and **Willis Richardson**; the poets **Lewis Alexander** and **Gwendolyn Bennett**; and, on occasion, Locke, Grimké, and Woodson. The Washingtonians who went to Harlem and other Black writers, such as Countee Cullen and **Claude McKay**, often participated in the salons when they were in the District. By providing opportunities for writers to share and discuss their work, "the circle," as Richard Bruce Nugent referred to the group, had a major impact on the development of the Harlem Renaissance (Beemyn 1997, 95).

Nearly fifty years later, another gathering place in Washington would help spark a new renaissance in African American literature. Although many Harlem Renaissance writers were attracted to members of their sex, few wrote about the subject and even fewer were open about their sexual identity. The question of Langston Hughes's sexuality, for example, remains a complicated one (Ostrom). But this silence began to be broken through major works by writers such as **James Baldwin** and **Audre Lorde**, and by the 1990s, a significant body of literature by openly lesbian, gay, and bisexual African Americans had developed. As with the Harlem Renaissance, many of the writers who contributed to this Black gay literary movement had ties to Washington.

Recognizing that there were few places in the District or elsewhere in the United States where lesbian, gay, and bisexual African Americans could regularly present their work, Ray Melrose, the president of the D.C. Coalition of Black Gays, turned a carriage house behind his home in Northeast Washington into a performance space in 1982. Referred to as the ENIK Alley Coffeehouse, after its location in an alley between Eighth and Ninth and I and K streets, the space hosted writers, artists, and musicians from Washington and around the country, providing them with a unique opportunity to hone their talents and develop an audience for their work.

Local writers who performed regularly at the Coffeehouse produced or contributed to many of the groundbreaking works on the experiences of Black lesbians, gay men, and bisexuals in the 1980s and early 1990s. The poet **Essex Hemphill**, who was raised in Washington, edited *Brother to Brother: New Writings by Black Gay Men* (1991) and published his own poetry and prose collection, *Ceremonies* (1992). He was also featured, along with Wayson Jones, Larry Duckette, and other Washington writers, in the acclaimed documentary about Black gay male life, *Tongues Untied* (1989), directed by Marlon Riggs. Another Washingtonian, the poet and filmmaker Michelle Parkerson, is best known for her video biographies of **Audre Lorde** and the District-based a cappella group Sweet Honey in the Rock. A number of other local writers, including Craig Reynolds and Cary Alan Johnson, contributed to *Brother to Brother* or its predecessor, **Joseph Beam**'s *In the Life: A Black Gay Anthology* (1986). (*See* **Gay Literature**; **Lesbian Literature**; **Williams, Edward Christopher.**)

Resources: Joseph Beam, ed., *In the Life: A Black Gay Anthology* (Boston: Alyson, 1986); Brett Beemyn, "A Queer Capital: Lesbian, Gay, and Bisexual Life in Washington, D.C., 1890–1955" (Ph.D. diss., University of Iowa, 1997); "The Black Renaissance in Washington, D.C., 1920–1930s" (District of Columbia Public Library, 2002), http://www.dclibrary.org/blkren; "Duke Ellington's Washington," Public Broadcasting System, http://www.pbs.org/ellingtonsdc/index.htm; Essex Hemphill, ed., *Brother to Brother: New Writings by Black Gay Men* (Boston: Alyson, 1991); Nathan Irvin Huggins, *Harlem Renaissance* (New York: Oxford University Press, 1971); George B. Hutchinson, "Jean Toomer and the 'New Negroes' of Washington," *American Literature* 63 (Dec. 1991), 683–692; Georgia Douglass Johnson Papers, Manuscript Division, Moorland-Spingarn Research Center, Howard University, Washington, DC; Ronald M. Johnson, "Those Who Stayed: Washington Black Writers of the 1920's," in *Records of the Columbia Historical Society of Washington, D.C.*, vol. 50, ed. Francis Coleman Rosenberger (Washington, DC: Columbia Historical Society, 1980), 484–499; Alain Locke, *The New Negro* (1925; repr. New York: Atheneum, 1970); Alain Locke Papers, Manuscript Division, Moorland-Spingarn Research Center, Howard University, Washington, DC; Rayford W. Logan, *Howard University: The First Hundred Years, 1867–1967* (New York: New York University Press, 1969); Hans Ostrom, "Sexuality and Hughes," in his *A Langston Hughes Encyclopedia* (Westport, CT: Greenwood Press, 2002), 350–352; Marlon Riggs, dir., *Tongues United* (Santa Monica, CA: Strand Releasing Home Video, 1991), VHS format; Mary Church Terrell, *A Colored Woman in a White World* (Washington, DC: Ransdell, 1940); Jean Toomer, *Cane* (1923; repr. New York: Norton, 1988); Edward Christopher Williams, *When Washington Was in Vogue: A Love Story—A Lost Novel of the Harlem Renaissance*, intro. Adam McKible, commentary by Emily Bernard (New York: Amistad, 2003).

Brett Beemyn

Waters, Ethel (1896–1977). Singer, actress, and autobiographer. Born in **Philadelphia, Pennsylvania**, Ethel Waters had one of the longest and most successful careers of a twentieth-century Black entertainer. As a child she lived largely with her grandmother and at an early age discovered a gift for mimicry. Starting out as a **blues** singer and dancer in traveling tent shows and vaudeville theaters with **Bessie Smith** in the post–**World War I** period, she went by "Sweet Mama Stringbean" due to her thin frame and signature shimmy. Waters secured a recording contact soon after her move to New York City in 1919. She first signed with Cardinal in 1921 and then switched to Black Swan, eventually settling at Columbia. On the blues circuit, she was often recognized for her "difference" from other blues singers, most notably Bessie Smith. Tall, skinny, and light-skinned, Waters had a "sweet" voice, as opposed to Smith's deep tones. For this reason, Waters is often credited with bridging the gap between blues and popular music. She moved her act to Broadway in the late 1920s and throughout the 1930s, performing in musicals such as *Africana* and *As Thousands Cheer*.

Waters also toured the United States and Europe, mostly with her longtime partner, dancer Ethel Williams. She was the first top-billed Black actress in a Broadway show. As she grew older, she began to take roles in "White" productions, most notably in *Member of the Wedding*, the Carson McCullers play that was later turned into a film (1952). Waters insisted on script approval for her character and demanded that Portia, the maid, become as religious as Waters herself had become, a stance she previously took when agreeing to star in the musical *Cabin in the Sky* (1943) alongside Lena Horne, with whom she reportedly had great tension on the set. In between these two plays adapted into films was her role in the feature film *Pinky*, for which she received an Oscar nomination for the best supporting actress in 1949; she earned her second for her work in *Member*.

Waters's first **autobiography**, *His Eye Is on the Sparrow* (1951), written with Charles Samuels, chronicles her life up to this point. The book was a best-seller, indicating how popular a figure Waters had become in American culture. Her autobiography frankly details her rise to fame, including accounts of her involvement in the **Harlem Renaissance** at **Carl Van Vechten**'s parties and drag balls, among other noteworthy events. Van Vechten, the White patron of many Black writers of the time, became a close friend. In her autobiography, Waters manages both to titillate with details of her well-traveled and often difficult life and to cast herself as "saved" by the text's end. Also in 1951, Waters starred in the first black-centered sitcom, *Beulah*. Over the next few years her larger frame and her repeated portrayal of maids or servants cast her out of favor with civil rights politics and Black audiences. Waters found herself with a lack of work and moved to California, where she became a follower of Rev. Billy Graham, a popular evangelical Christian preacher, in the late 1950s. In her capacity as one of Graham's disciples, Waters appeared at numerous events for Richard Nixon's presidential campaigns. Her second autobiography, *To Me It's Wonderful* (1972), chronicles her relationship to her religion in her later years. She died a member of Graham's church, and a fellow member, Twila Knaack, chronicled the last ten years of her life in the memoir *Ethel Waters: I Touched a Sparrow* (1978).

As a pioneer in Black popular music and film, Waters was one of the first "mainstream" or crossover successes from Black to White American culture.

This fact is often lamented or celebrated in profiles of the singer, with both sides engaging in problematic racial essentialisms to make their points. Carl Van Vechten famously remarked on how Waters's "refined" voice distinguished her from the "growl" of other Black performers. Susan McCorkle, in a long overdue profile in *American Heritage* that sought to recover Waters from relative obscurity, remarks that Waters's voice became too "mannered" later in her career, leaving out the "naturalness" of her vocal sensibility. **Amiri Baraka** (as LeRoi Jones), in his famous study of Black music and audiences, *Blues People* (1963), locates Waters and her Black-owned label Black Swan as a case study in the tensions between middle-class Black taste and Black audiences. As reissues of many blues women's recordings and **black feminist literary criticism** have brought such figures as "Ma" Rainey and **Bessie Smith** back into popular circulation for a whole new generation, Waters is still mostly forgotten except as the occasional sign of White appropriation of Black talent. Her recordings and performances mark subtle racial tensions in American culture throughout the twentieth century, leaving Waters an undeniably talented and complicated figure in African American culture and literature.

Resources: LeRoi Jones, *Blues People* (New York: Morrow, 1963); Twila Knaack, *Ethel Waters: I Touched a Sparrow* (Waco, TX: Word Books, 1978); Susannah McCorkle, "The Mother of Us All," *American Heritage*, Feb./Mar. 1994, 60–73; Ethel Waters, *To Me It's Wonderful* (New York: Harper & Row, 1972); Ethel Waters with Charles Samuels, *His Eye Is on the Sparrow* (Garden City, NY: Doubleday, 1951).

Samantha Pinto

Weatherly, Tom (born 1942). Poet, teacher, and editor. Born in Scottsboro, Alabama, Weatherly was the son of a teacher. He attended Morehouse College from 1958 to 1961 and Alabama Mechanical and Agricultural College in the 1961–1962 academic year. He subsequently became a minister in the African Methodist Episcopal Church, and for several years was an assistant pastor of the denomination's church in Scottsboro. He eventually found the responsibilities of his ministry and life in the Deep South to be constraining, however, and he moved to New York City to pursue his ambition of becoming a poet.

While honing his own skills as a poet, Weatherly began to conduct poetry workshops to promote self-expression among African Americans and other marginalized groups. In the mid-1970s, he began long associations with the **Brooklyn, New York**, Poetry Project and the St. Mark's Church Poetry Project. His work in developing poetry workshops has been supported by three grants from the National Endowment for the Arts.

Because of his success with these workshops, Weatherly considered a career in academia and became a somewhat itinerant instructor. In 1969–1970, he taught art as an adjunct instructor at Rutgers University; in 1970–1971, he was writer-in-residence at Bishop College in Dallas, **Texas**; in 1971–1972, he was poet-in-residence at Morgan State College in **Baltimore, Maryland**;

and in 1972–1973, he was a poetry teacher at the Webb School in Westchester County, New York. Then, in 1974, he entered the M.F.A. program at Columbia University, but he did not complete the degree. He has subsequently been a writer-in-residence at Grand Valley State College, poet-in-the-schools for the public school district of Richmond, Virginia, and an instructor at several penal institutions, including the Women's House of Detention in New York City.

In his own poetry, Weatherly has sought to fuse historical and cultural awareness with calls for progressive political and social action. In his first collection, *Maumau American Cantos* (1970), Weatherly links the Kenyan insurgency against British colonial rule and the American **Civil Rights Movement**, seeing them as parts of an international movement to assert the cultural value of the African heritage and the political possibilities in the African **diaspora**. In his second collection, *Thumbprint* (1971), he emphasizes the contributions of African and African American women not only in sustaining their families but also in supporting political and social activism and, historically, in preserving the cultural memory. His third collection, *Climate* (1972), is a chapbook-size group of poems bound with Ken Bluford's *Stream*.

Weatherly coedited *Natural Process: An Anthology of New Black Poetry* (1971). His own work has been included in the collections *The Poetry of Black America: An Anthology of the Twentieth Century* (1973) and *America: A Prophecy* (1973). (*See* **Scottsboro Boys.**)

Resources: Arnold Rampersad, "The Universal and the Particular in Afro-American Poetry," *CLA Journal* 25 (Sept. 1981), 1–17; Evelyn Hoard Roberts, "Tom Weatherly," in *Dictionary of Literary Biography*, vol. 41, *Afro-American Poets since 1955*, ed. Trudier Harris and Thadious M. Davis (Detroit: Gale, 1985); Tom Weatherly: *Climate* (Philadelphia: Middle Earth, 1972); *Maumau Cantos* (New York: Corinth, 1970); *Thumbprint* (Philadelphia: Telegraph, 1971).

Martin Kich

Weaver, Afaa Michael (born 1951). Poet, short story writer, playwright, editor, teacher, and factory worker. Weaver is known for substantial work in three genres: poetry, **short fiction**, and **drama**. He was born in **Baltimore, Maryland**, and originally named Michael S. Weaver. He attended public schools in Baltimore, and at age sixteen he started attending the University of Maryland in College Park, studying for two years before leaving to work in a factory. Factory work was his main occupation for the next fifteen years; during that time he wrote creatively, and also wrote occasionally for the *Baltimore Sun* ("Afaa M. Weaver"). In 1985 several of his poems were accepted by and published in the magazine **Callaloo**. In that same year Weaver was awarded a grant by the National Endowment for the Arts. Weaver went on to pursue an M.F.A. in creative writing at Brown University, which awarded him a fellowship. For his graduate thesis, he wrote the play *Rosa*, which was produced in **Chicago, Illinois**, in 1993. That same year his second play, *Elvira and the Lost Prince*, was produced in **Boston, Massachusetts**.

Weaver's books of poems include *Poems* (1985), *My Father's Geography* (1992), *Stations in a Dream* (1993), *Timber and Prayer: The Indian Pond Poems* (1995), *Talisman* (1998), *Ten Lights of God* (2000), and *Multitudes: Poems Selected and New* (2000). Of *Talisman*, the poet **Kalamu ya Salaam** said, "It is a brave little book of poems," and he praised Weaver's unflinching honesty. Weaver is clearly attuned to his working-class experience but also writes on a variety of other subjects, including memory, family, emotional loss, and regret. Weaver edited *These Hands I Know: African-American Writers on Family* (2002) and coedited the anthology *Gathering Voices* (1986). His short story "By the Way of Morning Fire" is included in the anthology *Children of the Night: The Best Short Stories by Black writers, 1967 to the Present*, edited by **Gloria Naylor**. Weaver teaches creative writing at Simmons College in Boston.

Resources: "Afaa M. Weaver," *African American Literary Book Club* (2004), http://aalbc.com/afaa.htm; Gloria Naylor, ed., *Children of the Night: The Best Short Stories by Black Writers, 1967 to the Present* (Boston: Little, Brown, 1995); Kalamu ya Salaam, Review of *Talisman*, *African American Literary Book Club* (1998), http://aalbc.com; Afaa Michael Weaver: *Multitudes: Poems Selected and New* (Louisville, KY: Sarabande Books, 2000); *My Father's Geography* (Pittsburgh: University of Pittsburgh Press, 1992); *Stations in a Dream* (Baltimore: Dolphin-Moon Press, 1993); *Talisman* (Chicago: Tia Chuca Press, 1998); *Ten Lights of God* (Lewisburg, PA: Bucknell University Press, 2000); *Timber and Prayer: The Indian Pond Poems* (Pittsburgh: University of Pittsburgh Press, 1995); Afaa Michael Weaver, ed., *These Hands I Know: African-American Writers on Family* (Louisville, KY: Sarabande Books, 2002); Afaa Michael Weaver, David Beaudoin, and James Taylor, eds., *Gathering Voices* (Baltimore: Dolphin-Moon Press, 1987).

Hans Ostrom

Webb, Frank J. (c. 1828–c. 1894). Novelist. Very little is known about Frank J. Webb, author of *The Garies and Their Friends* (1857), his one major work and the one upon which his literary reputation rests. Yet Eric Gardner's meticulous investigation of Webb's biography reveals valuable, if still incomplete, information about his life. According to **Harriet Beecher Stowe**'s Preface to *The Garies*, Webb, a free Black, was part of an extensive and prominent network of Black and mixed-race individuals in nineteenth-century **Philadelphia, Pennsylvania**. He was probably born in Philadelphia in 1828 and had familial ties to the Forten family, whom he visited several times in the 1850s (Gardner, 298).

Webb was well-read and understood popular literary conventions of the time, especially those associated with sentimental and domestic novels. According to Gardner, *The Garies* underscores Webb's keen "Pan-Africanist sense of Black history" and his astute observations of "the complexities of free Black life in the North" (297). Although Webb worked with Harriet Beecher Stowe in the 1840s, he turned to British abolitionists in the 1850s and became interested in various Black nationalist issues, moving to Jamaica for a short period to consider the possibilities of colonization (Gardner, 298). Webb married in 1845 and may have worked in the clothing business until his shop failed in 1854 (Gardner, 298). He traveled to England with his wife, **Mary Webb**, who was intimately acquainted with Harriet Beecher Stowe and gave readings of a dramatized *Uncle Tom's Cabin*. Those readings brought the Webbs to England for an extensive British tour and subsequent accolades by British society. Most likely writing the bulk of *The Garies* in England, Webb dedicated the novel to Lady Noel Byron and garnered a Preface written by Stowe, which probably helped secure the publication of the novel and an appointment in the post office of Kingston, Jamaica (Gardner, 300). Upon returning to the United States in the 1860s, Webb worked for the Freedmen's Bureau. He moved west to **Texas** by the late 1870s and stayed through the 1880s.

Webb published three works in his lifetime. In addition to *The Garies*, in 1870 he had two serialized novellas in the Philadelphia-based periodical *The New Era*: "Two Wolves and a Lamb" and "Marvin Hayle." Both of these short works draw upon his experience in the aristocratic circles of London, **Paris, France**, and Cannes, France. *The Garies and Their Friends*, however, constitutes Webb's significant contribution to African American literature in both theme and technique. Gardner contends that *The Garies* deserves serious scholarly and classroom attention because it "can tell us much about how antebellum Black authors 'talked back' to other texts that foreground race . . . experimented with form and genre to achieve broad socio-political and artistic (as well as individual and economic) goals, and began to shape a distinct African American literature" (297). In its chronicling of mixed-race and Black families in urban Philadelphia, the novel touches on a number of important themes addressed extensively in later nineteenth- and twentieth-century African American novels, including **William Wells Brown**'s *Clotel*, **Pauline Elizabeth Hopkins**'s *Contending Forces*, and **James Weldon Johnson**'s *Autobiography of an Ex-Colored Man*. Moving away from the North versus **South** dichotomy, Webb instead depicts the chief conflict in the mid-nineteenth-century as Black versus White rather than region against region (Simson, 450).

Webb was one of the first black novelists to treat **passing** and its implicitly "'destructive psychology'" (Candela, 242). Although some critics contend that he backed away from advocating Black militancy, they also note his emphasis on the necessity of fighting back and resisting accommodationist positions in order to survive in the White man's world (Simson, 450). Webb explores the various of dimensions of Black resistance in his use of humor, particularly through the **trickster** figure who plays a joke on the White dupe, giving the Black reader "'the dual pleasure of identifying with the player of the joke as well as laughing at the victim'" (Candela, 242). His use of **humor** is also prominent in his treatment of childhood. Some critics assert that his characterization of Charlie and Kinch, the two central child figures in the novel, are forerunners to **Mark Twain**'s *Tom Sawyer* and *Huckleberry Finn*. Of Webb, **Robert Reid-Pharr** argues that *The Garies and Their Friends* "functions as a complex nexus of sentimental ideology and emergent Black national-ism; and as the weaver of such a story, [he] demands careful study" (Gardner, 297).

Resources: Gregory Candela, "Frank J. Webb," in *Dictionary of Literary Biography*, vol. 50, *African-American Writers Before the Harlem Renaissance*, ed. Trudier Harris (Detroit: Gale, 1986), 242–245; Eric Gardner, "A Gentleman of 'Superior Cultiva-tion and Refinement': Recovering the Biography of Frank J. Webb," *African American Review* 35 (2001): 297–308; Rennie Simson, "Frank Webb," in *African American Authors, 1745–1945: A Bio-bibliographical Critical Sourcebook*, ed. Emmanuel S. Nelson (Westport, CT: Greenwood Press, 2000), 448–454.

Rebecca R. Saulsbury

Webb, Mary (1828–1859). Dramatic reader. One of the first African American dramatic readers, Webb gained brief fame both in the United States and Great Britain for her readings of a version of *Uncle Tom's Cabin* and, arguably through that fame, supported her husband's writing of the first African American novels.

Little is known of Webb's early life beyond the remnants from publicity materials and gossip. Accounts suggest that she was the daughter of a female slave and a wealthy Spaniard. Her maiden name remains unknown.

She married **Frank J. Webb** in 1845 in **Philadelphia, Pennsylvania**, and they moved on the fringes of Philadelphia's African American elite. When their clothing business failed in 1854, Webb, always noted for her love of poetry, turned to dramatic readings as a source of income. After brief training, she gave a successful private reading in early April 1855, and her first public reading on April 19. Her success in Philadelphia and in **Boston, Massachu-setts**, and Worcester, Massachusetts, brought her to the attention of White abolitionists. **Harriet Beecher Stowe**, who had previously resisted requests to dramatize *Uncle Tom's Cabin*, created an abbreviated version of the novel for Webb's use, titled *The Christian Slave* (1855).

Webb's debut reading of this text reportedly drew over 1,000 people to Boston's Tremont Temple on December 6, 1855, and initiated a six-month tour that included cities ranging from New York to Cleveland, Ohio, and allowed interaction with such abolitionists as **William Cooper Nell** and Amy Post. While attendance and reviews were uneven, Webb gained additional note by the addition—apparently sanctioned by the poet—of excerpts from Henry Wadsworth Longfellow's *Hiawatha* (1855), which she read in Native American garb.

Like many of her contemporaries, Webb turned next to Britain. Aided by her connection to Stowe and then by a circle of British abolitionists, Webb debuted in London on July 28, 1856. During the year that the Webbs stayed in Britain, her husband penned *The Garies* (1857), one of the first African American novels. Mary Webb's health rapidly declined, though, and, the Webbs eventually moved to Jamaica, where British friends obtained a post for Frank in hopes that the climate would aid Mary's recovery. While she offered a few readings in 1858 and 1859, her health continued to fail, and she died from consumption in Kingston. (*See* **Abolitionist Movement**.)

Resources: Eric Gardner, "Webb, Mary," *American National Biography Online* (Apr. 2003 update), http://www.anb.org/articles/18/18-03725.html; Phillip Lapsansky, "Afro-Americana: Frank J. Webb and His Friends," in *Annual Report of the Library Company of Philadelphia for the Year 1990* (Philadelphia: Library Company of Philadelphia, 1991), 27–43.

Eric Gardner

Weber, Carl (born 1970). Novelist. Weber's fiction often includes both comedic elements and dramatic situations, and it is often concerned with relationships as seen from African American males' points of view. Weber has said he enjoys creating characters "people love to hate" and writing novels that provide a chance for his audience to deal with "other people's problems" (*Shades of Romance*). Weber is a popular writer of "mass-market" or "commercial" fiction. He was born in the borough of Queens in New York City, and earned a B.S. in accounting from Virginia State University. Later he earned an M.B.A in marketing from the University of Virginia (Mullen). In the 1990s, while teaching business at the prison on Riker's Island in New York City, Weber started the African American Bookstore, first as a mail-order business (Mullen, 2004). He now has multiple stores in the New York City area. He is also the owner of Black Print Publishing, a publishing company, and has started Urban Books, a publishing company that focuses on the **drama** and grit of inner-city life. Its goal is to feature "edgy, and exciting new voices—writers who tell it like it is" (Urban books).

Since 2000, Weber has written four novels. His breakthrough novel, *Lookin' for Luv* (2000), chronicles the trials and tribulations people go through while dating and searching for true love. His next novel, *Married Men* (2001), is about African American men looking for love in untraditional places. *Baby Momma Drama* (2003) is written from a Black woman's point of view. It is about two Black sisters, the men in their lives, and the children from those relationships. He then wrote a novella, "Easy Street," with La Jill Hunt, which was published in the anthology *A Dollar and a Dream* (2003). The novella is about what people would do if they won the lottery. His most recent work is *Player Haters* (2004), which concerns the experiences of three siblings.

Resources: "Carl Weber," African American Literature Book Club (2001), http://authors.aalbc.com/carlweber.htm; Jennifer Cates, "Author of the Month: Carl Weber," *Romance in Color* (2001), http://www.romanceincolor.com/authormthweber.htm; Leah Mullen, "Carl Weber Gives 'Best Selling' Author a New Meaning," *Mosaic Books*, http://www.mosaicbooks.com/cw.htm; "Questions and Answers with Carl Weber," *Shades of Romance* (2004), http://www.bookremarks.com/CarlWeber2.htm; Urban Books Company, http://www.urbanbooks.net; Carl Weber: *Baby Momma Drama* (New York: Dafina, 2003); *Lookin' for Luv* (New York: Kensington, 2000); *Married Men* (New York: Dafina, 2001); *Player Haters* (New York: Dafina, 2004); Carl

Weber and La Jill Hunt, "Easy Street," in *A Dollar and a Dream* (New York: Dafina, 2003).

Catherine N. Anyaso

Wells-Barnett, Ida B. (1862–1931). Essayist, journalist, and political activist. Ida B. Wells-Barnett is best remembered as a groundbreaking journalist who exposed the horrors of **lynching** to an international audience. Born in Holly Springs, Mississippi, to enslaved parents, Wells was influenced by the decisive, independent character of her parents (Myrick-Harris, 70). Following her parents' death in 1878 during a yellow fever epidemic, sixteen-year-old Wells took primary responsibility for her six siblings. She later taught in a one-room school near Holly Springs. In 1882 or 1883, she left Mississippi for **Memphis, Tennessee**; she taught in the rural schools of Shelby County until she passed the qualifying examination to teach in Memphis city schools in 1884 (Wells-Barnett, *Crusade*, xvii). She was fired from her teaching position in 1891 after she published articles in her newspaper *Free Speech* which criticized Memphis school board members for conditions in separate colored schools (*Crusade*, xix).

Wells-Barnett's journalism career began in 1884 when she wrote an article for *The Living Way*, a Black church newspaper (Thompson, 15). The article detailed a lawsuit she had waged against a railroad that insisted she move to a smoking car. She won the 1884 case in the lower court, arguing that equal accommodation statutes had been violated (14). However, the Supreme Court of Tennessee overturned the ruling, saying that the smoking car was considered equal accommodation for colored people (14).

The article was the start of a weekly column in *The Living Way*, for which she wrote under the pseudonym "Iola" (Sterling, 73). In 1889, Wells-Barnett bought an interest in the Memphis Black newspaper *Free Speech and Headlight*. The name was later changed to *Free Speech*. It was in 1892 that Wells-Barnett published in her newspaper a scathing criticism of the lynchings of three Black Memphis businessmen, one of whom was a dear friend (*Crusade*, xix).

The lynchings led Wells-Barnett to research other lynchings, and she wrote an editorial on May 21, 1892, that reported her initial findings. She left for a planned trip to New York City on May 26, 1892, before the editorial had been typeset (Sterling, 82). By the time she reached New York, news of the editorial had

Ida B. Wells-Barnett, 1891. Courtesy of the Library of Congress.

preceded her to the city, as had an open call by two White newspapers in Memphis for Whites not to stand for the charges posed in the editorial (Sterling, 82). While Wells-Barnett was in New York, the office of the *Free Speech* was ransacked (Sterling, 83). She never returned to Memphis.

In the North, Wells-Barnett found a new audience. Within a week of her arrival in New York, she began writing a column for the *New York Age*, published by prominent Black journalist **Timothy Thomas Fortune** (Sterling, 85). One particular issue was sold throughout the country; in it, Wells wrote of lynching as a concerted effort by Whites to thwart Black progress (Sterling, 83). Soon after, on October 5, 1892, she gave her first major speech to hundreds of women from New York, **Philadelphia, Pennsylvania**, and **Boston, Massachusetts**, who had gathered to honor her, giving her a brooch and $500. She used the funds to expand the *New York Age* article into the pamphlet *Southern Horrors: Lynch Law in All Its Phases* (1892).

Schechter credits *Southern Horrors* as "a point of origin in American critical thought on lynching and racism" (85). In the pamphlet, Wells-Barnett chronicled incidents in which Black men were charged with raping White women, a frequent justification for lynching. She also included accounts in which White women admitted to consensual relationships with the accused, thus supporting her point that Black men were lynched without probable cause. In the pamphlet, she shared accounts of White men being protected by local militia and government leaders when they were charged with raping Black females, including little girls. She ultimately stressed that Black men must protect themselves against mob justice by doing so with their own firearms, boycotting, emigrating, and using the press.

For four months after her first major New York speech, she gave a speech titled "Lynch Law in All Its Phases" (Sterling, 85). Her speaking abilities had become so well known that in 1893 she was invited to Great Britain to speak on the topic of lynching (Sterling, 86). She returned to England on a speaking tour from March to July 1894 (Sterling, 86). Accounts of her tour were published in the *Chicago Inter-Ocean* (*Crusade*, xxi). An Anti-Lynching Committee was formed in Great Britain, and Wells continued to organize antilynching committees in the United States upon her return (*Crusade*, xxi).

In 1895, Wells-Barnett published *A Red Record: Tabulated Statistics and Alleged Causes of Lynchings in the United States, 1892–1893–1894*. *A Red Record* did much of what *Southern Horrors* had done in detailing incidents of lynchings and the purported reasons for them, but it also expanded the argument for cessation of lynching. She argued that as a leading world citizen concerned with the plight of humanity, America could not allow lynching to continue. She argued that if the same mob violence occurred in Africa, White Christians in the United States would consider the acts barbarism. In *A Red Record*, she also underscored the wide array of reasons given for lynching Blacks: a man beating his wife, suspicion of hog stealing, being "saucy to white people," and so on. In addition, she included a very detailed record of lynchings in 1894. According to Wells-Barnett, 197 people (both Black and White) were lynched in eighteen states. Women were among those lynched. She added that more men were put to death by mobs than by the due process of law in 1894.

Wells-Barnett's well-known antilynching work catapulted her onto the national scene and into association with other Black leaders. At least on one occasion, she was the houseguest of the poet and novelist **Frances Ellen Wilkins Harper**. The noted orator and journalist **Frederick Douglass** was familiar with her work and supported it. His own body of work included the essay "Lynch Law in the South" (1892). To protest that the World's Columbian Exhibition would not allow Black exhibitors, she published a collection of essays titled *The Reason Why the Colored American Is Not in the Columbian Exhibition: The Afro-American's Contribution to Columbian Literature*. Frederick Douglass contributed an essay to this collection. He was also a key figure for her, introducing her to several individuals who would aid in her antilynching campaign. Her early work with the **NAACP** put her in especially close proximity with an already familiar acquaintance, W.E.B. Du Bois. However, ideological differences made her association with the organization short-lived.

Although Wells-Barnett was a well-known national figure in promoting the rights of Blacks, her relationships with other national leaders were often contentious. She disagreed with **Booker T. Washington**'s insistence that Blacks work within Jim Crow laws to advance the **race**. She thought that protest was necessary for racial progress. Her aggressive approach was also ill suited to the more reserved agenda of **Mary Church Terrell** and the National Association of Colored Women.

In 1895, Wells-Barnett married attorney and founder of the **Chicago, Illinois**, newspaper *The Conservator*, Ferdinand Lee Barnett, and is therefore commonly referred to as Ida B. Wells-Barnett. Soon she assumed the helm of the paper (Myrick-Harris, 70). The Barnetts had four children, and after the second child was born, Wells-Barnett resigned from her work at *The Conservator* (*Crusade*, xxiii). Nonetheless, she was still very active in her community. She taught a Sunday School class and encouraged the young men in her class to form an organization that would right some of the wrongs in their communities (*Crusade*, xxv). This organization, the Negro Fellowship League, "provided sleeping quarters to homeless men and sponsored various community activities" (*Crusade*, xxv). Around 1897, Wells-Barnett led the Ida B. Wells Club, begun in 1893, to start the first kindergarten for Black children in Chicago (Fradin and Fradin, 103).

In spite of her controversial reputation among national leaders, Wells-Barnett remained active in public life even after the momentum behind her antilynching message had diminished. In January 1913, she organized the Alpha Suffrage Club, the first **Negro** suffrage club. In the years immediately leading to 1920 and in the early 1920s, Wells's reports on **race riots** appeared in several Black newspapers: the **Chicago Defender**, *The World*, *The Broad Ax*, and *The Whip*. The Negro Fellowship League distributed several pamphlets which Wells had written. In 1930, she was a candidate for the Illinois state senate (*Crusade*, xxix).

While other Black writers of the late nineteenth and early twentieth centuries were being published by presses or journals, Wells-Barnett published *A Red Record*, *Lynch Law in Georgia*, and *Mob Rule in New Orleans* (1900) at her own expense. The late twentieth and the early twenty-first centuries have been kinder to her reputation. The film *A Passion for Justice* chronicles her life, as does the stage play *Constant Star*. The "Princess of the Press," as Wells-Barnett is sometimes called, was inducted posthumously into the Tennessee Newspaper Hall of Fame.

Ida B. Wells-Barnett died on March 25, 1931, in Chicago after a brief illness.

Resources: Primary Sources: Ida B. Wells: *Crusade for Justice: The Autobiography of Ida B. Wells*, ed. Alfreda M. Duster (Chicago: University of Chicago Press, 1970); *The Memphis Diary of Ida B. Wells*, ed. Miriam DeCosta-Willis (Boston: Beacon, 1995); *Southern Horrors and Other Writings: The Anti-Lynching Campaign of Ida B. Wells, 1892–1900*, ed. Jacqueline Jones Royster (Boston: Bedford/St. Martin's, 1997). Secondary Sources: Dennis Brindell Fradin and Judith Bloom Fradin, *Ida B. Wells: Mother of the Civil Rights Movement* (New York: Clarion, 2000); Linda O. McMurry, *To Keep the Waters Troubled: The Life of Ida B. Wells* (New York: Oxford University Press, 1998); Clarissa Myrick-Harris, "Against All Odds: A New Play and Photo Exhibition Call Attention to Ida B. Wells and Her Brave Fight to End Lynching in America," *Smithsonian*, July 2002, 70; Patricia A. Schechter, *Ida B. Wells-Barnett and American Reform, 1880–1930* (Chapel Hill: University of North Carolina Press, 2001); Dorothy Sterling, *Black Foremothers: Three Lives* (Old Westbury, NY: Feminist Press, 1979); Mildred I. Thompson, *Ida B. Wells-Barnett: An Exploratory Study of an American Black Woman, 1893–1930* (Brooklyn, NY: Carlson, 1990); Catherine A. Welch, *Ida B. Wells-Barnett: Powerhouse with a Pen* (Minneapolis, MN: Carolrhoda Books, 2000).

Sharese Terrell Willis

Wesley, Dorothy Burnett Porter (1905–1995). Librarian, bibliographer, scholar, and archivist. For forty-three years, Dorothy Porter Wesley was curator for the Moorland-Spingarn Collection at Howard University in **Washington, D.C.** (1930–1973). Under her distinguished and aggressive leadership, a small collection of books, papers, and memorabilia grew into what is believed to be the world's largest single holding of information about the peoples of Africa and their descendants all over the world. Many well-known and respected writers called upon Wesley's expertise, including **Sterling A. Brown, Alain Locke, Langston Hughes, Alex Haley, Richard Wright**; the historians Lerone Bennett and John Henrik Clarke; thousands of graduate students, researchers, international scholars, museum exhibitors, journalists, and others.

Dorothy Porter Wesley was born on May 25, 1905, in Warrenton, Virginia, to Dr. Hayes J. Burnett, a doctor, and Bertha Ball Burnett, a tennis player. She was the eldest of four children. She obtained her early education in Montclair, New Jersey. Then she enrolled in the Miner Normal School, which later became the University of the District of Columbia. In 1926 she transferred to nearby Howard University, where she graduated in 1928 with a bachelor's degree. In 1931, she received a bachelor's degree in library science from Columbia University, and in 1932 a master's degree in library science (M.L.S.), also from Columbia. Wesley is widely regarded as the first African American woman to receive the M.L.S. from Columbia University.

Upon returning to the library at Howard University after her studies, Wesley ushered in a new era there. Before 1930, no American library seemed to have a clear classification system for Black materials, especially the pamphlets, brochures, pictures, correspondence, newspapers, tracts, programs from events, and other written formats that were characteristic of many documents about and by Blacks up to that time. Along with her colleagues Lula V. Allan, Edith Brown, Lula E. Connor, and Rosa Hershaw, Wesley developed a classification and cataloging system for this special Black collection. She developed a range of research tools and bibliographies, which laid the groundwork for a new field of study that evolved into Black or African American Studies. During her tenure, the collection increased from about 3,000 items to approximately 200,000 by the time she retired in 1973.

Perhaps the largest and single most significant materials which Wesley was responsible for acquiring was the private collection of the attorney Arthur B. Spingarn, who knew many participants in the **Harlem Renaissance**, including Langston Hughes. Spingarn had collected books and other written materials on, by, and about Africans in the **diaspora** as he traveled throughout the world for thirty-five years. At the time of the acquisition, bibliophiles proclaimed the collection unprecedented in its depth, quality, and quantity. Dr. Mordecai W. Johnson, the President of Howard University at the time, lauded the collection as the most comprehensive and interesting group of books about Blacks ever assembled. Among the many rare materials in the collection was **Armand Lanusse**'s *Les Cenelles* (1845), the first anthology of Black poetry in the United States, and **Phillis Wheatley**'s An *Elegiac Poem on the Death of That Celebrated Divine . . . George Whitfield* (1770).

Wesley wrote several books, articles, and book reviews, but she is remembered mostly for extensive bibliographies she compiled, some of which were published. Although Wesley retired in 1973, she continued to be active in several organizations and received many honors and awards. Among those were the **Olaudah Equiano** Award (1989) and honorary degrees from Susquehanna University (1971), Syracuse University (1989) and Radcliffe College (1990). She was a Ford Foundation Visiting Senior Scholar at the **W.E.B. Du Bois** Institute at Harvard University (1994) and a member of Phi Beta Kappa. President Bill Clinton honored her with the National Endowment for the Humanities Charles Frankel Award (1994). Wesley was married to James Amos Porter, a Howard University educator, artist, and writer, and later to Charles Harris Wesley, a distinguished educator and author of twelve books.

"Bibliomaniac" is the term Wesley often used to describe herself (Belt and Hall). Because of the early work that she did to build a world-class collection of books and materials on Africa and the African diaspora, many scholars, writers, public servants, and others have chosen to donate their libraries and papers to the Moorland-Spingarn Research Center at Howard University. The Moorland-Spingarn Library honors her memory with an annual Dorothy Porter Wesley lecture series.

Resources: Marva Belt and Tomasha P. Hall, *Dorothy Porter Wesley: A Selected Bibliography* (Washington, DC: Moorland-Spingarn Research Center, Howard University, 1996); Dorothy B. Porter: "A Library on the Negro," *American Scholar* 7 (Winter 1938), 115–117; *Negro Writing 1760–1837* (Boston: Beacon, 1971); *The Negro in the United States: A Selected Bibliography* (Washington, DC: Library of Congress, 1970); *North American Negro Poets: A Bibliographic Checklist of Their Writings, 1760–1944* (Hattiesburg, MS: Book Farm, 1945).

Betty W. Nyangoni

Wesley, Valerie Wilson (born 1947). Novelist, editor, and children's writer. Wesley is an award-winning writer with an international readership. She is best known for a series of mystery novels featuring the protagonist Tamara Hayle. Hale is an African American private investigator who used to be a policewoman. She is also a single parent who lives in New Jersey. The novels in the series include *When Death Comes Stealing, Devil's Gonna Get Him, Where Evil Sleeps, No Hiding Place, Easier to Kill,* and *The Devil Riding.* Wesley has written two novels that are not in the **crime and mystery fiction** genre: *Always True to You in My Fashion* and *Ain't Nobody's Business if I Do.* They focus on African American family issues and male-female relationships.

Wesley has also written children's books: *Where Do I Go from Here, How to Lose Your Cookie Money, How to Lose Your Class Pet,* and *How to Fish for Trouble.* The *Willimena* books are geared toward children from ages six to nine. Willimena is an African girl who is often in the midst of a humorous adventure. Wesley wrote *Afro-Bets Book of Black Heroes from A to Z: An Introduction to Important Black Achievers for Young Readers* with Wade Hudson.

In 2000 Wesley received an award for the novel *Ain't Nobody's Business if I Do* from the Black Caucus of the American Library Association. She was named Author of the Year by the Go On Girl! Book Club, and she received the Griot Award from the New York chapter of the National Association of Black Journalists.

Wesley has contributed to *Essence, Ms.,* the *New York Times,* and *Family Circle;* she is a former executive editor of *Essence.* She earned a B.A. from Howard University and M.A. degrees from the Columbia Graduate School of Journalism and the Bank Street College of Education.

Resources: Wade Hudson and Valerie Wilson Wesley, eds., *Afro-Bets Book of Black Heroes from A to Z: An Introduction to Important Black Achievers for Young Readers* (Orange, NJ: Just Us Books, 1988); Valerie Wilson Wesley: *Ain't Nobody's Business if I Do* (New York: Avon, 1999); *Always True to You in My Fashion* (New York: Morrow,

2002); *The Devil Riding* (New York: Putnam, 2002); *Dying in the Dark* (New York: One World/Ballantine, 2004); *Easier to Kill* (New York: Putnam, 1998); *How to Fish for Trouble* (New York: Jump at the Sun, 2004); *How to Lose Your Class Pet* (New York: Jump at the Sun, 2003); *How to Lose Your Cookie Money* (New York: Jump at the Sun, 2004); *No Hiding Place* (New York: Putnam, 1997); Web site, http://tamarahayle .com/biography.htm; *When Death Comes Stealing* (New York: Putnam, 1994); *Where Evil Sleeps* (New York: Putnam, 1996).

Shondrika L. Moss

West, Cheryl L. (born 1965). Playwright, screenwriter, and teacher. West has written several critically acclaimed plays that dramatize issues of **gender**, sexuality, ethnicity, and family. She is a versatile playwright, having written dramatic, comedic, and musical plays. West was born and grew up in **Chicago, Illinois**, and she earned a B.A. from the University of Illinois at Urbana-Champaign. Her play *Before It Hits Home* (1989) premiered in **Washington, D.C.** in 1991, followed by a production in New York City in 1992. Its protagonist is Wendal Bailey, a young bisexual African American man who is dying of complications from AIDS. The play concerns Bailey's complex relationships with former and current lovers, with his extended family, and with his immediate family, including his father. *Holiday Heart* (1994) concerns a gay, cross-dressing African American man, a drug-addicted woman, and the woman's young daughter. This play was turned into a motion picture of the same title; it was produced in 2000, starred Ving Rhames and Alfre Woodard, and was broadcast on the Home Box Office (HBO) television network. It was released in DVD format in 2004 (Townsend). At this writing, *Before It Hits Home* also is scheduled to be adapted to the screen. Filmmaker **Spike Lee** has acquired the film rights and asked West to write the screenplay (*Women of Color/Women of Words*). *Play On!* is a musical play for which West wrote the book and which features the music of **Edward Kennedy "Duke" Ellington**. It premiered in New York City in 1997. Other plays by West include *Jar the Door* (1991), a comedy which features four African American women characters representing different generations, and *Puddin 'n Pete* (1993).

Resources: "Cheryl L. West," *Women of Color/Women of Words*, http:// www.scils.rutgers.edu/~cybers/west2.html; Ann Russo, "Exploring AIDS in the Black Community," *Sojourner: The Women's Forum* 15, no. 1 (Sept. 1989), 38; Robert Townsend, dir., *Holiday Heart* (Los Angeles: MGM/United artists, 2004), DVD; Cheryl L. West: *Before It Hits Home* (New York: Dramatists' Play Service, 1993); *Jar the Door* (New York: Dramatists' Play Service, 2002).

Hans Ostrom

West, Cornel (born 1953). Philosopher, professor, activist, essayist, actor, and cultural critic. Scholar-activist Cornel West is one of the most widely recognized Black public intellectuals based in the U.S. academy today. His views have been articulated and disseminated through the main channels of the popular media. A philosopher by trade and liberation theologian in spirit, West has produced a body of social and cultural criticism that theorizes the ethical and political responsibilities to social justice in African Americanist scholarship. (*See* **Theology, Black and Womanist.**)

West was born in Tulsa, **Oklahoma**, in 1953. His parents were educated at Fisk University in **Nashville, Tennessee**, and worked hard to be part of the consolidated Black middle class at midcentury. His mother was a schoolteacher; his father worked for the U.S. Air Force. The family eventually moved to Sacramento, California, where West's precocious activities as a child were nurtured into a keen and outspoken intellect by continued involvement in the Baptist Church as well as contact with the militant politics of the **Black Panther Party**. West excelled in his studies and won a scholarship to Harvard University in 1970.

It took West only three years to graduate from Harvard magna cum laude with a degree in Near Eastern languages and literature. He went on to study Western philosophy at Princeton University, where he worked with Richard Rorty and earned an M.A. in 1975 and a Ph.D. in 1980. West's dissertation, which reflects the varied influences on his early liberationist thinking, was revised and published as *The Ethical Dimensions of Marxist Thought* in 1991. During his time at Princeton and Union Theological Seminary in New York City, where he began teaching in 1977, West developed a philosophical worldview that fused the most progressive elements of Christian theology, Marxist dialectics, and American pragmatism, with nods to Emersonian transcendentalism and insurgent Black politics (*see* **Marxism**). Teasing out the intricacies of this worldview led West to shun intellectual orthodoxy and dogmatism and to stress the modes by which critical theory and theology enable radical political praxis. Two early monographs prove instructive here: *Prophesy Deliverance!* (1982) and *The American Evasion of Philosophy* (1989).

The period since the 1980s has seen West continue to develop his liberationist thinking while occupying positions of enormous influence at the most prestigious institutions of higher education in the United States. Barely into his thirties, West was awarded a full professorship in religion and philosophy at Yale Divinity School, where he served from 1984 to 1987. In 1988 he returned to Princeton to direct its Program in Afro-American Studies. He solidified that department's standing in the U.S. academy with the support of a stellar community of scholars and artists, most notably the historian Nell Irvin Painter and the Nobel laureate **Toni Morrison**. In 1994 West was on the move again, leaving Princeton for his other Ivy League alma mater, Harvard, where **Henry Louis Gates, Jr.**, was in the process of assembling what many would later deem the nation's foremost group of Black public intellectuals in the Department of African and African American Studies and its **W.E.B. Du Bois** Institute for African and African American Research (*see* **Black Studies**). In 1998 West was named the first Alphonse Fletcher, Jr., University Professor.

He, Gates, and their philosophy colleague Kwame Anthony Appiah collaborated extensively on book, teaching, and popular media projects.

Given this string of successful academic appointments, culminating in his move to Harvard, it seemed as though West would be a mainstay among the Black public intellectuals working closely in and around Cambridge, Massachusetts. But in 2001 West was at the center of an academic dispute that made national headlines. Behind closed doors, newly appointed Harvard President and former U.S. Treasury Secretary Lawrence Summers allegedly questioned West's involvement in national politics—the Million Man March in 1995, **Russell Simmons**'s ongoing Hip-Hop Summit, the 2000 presidential campaigns of Bill Bradley and Ralph Nader—at the expense of his teaching duties and scholarly productivity. Also allegedly subjected to professional scrutiny was West's intriguing **hip-hop/soul**/spoken word record *Sketches of My Culture* (2001), produced by Derek "D.O.A." Allen and dedicated to "the preservation, persistence, and prevailing of our foremothers and forefathers." When news of the private meeting leaked, the news media were quick to pit West's defenders, who accused Summers of professional discrimination, against critics who branded West's extracurricular activities anti-intellectual. Even after an attempted reconciliation with Summers, West said that he had felt "attacked and insulted" by the President's words.

The fiasco left West disillusioned with Harvard, and in 2002 he returned to Princeton, where he is currently Class of 1943 University Professor of Religion and Professor of African American Studies. Unhampered by the heightened, at times disparaging, attention to his work as a scholar-activist, West has become even more of a star intellectual since leaving Harvard. A resolute critic of George W. Bush, he took up the banner of national politics once again by advising Al Sharpton's presidential campaign in 2004. West has also appeared in the much-lauded cameo role of Zion elder Councillor West in two parts of the Hollywood blockbuster *Matrix* trilogy, *The Matrix Reloaded* (2003) and *The Matrix Revolutions* (2003). The Wachowski brothers, who directed the heady yet entertaining **science fiction** series, enlisted West's help in recording philosophical commentary for the DVD release of all three films. A follow-up album titled *Street Knowledge* appeared in 2003.

In light of these developments, one might revisit the Summers debacle to note that what was stifled in the ensuing media frenzy was an account, critical or otherwise, of how West's creative production and political involvement seek to reconceptualize the terms by which the U.S. academy would define the role of the public intellectual in modern society. After all, the publication of his most famous book to date, the best-selling *Race Matters* (1993), sparked renewed interest in a multifaceted yet accessible national dialogue on **race** in the midst of the political conservatism of the post-Reagan "culture wars." The pithy collection of eight essays addresses topics ranging from **affirmative action** and the "crisis in black political leadership" to predominant myths of Black sexuality and the worrisome state of Black-Jewish relations. In granting everyday cultural and ethical practices (and not just large-scale political and economic policies) the capacity to uproot the nihilism that threatens to consume Black America, the book's political vision of social justice draws heavily from the sort of "prophetic pragmatism" that West forged early in his career. Indeed, *Race Matters* might be fruitfully compared with **James Baldwin**'s *The Fire Next Time* (1963) in the way it attempts to convey the African American sermon of liberation, delivered especially but not exclusively to an African American audience, in prose.

West mediated the popularity of *Race Matters* with more academic fare such as the two-volume *Beyond Eurocentrism and Multiculturalism* (1993) and *Keeping Faith* (1993). These occasional notes, essays, and interviews on political correctness, public intellectualism, and postmodern theory develop the argument outlined above in ways that have been arguably more useful to literary critics and cultural theorists. The first volume of *Beyond Eurocentrism*, for example, includes discussion of work by the historian George M. Frederickson, the Brazilian performance artist-activist Paulo Freire, and the British cultural studies theorist Raymond Williams.

The mid-to-late 1990s saw West author a handful of books with academic colleagues and other comrades in struggle. Two are explicitly geared toward changes and improvements in U.S. domestic policy: *The War Against Parents* (1998), with Sylvia Ann Hewlett, and *The Future of American Progressivism* (1998), with Roberto Mangabeira Unger. Two offer dialogues on the state of Black-Jewish and Black-on-Black relations in the United States: *Jews and Blacks* (1995), with Rabbi Michael Lerner, and *The Future of the Race* (1996), with Gates. West's millennial project with Gates, *The African-American Century* (2000), is the most difficult to categorize of these texts. Part critical argument about the achievements of Blacks in the twentieth century, part photographic exhibit of 100 African American celebrities and icons, it is perhaps best described as a wonderfully instructive coffee table book.

Over a decade after *Race Matters* was met with critical acclaim and widespread national interest, West published *Democracy Matters* (2004), which signals perhaps the most dramatic intellectual transformation in the career of this longtime critic of U.S. social relations. Here the focus is on the world stage: West explains how the ideals of American democracy have been compromised by the perpetuation of domestic racism and imperial expansion into the twenty-first century. He understands Islamic fundamentalism and U.S. militarism as two sides of the same terrible coin. In order to stem the tide of ideologically driven violence, West calls for a revitalization of the Christian universalist notion of democracy, a notion put into prophetic words by Dr. **Martin Luther King, Jr**.

Resources: Primary Sources: Cornel West: *The American Evasion of Philosophy: A Genealogy of Pragmatism* (Madison: University of Wisconsin Press, 1989); *Beyond Eurocentrism and Multiculturalism*, vol. 1, *Prophetic Thought in Postmodern Times* (Monroe, ME: Common Courage, 1993); *Democracy Matters: Winning the Fight Against Imperialism* (New York: Penguin, 2004); *The Ethical Dimensions of Marxist Thought* (New York: Monthly Review, 1991); *Keeping Faith: Philosophy and Race in America*

(New York: Routledge, 1993); *Prophesy Deliverance! An Afro-American Revolutionary Christianity* (Philadelphia: Westminster, 1982); *Race Matters* (Boston: Beacon, 1993); *Street Knowledge* (Rancho Murieta, CA: Roc Diamond Records, 2003), CD; Cornel West and Henry Louis Gates, Jr.: *The African-American Century: How Black Americans Have Shaped Our Country* (New York: Free Press, 2000); *The Future of the Race* (New York: Knopf, 1996); Cornel West and Sylvia Ann Hewlett, *The War Against Parents: What We Can Do for America's Beleaguered Moms and Dads* (Boston: Houghton Mifflin, 1998); Cornel West and bell hooks, *Breaking Bread: Insurgent Black Intellectual Life* (Boston: South End, 1991); Cornel West and Michael Lerner, *Jews and Blacks: Let the Healing Begin* (New York: Putnam, 1995); Cornel West and Roberto Mangabeira Unger, *The Future of American Progressivism: An Initiative for Political and Economic Reform* (Boston: Beacon, 1998). **Secondary Sources:** Rosemary Cowan, *Cornel West: The Politics of Redemption* (Malden, MA: Polity, 2003); Clarence Sholé Johnson, *Cornel West and Philosophy: The Quest for Social Justice* (New York: Routledge, 2003); Anders Stephanson, "Interview with Cornel West," in *Universal Abandon? The Politics of Postmodernism*, ed. Andrew Ross (Minneapolis: University of Minnesota Press, 1988), 269–286; Mark David Wood, *Cornel West and the Politics of Prophetic Pragmatism* (Urbana: University of Illinois Press, 2000).

Kinohi Nishikawa

West, Dorothy (1907–1998). Novelist, short story writer, columnist, and editor. Dorothy West's death in 1998 marked the passing of the last surviving member of the **Harlem Renaissance** and the end of a seventy-year writing career. West was the only child of Rachel Benson and Isaac West, members of the Black middle class in **Boston, Massachusetts**. Both were grandchildren of slave masters in South Carolina and Virginia, respectively; her father, a generation older than her mother, was emancipated during the **Civil War**. Industrious, he was known as Boston's Black Banana King; her mother presided over a household that included three of her sisters and their children. West therefore grew up within a transplanted Southern household that nevertheless exuded the decorum of Boston's exclusive Brahmin caste. By the age of seven she knew she wanted to be a writer; by her 1923 graduation from the Girls Latin School, she had established herself.

West's career began with the *Boston Post*. She recalled, "I don't think I was anymore than fourteen or fifteen when the *Post* did a daily short story. At the end of the week, they gave $2, $5, and $10 prizes.... Eight times out of ten or seven times out of ten, I got the $10 prize and contributed to the family pot. When I got the $2 or the $5 prize, everybody in the family was indignant" (McDowell, 269). Her future was secured in 1926 when she tied with **Zora Neale Hurston** for second place in the short story category of the *Opportunity* Awards. West was accompanied to New York by **Helene Johnson**, a cousin with whom she'd been raised, and who had merited an honorable mention in the poetry category.

The Harlem Renaissance welcomed the two, whom **Wallace Thurman** pleasantly memorialized in his otherwise biting novel *Infants of the Spring*:

"They were characterized by a freshness and naiveté which he and his cronies had lost. And, surprisingly enough for Negro prodigies, they actually gave promise of possessing literary talent.... He was also amused by their interest and excitement" (230–231). Hurston became attached to the cousins, sharing her apartment and forming a genuine friendship with West. Others also took interest in the young, quiet girl whom they perceived as in need of their protection and guidance. A'Lelia Walker (African American bon vivant and patron of the arts) chastised **Carl Van Vechten** (art critic, novelist, patron, and friend of **Langston Hughes**) for his improper advances to West, who received marriage proposals from **Countee Cullen, Claude McKay**, and Langston Hughes—among others (Dalsgard, 33; Steinberg, 35; McDowell, 270; Roses, 49). While she admitted that she loved them all, she credited McKay with the greatest influence upon her writing: "I don't know how much I would have written, if it hadn't been for him" (Dalsgard, 33). West's short story "The Typewriter" is considered one of the most memorable pieces of short fiction to have been written during the Harlem Renaissance.

Like many writers of the era, West depended upon other sources for income: in 1929 she became an extra in the Theatre Guild's original production of *Porgy* by **DuBose Heyward**, traveling to London for three months (Newson, 22). Three years later, West was one of twenty-two African Americans who journeyed to Russia. The group included Langston Hughes, Henry Lee Moon, and Ted Poston. A group in Russia planned to make a film about American racism as a means of advancing Communist interests, but was thwarted by American threats to stall the building of the Dnieper Dam (McDowell, 272). Langston Hughes noted that the Russians seemed to know nothing about African Americans (*I Wonder*). West nevertheless remembered that year as her most carefree, and recorded her memories of Sergei Eisenstein in "An Adventure in Moscow."

West's return to America was precipitated by the death of her father, followed by that of Thurman. West recalled, "For me, Wally's [Thurman] death in [1934] meant the end of the Harlem Renaissance" (Roses, 49). Disappointed by the **Great Depression**'s impact upon creative writers, in 1934 West launched

Photograph of Langston Hughes and Dorothy West traveling to Russia, 1933. Yale Collection of American Literature, Beinecke Rare Book and Manuscript Library.

the magazine *Challenge*, promoting it as "an organ for the new voices…to bring out the prose and poetry of newer Negroes…by those who were the new Negroes now challenging them to better our achievements. For we did not altogether live up to our fine promise." While some disliked the suggestion that they had failed, West received support from Cullen, Hughes, Hurston, McKay, Van Vechten, and others (Cromwell, 354–355). The larger detractions came from those who demanded an explicitly socialist production. Accordingly, *Challenge* became *New Challenge* in 1937, with West as coeditor and **Richard Wright** as associate editor, and included **Ralph Ellison**'s first published piece and Wright's "Blueprint for Negro Writing" (*see* **Marxism**). Opposed to communism, West ultimately ceased its publication.

While unsupportive of the Left, West was sympathetic to America's poor. Two years with the Public Welfare Department during the Depression exposed her to the extremes of poverty (Cromwell, 353). Her time with the Works Progress Administration's **Federal Writers' Project** allowed her to chronicle the effects of the Depression had upon the residents of **Harlem, New York**, and the strategies they deployed to preserve their dignity in the face of economic and spiritual stress. West dated the end of her apprenticeship to this era: "My own writing was now more mature. I saw life with a larger eye. But important magazines were not in the market for stories about blacks. They surmised that neither were their readers." A chance submission to the *New York Daily News* in 1940 led to West's arrangement to provide the newspaper with two stories a month, thus keeping her "writing hand ready and her mind alert" and initiating a relationship that lasted almost twenty years (*The Richer, the Poorer*, 3–4).

Throughout the excitement of the 1920s and the hardship of the 1930s, West remained sustained by memories of her childhood and summers at Oak Bluffs, Martha's Vineyard. West retired to Oak Bluffs in 1947 to write her first novel, *The Living Is Easy*. It was originally to have been serialized by the *Ladies' Home Journal*, but editors feared subscription cancellations by Southern readers (Steinberg, 35). Nevertheless, reviews were favorable: drawn from West's family, the novel chronicles the manipulations of a young matron to gather her Southern sisters and their children around her in Boston, exploiting her husband's financial success. The novel also included a thinly veiled portrait of Monroe Trotter—West had been a pupil of his sister Bessie and a goddaughter of his sister Maude (Roses, 48).

Following the publication of her first novel, West, who had returned to her youth in so much of her writing, permanently moved to her childhood summer home. While continuing to write, West also became a clerical worker at the *Vineyard Gazette* in 1965 (Cromwell, 350). She soon replaced the local bird columnist, and in 1968 began a regular column, "Cottagers' Corner," covering the activities of vacationing African Americans (Saunders and Shackelford, 6). By 1973, West was reporting on all Oak Bluffs residents—human and animal. From the late 1960s through the 1980s, West spent summers as a restaurant cashier, leaving her little time for work on her novel *The Wedding*, begun in the 1960s (Cromwell, 351). West acknowledged that the politics of the 1960s also negatively affected its completion. Admitting she cared "very deeply" about the goals of the Black Revolution, she disliked its contempt for the bourgeois: "I had a suspicion that the reviewers, who were white, would not know how to judge my work in that prevailing climate" (McDowell, 278; Steinberg, 35). Publishers likewise proved hesitant to risk a novel about the Black middle class (McDowell, 277–278) (*see* **Black Arts Movement; Black Power**).

Despite these setbacks, West's writings for *Vineyard Gazette* eventually brought her to the attention of another Vineyard vacationer, an editor at Doubleday. She urged West to return to *The Wedding*, and they forged a friendship evident in the novel's dedication: "To the memory of my editor, Jacqueline Kennedy Onassis. Though there was never such a mismatched pair in appearance, we were perfect partners." Whereas the republication of *The Living is Easy* in 1982 generated academic interest in West, this second novel secured popular interest in the last surviving writer of the Harlem Renaissance, and several collections of various works followed, as well as a miniseries of *The Wedding*. West died in 1998, content with her belated recognition: "It gratifies me now at the end of my life that I am not afraid of dying. I'm leaving you my legacy" (McDowell, 282).

Resources: Primary Sources: Dorothy West: *The Dorothy West Martha's Vineyard: Stories, Essays and Reminiscences by Dorothy West Writing in the* Vineyard Gazette, ed. James Robert Saunders and Renae Nadine Shackelford (Jefferson, NC: McFarland, 2001); *The Living Is Easy* (1948; repr. Old Westbury, NY: Feminist Press, 1982); *The Richer, the Poorer: Stories, Sketches, and Reminiscences* (New York: Doubleday, 1995); *The Wedding* (New York: Doubleday, 1995). **Secondary Sources:** Lionel C. Bascom, ed., *A Renaissance in Harlem: Lost Voices of an American Community* (New York: Avon, 1999), includes work by West; Adelaide M. Cromwell, "Afterword," in West's *The Living Is Easy*, 349–364; Katrine Dalsgard, "Alive and Well and Living on the Island of Martha's Vineyard: An Interview with Dorothy West, October 29, 1988," *Langston Hughes Review*, Fall 1993, 28–44; Langston Hughes, "Moscow Movie," "Scenario in Russian," and "The Mammy of Moscow," in *I Wonder as I Wander* (New York: Rinehart, 1956), 69–86; Deborah E. McDowell, "Conversations with Dorothy West," in *The Harlem Renaissance Re-examined*, ed. Victor A. Kramer (New York: AMS, 1987), 265–282; Lorraine Elena Roses, "Interviews with Black Women Writers: Dorothy West at Oak Bluffs; Massachusetts," *Sage*, Spring 1985, 47–49; James Robert Saunders and Renae Nadine Shackelford, "Introduction," in *The Dorothy West Martha's Vineyard*, pp. 1–11; Sybil Steinberg, "Dorothy West: Her Own Renaissance," *Publishers Weekly*, July 3, 1995, pp. 34–35; Wallace Thurman, *Infants of the Spring* (1932; repr. New York: AMS, 1975).

Jennifer Harris

Wheatley, Phillis (c. 1753–1784). Poet and literary pioneer. Wheatley was the second woman and the first African American to publish in colonial America. Even though Africans had published previously in America, her work arguably started "African American literature" because of the United States' shift from a British colony to a free country during her lifetime. Although many scholars place her birth in Senegal, Wheatley claimed in her work that she was born in Gambia, West Africa. Little is known of Wheatley's childhood in Africa. She claimed to have remembered only her mother pouring water on the ground to honor the rising sun every morning. This ritual suggested that her mother adhered to sun worship, perhaps Islam. However, when she was around seven years old, Wheatley was captured and sold into **slavery** on July 11, 1761. She was bought by the Wheatley family, who resided in **Boston, Massachusetts**, and was named for the slave ship, the *Phillis*, upon which she arrived (Gates; Robinson).

The Wheatleys were a wealthy family who provided Phillis with the sort of thorough education that was usually reserved for the Caucasian elite of that time. Her adjustment to her new life was so phenomenal that she learned to read and write English and Latin in four years, and at around fourteen she published her first poem, "On Messrs. Hussey and Coffin," on December 21, 1767, in the *Newport Mercury*. Wheatley utilized her classical training to enhance her poetry. Besides becoming a budding classical scholar and poet, she converted to Christianity on August 18, 1771 (Robinson).

In 1772, she tried to publish her first volume of poetry in America. Because of her **race** and **gender**, many learned people of the time period doubted that Wheatley actually wrote the poems, especially because of her command of the English language and her references to Greek and Roman figures and mythology. Therefore, Wheatley appeared in a room filled with men of the Boston elite (including Governor John Hancock and Rev. Mather Byles) to prove that she knew English and Latin and that she wrote the poems. The fact that the men were a mixture of loyalists and patriots suggests that her work transcended the boundaries of politics or that it at least appealed to readers of both political persuasions. Little is known about that meeting except that she impressed the men so much that they added an attestation page to her volume to inform the public that it was her work (Robinson). Even with this ringing endorsement, however, Wheatley still could not get published in America and had to turn to England. Fortunately, Selena Hastings, the Countess of Huntingdon, financed the publishing. Wheatley's first volume of poetry, *Poems on Various Subjects, Religious and Moral*, appeared in 1773. This publication made her the first African American to gain freedom from slavery through literary work.

Wheatley's poems demonstrate not only classical learning but also an awareness of the changing world around her. As a history maker herself, she was very popular with the elite in America and in Europe, the first African American to gain this acknowledgment. Most of her poems were elegies, poems dedicated to the memory of important people she knew in colonial America. Furthermore, she dedicated poems to such historical figures as George Washington and Benjamin Franklin, and eventually she regularly corresponded with both. Besides her first volume of poetry, many of her letters and miscellaneous poems still exist.

Unfortunately for Wheatley, her freedom did not bring her happiness because she encountered many new problems. In 1778, she married John Peters, a free African American. Her first two children died as infants. Peters left Wheatley after she gave birth to their last child. Because of the Revolutionary War (and the death of many of the people who signed the attestation), Wheatley's fame diminished greatly. In vain, Wheatley tried numerous times to garnish subscribers to a new volume of poetry dedicated to Benjamin Franklin in 1779. After her husband abandoned her, she was forced to work as a domestic. In September 1784, her last advertisement for subscribers appeared. In December of that year, because of her hardships and lifelong poor health, Wheatley was found dead with her third child. She was in her thirties. After her death, it is believed that Peters sold the only copy of her second volume of poetry. Most of these poems are still undiscovered.

Phillis Wheatley, 1773. Courtesy of the Library of Congress.

Wheatley's legacy has possibly been the most reviled of any African American writer. Dismissed by Caucasian scholars such as Thomas Jefferson as not a good poet because of her race, Wheatley has also been maligned by African American critics such as **James Weldon Johnson** and **Amiri Baraka**. Initially embraced by African American readers because of her history-making attributes, Wheatley was subsequently seen by some as having denounced her African heritage when she converted to Christianity. Her life and career, at any rate, became points of contention. To be fair, most of Wheatley's poetry has been rediscovered slowly over the centuries, so many scholars were not aware of her acknowledgment, in some of her poems, of her heritage. Now, since most of her extant poems were put into a collection titled *The Collected Works of Phillis Wheatley* in 1988, scholars have a clearer view of her work. Since the 1980s, some scholars, such as John C. Shields and James A. Levernier, have reexamined her work to the extent that some perceive a strain of subversiveness in her verse. They do not view Wheatley as catering to her "betters." Indeed, even though she became a Christian, she criticized slavery and racism in her poetry. No matter what point of view one takes on her Christian conversion, the style of her poetry, or how subversive she was, Wheatley's contributions to African American literature and culture cannot be ignored or denied.

Resources: Henry Louis Gates, Jr., *The Trials of Phillis Wheatley* (New York: Basic Civitas Books, 2003); James Weldon Johnson, *The Book of American Poetry* (New

York: Harcourt Brace, 1922); LeRoi Jones (Amiri Baraka), "The Myth of 'Negro Literature,'" in *Within the Circle: An Anthology of African American Literary Criticism from the Harlem Renaissance to the Present*, ed. Angelyn Mitchell (Durham, NC: Duke University Press, 1994), 165–171; James A. Levernier, "Style as Protest in the Poetry of Phillis Wheatley," *Style* 27, no. 2 (Summer 1993), 173–193; William H. Robinson, *Phillis Wheatley and Her Writings* (New York: Garland, 1984); John C. Shields, *The American Aeneas: Classical Origins of the American Self* (Knoxville: University of Tennessee Press, 2001); John C. Shields, ed., *The Collected Works of Phillis Wheatley* (New York: Oxford University Press, 1988).

Devona Mallory

Whipper, William (1804–1876). Activist, entrepreneur, and journalist. A noted abolitionist, Whipper founded one of the earliest African American periodicals and wrote for the abolitionist press for three decades.

Born in Lancaster County, Pennsylvania, to a White father and a Black mother, Whipper moved to **Philadelphia, Pennsylvania**, in the 1820s and quickly achieved notice through his work with the African American Reading Room Society, of which he was the first secretary. His *Address Before the Colored Reading Society of Philadelphia*, published as a pamphlet in 1828, was his first publication and was a signal of a long commitment to African American education and self-sufficiency. He later became one of the first members of the Philadelphia Library Company of Colored Persons.

In the early 1830s, Whipper had already made a name as a reform activist—not just in abolitionist circles but in temperance organizations as well. He published another pamphlet, *Eulogy on William Wilberforce*. He had delivered the eulogy on the abolitionist Wilberforce at the Second African Presbyterian Church in Philadelphia on December 6, 1833.

Whipper later opened a "free produce" store. He became an important figure in both the growing African American convention movement and the new American Moral Reform Society. Whipper moved to Columbus, Pennsylvania, in 1835. There, he partnered with a cousin, Stephen Smith, in a lumber business that later grew into a very successful, multifaceted enterprise that had interests in both Pennsylvania and Canada. His wealth allowed him to aid fugitive slaves (his house became a key stop on the **Underground Railroad**) and various societies. In 1838, he became the founding editor of the *National Reformer*, the organ of the American Moral Reform Society and one of the earliest **African American newspapers** in Pennsylvania. Though it lasted only a little over a year, it was an important outlet for Whipper's work, which other abolitionist periodicals were also beginning to publish.

Whipper grew into a firm follower of William Lloyd Garrison, a leader of the **Abolitionist Movement**. He continued to lecture and write for the abolitionist press throughout the 1840s and 1850s. He gradually shifted his position on the moral reform central to the Moral Reform Society because the organization failed to actively consider racism. In the wake of the Fugitive Slave Law, he also reconsidered his attitude toward recolonizing African

Americans outside the United States. Nonetheless, when the **Civil War** came, he decided to stay in the United States, working first to help enlist African American troops and then for equal rights. Late in life, he spent a brief period in New Brunswick, New Jersey, and another brief period as a cashier in the Philadelphia branch of the Freedmen's Savings Bank. (*See* **Back-to-Africa Movement**.)

Resources: Penelope L. Bullock, *The Afro-American Periodical Press, 1838–1909* (Baton Rouge: Louisiana State University Press, 1981); Jane H. Pease and William H. Pease, *They Who Would Be Free* (Urbana: University of Illinois Press, 1990); C. Peter Ripley, ed., *The Black Abolitionist Papers*, 5 vols. (Chapel Hill: University of North Carolina Press, 1985–1992); William Still, *The Underground Rail Road* (1877; repr. New York: Arno, 1968); William Whipper, *Eulogy on William Wilberforce, Esq., Delivered at the Request of the People of Colour of the City of Philadelphia, in the Second African Presbyterian Church, on the Sixth Day of December, 1833* (1833; repr. Philadelphia: Rhistoric Publications, 1969).

Eric Gardner

White (Racial Designation). "White" is a racial coding or category that is putatively self-evident to the naked eye, yet on further inspection, it appears to be rigorously and methodically constructed as an ideological category of supremacy over variously defined, nonwhite "others." Though White is frequently understood to exist in complex, dialectical relation to Black, the coding is not without its internal fissures and divisions based on historical contingency.

African American literature registers the violence and degradation visited upon Black subjects by White subjects who claim exclusive right to "universal" notions of reason, sentiment, beauty, and progress. Critics have suggested that early African American writing in particular—from the poetry of **Phillis Wheatley** to **Frederick Douglass**'s *Narrative*—was produced in part to "prove" Black humanity to Whites, even those who were committed abolitionists. Antebellum U.S. culture upheld White as the standard by which African or slave selfhood was to be measured.

The decades immediately following emancipation saw little that altered this dynamic. "White" was legally codified under what came to be known as Jim Crow laws, and thus it was anxiously policed as White supremacy over Blacks. Despite such measures, the literature of **passing** flourished during Jim Crow segregation, providing transgressive narrative crossings between Black and White. Moreover, **labor** and cultural historians have shown how the White demographic underwent confounding self-division as eastern European immigrants, among other ethnic Whites, arrived in the United States in record numbers well into the twentieth century. In his 1953 essay "Twentieth-Century Fiction and the Black Mask of Humanity," **Ralph Ellison** situates Black and White conflict within "that larger conflict between older, dominant groups of white Americans, especially the Anglo-Saxons, on the one hand, and the newer white and non-white groups on the other, over the major group's attempt to impose its ideals upon the rest, insisting that its exclusive image be accepted as *the* image of the American" (*Shadow and Act*, 26). Increasing cultural diversity forced White subjects to identify themselves not simply against Black subjects but also within a matrix of competing and overlapping identities, including Irish, Italian, and Jewish.

Bolstered by the **Civil Rights Movement** and the emergence of **Black nationalism**, African American writers in the 1960s sought to undercut the assumed superiority of White categories of being. In his 1962 essay " 'Black' Is a Country," LeRoi Jones (**Amiri Baraka**) declares, "America is as much a black country as a white one. The lives and destinies of the white American are bound up inextricably with those of the black American, even though the latter has been forced for hundreds of years to inhabit the lonely country of black" (*Home*, 85). Jones's recasting of the master-slave dialectic, which the German philosopher Hegel had put forward, renders White a contingent social discourse by denying its essential racial signification. Much postmodern African American literature lies at the juncture of denaturalized racial categories, as do academic interrogations of White. Academic investigations of White mainly fall under the heading "Whiteness Studies." Writers and critics stress, however, that critiquing the empirically fictional grounds for White supremacy entails recognition of the very real effects that practices of racial coding have on U.S. subjects even today. (*See* **Color of Skin**; **Race**.)

Resources: Richard Dyer, *White* (New York: Routledge, 1997); Ralph Ellison, *Shadow and Act* (New York: Random House, 1964); Frantz Fanon, *Black Skin, White Masks*, trans. Charles Lam Markmann (1952; repr. New York: Grove, 1967); Ian F. Haney-López, *White by Law: The Legal Construction of Race* (New York: New York University Press, 1998); Matthew Frye Jacobson, *Whiteness of a Different Color: European Immigrants and the Alchemy of Race* (Cambridge, MA: Harvard University Press, 1998); LeRoi Jones, *Home: Social Essays* (New York: Morrow, 1966); Toni Morrison, *Playing in the Dark: Whiteness and the Literary Imagination* (Cambridge, MA: Harvard University Press, 1992); David R. Roediger, *The Wages of Whiteness: Race and the Making of the American Working Class* (New York: Verso, 1991).

Kinohi Nishikawa

White, Edgar Nkosi (born 1947). Playwright and novelist. White was born on the Caribbean island of Montserrat, and in 1952 he moved to New York City, where his mother was already living. He grew up in the borough of the Bronx. Beginning in 1964, he studied for a year at the City College of New York and then went on to study at New York University through 1968. At age eighteen he wrote *The Mummer's Play*, which was produced, partly through the assistance of the actor Martin Sheen, by Joseph Papp at the Public Theatre in New York City. From 1971 to 1973 White studied at the Yale University School of Drama, where he later founded a **drama** group initially known as the Yale Black Players and subsequently called the Yardbird Players Company (Casado). White spent much of the 1980s in London. He has written over thirty plays, most of which have been produced, chiefly in the United States,

Great Britain, and the Caribbean. Some of his plays are historical; for example, *The Burghers of Calais* (1970) concerns the **Scottsboro Boys**, eight Black Alabama youths falsely accused, tried, and convicted of rape in the 1930s. Other plays are contemporary, including *Les Femmes Noires* (1972). Other titles include *Black* (1971), *The Black Woman* (1978), and *The Cathedral of Chartres* (1969). White has also published two novels, *Children of the Night* (1974) and *The Rising* (1988), the latter set in the Caribbean.

Resources: Stephen R. Carter, "Edgar B. [*sic*] White," in *Dictionary of Literary Biography*, vol. 38, *Afro-American Writers after 1955: Dramatists and Prose Writers*, ed. Thadious M. Davis and Trudier Harris (Detroit: Gale, 1985), 278–283; Núria Casado, "White, Edgar Nkosi," in *Black Drama Biography*, http://www.alexander street2.com; "Edgar Nkosi White," http://www.doolee.com, list of plays and productions; Judy S. J. Stone, "Black British Theatre. The Theatre of Exile: Edgar White, Mustapha Matura, Caryl Phillips," in *Theatre Studies in West Indian Literature* (London: Macmillan, 1994), 61–79.

Hans Ostrom

White, Paulette Childress (born 1948). Poet and short fiction writer. A native of **Detroit, Michigan**, White early on had wanted to become an artist, but she attended art school for only one year. After she married an artist, and started a family of five boys, she began to write. At age thirty, she published her first poem in *Deep Rivers* (1972). White attended a writers' workshop where poet **Naomi Long Madgett** was conducting a session on poetry, and with Madgett's support, **Lotus Press** in Detroit published White's first collection of poems, *Love Poem to a Black Junkie* (1975). Further support came from a small group of talented, dedicated Black writers, including **Mary Helen Washington**, and led to the publication of her first short story, "Alice," in *Essence* (January 1977), and her second, "The Bird Cage," in *Redbook* (June 1978). Of these two stories written in the 1970s, Washington observes that White's "fiction recalls Gwendolyn Brooks's 1953 novel *Maud Martha*" (37). After her creative burst of energy, White published her narrative poem *The Watermelon Dress: Portrait of a Woman* (1984), which traces the author's development as a closet artist from adolescence to her eventual awareness of selfhood. White's poetry has been collected in the *Broadside Annual* (1974) and *Blacksongs: Series I and Dear Dark Faces* (1977), edited by **Jill Witherspoon Boyer**. Both her fiction and poetry have appeared in **Callaloo**, *Michigan Quarterly Review*, and *Harbor Review*, and in several anthologies, including *Sturdy Black Bridges* (1979), *Black-Eyed Susans/Midnight Birds* (1990), *The Jazz Poetry Anthology* (1991), and *Women: Images and Realities* (1995). Of White, Madgett writes, "When her schedule permits her more time for creativity, this unique voice may well encourage other writers to trust the validity of their own experiences as women emerging from the darkness of restriction and concealment into the sunlight of their own personhood and to express those realized selves with sensitivity, insight, and lyrical beauty" (773).

Resources: Jill Witherspoon Boyer, ed., *Blacksongs, Series I: Four Poetry Broadsides by Black Women* (Detroit: Lotus Press, 1977); Naomi Long Madgett, "White, Paulette Childress," in *The Oxford Companion to African American Literature*, ed. William L. Andrews, Frances Smith Foster, and Trudier Harris (New York: Oxford, 1997), 772–773; Mary Helen Washington, "Paulette Childress White," in *Black-Eyed Susans/Midnight Birds*, ed. Washington (New York: Anchor, 1990), 35–53; Paulette Childress White, *The Watermelon Dress: Portrait of a Woman* (Detroit: Lotus Press, 1984).

Loretta G. Woodard

White, Walter Francis (1893–1955). Novelist, essayist, and civil rights leader. Walter White is considered one of the most influential civil rights leaders of the early twentieth century. Born in **Atlanta, Georgia**, on July 1, 1893, Walter White literally and figuratively grew up on the boundary between White and Black America. The White family home was located on the border between the White community and the African American community in Atlanta. The son of light-skinned African Americans, White was a blue-eyed, blonde-haired, white-skinned boy whose appearance belied his African American heritage. As a consequence of their light coloring, the White family often came face to face with the perils of **passing**. Despite a concerted effort to avoid such duplicity, the Whites were often placed in a double bind as a result of the collective anxiety of both the White and Black communities stemming from the Jim Crow system of segregation. In his autobiography, *A Man Called White* (1948), White illustrates the kind of hostilities his family frequently encountered as a result of unwittingly "crossing the line." The White's ambiguous racial identity made something as commonplace as riding the streetcar a daunting experience. In order to avoid ridicule from White and Black passengers alike, the family had to straddle the imaginary line that divided the front of the streetcar from the rear. If they sat at the back of the car, they were scorned by White passengers who assumed they were White. Had they sat at the front of the car, they would have been guilty of passing and spurned by Black passengers who knew they were Black.

Throughout his **autobiography**, White recounts instances in which he had to convince others of his racial identity. Conditioned to believe that "there is magic in a white skin," and only "tragedy, loneliness, exile, in a black skin" (3), many could not comprehend White's willingness to forsake the power and privilege of the dominant culture to align himself with the oppressed and persecuted. White's conscious decision to shed his "magical" White skin and embrace his racial heritage was not one he came to lightly. Recalling that pivotal moment in his youth when he first discovered what it meant to be an African American, White wrote, "I know the night when, in terror and bitterness of soul, I discovered that I was set apart by the pigmentation of my skin (invisible though it was in my case) and the moment at which I decided that I would infinitely rather be what I was than, through taking advantage of the way of escape that was open to me, be one of the race which had forced the decision upon me" (4–5).

Thirteen years old at the time, White admits to being too naïve to fully appreciate the ramifications of the mounting racial tension that preceded the Atlanta **race riot** and the pivotal moment of which he speaks. Barricaded in their home, the White family listened to the mob's cries reverberate through the silent house. Engulfed in a darkness lessened only by the light of the torches borne by the mob, White was enlightened to the fact that he belonged to a race condemned to suffering and abuse for no less a reason than the pigmentation of skin. Yet, even as a boy, White recognized the inexplicable: that his skin was as white as the skin of his attackers. What the young man did not realize was that his status as an African American was determined not by the pigmentation of his skin but by the figurative single drop of black blood coursing through his veins. White's epiphany on that fateful day signaled more than his transition from boyhood to manhood, it cemented his loyalty to the Black community.

Encouraged by his parents in his pursuit of higher education, White enrolled in Atlanta University, where he received his Bachelor of Arts degree in 1916. That same year, he began a crusade against the Atlanta Board of Education for its continued maltreatment of Black students. White's dedication to the African American community attracted the attention of the **NAACP**'s **James Weldon Johnson**, who offered White the position of assistant secretary with the organization. Within two weeks of accepting his job with the NAACP, the twenty-five-year-old White requested permission to investigate firsthand the **lynching** of an African American sharecropper in Tennessee. Despite the harrowing nature of this experience, White continued to pass for white in an attempt to expose the epidemic of **lynching** in **the South**. Through his manipulation of the color line, White was able to expose the atrocities committed against members of his race and sway public opinion against the perpetrators of such crimes. Although he did not attain his ultimate goal—the enactment of a federal antilynching law—White's investigations, exposés, and fervent advocacy succeeded in drastically reducing the number of lynchings in the United States.

In 1924, White published his first novel, *The Fire in the Flint*, which was inspired by his undercover work with the NAACP. *The Fire in the Flint* tells the story of Kenneth Harper, an African American doctor whose plans to help his community are thwarted by a series of family tragedies. Harper's sister is raped by a gang of White boys, and then his brother is brutally murdered for trying to avenge her. Harper meets his own tragic end when he tries to save an ailing young White girl. Falsely accused of trying to assault the girl's mother, Harper is shot and then lynched by a mob of White men. Following the publication of *The Fire in the Flint*, White became increasingly involved in what became known as the **New Negro** movement or the **Harlem Renaissance**. In addition to the articles he produced for newspapers and magazines such as the *New York Evening Post*, the *Chicago Daily News*, **The Crisis**, and *American Mercury*, White aided fledgling writers in their artistic pursuits.

In 1926, White published his second novel, *Flight*, which centers on the life of Mimi Daquin, a light-skinned African American woman who passes for

White in an effort to escape a life of pettiness and despair. Although she prospers as a member of White society, Mimi is unable to quell the yearning she feels for her own people. Her newfound appreciation for her rich cultural heritage prompts her to return to the African American community. In the same year that he published *Flight*, White was awarded a Guggenheim Fellowship. The following year, he moved to France with the intention of writing a third novel. Instead, he produced a book-length treatise on lynching in the United States, titled *Rope & Faggot: The Biography of Judge Lynch* (1929). In 1931, White became Executive Secretary of the NAACP, a position he held until his death in 1955. In addition to his **autobiography** and several articles, White produced two more literary works in the last ten years of his life: *A Rising Wind* (1945) and *How Far the Promised Land?* (1955). The first scrutinized the impact of Jim Crow segregation on African American soldiers fighting in Europe. The second chronicled the history of the NAACP under White's direction.

During his thirty-seven years with the NAACP, Walter White spearheaded a national campaign to ensure the social, political, and economic freedom of all African Americans. In *"New World A-Coming": Inside Black America* (1943), Roi Ottley claimed that under White's leadership "the N.A.A.C.P. is carrying on a fight begun during W.E.B. Du Bois's day, to win complete equality for Negroes" (244). Another prominent African American leader, Adam Clayton Powell, Jr., insisted that without Walter White, civil rights might have become a thing of the past. White's years of dedication to the NAACP and his active involvement in the Harlem Renaissance serve as a testament to his commitment to the African American community.

Resources: Kenneth Robert Janken, *White: The Biography of Walter White, Mr. NAACP* (New York: New Press, 2003); Roi Ottley, *"New World A-Coming": Inside Black America* (Boston: Houghton Mifflin, 1943); Edward E. Waldron, *Walter White and the Harlem Renaissance* (Port Washington, NY: Kennikat, 1978); Walter White: *The Fire in the Flint* (New York: Knopf, 1924); *Flight* (New York: Knopf, 1926); *How Far the Promised Land?* (New York: Viking, 1955); *A Man Called White* (New York: Viking, 1948); *The Negro's Contribution to American Culture: The Sudden Flowering of a Genius-Laden Artistic Movement* (Girard, KS: Haldeman-Julius, 1928); *A Rising Wind* (Garden City, NY: Doubleday, Doran, 1945); *Rope & Faggot: A Biography of Judge Lynch* (New York: Knopf, 1929); *What Caused the Detroit Riot? An Analysis* (New York: NAACP, 1943).

Carol Goodman

Whitehead, Colson (born 1969). Novelist and short story writer. A native of New York City, Whitehead graduated from Harvard in 1991 and then returned to New York, where he worked as a journalist, writing for the *Village Voice* for five years, including a stint as television critic. At this writing, he lives in **Brooklyn, New York**. Whitehead did not find a publisher for his first book, a "black Gen-X tale that incorporated a lot of pop culture" (Whitehead and Mosely, 47). However, his first published novel, *The Intuitionist*, appeared to great acclaim in 1999. In an unnamed metropolis, elevators are about to enter a period of technological innovation, but African Americans are called "colored" and people still use rotary phones.

The novel employs the form of **crime and mystery fiction**, specifically the detective novel, to tell the story of Lila Mae Watson, an "intuitionist" elevator inspector who must brave danger to locate the papers of an elevator visionary. According to Whitehead, the novel is deliberately dislocated in time and space: "I think there's an interesting tension when you can't pin it down and there are these different kinds of inputs that are telling you one thing on one page and another thing on another page. I think that confusion mimics racial confusion at large in the country.... You can read the newspaper and feel that same confusion" ("Fiction Writers"). His second novel, *John Henry Days* (2001), tells the story of freelance journalist J. Sutter, who visits a West Virginia town in 1996 to celebrate the eponymous festival and the concomitant unveiling of a U.S. Postal Service stamp honoring the folk hero. Various chronological layers make up the novel, including **John Henry**'s story, **Paul Robeson**'s participation in a musical version of it, the first work assembling versions of the folk song by a Black folklorist, and the composition and recording of various songs describing John Henry's deeds. The novel's style varies greatly from chapter to chapter, shifting perspectives and voice and including **drama** and journalistic prose (*see* **Folklore**).

A book of brief, interconnected short stories, *The Colossus of New York: A City in Thirteen Parts*, was published in late 2003. It offers anonymous impressionistic glimpses of early twenty-first-century New York City from numerous perspectives, switching constantly between first-, second- and third-person points of view. Most of the stories have location-based titles such as "Port Authority" and "Coney Island," although three of them are called "Morning," "Rain," and "Rush Hour." Whitehead espouses an American postmodern sensibility, citing as influences Thomas Pynchon, Don DeLillo and John Dos Passos alongside **Ralph Ellison**, **Jean Toomer**, **Ishmael Reed**, **Charles S. Wright**, and **Clarence Major** ("Fiction Writers"; "Salon"; "Table Talk"). Whitehead has received numerous awards for his writing, including the QPB New Voices Award (for *The Intuitionist*, which was also a finalist for the Ernest Hemmingway/PEN Award for first fiction), the Whiting Writers Award (2000), and the New York Public Library's Young Lions Fiction Award (2002). He was named a MacArthur Foundation Fellow (the MacArthur "genius" grant) in 2002.

Resources: Colson Whitehead: *The Colossus of New York: A City in 13 Parts* (New York: Doubleday, 2003); "Fiction Writers on Writing: Colson Whitehead," *WriteNet* (Spring 2003), http://www.writenet.org/fiction_writers/fiction-colson_whitehead .html; *The Intuitionist* (New York: Anchor, 1999); *John Henry Days* (New York: Doubleday, 2001); "The Salon Interview," *Salon* (Jan. 21, 1999), http://archive.salon .com/books/int/1999/cov_si_12int.html; "Table Talk," *Village Voice*, Oct. 6, 2003, http://www.villagevoice.com/issues/0341/tepper.php; Colson Whitehead and Walter Mosley, "Eavesdropping," *Book* 16 (May/June 2001), 44–47.

Ian W. Wilson

Whitfield, James Monroe (1822–1871). Poet. Whitfield was one of only a handful of antebellum African Americans to publish a collection of poetry and thus is considered a pioneer in African American literature.

Born to free parents in Exeter, New Hampshire, Whitfield seems to have been related to the noted Paul family of African American clergy. He briefly attended school in New Hampshire, traveled to **Boston, Massachusetts,** and eventually settled in Buffalo, New York, about 1839. There, he worked as a barber and became active in the colonization movement. During the late 1840s and early 1850s, he contributed poetry to both the *North Star* and *Frederick Douglass's Paper*; at least one of his poems was also copied in *The Liberator*. By 1853, he was well known not only to Buffalo's African Americans but also to several leaders among Northern free Blacks—**Frederick Douglass, Martin R. Delany,** and **William Wells Brown,** among others. Though some differed with him on his colonization politics (as seen in an exchange of letters in the *North Star* in late 1853), all praised his poetic talent.

Whitfield's first and only collection of poetry, *America and Other Poems,* was published in 1853 and was dedicated to Delaney. The poems are, for the most part, traditional **formal verse,** though they do show some skill in terms of metrics. There are several religious poems, a handful of love poems, and a few occasional poems, but the most striking texts are those that focus on abolitionism and race, including the title poem, "Lines on the Death of John Quincy Adams," and "How Long?"

Though the collection's introduction prayed that readers would support Whitfield in further work, economics and his increasing interest in the colonization movement (including planning for a National Emigration Convention in 1854) pulled him from writing—though he did circulate a prospectus for a periodical that seems not to have been published, the *Afric-American Repository,* in 1856 and 1857. Biographer Joan Sherman claims that the next few years saw Whitfield traveling out of the country in hopes of identifying a potential Central American or South American colony for African Americans.

Whitfield settled in **San Francisco, California,** in 1861, where he continued working as a barber, became active in Black masonry in the region, and occasionally wrote poetry. Except for extended stays in Portland, Oregon, Placerville and Centerville, Idaho, and Elko, Nevada, Whitfield made San Francisco his home. His most notable work from this later period was a long, untitled poem published in 1867 alongside Ezra R. Johnson's "Emancipation Oration . . . in Honor of the Fourth Anniversary of President Lincoln's Proclamation of Emancipation." (*See* **Hall, Prince.**)

Resources: Doris Lucas Laryea, "James Monroe Whitfield," in *Dictionary of Literary Biography,* vol. 50, Afro-American Writers before the Harlem Renaissance (Detroit:

Gale, 1986), 260–263; Joan R. Sherman, "James Monroe Whitfield," in her *Invisible Poets*, 2nd ed. (Urbana: University of Illinois Press, 1989), 42–52.

Eric Gardner

Whitfield, Van (born c. 1964). Novelist. Whitfield has published several popular novels that feature comedic elements and sharp observation and that concern the relationships between Black men and women and how society affects an individual's perspective. Whitfield was born in **Baltimore, Maryland**. His father was a probation officer in the Maryland state prison system, and his mother was a special-education teacher. As a child, Whitfield was misdiagnosed as learning-disabled and placed in the St. Ambrose School, a remedial institution run by the Catholic Church. School personnel later identified a hearing problem as the cause of his academic difficulty. Corrective surgery improved his hearing, and his academic performance improved. A nun at his school instilled in him a love of reading and writing. After becoming a successful writer, therefore, Whitfield established the Van Whitfield Education Works Foundation, a program to help children learn to read and write (Henderson).

Whitfield followed his father into the corrections profession and worked at Lorton Prison. In 1995, Whitfield worked in a youth program in the mayor's office in **Washington, D.C.** (Henderson). His first novel, *Beeperless Remote* (1996), is a fictional account of an unsuccessful blind date he once had. The novel was published by the Alexander Publishing Group, a small, Baltimore-based firm, and earned six Ben Franklin Award nominations, including Best Author and Best New Voice in Books ("Van Whitfield"). His relationship with Alexander ended in a lawsuit over royalties, and Pines One Publications republished the book in 1997. He then signed a multibook contract with Doubleday-Random House ("Van Whitfield").

Whitfield's other novels include *Something's Wrong with Your Scale!* (1999), which is about weight gain and loss and their effect on romantic relationships, careers, and self-esteem. His next novel was *Guys in Suits* (2001), a novel about relationships and issues of social class. His most recent novel, *Dad Interrupted* (2004), is a follow-up to *Beeperless Remote* and deals with romantic relationships and Black fatherhood. Whitfield expanded his talents into screenwriting by writing for the UPN network series *Grown Ups*. He has also written for the Black Entertainment Television netowork's "profile" show, *Turnstyle*. He is currently working on the authorized biography of former Washington, D.C., Mayor Marion Barry (Random House home page).

Resources: Steve Hammer, "Van Whitfield Takes on a Big Problem: Author Gets Inside the Overweight World," *Nuvo* (1999), http://www.nuvo.net/archive/040199/040199_ahammer.html; Ashyia Henderson, "Van Whitfield," in *Contemporary Black Biography*, vol. 34, ed. Gale Group (Detroit: Gale, 2002), reproduced in *Biography Resource Center*, Gale Group (2004), http://galenete.galegroup.com/servlet/Biorc; Random House home page, http://www.randomhouse.com/catalog/display.pperl?isbn=0385508182; "Van Whitfield," African American Literature Book Club (1999), http://www.aalbc.com; Van Whitfield: *Beeperless Remote* (Los Angeles: Pines One, 1997); *Dad Interrupted* (New York: Harlem Moon, 2004); *Guys in Suits* (New York: Doubleday, 2001); "Home page," http://www.vanwhitfield.com; *Something's Wrong with Your Scale!* (New York: Doubleday, 1999).

Catherine N. Anyaso

Whitman, Albery Allson (1851–1901). Poet. Although Whitman's poems have often been regarded as digressive and shallow, Whitman is also praised as one of the most important poets of his age. After studying at Wilberforce College, he became the pastor at churches in several states, including Ohio and Georgia. He died of pneumonia in 1901.

Whitman's earliest work, *Essays on the Ten Plagues and Miscellaneous Poems* (1871?), is lost, and his 1873 poem *Leelah Misled*, the story of a white woman seduced by a philanderer, has received little critical attention. The publication of *Not a Man, and Yet a Man* (1877) established Whitman's reputation.

Not a Man, and Yet a Man is a 5,000-line epic that spans the life of Rodney, the poem's hero, who, although "eighty-five percent white," is still considered Black. The poem focuses on Rodney's manly exploits. Whitman's focus on African American advancement through self-improvement, and his avoidance of overt political rhetoric, are identifying features of his work (*see* **Epic Poetry/The Long Poem**).

The Rape of Florida (1884), revised as *Twasinta's Seminoles; or, Rape of Florida* (1885), is Whitman's best-known work. This tale of Seminole Indians expelled from Florida is thought to be the first poem by an African American to use Spenserian stanzas (*see* **Formal Verse**).

Whitman also experimented with poetic forms not often seen in contemporary African American poetry in "The Octoroon," included in *An Idyl of the South* (1901). The story of Maury and Lena is told in ottava rima, a form popularized by the British poet, Lord Byron. Often praised as Whitman's finest poem, "The Octoroon" comes closest of his poems to social protest in its focus on **color of skin** as a barrier. Whitman was a light-skinned Black man, and his characters are invariably light-skinned as well. A planned sequel to the poem, which was to address additional problems in **the South**, never appeared.

Whitman was called a "mockingbird poet" (Jackson, 266), and his style is imitative of the Romantics in general and of poets such as Henry Wadsworth Longfellow and William Cullen Bryant in particular. Longfellow's influence is seen in the *Hiawatha*-like verses of *Not a Man, Yet a Man*, while poems such as his "Boatman's Song," from *The Rape of Florida*, are praised for their creativity.

Resources: Blyden Jackson, "Albery Allson Whitman," in *Dictionary of Literary Biography*, vol. 50, *Afro-American Writers before the Harlem Renaissance* (Detroit: Gale, 1986), 263–267; Joan R. Sherman, *Invisible Poets: Afro-Americans of the Nineteenth Century*, 2nd ed. (Urbana: University of Illinois Press, 1989), 112–129; Albery Allson Whitman: *An Idyl of the South* (New York: Metaphysical Publishing, 1901); *Not a*

Man, and Yet a Man (Springfield, OH: Republic, 1877); *Twasinta's Seminoles; or, Rape of Florida* (St. Louis: Nixon-Jones, 1885).

Patricia Kennedy Bostian

Wideman, John Edgar (born 1941). Novelist, short story writer, essayist, professor, and editor. Born in **Washington, D.C.**, John Edgar Wideman spent his early childhood in the African American community of Homewood in **Pittsburgh, Pennsylvania**. He studied English at the University of Pennsylvania, where he captained the basketball team and won all–Ivy League status, and later was inducted into Philadelphia's Big Five Basketball Hall of Fame. (The importance of **basketball** emerges in Wideman's works, in which the physical and symbolic space of the basketball court represents a space of infinite potential, though it is never idealized or utopian). In 1963, Wideman won a Rhodes Scholarship; the only other African American to have done so was **Alain Locke**. He completed his M.A. at Oxford University in 1966, writing a thesis on the beginnings of the novel form. He is the only writer to have won the PEN/Faulkner Award twice, in 1983 for *Sent for You Yesterday* and in 1990 for *Philadelphia Fire*. Wideman also numbers the American Book Award, the MacArthur Award (1993), and a Lannan Foundation Fellowship (1991) among his accolades.

In 1966, Wideman began work on his first novel, *A Glance Away*, which was published in 1967. Both *A Glance Away* and *Hurry Home* (1970), Wideman's second novel, are experimental, fractured narratives in which the structures reflect the characters' feelings of communal and existential alienation and dislocation. The struggles of the protagonists are at times all but overshadowed by the density of Wideman's literary allusions, which cover everything from the work of Goethe to **spirituals**. At this time, Wideman lectured at the University of Pennsylvania; at his students' request, in 1968 he fashioned the university's first African American literature course. He spent three years as director of the university's Afro-American Studies program (*see* **Black Studies**).

In *The Lynchers* (1973), Wideman produced a more raw, less obviously wrought novel. The bleak lyricism of the first two novels was transformed into a powerful, claustrophobic evocation of the pressures that accumulate during centuries of racial oppression. In this tale of Black conspirators planning what proves to be an abortive **lynching** of a White police officer, Wideman, like **Richard Wright** and **Chester Himes** before him, mused on the relationship among violence, community creation, and revolution. In 1975, Wideman, his wife, and his three children moved to Laramie, where he spent eleven years as a professor of English at the University of Wyoming.

Wideman describes the eight-year hiatus between the publication of *The Lynchers* and his next works, the novel *Hiding Place* and the short story collection *Damballah* (both 1981), as a time in which he explored the breadth of African American literary production. The later works formed two parts of

Wideman's Homewood Trilogy (which concluded with *Sent for You Yesterday*). Wideman's literary Homewood remains a central presence in his writing, reappearing in various guises in the memoir *Brothers and Keepers* (1984) and the novel *Reuben* (1987). This literary return to the landscape of his childhood has led critics to suggest that Wideman moved away from the high modernist model of his first three works, dominated by references to a traditional White, European canon, to explore a more African American voice (*see* **Modernism**). Wideman, however, suggests that all of his works represent an ongoing experimentation with the novel form and exploration of the functions of community. Thus, the Homewood Trilogy pays tribute to the ways in which voices of larger-than-life figures in the family and community maintained the Homewood of his childhood, through the circulation of foundational and everyday stories. Through this exchange of stories, Wideman explores what community can mean, as well as the difficulties of maintaining a true, open exchange between individuals which represents the ideal of community.

Wideman's writing shows an unflinching personal bravery; his fiction (in the novels *Hiding Place* and *Philadelphia Fire*, as well as short stories from *Damballah*) and memoirs (*Brothers and Keepers*) address the imprisonment of his brother Robby (who was imprisoned for life in 1976 for his part in an armed robbery that turned into a murder) and of Wideman's son Jacob, sentenced to life in prison for the murder of a bunkmate while at camp. Wideman acknowledges the potential for pain on the parts of both writer and subject when working with biographical material, while underlining the potential of storytelling to allow people to face traumatic separations and to reconnect. Indeed, Wideman states that *Brothers and Keepers*, which is arguably his best-known work, began as an attempt to describe his exchange of stories with his imprisoned brother Robby, an exchange that overcame the distance which had grown between them since John left for university.

In 1986, Wideman moved to the University of Massachusetts at Amherst, where he still teaches as a professor in the creative writing program. In the title short story of his collection *Fever* (1989), Wideman began to explore in depth the concept that history repeats itself in the present. Patterns of violence and racial oppression in the past cannot be forgotten, he claims, because they hold the keys to understanding similar violence in the present.

In *Philadelphia Fire*, Wideman dwells on the bombing of the MOVE house on Osage Avenue on May 13, 1985. The bombing, ordered by Mayor Wilson Goode, resulted in the deaths of eleven of the house's thirteen inhabitants. In *The Cattle Killing* (1996), Wideman continues to draw on historical sources, using **Richard Allen**'s *The Life, Experience, and Gospel Labours of the Rt. Rev. Richard Allen* to focus on the yellow fever epidemic in Philadelphia in 1793, and the ways in which the biological contagion mirrors the sickness of racism. Wideman contrasts these sicknesses by having his narrator relate the events as a story told to a dying woman, suggesting that the story is not only keeping the woman alive but also, perhaps, helping her to recover.

In his most recent work, the novel *Two Cities: A Love Story* (1998), the basketball memoir *Hoop Roots* (2001), and the travel memoir *The Island: Martinique* (2003), Wideman focuses on love and its role in community formation. Once again, these texts show Wideman's signature blurring of the boundaries between **autobiography**, biography and fiction. In 2001, he edited the anthology *My Soul Has Grown Deep: Classics of Early African-American Literature*.

Despite Wideman's examination of love, his literary vision is often criticized as bleak, perhaps even nihilistic. His vision, though certainly unflinching when regarding material forms of oppression and suffering, is nonetheless idealistic, as his characters find ways to negotiate personal connections, even love, across class divides, prison walls, years of separation, and even beyond death. At the core, Wideman's work, like that of **Alice Walker, Gloria Naylor**, and **Toni Morrison**, displays a faith in such personal connections and in the sense of belonging created by inclusive community models which are not based on racial, gendered, or class exclusion.

Resources: Primary Sources: John Edgar Wideman: *All Stories Are True* (New York: Vintage, 1993); *Brothers and Keepers* (New York: Holt, Rinehart and Winston, 1984); *The Cattle Killing* (Boston: Houghton Mifflin, 1996); *Damballah* (1981; repr. New York: Vintage, 1988); *Fever: Twelve Stories* (New York: Henry Holt, 1989); *A Glance Away* (1967; repr. New York: Holt, Rinehart and Winston, 1985); *God's Gym* (Boston: Houghton Mifflin, 2005); *Hiding Place* (1981; repr. New York: Vintage, 1988); *The Homewood Trilogy* (New York: Avon, 1985); *Hoop Roots* (Boston: Houghton Mifflin, 2001); *Hurry Home* (New York: Harcourt, Brace & World, 1970); *Identities: Three Novels* (New York: Henry Holt, 1994); *The Island: Martinque* (Washington, DC: National Geographic, 2003); *Lynchers* (New York: Harcourt Brace Jovanovich, 1973); *Philadelphia Fire: A Novel* (New York: Henry Holt, 1990); *Reuben* (New York: Henry Holt, 1987); *Sent for You Yesterday* (New York: Avon, 1983); *The Stories of John Edgar Wideman* (New York: Pantheon, 1992); *Two Cities* (Boston: Houghton Mifflin, 1998); John Edgar Wideman, ed., *My Soul Has Grown Deep: Classics of Early African-American Literature* (Philadelphia: Running Press, 2001). **Secondary Sources:** James W. Coleman: *Black Male Fiction and the Legacy of Caliban* (Lexington: University Press of Kentucky, 2001); *Blackness and Modernism: The Literary Career of John Edgar Wideman* (Jackson: University Press of Mississippi, 1989); Bonnie TuSmith, ed., *Conversations with John Edgar Wideman* (Jackson: University Press of Mississippi, 1998).

Scott Bunyan

Wilkins, Roy (1901–1981). Journalist, organizational leader, political activist, editor, and autobiographer. As the editor of **The Crisis** and then the Executive Secretary of the National Association for the Advancement of Colored People (**NAACP**), Wilkins was a key figure in the **Civil Rights Movement**. Wilkins was born in **St. Louis, Missouri**, but he grew up in St. Paul, Minnesota, where an outdoor memorial commemorates him and his achievements. Wilkins graduated from the University of Minnesota in 1923, and shortly thereafter he began working as a journalist for an African American newspaper, the *Kansas City Call*. In the 1930s he became involved with the NAACP and served as the editor of the organization's magazine, *The Crisis*, from 1934 through 1949. In 1955, in the midst of the Civil Rights Movement, he served as the NAACP's Executive Secretary. In the 1960s and early 1970s, Wilkins and other moderate African American leaders were perceived as insufficiently militant by younger leaders, including **Malcolm X** and **Stokely Carmichael** (Valade, 380). Wilkins comments on such tension in his book *Standing Fast: The Autobiography of Roy Wilkins* (1982), which also surveys his involvement with journalism, social activism, and progressive politics over four decades. In addition, it discusses his connection to Thurgood Marshall, arguably the most important legal mind in the Civil Rights Movement, as well as to **Walter Francis White** and **Martin Luther King, Jr.**, and to Presidents John F. Kennedy and Lyndon Baines Johnson, with whom he consulted. Wilkins was awarded the Presidential Medal of Freedom in 1969. He retired from the NAACP in 1977.

Resources: G. B. Current, "Review of *Standing Fast: The Autobiography of Roy Wilkins*," *The Crisis* 89 (June 1982), 53; A. Meier, "Review of *Standing Fast: The Autobiography of Roy Wilkins*," *Journal of Southern History* 49 (May 1983), 326–327; Roger M. Valade III, *The Essential Black Literature Guide* (Detroit: Visible Ink, 1996), 380–381 (includes photo of Wilkins); Roy Wilkins, with Tom Matthews, *Standing Fast: The Autobiography of Roy Wilkins* (1982; repr. New York: Da Capo, 1994).

Hans Ostrom

Wilks, Talvin Winston (born 1961). Playwright, director, and dramaturge. For Wilks, politics and history become places in which to examine, by means of **drama**, identities continually divided by **race**, class, **gender**, and sexuality. According to Roger Downey, Wilks's plays continue the dramatic conversations begun by **Lorraine Hansberry**, LeRoi Jones (**Amiri Baraka**), **Ntozake Shange**, and **George C. Wolfe** (Downey, 3). From **affirmative action** debates to "culture wars," Wilks's original work addresses the complicated terrain of what it means socially, politically, and individually to be an African American (*see* **Drama**).

Wilks was born on December 10, 1961, in Dayton, Ohio. He attended Princeton University and began his undergraduate work in biochemistry, but soon realized that his academic path was in theater. At Princeton, Wilks was introduced to the practices of The Open Theater, where he worked with Jean Claude van Itallie, Tina Sheppard, and Steve Gomer. Wilks graduated cum laude with a degree in English literature in 1985, and his senior thesis, *INCUBUS: An American Dream Play*, premiered soon after his graduation at the Edinburgh Fringe Festival. That same year, Wilks began fund-raising for Crossroads Theatre Company in New Brunswick, New Jersey, which later served as the site for the 1990 world premiere of his second and best-known play, *Tod, the Boy, Tod*.

Tod focuses on a seemingly assimilated, middle-class African American protagonist whose father is a former political activist and whose mother is a former member of the **Black Panther Party**. He is experiencing an identity crisis, and the play begins with his suicide attempt. The plot then moves to a multiple-character debate about Tod's identity crisis. Wilks's play *The Trial of Uncle S&M*, a work about social repression and dominance, also opened in 1990. *The Trial of Uncle S&M* was part of Wilks's work with Spin Lab, a six-person collaborative theater group of which he was a founding member.

While at Crossroads, Wilks made his professional directorial debut in 1992 with Ntozake Shange's *The Love Space Demands*, a multimedia, multigenre dramatic piece that included poetry, music, and photography. Wilks was also involved in the African American College Initiative Program (1991–1994), where he developed dramatic works in several historically Black colleges across the United States. In 1993, *Tod, the Boy, Tod* received its West Coast premiere at The Group Theatre in Seattle, Washington. Following this second production of *Tod*, Wilks served as The Group's playwright-in-residence/dramaturge (1994–1996).

Since 1996, Wilks has worked primarily as a freelance collaborative director for several artists, including **Carl Hancock Rux**, Sekou Sundiata, Migdalia Cruz, Kia Corthron, Stephanie Berry, Mildred Ruiz, and Steven Sapp. He also has served as coauthor of Ping Chong's bicultural, bilingual, community-based series *Undesirable Elements*, a work that has been staged in several cities within and outside the United States. Wilks has worked with Chong on seven productions in the series, including *Undesirable Elements/Seattle* (1995), *Secret Histories/Charleston* (Spoleto Festival, 2000), *Undesirable Elements/Atlanta* (2001), *UE: 92/02* (a thirtieth anniversary production at La Mama Theater, New York City), and *Undesirable Elements/Pioneer Valley* (2003). According to Wilks, collaborating with Ping Chong made him think of being an "artist of the world," prompting him to break through traditional identity boundaries in his own work. This idea of breaking through boundaries is also present in his recent collaborations with the choreographer Bebe Miller. Wilks provided text and dramaturgy for Miller's *Verge* (2000), a Bessie Award-winning dance piece that examines the spaces in relationships and between individuals.

From 2002 to 2004, Wilks was the interim Artistic Director of New WORLD Theater, a multicultural theater company located in Amherst, Massachusetts.

Resources: Primary Sources: Talvin Wilks: "Elijah's Journey: Introduction to *Elijah*," in *The Color of Theater: Race, Culture, and Contemporary Performance*, ed. Roberta Uno and Lucy Mae San Pablo Burns (New York: Continuum, 2002), 385–388; *Tod, the Boy, Tod*, in *Colored Contradictions: An Anthology of African-American Plays*, ed. Harry Justin Elam and Robert Alexander (New York: Plume, 1996), also in *The National Black Drama Anthology: Eleven Plays from America's Leading African-American Theaters*, ed. Woodie King, Jr. (New York: Applause, 1995). *Plays Produced But Unpublished: Bread of Heaven* (1994); *Incubus: An American Dream Play* (1985);

Occasional Grace (1991); *Sarajevo: Behind God's Back* (1995); *The Trial of Uncle S&M* (1990); *Undesirable Elements/Seattle*, with Ping Chong (1995). **Secondary Sources:** Roger Downey, "Darkness of the Soul," review of *Tod, the Boy, Tod, Seattle Weekly,* Mar. 5, 1993, p. 3; Shelley Jiggetts, "*The Love Space Demands,*" in *The Production Notebooks: Theatre in Process*, vol. 1, ed. Mark Bly (New York: Theatre Communications Group, 1996), 125–173; Cathy J. Schlund-Vials, "Interview with Talvin Wilks," Amherst, MA, June 25, 2004.

Cathy J. Schlund-Vials

Williams, Bert (1874–1922). Theatrical performer and singer. Two well-known quotations appear repeatedly in the biographical literature about Egbert Austin "Bert" Williams, including the biographies by Charters and Smith. Tuskegee Institute founder and president **Booker T. Washington** claimed that "Bert Williams has done more for the race than I have. He has smiled his way into people's hearts. I have been obliged to fight my way." And Williams's *Ziegfeld Follies* colleague W. C. Fields said, "He was the funniest man I ever saw, and the saddest." Williams's theatrical career straddled the tenuous line between humor and pathos, between tragedy and comedy, and between accommodation and racial protest. He was possibly the most important American actor during the pre–**World War I** period. Along with his partner, George Nash Walker, Williams brought the blackface minstrel performance to its most sophisticated level (*see* **Minstrelsy**).

Many of the facts of Williams' life are still in dispute. He was born in 1874 in New Providence, Nassau, the Bahamas, and he died in New York City of pneumonia two weeks after collapsing in **Detroit, Michigan**, during a stage performance of *Under the Bamboo Tree*. His family moved to Riverside, California, in 1885, and Bert later abandoned his engineering studies in order to pursue a theatrical career in **San Francisco, California**. In 1893, Williams joined Martin & Seig's Mastodon Minstrels, where he met George Walker. In 1895 the pair went to **Chicago, Illinois**, where they developed their unique, two-man minstrel act—Williams, in blackface, playing the shuffling straight man to Walker's well-dressed dandy. They billed themselves as "The Two Real Coons," and appeared to embrace the coon stereotypes of African Americans. But like other aspects of Williams's career, the name is more complicated than it seems (Brown). Rather than representing a capitulation to insulting White supremacist stereotypes, Williams and Walker chose the name "The Two Real Coons" to emphasize the fact that most of the minstrel performers were White men creating an insulting, spurious version of Black life. For the fourteen years the team was together, they attempted to stretch the artistic and interpretive possibilities of **minstrelsy** and, to the extent possible, render it useful for a serious expression of and investigation into Black thought and life.

Williams's career had many highlights. He and Walker, with their future wives Lottie Thompson and Aida Overton, popularized the cakewalk in an 1896 musical farce titled *The Gold Bug*. In 1901 the pair became the first

African American recording artists when they made their initial recordings for the Victor label. From 1902 to 1905 they brought the first African American show to Broadway when they collaborated with Will Marion Cook, **Paul Laurence Dunbar**, and Jesse Schipp to produce *In Dahomey*. The show toured Europe, where it was featured at Buckingham Palace in a command performance for Edward VII, and where Williams and Walker made the cakewalk the rage of the London and **Paris, France**, social sets. In 1906 the team was instrumental in establishing the first African American actors' union, called The Negro's Society.

In 1909 Walker contracted syphillis, and he died two years later. Williams continued performing as a solo act, and in 1910 Florenz Ziegfeld invited him to be the first African American regular in the *Ziegfeld Follies*, where he performed steadily until the end of his life. Williams's colleagues in the *Follies* were, among others, Fanny Brice, W. C. Fields, and Eddie Cantor. Cantor credited Williams with teaching him all he knew about timing on the comic stage. In 1916 Williams was the star of a film titled *The Natural Born Gambler*. During the final two decades of his life, Williams recorded over fifty songs, the most famous being "Nobody," a tune that expresses the ironic, aching humor that characterized Williams's own career and the bittersweet plight of the African American minstrel performer.

Bert Williams in blackface, undated. Yale Collection of American Literature, Beinecke Rare Book and Manuscript Library.

It may be difficult to convince the modern-day student of the history of the American stage that Bert Williams's career served any useful purpose. He performed "darky" material, and did so behind the debilitating veneer of a corked blackface. But in his life and work are echoes of an idea that several generations of serious African American artists and intellectuals have addressed. Williams's effort to bring a greater sophistication and variety to the most limiting kinds of demeaning stereotypes embodies the inspiration behind such work as **Paul Laurence Dunbar**'s poems "We Wear the Mask" (1895), "Sympathy" (1899), and "The Poet" (1903); **Langston Hughes**'s poems "Minstrel Man" (1925) and "Trumpet Player" (1947); **Jacob Lawrence**'s 1963 painting *Clown*; and even such popular songs as The Platters' "The Great Pretender" (1955) and Smokey Robinson and the Miracles' "Tracks of My Tears" (1965) and "Tears of a Clown" (1967). Three years after Williams died, **Jessie Redmon Fauset**, the artistic editor of the **NAACP**'s magazine, *The Crisis*, captured the contradictions and achievements of Williams's career when she memorialized him in her conclusion to an essay titled "The Gift of Laughter" that appeared in **Alain Locke**'s *The New Negro* (1925):

> All this beyond any doubt will be the reward of the "gift of laughter" which many black actors on the American stage have proffered. Through laughter we have conquered even the lot of the jester and the clown. The parable of the one talent still holds good and because we have used the little which in those early painful days was our only approach we find ourselves slowly but surely moving toward that most glittering of all goals, the freedom of the American stage. I hope that Hogan realizes this and Cole and Walker, too, and that lastly Bert Williams the inimitable, will clap us on with those tragic black-gloved hands of his now that the gift of his laughter is no longer tainted with the salt of chagrin and tears. (167)

Resources: Janet Brown, " 'Coon-Singer' and the 'Coon-Song': A Case Study of the Performer-Character Relationship," *Journal of American Culture* 7, no. 1–2 (Spring–Summer 1984), 1–8; Ann Charters, *Nobody: The Story of Bert Williams* (New York: Macmillan, 1970); Jessie Redmon Fauset, "The Gift of Laughter," in Alain Locke, ed., *The New Negro* (1925; New York: Atheneum, 1992); Nathan Irvin Huggins, *Harlem Renaissance* (New York: Oxford University Press, 1971); Alain Locke, ed., *The New Negro: An Interpretation* (New York: Albert & Charles Boni, 1925); Mabel Rowland, ed., *Bert Williams: Son of Laughter* (New York: Negro Universities Press, 1969); Eric Ledell Smith, *Bert Williams: A Biography of the Pioneer Black Comedian* (Jefferson, NC: McFarland, 1992); Stephen C. Tracy, " 'Something You Don't Expect': The Recordings of Bert Williams," *MELUS* 29, no. 2 (Summer 2004), 290–301.

Mychel J. Namphy

Williams, Billy Dee (born 1937). Actor, painter, and science fiction writer. Though recognized mainly for his work on stage and screen, Billy Dee Williams has coauthored three best-selling novels that are of some import to a subgenre that combines espionage and **science fiction**.

He was born William December Williams in New York City. Committed to a career in the arts from an early age, Williams initially wanted to become a painter. But landmark performances in the television film *Brian's Song* (1971) and the motion picture *Lady Sings the Blues* (1972) assured Williams's status as one of Hollywood's most desirable Black male actors. He is perhaps best known for his role as the rogue double-dealer Lando Calrissian in two parts of the phenomenally popular *Star Wars* trilogy, *The Empire Strikes Back* (1980) and *Return of the Jedi* (1983).

Williams's novels *PSI/Net* (1999) and *Just/in Time* (2000) introduce readers to former Air Force Major Trent Calloway, whose involvement in a government "remote-viewing" project entails becoming a psychic spy for the CIA. Combining classic espionage writing with high-tech science fiction, the books document Calloway's struggle to discover the "truth" of his psychic condition as he combats such state enemies as New Age cult leader Justin Logos. *Twilight* (2002), written with Elizabeth Atkins Bowman, is a very different novel, drawing from Hollywood pulp, contemporary romance, and courtroom **drama** to create narrative tension. Williams and Bowman effectively work across genres to imagine a uniquely troubled erotic love story whose Black male lead bears a striking resemblance to Williams himself.

Resources: Billy Dee Williams and Elizabeth Atkins Bowman, *Twilight* (New York: Forge, 2002); Billy Dee Williams and Rob MacGregor: *Just/in Time* (New York: Forge, 2000); *PSI/Net* (New York: Tor, 1999).

Kinohi Nishikawa

Williams, Crystal (born 1970). Poet, essayist, and professor. A performance poet who toured on the competitive poetry-slam circuit before making the transition from spoken word to printed page, Crystal Williams has combined a dramatic insistence on immediacy and accessibility with a reverence for the amplitude of the lyric tradition. Her signature performance piece, "In Search of Aunt Jemima" (from her 2000 collection, *Kin*), early established her thematic preoccupations with **race**, self-image, class, and cultural/familial kinship. Expressing a varied repertoire of moods, from the wryly ironic to the disturbingly grim and caustic, to the delicately self-reflective, her voice is always determinedly clear and unambiguously humane.

Adopted and raised in **Detroit, Michigan**, by a progressive, education-minded interracial couple, Williams profited from her father's musicality and her mother's belief in language training and lessons of all sorts. Her father, a charismatic **jazz** pianist, died when Williams was eleven. Her mother, a psychologist, then took her daughter to live for two years in Spain, where she developed Spanish language proficiency and a more worldly outlook than most of her Detroit peers, prompting an early interest in the ways class and race converge.

Williams returned to the United States and continued the theater training she had begun as a child, becoming a member of Detroit's Performing Arts Guild and attending a performing arts high school. She was especially drawn to the writers of the **Black Arts Movement** (BAM), including **Sonia Sanchez** and **Nikki Giovanni**. The BAM writers' belief in using art and performance as a means of instigating political and community change was particularly relevant to Williams, who combined her dramatic arts background with her early poetic efforts.

Williams moved to **Washington, D.C.**, and then to New York City, where she studied creative writing at New York University, completing her B.A. in 1997. She continued to refine her craft and her delivery style, gaining a reputation as a writer/performer of great dramatic power. She became a regular at the **Nuyorican Poets Café** and was a member of the 1995 championship Nuyorican Slam Team along with Poppy, Xavier Cavazos, and Hil Cato.

Though no longer exclusively associated with spoken word or **performance poetry**, Williams continues to do public readings of her work at colleges, festivals, and community centers across the country, "performing" her written words with heartfelt precision. Her second collection, *Lunatic* (2002), further demonstrates her lyric range and complexity. She received her M.F.A. in creative writing from Cornell University in 2000 and is now assistant professor of creative writing at Reed College in Portland, Oregon.

Resources: Crystal Williams: "In the Belly of a Clothes Rack," in *Children of the Dream: Our Own Stories of Growing Up Black in America*, ed. Laurel Holiday (New York: Pocket Books, 1999); "Jemima in the Mirror," *Ms.*, Dec. 2000/Jan. 2001, 41–44; *Kin: Poems* (East Lansing: Michigan State University Press, 2000); *Lunatic: Poems* (East Lansing: Michigan State University Press, 2002); Jeff Zaleski, "Review of *Kin*," *Publishers Weekly*, May 29, 2000, p. 79.

Kate Falvey

Williams, Edward Christopher (1871–1929). Novelist, librarian, and playwright. Until the republication of *When Washington Was in Vogue*, a **novel** set in the District of Columbia during the **Harlem Renaissance**, Williams was known primarily as the first professionally trained Black librarian in America. Born in Cleveland, Ohio, to an African American father and a white mother, he graduated from Cleveland public schools with honors and attended Western Reserve University (now Case Western Reserve University), where he was both Phi Beta Kappa and class valedictorian. Shortly after his 1892 graduation, Williams became an assistant librarian at Western Reserve's Hatch Library, and by 1901 he rose to the position of head librarian. Williams attended the New York State Library School in Albany in 1899–1900, where he completed the two-year course in a little over a year. In 1902, he married Ethel Chesnutt, the daughter of the author **Charles Waddell Chesnutt**.

Williams resigned his position at Western Reserve in 1909 and moved to **Washington, D.C.**, where he became principal of the M Street School (now **Paul Laurence Dunbar** High School). He served in this capacity until 1916, when he began work as head librarian at Howard University; he also taught courses in library science and foreign languages while there. Williams enjoyed an active literary life while in Washington. Three of his plays—*The Chasm, The Exile*, and *The Sheriff's Children* (an adaptation of the Chesnutt story)— were performed at Howard, and he contributed a number of anonymous pieces to little magazines, perhaps under the pseudonym "Bertuccio Dantino" (Porter, 320).

Most significantly, Williams published his novel *The Letters of Davy Carr: A True Story of Colored Vanity Fair*, serially and anonymously in the African American magazine **The Messenger**, from January 1925 through June 1926. This novel was republished in book form in 2004 under the title *When Washington Was in Vogue*, an allusion both to **Langston Hughes**'s "When the Negro Was in Vogue," a chapter in his first **autobiography**, *The Big Sea*, and to David Levering Lewis's book *When Harlem Was in Vogue*. The first African American **epistolary novel**, it tells the story of Davy Carr, a fair-skinned **World War I** veteran, who comes to Washington to research the slave trade. While there, he writes to a friend about the culture and mores of the Black bourgeoisie, and he eventually falls in love with the younger, darker, and more socially adventurous Caroline Rhodes. *When Washington Was in Vogue* is one of the first novels to offer an extensive and realistic portrayal of Black life in Washington, D.C.; as Emily Bernard notes in her commentary on the novel (Williams, 2003), Williams' achievement is that he depicts this world in all of its "style, wit, and charm," as well as in its occasional heartlessness and "bad behavior." Williams died in New York City in 1929 while pursuing a Ph.D. in library science at Columbia University. Archival material, including copies of his plays *The Exile* and *The Sheriff's Children*, are available at Howard University's Founders Library.

Resources: E. J. Josey, "Edward Christopher Williams: Librarian's Librarian," *Negro History Bulletin* 33 (1970), 70–77; Dorothy B. Porter, "*Phylon* Profile, XIV: Edward Christopher Williams," *Phylon* 7 (1947), 315–321; Christina Simmons, "'Modern Marriage' for African Americans, 1920–1940," *Canadian Review of American Studies* 30, no. 3 (2000), 11–25; Edward Christopher Williams, *The Letters of Davy Carr: A True Story of Colored Vanity Fair*, *The Messenger*, Jan. 1925–June 1926, reprinted as *When Washington Was in Vogue: A Love Story—A Lost Novel of the Harlem Renaissance*, introd. Adam McKible, commentary by Emily Bernard (New York: Amistad, 2003).

Adam McKible

Williams, George Washington (1849–1891). Historian and political activist. George Washington Williams's seminal works of African American history synthesized a wide array of archival information, attested to the roles played by African Americans in the nation's history, and challenged widespread misconceptions about emerging forms of Black community. Born in Bedford Springs, Pennsylvania, Williams spent his childhood in various parts of the state. In 1863, at the age of fourteen, his enthusiasm led him to try enlisting in the Union Army under a false name; after several attempts, he was accepted the next year. Wounded in the **Civil War** battle at Harrison, Virginia, Williams later joined the Mexican Army, and then returned to the U.S. Army as a cavalryman in the Comanche campaigns. In 1868, after baptism at **St. Louis, Missouri**, Williams studied to become a preacher, attending Howard University, Wayland Seminary, and finally the Newton Theological Seminary in Massachusetts; **John Hope Franklin** notes that "semiliterate as an entrant, he became a polished writer and speaker within five years" (xvi). Having graduated from Newton in 1874, Williams worked at the Twelfth Street Baptist Church in **Boston, Massachusetts**. He moved in 1875 to **Washington, D.C.**, where he founded and edited the journal *The Commoner*, and to Cincinnati, Ohio, in 1876, where he served as pastor at the Union Baptist Church. In Ohio he attended the Cincinnati Law School, worked for Judge Alphonso Taft, wrote for the *Cincinnati Commercial*, and, in 1879, became the first African American elected to the Ohio House of Representatives. While conducting research for a Fourth of July oration, "The American Negro from 1776 to 1876," Williams found abundant material on Black history and, rather than stand for reelection in 1881, he decided to work full-time as a historian.

Williams drew on over 12,000 sources (of which over 1,000 are cited) and spent over seven years writing the sixty-chapter *History of the Negro Race in America, 1619–1880* (1883). It was a landmark in African American scholarship, offering a sweeping account from "African antecedents" to the **Reconstruction** era. In the wake of publicity generated by the book, Williams attended the 1884 World Conference on Foreign Missions in London, served briefly as U.S. minister to **Haiti** in 1885, and met King Leopold of Belgium at an antislavery conference in Brussels. His second book, *A History of the Negro Troops in the War of the Rebellion 1861–1865* (1888), focused on the experiences of Black soldiers who battled to preserve the Union and covered debates among military and civilian leadership over the use of Black troops. The more scholarly tone of Williams's second history demonstrated his mastery of the conventions of academic historians, and earned it a warm critical response. In 1889, Williams traveled to the Congo and wrote several pieces in favor of its independence from Belgium, including an 1890 report for President Benjamin Harrison. In 1891, he left for England to begin a book on the Congo, and died later that year at the age of forty-two.

Resources: John Hope Franklin, *George Washington Williams: A Biography* (Chicago: University of Chicago Press, 1985); Linda O. McMurry, "George Washington Williams," in *Dictionary of Literary Biography*, vol. 47, *American Historians, 1866–1912* (Detroit: Gale, 1986), 337–343; Earl E. Thorpe, *Black Historians: A Critique* (New York: Morrow, 1971), 549–566; George Washington Williams, *History of the Negro Race in America, 1619–1880* (1883; repr. New York: Arno, 1968).

Alex Feerst

Williams, John A. (born 1925). Novelist, journalist, editor, and professor. Williams's literary reputation rests chiefly on one novel, *The Man Who Cried I Am* (1967), but he is in fact a remarkably versatile, prolific writer. He was born in Mississippi but grew up in Syracuse, New York, where he attended Syracuse University after having served in the Navy during **World War II**. He graduated from Syracuse in 1950, and shortly thereafter began publishing articles in magazines, including **Ebony** and *Jet*. Williams's early novels are *The Angry Ones* (1960), *Night Song* (1961), and *Sissie* (1963), which deal in different ways with African Americans' predicament in a racist, oppressive society. The most controversial moment of his literary career came in 1962, when the American Academy of Arts and Letters was poised to bestow the prestigious Prix de Rome Award but withdrew the prize after members of the Academy had conducted an interview with him (Nash, 778). A withdrawal of the award was unprecedented, and has not happened to any writer since then.

In writing *The Man Who Cried I Am*, Williams made use of this experience. The novel concerns three male African American writers, one of whom, Max Reddick, is dying of cancer; the other two characters are thought to be fictional incarnations of **Richard Wright** and **James Baldwin** (Gates and McKay, 1876). *The Man Who Cried I Am* is an intellectually and stylistically sophisticated novel that addresses a wide variety of issues and subjects, including aesthetics and philosophy, **jazz** and politics, friendship, memory, sexuality, and **race**. It is considered one of the most important works to come out of the **Black Arts Movement**, even though critics tend not to associate Williams with that movement.

As a journalist, Williams worked for the CBS and NBC television networks, as well as for *Newsweek* magazine. *Flashbacks* (1973), a nonfiction book, concerns his career as a print journalist. Williams's other novels include *Sons of Darkness, Sons of Light: A Novel of Some Probability* (1969), *The Junior Bachelor Society* (1976), and *Jacob's Ladder* (1987). With Gilbert H. Muller, who wrote a book-length critical study of Williams's work, he edited the anthology *Bridges: Literature Across Cultures* (1994). Williams has taught at Sarah Lawrence College and the University of California at Santa Barbara, among other institutions.

Resources: Henry Louis Gates, Jr., and Nellie Y. McKay, eds., *The Norton Anthology of African American Literature*, 2nd ed. (New York: Norton, 2004), 1876–1895; Gilbert H. Muller, *John A. Williams* (New York: Twayne, 1984); Gilbert H. Muller and John A. Williams, eds., *Bridges: Literature Across Cultures* (New York: McGraw-Hill, 1994); William R. Nash, "John A. Williams," in *The Oxford Companion to African American Literature*, ed. William L. Andrews, Frances Smith Foster, and Trudier Harris (New York: Oxford University Press, 1997), 778–779; John A. Williams: *The Angry Ones* (1960; repr. New York: Norton, 1996); *Flashbacks: A Twenty-Year Diary of Article Writing* (New York: Anchor, 1973); *Jacob's Ladder* (New York: Thunder's Mouth Press, 1987); *The Junior Bachelor Society* (Garden City, NY: Doubleday, 1976); *The Man Who Cried I Am* (Boston: Little, Brown, 1967); *Night Song* (1961; repr. New York: Chatham Bookseller, 1975); *Sissie* (1963; repr. New York: Thunder's Mouth Press, 1988); *Sons of Darkness, Sons of Light: A Novel of Some Probability* (1969; repr. Boston: Northeastern University Press, 1999).

Hans Ostrom

Williams, Patricia J. (born 1951). Legal scholar, cultural critic, columnist, and memoirist. Though broadly aligned with **Derrick Bell** in initiating critical **race** theory, Patricia J. Williams has produced a singular body of work that confounds technical and stylistic distinctions among legal scholarship, memoir, anecdote, and even speculative fiction. Her books and the regular column she writes for *The Nation*, "Diary of a Mad Law Professor," employ the details and wonderings of everyday life to give body to frequently abstracted notions of property and personhood, politics and rights.

Williams was born in **Boston, Massachusetts**, in 1951. She received her B.A. from Wellesley College in 1972, one of the first Black women to graduate from that school, and went on to earn her J.D. from Harvard University in 1975. Williams began her career as a lawyer working for the Los Angeles City Attorney's Office and the Western Center on Law and Poverty. She returned to the academy in 1980, and after stints at the City University of New York and the University of Wisconsin, in 1991 she became a faculty member at the Columbia Law School, where she is currently James L. Dohr Professor of Law.

In 2000 Williams won the prestigious MacArthur Fellowship, known informally as the "genius grant," in recognition of her contributions to legal scholarship and inquiry.

The Alchemy of Race and Rights (1991) is Williams's first book; in it she sheds the objective formality of the law profession's mode of discourse to offer metaphors, parables, and thought pieces on the textual valences of legal and political subject positioning. Williams endures a "blizzard of rage" upon being denied entry into a New York City Benetton store, thanks to a staff member's suspicious, judgmental gaze. She describes being jostled by teenage basketball players on the campus of Dartmouth College as a peculiar confrontation with polar bears: "White wilderness of icy meateaters heavy with remembrance; leaden with undoing; shaggy with the effort of hunting for silence; frozen in a web of intention and intuition" (236). Though these wonderfully illustrative moves are informed by Williams's engagement with literary aesthetics, they are also products of her reimagining the law through the racialized and gendered logics of everyday practice. She notes, "The question . . . remains whether the law can truly exist apart from the color-conscious society in which it exists, as a skeleton devoid of flesh; or whether law is the embodiment of society, the reflection of a particular citizenry's arranged complexity of relations" (120). For Williams, literary textuality reveals how the law emboldens everyday discriminatory acts by legitimating the color- and **gender**-coded lenses through which we see each other.

Williams delves into more personal territory in *The Rooster's Egg* (1995) and *Open House* (2004). Here she attends to her upbringing and extended family, particularly her adopted son, as well as the domestic and public spaces through which she and her relatives have resisted the sort of everyday racism that the law engenders. These books continue to address the "large" political issues—Clarence Thomas's confirmation as a U.S. Supreme Court justice and Dan Quayle's reactionary defense of "family values," to name two—but in a more intimate, less allegorical, fashion than *Alchemy*. In this regard, Williams's recent writings have taken to heart the powerful story she recounts toward the end of her first book: that of coming to possess the contract for sale of her great-great-grandmother Sophie, an adolescent slave made pregnant by her owner, Austin Miller, a renowned lawyer.

Resources: Primary Sources: Patricia J. Williams: *The Alchemy of Race and Rights: Diary of a Law Professor* (Cambridge, MA: Harvard University Press, 1991); *Open House of Family, Friends, Food, Piano Lessons, and the Search for a Room of My Own* (New York: Farrar, Straus and Giroux, 2004); *The Rooster's Egg: On the Persistence of Prejudice* (Cambridge, MA: Harvard University Press, 1995); *Seeing a Color-Blind Future: The Paradox of Race* (New York: Noonday, 1998). **Secondary Sources:** Janis Greve, "Legal Bodies, Racial Bodies: Autobiography and Autonomy in Patricia Williams's *Alchemy of Race and Rights*," in *Bodies of Resistance: New Phenomenologies of Politics, Agency, and Culture,* ed. Laura Doyle (Evanston, IL: Northwestern University Press, 2001), 195–216; Barbara Johnson, "The Alchemy of Style and Law," in *The Rhetoric of Law,* ed. Austin Sarat and Thomas R. Kearns (Ann Arbor: University of Michigan Press, 1994),

261–274; Charles H. Rowell, "An Interview with Patricia J. Williams," *Callaloo* 19, no. 4 (1996), 823–834; Richard Schur, "Critical Race Theory and the Limits of Auto/ Biography: Reading Patricia Williams's *The Alchemy of Race and Rights* Through/Against Postcolonial Theory," *Biography* 25, no. 3 (2002), 455–476.

Kinohi Nishikawa

Williams, Samm-Art (born 1946). Playwright. Williams is best known for having written *Home*, a play first produced by the Negro Ensemble Company in 1979. He was born in 1946 in **Philadelphia, Pennsylvania**, but he has always considered Burgaw, North Carolina, his hometown. He has commented that he would never have left the small town in the southeastern part of the state if not for the necessity of employment. He went to Morgan State College in **Baltimore, Maryland**, where he earned a B.A. in political science in 1968, then studied extensively at the Freedom Theater's Acting Workshop in Philadelphia. In 1973, Williams became a member of the Negro Ensemble Company's Acting Repertory.

Home was directed by **Douglas Turner Ward** and received a Tony nomination for Best Broadway Play, the Outer Critics Circle Award, a Drama Desk nomination, the NAACP Image Award and the North Carolina Governor's Award. *Home* has toured Australia, the Philippines, England, Japan, and Ireland.

Home is a very personal play which had its origin in Williams's longing for Burgaw in the 1970s. He was living in New York at the time, acting with the Negro Ensemble Company and feeling a little homesick. Traveling home for Christmas on a Greyhound bus, he began to write a poem that later grew into the play, which he dedicated to his mother and the people of Burgaw. After a stint in Hollywood as a successful, award-winning television writer, Williams returned home to Burgaw, where he lives today.

Williams's other plays include *Woman from the Town, Cork, A Love Play, Welcome to Black River, Eyes of the American, Brass Birds Don't Sing, Friends, In My Father's House, Eve of the Trial, Conversations on a Dirt Road*, and *The Dance on Widow's Row*. Both *Home* and *Eyes of the American* have been published. Williams has received a Guggenheim Fellowship, the National Endowment for the Arts Fellowship for playwriting in 1981, and the Roanoke Island Historical Association's Morrison Award. For television, Williams has written *Northup's Odyssey, John Henry, Badges*, and episodes of *Cagney and Lacey, The New Mike Hammer*, and *Miami Vice*. He was twice nominated for the Emmy. He also has been an executive producer for *Martin, The Fresh Prince of Bel-Air*, and *Good News*.

Williams has performed at the New Federal Theater, the Arena Stage, the Pittsburgh Public Theater, and the Kennedy Center. His film acting credits include *Blood Simple, Huckleberry Finn*, and *A Rage in Harlem*. On television he has appeared in *Women of Brewster Place, Fresh Prince of Bel-Air, 227, Race to the Pole, Search for Tomorrow, The New Mike Hammer, Miami Vice, Denmark Vesey*, and *Equal Justice*.

Resources: Samm-Art Williams: *Eyes of the American* (New York: Samuel French, 1986); *Home* (New York: Dramatists' Play Service, 1980).

Laura Grace Pattillo

Williams, Sherley Anne (1944–1999). Novelist, poet, children's book author, professor, critic, and playwright. Sherley Anne Williams remains one of the most acclaimed African American women writers of the twentieth century. Her death from cancer in 1999 meant the early loss of a gifted, compelling writer of **historical fiction**, poetry, criticism, **drama**, and **children's literature**. Known as both a generator and a preserver of African American history and culture, she produced texts that feature African American **folklore**, the **blues**, and other elements of folk culture, as well as careful interrogations of history and memory. Williams was committed to recording and preserving African American history and its legacies, and this resonates throughout her diverse body of critical and creative work.

Williams was born in Bakersfield, California, on August 25, 1944, to Lena-Leila Siler and Jesse Winson Williams, and she lived and worked in California for much of her life. She earned a Bachelor of Arts in English in 1966 from California State University at Fresno and a master's degree in English from Brown University in 1971. Her productive literary career began with the publication of her short story "Tell Martha Not to Moan" in 1967, at a time when scant attention was paid to the literary achievements of African American women. Five years later her critical literary study, *Give Birth to Brightness: A Thematic Study in Neo-Black Literature* (1972), was published, a text that explores the figure of the hero and the role of heroism in modern African American literature and culture.

Williams's creative and intellectual contributions increasingly earned acclaim in the late 1970s and early 1980s. She began teaching at the University of California at San Diego in 1973, and became the first African American literature professor at the university. In 1975 she published her first volume of poetry, *The Peacock Poems*, which was nominated for both a National Book Award and a Pulitzer Prize. Williams received an Emmy for a television performance of her second volume of poetry, *Some One Sweet Angel Chile* (1982), and the book was nominated for a National Book Award. In her poetry, Williams continually reinforces the importance of sisterhood, self-affirmation, and reclaiming historical figures in the building of a more equitable and just world. Many of her poems are infused with elements of folk life, the blues, **spirituals**, and African American folk traditions, with individuals such as Bessie Head appearing prominently in several poems.

The 1990s brought success for Williams as a playwright and children's author. Her full-length drama *Letters from a New England Nun* was featured at the National Black Theatre Festival in 1991 and the International Theatre Festival at **Chicago, Illinois**, in 1992. Her first children's book, *Working Cotton*, also appeared in 1992, and received both an American Library Association Caldecott Award and a Coretta Scott King Book Award. Considered a highly autobiographical work, it focuses on the life of a young girl, Shelan, who rises early and works late picking cotton alongside her family and the other children who work in the fields. Williams, who helped her parents pick fruit and cotton as a child, writes in the Author's Note to the book: "Our shame as a nation is not that so many children work the fields but that so few of them have other options, that the life chances of too many are defined by the cycle of the seasons" (*see* **Nature**). Williams continues: "In environments characterized by minimums—minimum wages, minimum shelters, minimum food and education—individual character, the love of a family, can only do so much; the rest is up to the country." Williams's second children's book, *Girls Together*, was published shortly before her death in 1999.

Williams may be best known for her celebrated novel *Dessa Rose* (1986), a carefully crafted text that centers on the convergence of two women's stories: Dessa Rose (Odessa), a pregnant slave woman who is condemned to die for her participation in a slave rebellion, and Miss Rufel, a White woman who provides refuge for several runaway slaves on her plantation. Alternately labeled a neo-**slave narrative** and a work of **historical fiction**, it traces the intersection of these two women's lives, their evolving relationship, and the obstacles each must confront to become truly free. *Dessa Rose* has many important themes, including the malleability of history, the preservation of intimate relationships during **slavery**, the role of resistance in establishing female agency, and the importance of names and rightful **naming**.

Williams's desire to reclaim and reestablish African American culture and history is especially evident in *Dessa Rose*, which expresses and validates a slave woman's voice, love, history, and vision. The novel can also be read as a response to William Styron's controversial portrayal of a slave uprising in the novel *The Confessions of Nat Turner* (1967). Williams writes in the Author's Note that she "loved history as a child, until some clear-eyed young **Negro** pointed, out, quite rightly, that there was no place in the American past I could go and be free" (ix–x). Williams is able to help reconstruct that history and infuse it with greater depth in *Dessa Rose*, in part because the text asks its readers to question how the nature of truth is constructed and how many of the participants of history have been misnamed and misconstrued along the lines of **gender**, **race**, and class. Like her other writing, the novel attests to Williams's investment in and commitment to (re)writing historical fallacies and claiming African American historical legacies that can be passed down to later generations.

At the time of her death at age fifty-four, Williams was working on another novel and a sequel to *Dessa Rose*. In addition to teaching for over twenty-five years at the University of California at San Diego, she was a visiting professor at a number of universities, including Cornell and the University of Southern California, and was a Senior Fulbright Lecturer at the University of Ghana. In 1987 she was named Distinguished Professor of the Year by the University of California San Diego Alumni Association.

Resources: Sherley Anne Williams: *Dessa Rose* (New York: Morrow, 1986); *Girls Together* (San Diego: Harcourt, Brace, 1999); *Give Birth to Brightness: A Thematic*

Study in Neo-Black Literature (New York: Dial, 1972); "The Lion's History: The Ghetto Writes Back," Soundings 76, no. 2 (1993), 245–259; The Peacock Poems (Middletown, CT: Wesleyan University Press, 1975); "Some Implications of Womanist Theory" (1986), in African American Literary Theory: A Reader, ed. Winston Napier (New York: New York University Press, 2000), 218–223; Some One Sweet Angel Chile (New York: Morrow, 1982).

Amanda Davis

Williams-Garcia, Rita (born 1957). Author of children's and young adult literature. Born in the borough of Queens in New York City, Williams-Garcia and her family settled in Jamaica, New York, when she was twelve. Encouraged by family members and teachers, she began writing at an early age. By fourteen, she was an author—her first short story was published in *Highlights* magazine. While in college, Williams-Garcia wrote an initial draft of her first novel, *Blue Tights* (1988), which is loosely based on her own experiences as a dancer. (She studied dance under Alvin Ailey and Phil Black.) Originally titled *Blue Tights, Big Butt*, it took nearly ten years to get published.

The majority of Williams-Garcia's works are set in the inner city and feature teenage protagonists who deal with realistic and sensitive issues related to identity formation. Other topics of interest to adolescents, such as sexuality, teen pregnancy, dating, family relationships, and African American history and culture, are also explored in her work. Her novels include such memorable characters as class valedictorian Denzel Watson, the protagonist of her second novel, *Fast Talk on a Slow Track* (1991), which earned Williams-Garcia the PEN Literary Citation and a Parents' Choice Award, and Gayle, who was first introduced in *Blue Tights*, the protagonist of *Like Sisters on the Homefront* (1995). When Gayle becomes pregnant with her second child, her mother forces her to do two things that change the direction of her life: Gayle has an abortion and she goes "down South" to live with relatives. In Georgia, she learns the rich history of her family and the importance of taking responsibility for oneself. *Like Sisters on the Homefront* was named a Coretta Scott King Honor Book and was chosen as an ALA Best Book for Young Adults and a Best Book of the Year by *ALA Booklist, School Library Journal, Bulletin of the Center for Children's Books, Horn Book*, and *Publishers Weekly*. Her other novels include *Every Time a Rainbow Dies* (2001) and, most recently, *No Laughter Here* (2004). *No Laughter Here* is one of only a few novels for young people that explore the issue of female genital mutilation. The protagonist, Akilah, learns that her best friend Victoria was circumcised while on summer vacation in Nigeria.

Besides young adult novels, Williams-Garcia has written a picture book, *Catching the Wild Waiyuuzee* (2000), and contributed short stories to a number of noteworthy young adult collections, such as *No Easy Answers: Short Stories About Teenagers Making Tough Choices* (1997), edited by Donald R. Gallo; *Stay True: Short Stories for Strong Girls* (1998), edited by Marilyn Singer; and *Necessary Noise: Stories About Our Families as They Really Are* (2003), edited by Michael Cart. Sims Bishop summed up Williams-Garcia's talent as a writer precisely when she wrote that Williams-Garcia is one of the few contemporary writers who "may well turn out to be among the most prominent Africa-American literary artists of the next generation" (616).

Resources: Rudine Sims Bishop, "Books from Parallel Cultures: New African American Voices," *Horn Book* 68, no. 5 (Sept.–Oct. 1992), 616–620; Hazel Rochman, "The Booklist Interview: Rita Williams-Garcia," *Booklist*, Feb. 15, 1996, 1002–1003; Rita Williams-Garcia: *Blue Tights* (New York: Lodestar, 1988); *Every Time a Rainbow Dies* (New York: HarperCollins, 2001); *Fast Talk on a Slow Track* (New York: Dutton, 1991); *Like Sisters on the Homefront* (New York: Lodestar, 1995); *No Laughter Here* (New York: HarperCollins, 2004).

KaaVonia Hinton-Johnson

Wilson, August (born 1945). Playwright and cultural critic. August Wilson is at this writing the most popular American playwright currently producing new works, and the only African American playwright to win the Pulitzer Prize for **drama** twice in his career. He is absorbed in a project to chronicle the African American experience in the twentieth century, through an ongoing series of plays capturing specific moments in each decade. His most important plays include *Ma Rainey's Black Bottom* (1985), *Fences* (1986), *Joe Turner's Come and Gone* (1988), *The Piano Lesson* (1990), *Two Trains Running* (1992), *Seven Guitars* (1996), *Jitney* (1996), and *King Hedley II* (2000).

Wilson was born Frederick August Kittel on April 27, 1945. His youth was spent on "The Hill," a racially mixed, low-income neighborhood in **Pittsburgh, Pennsylvania**, a location that would become the setting for nearly all of his major dramas. His father was a White German baker named Frederick Kittel; his mother was Daisy Wilson, a Black domestic worker. The elder Kittel, an absent father to August, died in 1965. His relationship with his stepfather, David Bedford, was a difficult one as well. Growing up without a positive male role model, Frederick eventually abandoned his biological father's name, adopting August Wilson to represent his far deeper connection to his mother (Bogumil, 1). The paternal influences in his life would later be mirrored in such roles as Troy Maxson in *Fences*.

While in high school, Wilson wrote a paper on Napoleon Bonaparte and was falsely accused of plagiarism. Considering this the final humiliation at the hands of an educational system with which he was already discouraged, Wilson dropped out of school and began a regimen of independent study, devouring works by **Langston Hughes, James Baldwin, Ralph Ellison**, and **Richard Wright**. The year of his father's death, he moved into a boardinghouse in his hometown to pursue writing. He listened carefully to the oral histories that the people in his neighborhood had to share, and took note of their everyday activities. He built a large collection of music, and felt transformed the first time he heard a **Bessie Smith** recording. The **blues** would become a central feature of his dramatic works.

Wilson became interested in theater before he ever saw or wrote a play, founding, with his writer/teacher friend **Robert Lee Penny**, the Black

Horizons Theater (1968). He directed a play by Penny, and began to explore poetry and drama more vigorously, including works by Dylan Thomas, John Berryman, and **Amiri Baraka**. His marriage to a Muslim woman named Brenda Burton began and ended around this time (1969–1973), though not before the birth of his first daughter, Sakina Ansari. His first drama, *Recycle*, was a semiautobiographical piece about his first marriage. In 1976, he was inspired to write his first major work while listening to a "Ma" Rainey album.

Ma Rainey's Black Bottom simultaneously criticizes White commercialization of Black culture and the way violent behavior compromises Black unity. In **Chicago, Illinois**, in 1927, Ma Rainey's band is preparing to record the song "Black Bottom" but Ma takes some time to arrive, and once she does, she makes a number of difficult demands of the White producer, Sturdyvant. During the various delays, the band members share stories from family histories, such as the trumpeter Levee's tale of his father, who was lynched for killing a number of White men who had raped his wife. As the play progresses, discussions lead to arguments. Levee draws a knife when an argument about whether God hates Black people erupts into violence. Ma fires Levee; Sturdyvant tries to swindle him while ridiculing his talent. A furious Levee reacts to having his shoe stepped on by murdering a fellow band member.

Ma Rainey demonstrates what many critics recognized early about Wilson's work. While the author's talents were nursed on the radical, sometimes "agit-prop" dramas of the **Black Arts Movement**, his craft became one that is conscious of the burdens of **slavery** and segregation, without the alienating excesses of overt denunciation of Whites (Shafer, 9). In a 1990 article in *Applause* magazine, Wilson articulated values of responsibility and a new concern for culture that he felt were becoming paramount during his entry into adulthood. It is almost certainly his deep historical and cultural awareness, married to profoundly moral themes that challenge both Whites and Blacks to take responsibility for the effects of their actions on society, that have garnered Wilson his mainstream critical and financial success. *Ma Rainey* was originally produced by the O'Neill Workshop in Waterford, Connecticut (1982). The first collaboration of Wilson and his director, Lloyd Richards, the production established a system of workshops, readings, and revisions that would be an integral part of Wilson's future successes. Richards, already a major African American stage director (he directed the original production of **Lorraine Hansberry**'s *A Raisin in the Sun*), went on to collaborate on all of Wilson's major plays.

Fences, Wilson's first Pulitzer winner, depicts the family conflicts in the household of Troy Maxson, a Pittsburgh garbage collector. A flawed hero, Troy articulates the systematic forms of racial oppression in the 1950s, especially targeting professional baseball—he was once a hopeful in the Jackie Robinson tradition—and achieves equal opportunity in his workplace. He lectures his son about the importance of responsibility over feelings, yet fathers a child with a woman who is not his wife. Rose, his wife, is a strong and well-drawn foil to Troy, challenging his self-serving platitudes and asserting her dignity against her husband's humiliations. *Fences* was a marked success, earning Wilson a Drama Critics Circle Award and a Tony Award for Best New Play. It was nearly made into a feature film, but Wilson ultimately rejected the offer from Paramount Studios because the producers were unwilling to meet his demand for a Black director. It is currently one of the most commonly anthologized plays by an African American author.

By the time *Joe Turner's Come and Gone* premiered on Broadway, Wilson's income had exceeded $1 million per year, and he was already being hailed as the foremost Black playwright in the United States. This play showcases the personal histories and personalities of a group of people at a 1911 Pittsburgh boardinghouse. The main character, Herald Loomis, is deeply wounded by years of forced labor on a chain gang and the unlawful conviction that put him there. In a series of spiritual revelations, involving a mysterious "shiny man" and the boardinghouse's resident shaman, he discovers the inner strength to persevere against the injustices of the world.

The Piano Lesson earned Wilson his second Pulitzer, his second Tony Award, and his fourth Drama Critics Circle Award. The action centers on a piano that has been in the Charles family since being stolen from its White owners. During **slavery**, a grandfather decorated it with images memorializing the abuses of enslavement and the family's history. In the present (1936), Berniece Charles, the current owner of the piano, and her brother, Boy Willie, disagree about its future. Boy Willie has been offered a good price for it by a White man, but Berniece cannot give up what her ancestor died for (he had been burned to death in retribution for the theft). Boy Willie tries to sell it without her permission, but in the end the piano remains the family's treasured possession. The presence of a threatening apparition called Sutter (the name of the slave-owning family of the Charles' past) adds a supernatural undercurrent to an other-

August Wilson, the Pulitzer Prize–winning author of *Fences*, 2003. AP/Wide World Photos.

wise realistic drama. The play began a controversy over Wilson's craft; reviews in such periodicals as the *New Republic*, *The New Yorker*, and *USA Today* claimed that the play was too long, questioned its deviations from realism, and derided its prose (Shafer, 36–37). Nonetheless, the majority of critical response was positive, and *The Piano Lesson* has enjoyed a healthy production history, becoming the only Wilson play to be adapted into a feature film (1995).

Wilson's last four plays deal with the shared psychic trauma of racism and the spiritual/familial strategies African Americans use to empower themselves while retaining a commitment to preserving history and a complex critique of American Black and White society. *Two Trains Running* uses the imminent closing of the restaurant of Memphis Lee (part of Pittsburgh city renovation), in the 1960s, to explore the consequences of Black migration to the North. *Seven Guitars*, set in the 1940s, depicts an older man named Hedley, who believes owning a plantation will serve as recompense for his father's suffering at the hands of White people. *Jitney*, a revamp of Wilson's 1980 drama, deals with an unsuccessful father/son reconciliation involving a taxi service owner, Becker, who dies before he can articulate his feelings for his ex-convict son, Booster. Despite heavy bitterness and near pathos, the play is rich in atmosphere; Wilson dexterously portrays the racial divisions and economics of urban renewal in his hometown (Sternlicht, 209). His most recent play, *King Hedley II*, struggles with the need for forgiveness. Hedley, a recently released murderer (he killed a man who assaulted him), tries to leave behind his criminal life by starting a business. Hedley is destitute and his wife is pregnant, but his planting of a garden symbolizes undying possibility (Sternlicht, 212). In both *Two Trains* and *Seven Guitars*, characters either manage to retain or rediscover hope, to achieve security in the face of adversity, or to believe in the future against the losses of the past.

Several motifs are visible throughout Wilson's many dramas. Music is central to his craft, serving as a ritual for unity and empowerment. In *Piano Lesson*, the male characters share their memories of forced labor by singing a work song. In both *Fences* and *Seven Guitars*, the main female characters use songs to heal their souls at the funerals of loved ones. Wilson's drama continues to be conscious of the problems of violence in Black communities; many of his characters resort to weapons to solve their crises. Yet, while Hedley kills, Berniece shuns violence. The aggregate of Wilson's dramas offers alternatives to violence. His plays also share a rich picture of the intercultural background of African American religion, exposing its roots in Yoruba, Caribbean, and Christian traditions.

Wilson has had many successes, from Pulitzer Prizes to Tony Awards, from a Guggenheim Fellowship (1986) to membership in the American Academy of Arts and Letters (1995). Nevertheless, he has considerable misgivings about the sincerity of those successes, suspecting his career is a mere token when set against the generally limited support for Black artists. At his keynote address to the Theatre Communications Group National Conference (1996), Wilson criticized funding of White theaters for Black plays, arguing that those monies should go to legitimate Black theaters. He also challenged the American stage's dependence on colorblind casting to give roles to Black actors, saying it distracted the theater from encouraging more new Black playwrights. He attacked Robert Brustein for charging him with "separatism" and for his "sophomoric assumptions" about theater outside à White tradition (Bogumil, 7). The speech, and Brustein's response, led to a heated debate that culminated in a public forum moderated by **Anna Deveare Smith** (1997). Despite the unusual opportunity for a playwright and critic to discuss the purpose and future of drama, the event turned into a public heckling and a hostile stand-off (Shafer, 14). Wilson continues to advocate and focus public efforts on increasing opportunities for African American playwrights, while standing as one of the world's most important active dramatists. (*See* **Drama**; **Vernacular.**)

Resources: Primary Sources: August Wilson: "August Wilson Responds," *American Theatre*, Oct. 1996, pp. 101–107; *Fences* (New York: New American Library, 1986); *The Ground on Which I Stand* (New York: Theatre Communications Group, 2001); "In His Own Words," *Applause*, Jan. 1990, p. 5; "The Janitor," in *Short Pieces from the New Dramatists*, ed. Stan Chervin (New York: Broadway Play Publishing, 1985); *Jitney* (New York: Samuel French, 2002); *Joe Turner's Come and Gone* (New York: New American Library, 1988); *King Hedley II* (New York: Theatre Communications Group, 2005); "The Legacy of Malcom X," *Life*, Dec. 1992, 84; *Ma Rainey's Black Bottom* (New York: New American Library, 1985); *The Piano Lesson* (New York: Plume, 1990); *The Piano Lesson*, dir. Lloyd Richards (Artisan Pictures, 1995); *Seven Guitars* (New York: Dutton, 1996); *Two Trains Running* (New York: Dutton, 1992). Secondary Sources: Harold Bloom, ed., *August Wilson* (Broomall, PA: Chelsea House, 2002); Mary L. Bogumil, *Understanding August Wilson* (Columbia: University of South Carolina Press, 1999); Margaret Booker, *Lillian Hellman and August Wilson: Dramatizing a New American Identity* (New York: Peter Lang, 2003); Keith Clark, *Black Manhood in James Baldwin, Ernest J. Gaines, and August Wilson* (Urbana: University of Illinois Press, 2002); Harry Justin Elam, *The Past as Present in the Drama of August Wilson* (Ann Arbor: University of Michigan Press, 2004); Marilyn Elkins, ed., *August Wilson: A Casebook* (New York: Garland, 1994); Joan Herrington, *I Ain't Sorry for Nothin' I Done: August Wilson's Process of Playwriting* (New York: Limelight Editions, 1998); Alan Nadel, ed., *May All Your Fences Have Gates: Essays on the Drama of August Wilson* (Iowa City: University of Iowa Press, 1994); Kim Pereira, *August Wilson and the African American Odyssey* (Urbana: University of Illinois Press, 1995); Yvonne Shafer, *August Wilson: A Research and Production Sourcebook* (Westport, CT: Greenwood Press, 1998); Sandra G. Shannon: *August Wilson's Fences: A Reference Guide* (Westport, CT: Greenwood Press, 2003); *The Dramatic Vision of August Wilson* (Washington, DC: Howard University Press, 1995); Sanford V. Sternlicht, *A Reader's Guide to Modern American Drama* (Syracuse, NY: Syracuse University Press, 2002); Qun Wang, *An In-depth Study of the Major Plays of African American Playwright August Wilson: Vernacularizing the Blues on Stage* (Lewiston, NY: Edwin Mellen, 1999); Peter Wolfe, *August Wilson* (New York: Twaye, 1999).

Ben Fisler

Wilson, Edward Everett (1867–1952). Lawyer and essayist. Wilson graduated from Williams College and Howard University's law school, and served for forty-six years (1902–1949) as an Assistant State's Attorney in Cook County, Illinois. A resident of the **Chicago, Illinois**, area for most of his adult life, Wilson died in **Paris, France**, in 1952 (Titcomb).

Wilson's first **essay** to appear in print, "The Joys of Being a Negro," was published in the January 1906 issue of the *Atlantic Monthly*. A furious indictment of the social institutions that perpetuated American racism, "The Joys of Being a Negro" represents a striking departure from the calm and muted critiques that characterized most magazine writings on **race** in the early twentieth century that were published in magazines with primarily White readers. Wilson reads myriad aspects of American culture as examples of structural racism, taking on in turn Pullman cars, magazine publishers, newspaper editors, "sympathetic" Whites, voting rights, and accomodationist African Americans. He also highlights how representations of African Americans in print culture have solidified America as a White man's country. He scornfully proclaims, "Without the Negro as a foil, Americans would be nothing but plain white men." While the overall tone of the essay is one of equal parts anger and despair, Wilson finds hope in a highly qualified sense of African American community. The concluding paragraphs imagine Blacks exploiting senseless racial categories such as "white **Negro**" to insinuate themselves into cultural and social spaces reserved for Whites, an insertion that would ultimately lead to the demise of Jim Crow.

Wilson's first essay for an African American periodical, *The Voice of the Negro*, appeared later in 1906. "The Negro in the President's Message" analyzes national race politics in a manner reminiscent of his argument in "The Joys of Being a Negro." Arguing that the Presidential Address represents the ugliest racist sentiments of the nation in an attempt to appeal to Southern voters, Wilson links the President's speech to the views of the popular Southern writer Thomas Nelson Page, drawing a distinct connection between literary and political representation. Wilson continued to develop a nuanced sense of African American life while condemning racist oppression in his remaining essays for Black periodicals. "Negro Society in Chicago" (*Voice of the Negro*, 1907) examines the lives of middle-class Chicagoans; another essay for the *Voice*, "The Chicago Negro in Politics" (1907), chronicles all of the Black politicians at work in Chicago. His final essay for Black periodicals appeared in **Opportunity**; in "The Responsibility for Crime," Wilson returns to his analysis of Chicago to criticize characterizations of the Black community as inherently criminal. He carefully distinguishes various types of Black criminals with an eye to delineating a clear boundary between the African American criminal and the African American community, emphasizing that Black criminals deviate from the norms of Black Chicagoans.

Wilson's oeuvre as a writer, while small, is striking for its outspoken criticism of White America in the era of Jim Crow. "The Joys of Being a Negro" is particularly significant because its blistering critique of White privilege and Black oppression expands our sense of what Black writers could say to White audiences in this most oppressive time in American history.

Resources: Charles Brahham, "Black Chicago: Accomodationist Politics Before the Great Migration," in *Ethnic Chicago*, ed. Melvin G. Holli and Peter d'A. Jones, rev. and enl. ed. (Grand Rapids, MI: Eerdmans, 1984); Allan H. Spear, *Black Chicago:*

The Making of a Negro Ghetto (Chicago: University of Chicago Press, 1967), 61–62, 85, 192–193; Caldwell Titcomb, "The Earliest Black Members of Phi Beta Kappa," *Journal of Blacks in Higher Education* 33 (Oct. 31, 2001), 92; Edward Everett Wilson: "The Chicago Negro in Politics," *Voice of the Negro*, Mar. 1907, 99–103; "The Joys of Being a Negro," *Atlantic Monthly*, Jan. 1906, 245–250; "The Negro in the President's Address," *Voice of the Negro*, Dec. 1906, 575–579; "Negro Society in Chicago," *Voice of the Negro*, Dec. 1907, 306–309; "The Responsibility for Crime," *Opportunity*, Mar. 1929, 95–97.

Heather Tirado Gilligan

Wilson, Ernest James, Jr. (1920–1990). Poet, academician, and orator. A longtime resident of **Washington, D.C.**, Wilson was a proponent of the "everyman" style of poetry exemplified by the work of **Langston Hughes**. He was born March 15, 1920, in Greenwich, Connecticut, the eldest of four children. His brother Calvin became a judge, and young "Billy," an internationally recognized choreographer.

Wilson graduated as salutatorian from Central High School in **Philadelphia, Pennsylvania**, in 1937 with an Elks scholarship for oratory. He received a B.S. in zoology in 1942 from Howard University and in 1943 was drafted into the armed forces, which halted his work toward a master's degree in psychology. Discharged in 1946 after two years in the Pacific as an Army medical corpsman, "Corporal Chico" received the Battle Star.

In 1947, Wilson married Mignon Gregory of Atlantic City, New Jersey. Her father, Thomas Montgomery Gregory, was a former professor of dramatic art and public speaking at Howard University, and editor—with **Alain Locke**—of *Plays of Negro Life* (1927), the first anthology of African American theater. Wilson's focus now shifted to counseling, and he received his M.A. in psychology and guidance from American University in 1952.

From 1946 to 1955, Wilson was assistant dean of Cook Hall, where he penned his "Creed" for the men in his charge. In 1950, Wilson's poetry was published in the winter issue of the magazine *Voices*, titled "Negro Poets" an issue edited by **Langston Hughes**. Wilson's poems were included in *The Poetry of the Negro, 1746–1949* (1949), an anthology edited by Hughes and **Arna Bontemps**.

In 1955, Wilson became Assistant Director of Admissions at Howard, traveling the Southeast to recruit high school students for his alma mater. He later became the foreign student adviser, then Howard's first Director of International Student Services. In the mid-1960s Wilson shared with school administrators in Africa and Asia how to prepare their students for university life in the United States. He retired in 1976.

Wilson maintained a close relationship with **Sterling A. Brown**, Chuck Stone, and others in the Washington arts scene. In the 1980s, he was appointed poet-in-residence at the National Park Service's Art Barn, and conducted writing workshops in the Washington area. In collaboration with his longtime friend Walter Ray, he privately published two books of poems, *We*

Two Is Working Men! and *The Pilgrimage of Two Friends.* In 1989, Wilson served as editor for Howard University's resurrected *Stylus* literary magazine, founded in 1916 by **Alain Locke** and Wilson's late wife, Mignon Gregory. Composing poems to the very end, Wilson passed away on Halloween, 1990.

Resources: Langston Hughes and Arna Bontemps, eds., *The Poetry of the Negro, 1746–1949* (Garden City, NY: Doubleday, 1949); Ernest J. Wilson Papers, Moorland-Spingarn Research Center, Howard University; Ernest J. Wilson Papers, S. Greg Wilson Private Collection.

Sule Gregory C. Wilson

Wilson, Francis H. [Frank] (1886–1956). Playwright, singer, and actor. A well-known actor and playwright, Wilson cultivated a career in theater that spanned more than four decades. His play *Meek Mose* (1928) was the third play by an African American playwright to be produced on Broadway, and helped establish him as a serious actor and writer in the American theater.

Wilson was born in New York City; little is known of his childhood. At the age of twenty-two he founded the vaudeville group Carolina Comedy Four. After a few years, Wilson became a mail carrier for the U.S. Post Office (1911–1914). He filled his days writing short plays about his experiences, and soon organized another theater group, the Lincoln Players, so that he could write, direct, and act in his plays.

In 1917, Wilson joined the Lafayette Players, a group of African Americans who strove to gain acceptance as legitimate stage artists and trained many African American theater professionals. In addition to casting Wilson in a series of acting roles, the Lafayette Players produced several of his plays including *The Heartbreakers* (1921) and *Pa Williams' Gal* (1923).

Wilson continued acting and writing; in 1925, his one-act play *Sugar Cane* won the **Opportunity** Contest Award. Wilson's popular Broadway comedy *Meek Mose* (1928) followed. In 1936 Wilson revised *Meek Mose* (retitled *Brother Mose*) for production by the **Federal Theatre Project** (FTP) **Negro units** in **Boston, Massachusetts,** Newark, New Jersey, and New York City. Set on a slave plantation in 1851 and augmented by **spirituals** such as "Go Down Moses," *Brother Mose* is the story of a pious, old-fashioned man who "inherits the earth" (Wilson, 133; Fraden, 160–162).

Walk Together, Chillun (1936), one of Wilson's last and best-known works, was the debut production of the FTP Negro unit in New York. Like *Brother Mose, Walk Together, Chillun* was a popular production containing African American spirituals, comedic characters, and a social message.

Wilson continued to play a prominent role in the arts for the rest of his life, writing screenplays for the independent films *Paradise in Harlem* (1940), *Murder on Lenox Avenue* (1941), and *Sunday Sinners* (1941), and acting well into his sixties.

Resources: Rena Fraden, *Blueprints for a Black Federal Theatre, 1935–1939* (New York: Cambridge University Press, 1994); Alain Locke and Montgomery Gregory, eds., *Plays of Negro Life: A Source-Book of Native American Drama* (New York: Harper and Bros., 1927); Bernard L. Peterson, Jr., *Early Black American Playwrights and Dramatic Writers* (Westport, CT: Greenwood Press, 1990); Frank H. Wilson: *Brother Mose*, electronic ed. (Alexander Street Press, 2002), www.alexanderstreetpress.com; *Sugar Cane*, electronic ed. (Alexander Street Press, 2002), www.alexanderstreetpress.com.

Elizabeth A. Osborne

Wilson, Harriet E. (c. 1827–c. 1863). Novelist. Originally published in 1859, Harriet Wilson's *Our Nig; or, Sketches from the Life of a Free Black* (*Our Nig*) was the first **novel** published by a free African American woman. (**Hannah Crafts** is now likely the very first African American woman to write a novel.) Written as plea for financial support, *Our Nig* garnered little critical attention at the time of its publication and remained in obscurity until **Henry Louis Gates, Jr.,** rediscovered the novel in 1981 and republished it in 1983. Many of the scant facts known about Wilson's life are the result of painstaking research by Gates and more recent investigative work by Barbara White. We still know nothing about her parents, and her birth and death dates remain uncertain (Nelson, 483). Harriet Wilson was most likely born Harriet Adams in New Hampshire, in 1827 or 1828. She was a servant in the wealthy Milford, New Hampshire, household of Nehemiah and Rebecca Hayward, and she endured both physical and psychological abuse inflicted upon her by Mrs. Hayward. That abuse would later become the focus of *Our Nig*. On October 6, 1851, Wilson married Thomas Wilson, who was from Virginia. By the time her novel was published, she was living in **Boston, Massachusetts**, poverty-stricken, her husband apparently deceased, and struggling to support her ill son, George Mason Wilson. Wilson wrote her novel in an effort to raise funds for George's medical care. Her son died in 1860, shortly after its publication. At this writing, Wilson's life has not been traced beyond 1860. Ironically, one of the most pioneering African American writers is one about whom relatively little is known.

Alice Walker's response to *Our Nig*, which appeared on the front cover of the 1983 edition, best sums up the book's significance to African American literature: "I sat up most of the night reading and pondering the enormous significance of Harriet Wilson's novel *Our Nig*. It is as if we'd just discovered Phillis Wheatley—or Langston Hughes. . . . She represents a similar vastness of heretofore unexamined experience, a whole new layer of time and existence in American life and literature." Indeed, *Our Nig* launched the literary tradition in fiction by African American women writers. Its distinctiveness lies in its narrative hybridity; like Hannah Crafts's *The Bondwoman's Narrative*, *Our Nig* is at once a sentimental novel, a domestic novel, a **slave narrative**, and an **autobiography**. Wilson makes use of overtly sentimental language to elicit an emotional response from her readers to sympathize with the plight of Frado, the abandoned and then orphaned "tragic mulatta" (*see* **Mulatto**). Borrowing from what Nina Baym terms the overplot, a stock device in popular domestic novels by White women, Wilson features Frado's long and difficult journey to self-realization and independence. That journey includes regular beatings by her mistress, Mrs. Bellmont. And unlike White heroines such as Gertrude Flint in *The Lamplighter*, Frado's hard work and virtue are not rewarded with a happy marriage and stability. Instead, debilitated by ill health as a result of overwork and extreme poverty, she leaves readers responsible for her fate (and by this time we know that Frado and Wilson are doubles): "Reposing on God, she has thus far journeyed securely. Still an invalid, she asks for your sympathy, gentle reader" (Wilson, 130).

Our Nig's hybridity positions the novel "in an indeterminate space where a variety of literary forms intersect" (Nelson, 485). Its hybridity also signifies Wilson's effort "to find a new narrative form and to begin the African American women's tradition in fiction" (Nelson, 485). Indeed, Wilson appropriates these genres for both subversive and practical purposes, as indicated in the novel's long subtitle and its Preface: that racism and religious hypocrisy are just as prevalent (and violent) in the North as they are in **the South** (Nelson, 484). The full subtitle, *Sketches from the Life of a Free Black, in a Two-Story White House, North, Showing that Slavery's Shadows Fall Even There* references both the literal White House in **Washington, D.C.**, site of the federal government that endorses **slavery**, and the Bellmont family's white house that bears more than a passing resemblance to a Southern plantation mansion. Wilson explains that writing the novel is an "experiment which shall aid me in maintaining myself and child without extinguishing this feeble life." As several critics have noted, she also indicts abolitionists: "I would not from these motives even palliate slavery at the South, by disclosures of its appurtenances North. My mistress was wholly imbued with *southern* principles" (*see* **Abolitionist Movement**).

Since its second edition in 1983 (and a reissue in 2002), *Our Nig* has inspired a variety of scholarship. Eric Gardner provides a comprehensive overview of its publishing history, and Carla Peterson argues that the function of the narrative is to "expose the romanticization of this figure [the tragic mulatta] and point to its economic basis" (165). Cynthia Davis argues that "it is pain, not sexuality, which explicitly determined Frado's physical experiences, which makes her body visible" (393). And Lois Leveen focuses on the racial and spatial implication of the Bellmont house, contending that "Wilson's authorial strategy in depicting the house of oppression contests the very assumptions that serve as the foundation for the racial and spatial practices in that house" (570).

Resources: Nina Baym, *American Women Writers and the Work of History, 1790–1860* (New Brunswick, NJ: Rutgers University Press, 1995); Cynthia J. Davis, "Speaking the Body's Pain: Harriet Wilson's *Our Nig*," *African American Review* 27 (Fall 1993), 391–404; Eric Gardner, " 'This Attempt of Their Sister': Harriet Wilson's *Our Nig* from Printer to Readers," *New England Quarterly* 66, no. 2 (June 1993), 226–246; Henry Louis Gates, Jr., "Introduction," in *Our Nig; or, Sketches from the Life of a Free Black*, by Harriet Wilson (New York: Vintage, 1983), xi–lv; Lois Leveen, "Dwelling in the House of Oppression: The Spatial, Racial and Textual Dynamics of Harriet Wilson's *Our Nig*," *African American Review* 35, no. 4 (Winter 2001),

561–581; Emmanuel S. Nelson, "Harriet E. Wilson," in *African American Authors, 1745–1945: A Bio-Bibliographical Critical Sourcebook*, ed. Nelson (Westport, CT: Greenwood Press, 2000), 483–487; Carla L. Peterson, *"Doers of the Word": African-American Women Speakers and Writers in the North* (New Brunswick, NJ: Rutgers University Press, 1998); Alice Walker, Comment on back cover of *Our Nig; or, Sketches from the Life of a Free Black*, ed. Henry Louis Gates, Jr. (New York: Vintage, 1983); Barbara A. White, "Afterword: New Information on Harriet E. Wilson and the Bellmont Family," in *Our Nig; or, Sketches from the Life of a Free Black*, 2nd ed., ed. Henry Louis Gates, Jr. (New York: Vintage, 2002), iii–liv; Harriet E. Wilson, *Our Nig; or, Sketches from the Life of a Free Black*, ed. Henry Louis Gates, Jr. (New York: Vintage, 1983).

Rebecca R. Saulsbury

Winbush, Raymond (born 1948). Professor, college administrator, and nonfiction writer. Born in Cleveland, Ohio, Winbush studied psychology at Oakwood College in Huntsville, Alabama, and graduated with honors in 1970. He obtained the M.A. (1973) and the Ph.D. (1976) in psychology from the University of Chicago. From 1973 to 1980 Winbush was an instructor at Oakwood College, where he developed research interests including the infusion of African American students into school curricula, African American adolescent development, and Black male and female relationships. In 1991 he served as Assistant Provost and Director of the Johnson Black Cultural Center at Vanderbilt University. From 1995 to 2002, Winbush was Benjamin Hooks Professor of Social Justice at Fisk University. During his tenure he wrote numerous academic articles that focused largely on the "politics" of **Afrocentricity** and the resistance it encounters among scholars. This work led to the publication in 2001 of *The Warrior Method: A Program for Rearing Healthy Black Boys*. Winbush presented a guide for parents and teachers to assist African American boys in becoming capable, self-reliant men. Through modern variations of tribal customs and his own private reflections, Winbush used his book as a vehicle to enhance traditional African concepts to help boys as they make the transition into manhood by instilling the values of honor, dignity, and self-respect.

Later Winbush edited *Should America Pay? Slavery and the Raging Debate on Reparations* (2003). This comprehensive collection deals head-on with the explosive issue of **slavery** reparations. Winbush masterfully presents cogent material from a diverse array of contributors covering all aspects of the sensitive issue. His inclusion of those opposing reparations, however, does not mask the underlying rhetorical force presenting the historical foundation for reparations. Winbush's dedication to the issue of **race** led to the award of a $2.6 million grant by the Kellogg Foundation that was used to restructure the Race Relations Institute at Fisk University. His philanthropic involvement also includes sitting on the Executive Board of the National Council for Black Studies, and extensive travels to such places as Nigeria, Togo, Ghana, Senegal, Cote d'Ivoire, Jamaica, England, and France have enabled Winbush to gain insight into the influence African people have had on world culture. He currently serves as the Director of the Institute for Urban Affairs at Morgan State University.

Resources: "Raymond Winbush," *Emdarkment,* http://www.emdarkment.com/eap/legacy/9610winbush.htm; Raymond Winbush: *Should America Pay? Slavery and the Raging Debate on Reparations* (New York: Amistad, 2003); *The Warrior Method: A Program for Rearing Healthy Black Boys* (New York: Amistad, 2001); "Website," www.raymondwinbush.com/_wsn/page3.html.

Christine Marie Hilger

Winfrey, Oprah (born 1954). Talk show host, actor, and humanitarian. By promoting her own book club and inviting the authors of the books to appear on her talk show, Winfrey not only has popularized reading but also has popularized and championed the emotional struggles of women. Her appeal derives from her own life. She was born in Mississippi. Her parents were not married, and she was moved around to various relatives' homes. Winfrey was raped at an early age by two male members of her family. She cites the hardship as what pushed her toward personal success.

Winfrey began her career on the radio, then moved to **Nashville, Tennessee**'s WTVF-TV at the age of nineteen as the youngest, and only African American, anchor the station had had. At twenty-two, she became an anchor at a **Baltimore, Maryland**, TV station, and then cohosted the station's talk show, *People Are Talking.* In 1984, she moved to **Chicago, Illinois**, and hosted *AM Chicago.* The show eventually was renamed the *Oprah Winfrey Show,* and soon became nationally syndicated. Her first national show aired in 1986 as one of many daytime talk shows. In reaction to the criticism directed at talk shows in general, in 1995 Winfrey attempted to make the show more acceptable to a middle-class audience.

One of the changes included introducing her book club in 1996, which promoted reading, particularly of books bearing Winfrey's signature book club emblem. Influenced by **Maya Angelou**'s **autobiography**, *I Know Why the Caged Bird Sings,* even referring to Angelou as her "mother in another life" (Lowe, 10), Winfrey bridged the gap between critical reading and personal therapy, which had been a popular element in her show.

In a similar melding of real life and fictional trauma, Winfrey starred in the film adaptations of **Alice Walker**'s *The Color Purple* (1985) and **Toni Morrison**'s *Beloved* (1998), as well as the television miniseries based on **Gloria Naylor**'s *The Women of Brewster Place* (1989). As Illouz comments, Winfrey's choice of novels reflects her "cultural taste": almost every novel includes a female protagonist, who is rarely beautiful or wealthy, and who has to overcome hardship in her personal and social life (104). One of the results of Winfrey's inclusion of literature in her show is that reading has once again become socially acceptable, particularly for those in women's reading groups. Winfrey's book club and public discussion of her troubles have legitimized reading from an emotional and confessional point of view rather than from an academic point of view. Secondly, by allying herself with Black feminists such as Morrison, Winfrey has encouraged and molded contemporary discourse about the struggles of Black women. Much like **Frederick Douglass**, Winfrey uses literacy as a way of dealing with struggle. For instance, Illouz explains, "Oprah's way of interweaving orality and literacy into a narrative in which both suffering and hope are inscribed is a distinct mark of black culture and is at the heart of the Book Club" (199).

Beyond her various lifetime achievement awards and her thirty-nine Daytime Emmy Awards, the publishing industry recognized Winfrey for her contribution to reading and books when she received the National Book Foundation's 50th Anniversary Gold Medal (1999) and the Association of American Publishers' AAP Honors Award (2003). Winfrey has also showed her literary influence by using her production company, Harpo Productions, to produce several adaptations of novels, such as **Zora Neale Hurston**'s *Their Eyes Were Watching God*. After a short hiatus, Winfrey's book club has recently returned. Rather than promoting contemporary authors and issues, Winfrey's picks are "classics." In this way, her powerful influence moves beyond novels that reflect her personal experience to those whose receptions have long been influenced by academia.

Resources: Eva Illouz, *Oprah Winfrey and the Glamour of Misery* (New York: Columbia University Press, 2003); Janet C. Lowe, *Oprah Winfrey Speaks: Insight from the World's Most Influential Voice* (New York: Wiley, 1998); "A Novelist, a Talk-Show Host, and Literature High and Low," *Chronicle of Higher Education*, Nov. 30, 2001, p. B4; Sarah McIntosh Wooten, *Oprah Winfrey: Talk Show Legend* (Berkeley Heights, NJ: Enslow, 1999).

J'Lyn Simonson

Wolfe, George C. (born 1954). Playwright and director. A native of Frankfort, Kentucky, Wolfe attended predominantly Black elementary and secondary schools prior to enrolling in Pomona College in Claremont, California. As a theater (directing) major, Wolfe was twice named regional winner of the American College Theatre Festival for playwrighting. He later enrolled in the dramatic writing/musical theater M.F.A. program at New York University, and following graduation (1983) he pursued a career as a librettist and playwright. The success that Wolfe experienced as a student in the 1970s continued into the 1980s. In fact, one could argue that his career and reputation were launched in the 1980s. In 1985, *Paradise*, his full-length musical, which originally was staged in Cincinnati, Ohio, opened Off-Off-Broadway. The following year, his musical *Queenie Pie*, about the fantasy world of an aging beauty queen, premiered at the Kennedy Center in **Washington, D.C.** The same year, Wolfe's *The Colored Museum*, his postmodern play depicting the experience of the Black body both onstage and offstage, was first produced by the Crossroads Theatre in New Brunswick, New Jersey.

By the early 1990s, Wolfe's career seemed to be on autopilot. His play *Jelly's Last Jam*, about the legendary jazz musician Jelly Roll Morton, opened on

Broadway in 1992, featuring the actor/dancer Gregory Hines. The following year, he was named artistic director of the prestigious New York Shakespeare Festival/Public Theatre (NYSF/PT). The same year he directed Tony Kushner's *Angels in America: The Millennium Approaches* and was awarded the Tony for direction. Three years later, he won the Tony for best direction again for his musical *Bring in da Noise/Bring in da Funk*. Since the mid-1990s, Wolfe has remained active. He directed *The Tempest*, starring Patrick Stewart, for the NYSF. The production proved so popular that following its free run in Central Park, it moved to Broadway.

Wolfe has used his influence at the Public Theatre to nurture the talents of new playwrights. One of his protégées, **Suzan Lori Parks**, whose plays have been staged at the Public since the beginning of Wolfe's directorship, was awarded the 2002 Pulitzer Prize for **drama** for her play *Topdog/Underdog*. Wolfe directed the original production of *Topdog/Underdog* and received an Obie for his efforts. While mentoring the next generation of theater practitioners, he has worked to preserve the history and heritage of African American theater. In 2002, he wrote and directed *Harlem Song*, a musical based on twentieth-century Black culture in **Harlem, New York**, and staged it in the Apollo Theatre, Harlem's most revered theater.

Wolfe has worked with the brightest stars on the theatrical stage and has won just about every award imaginable. He directed Elaine Stritch's one-woman show, *Elaine Stritch at Liberty*; **Anna Deveare Smith**'s performance piece on the **Los Angeles, California**, riots, *Twilight—Los Angeles, 1992*; both parts of Tony Kushner's Tony-winning play *Angels in America*; and the opera *Amistad* at the Lyric Opera in **Chicago, Illinois**. (*See* **Drama**; **Postmodernism**.)

Resources: KET, The Kentucky Network, *Signature: George C. Wolfe* (1997), video; Ed Morales, "Theatre and the Wolfe," *American Theatre* 11, no. 10 (Dec. 1994), 14–20; John Simon, "Wolfe at the Door," *New York Magazine*, Nov. 17, 1986, pp. 119–120; George C. Wolfe, *The Colored Museum* (New York: Grove Press, 1988).

Harvey Young

Women's Clubs. Women's clubs were the site of local and national social reform work, particularly in the areas of education and home economics. They also supported literacy initiatives and helped popularize African American writers' work. *Woman's Era*, the first national periodical published by African American women, emerged from the women's clubs movement.

Local clubs were a major site of informal education and social activism for women of many backgrounds in the mid-to-late 1800s. Although women's clubs had roots in the racially integrated antislavery societies, in the years during and after **Reconstruction**, women's clubs became firmly entrenched as entities segregated not only by **race** but also by religion and class. In addition to the General Federation of Women's Clubs (the national organization for White, middle-class Protestant women), separate national organizations existed in the late 1800s and early 1900s for a variety of other social groups, including the National Council of Jewish Women and the National League of Women Workers.

African American women attempted in the late 1880s and early 1990s to collaborate with women in the General Federation clubs; however, the 1893 World's Columbian Exposition in **Chicago, Illinois**, marked a watershed moment regarding the question of whether African American clubwomen should aim for inclusion in White clubs or for their own separate club movement. In preparation for the 1893 Exposition, women (and particularly clubwomen) were for the first time given an official planning role when the U.S. Congress created the Board of Lady Managers to coordinate with women's organizations in the creation of exhibits and programs at the Women's Building. African American clubwomen requested representation on the Board, but their request was denied and their work was not represented at the Women's Building. Responding to this and other exclusions of African Americans from the planning of the exposition, clubwoman **Ida B. Wells-Barnett** collaborated with other African American writers to issue a pamphlet titled *The Reason Why the Colored American Is Not in the World's Columbian Exposition*, which was circulated widely among fairgoers.

The Columbian Exposition debacle and other widely publicized instances of racial segregation and repression led to several attempts by African Americans in the 1890s to create national vehicles for organizing efforts to gain civil and political rights. Two local African American women's clubs were especially influential in these organizing efforts: the **Washington, D.C.**, Colored Women's League, established in June 1892, and the **Boston, Massachusetts**, Women's Era Club, established in February 1893. The Women's Era Club's newsletter, *Women's Era*, was the first national publication by African American women.

No truly national organization existed, however, until 1895, when Woman's Era President Josephine Ruffin organized a national convention of 100 delegates representing twenty clubs from ten states. The immediate impetus for this convention was a letter that Missouri Press Association President John W. Jacks had written to the British antilynching activist Florence Belgarnie, in an attempt to discourage her from her work in America. In his letter, Jacks wrote, "The Negroes of this country are wholly devoid of morality, the women are prostitutes and are natural thieves and liars" (Jones, 19).

African American clubwomen wanted to respond univocally to Jacks's letter; at the same time, though, Ruffin's invitations to the convention and many of the letters sent by clubs across the nation demonstrate the strong desire not to let that response overshadow their long-term attempts to unite under a national organization. One example of this sentiment was expressed by the clubwomen of Bethel Church, New York: "We are sorry that the 'Jacks letter' should seem to be the prick which stung to activity.... We would desire the world to know that long before the base slanders... were uttered, our women were actively at work among the masses of our people, seeking to ground them in the fundamental principles of true progress" (NACW, 19).

Building on the groundwork of the 1895 convention, a smaller group of women met in 1896 to finalize plans for a national organization which would combine efforts behind the Colored Women's League and the Women's Era Club, and formed as the National Association of Colored Women (NACW). **Mary Church Terrell** was elected as the first president, and she served in that role until she stepped down in 1901.

From its inception in 1896, the NACW has functioned on a national level, through the local work of individual African American women's clubs. By the 1904 NACW biennial meeting, the efforts of individual clubs had been organized on a national scale into twelve national departments: Social Science, Domestic Science, Mother's Clubs, Kindergarten, Business Women, Professional Women, Rescue Work, Art, Literature, Music, Temperance, and Church Clubs (Davis, 43). Although the composition of departments has changed over time, the strong departmental structure remains. The NACW's official national publication, *National Association Notes*, has disseminated advice to local clubs about effective work within each of the national departments and has given a sense of unity to the clubs spread across the country, particularly in the early days when the clubwomen could not travel freely because of Jim Crow regulations.

The NACW motto, coined by Terrell and adopted in 1900, is "Lifting as We Climb." Early leaders in the organization, including Margaret Murray Washington (wife of **Booker T. Washington**), realized that educated Black women like themselves were judged on the basis of all members of their race; consequently, they were anxious for the NACW to do work that would elevate the social standing of all African Americans. As the first NACW president, Terrell set a precedent for integrating Booker T. Washington's industrial education philosophy with **W.E.B. Du Bois**'s notion of the **"Talented Tenth."**

In keeping with this philosophy, most local clubs in the NACW organized activities around both "lifting" through social welfare programs and "climbing" through self-improvement. Member clubs of the NACW started kindergartens for poor Black children, educated young girls on personal hygiene and moral improvement, donated books by Black authors to local libraries, distributed pamphlets on woman suffrage, created day care facilities for working mothers and boardinghouses for single young women, offered employment services to women working as domestic servants, and instituted countless other new programs for African American mothers and children. Together, the facilities and programs of NACW clubs formed one of the most extensive nongovernmental aid networks in the history of the United States.

Promotion of literacy and literature was a significant part of NACW clubs' self-improvement work. Many NACW clubs worked to make literature more accessible to their members and to other African Americans in their communities. A list of "don'ts" concerning the use of books that was published in the January 1899 *National Association Notes* advised, "Don't forget that good books are the best company in the world, if read understandingly and appreciatively" (NACW Reel 23). Reading rooms were created in several clubs to facilitate reading and exchange of books, as well as to provide alternatives to Jim Crow public libraries. Club names alone give an indication of the importance of literature to the NACW: in the annual listing of NACW clubs, numerous club names include the word "literary," and **Phillis Wheatley** Club is one of the most common club names.

Literary clubs studied literary works and wrote on more general topics. Clubwoman Josephine Washington explained that clubwomen "study standard authors, read the latest books, discuss current events and compare opinions on questions of interest" (Knupfer, 114). Many club records indicate that members read widely within literature, including standard White canonical authors such as Shakespeare, Ruskin, and Emerson along with such African American writers as Wheatley, DuBois, and **Paul Laurence Dunbar**. For clubwomen, writing and discussing papers was a way to cultivate one's mind after the completion of—or sometimes in place of—formal schooling. Literary clubs and the national biennial NACW meetings featured papers by clubwomen with such varied titles as "The Value of Race Literature," "How Are Our Professional Women Moulding Public Sentiment?" and "Mothers Clubs and the Schools." Some clubs published collections of clubwomen's poetry and sponsored essay contests.

An especially noteworthy NACW accomplishment in terms of the African American literary heritage was its major 1916 fund-raising campaign to pay off the mortgage of **Frederick Douglass**'s former home in **Washington, D.C.**, preserve his personal papers, and open the home to visitors. At the urging of the NACW, the Douglass home was placed within the National Parks system in 1962 and was designated as a National Historic Site in 1988.

Early clubwoman Elizabeth Lindsay Davis writes in her 1933 NACW history, *Lifting as They Climb*, that the NACW began with a membership of 5000 and by 1904 included 15,000 women from thirty-one states (44). Dorothy Salem reports membership in 1924 at 100,000.

By the mid-1920s, though, the NACW's mode of conservative social change through the domestic sphere was being challenged. Passage of the Nineteenth Amendment in 1920, granting women the right to vote, along with other changes in women's opportunities led to a decline in membership in NACW and other women's clubs nationwide. Furthermore, the formation of the National Association for the Advancement of Colored People (**NAACP**) in 1909, the cultural and political changes associated with the **Harlem Renaissance**, and Garveyism and other modes of radical Black expression challenged NACW conceptions of how to improve the position of African Americans, thus drawing clubwomen and would-be clubwomen away from the NACW. In 1935, former NACW President Mary McLeod Bethune formed the National Council of Negro Women (NCNW), a national organization that was focused on political rather than moral change and had a constituency that was more radical and less socially elite than that of the NACW. This new organization signaled an important departure from the NACW as the central organization for African American women (see White for an extended discussion of this shift).

Despite its changed role, the NACW still exists (renamed as the National Association of Colored Women's Clubs, Inc.) and is the oldest African American secular organization in existence, with member clubs across the nation. Under the presidency of Mary McLeod Bethune, the NACW dedicated a headquarters in Washington in 1928. The current headquarters, at 1601 R Street, NW, in Washington, was purchased in 1954; it was rededicated in 2000 after a $1.4 million restoration and renovation.

Perhaps the NACW's most important contribution to African American literature has been its cultivation of a ready audience for work by African American writers, as well as its educational assistance to countless African Americans who might otherwise not have achieved basic literacy. Beyond basic literacy, the NACW has offered scholarships for college-bound African American women—most notably the scholarship in honor of **Hallie Quinn Brown**, NACW president from 1920 to 1924. In many ways, the work of African American women through women's clubs has had a significant and lasting effect on African American literature and life. (*See* **Feminism/Black Feminism.**)

Resources: Elizabeth Lindsay Davis, *Lifting as They Climb* (1933; repr. New York: G. K. Hall, 1996); Lynda F. Dickson, "Lifting as We Climb: African American Women's Clubs of Denver, 1890–1925," in *Writing the Range: Race, Class, and Culture in the Women's West*, ed. Elizabeth Jameson and Susan Armitage (Norman: University of Oklahoma Press, 1997); George Washington Carver Day Care Center Collection, Western History Room, Denver Public Library; Anne Ruggles Gere, *Intimate Practices: Literacy and Cultural Work in U.S. Women's Clubs, 1880–1920* (Urbana: University of Illinois Press, 1997); Beverly Washington Jones, *Quest for Equality: The Life and Writings of Mary Eliza Church Terrell, 1863–1954* (Brooklyn, NY: Carlson, 1990); Anne Meis Knupfer, *Toward a Tenderer Humanity and a Nobler Womanhood: African American Women's Clubs in Turn-of-the-Century Chicago* (New York: New York University Press, 1996); NACW, *A History of the Club Movement Among the Colored Women of the United States of America*, 1902; NACWC, *Records of the National Association of Colored Women's Clubs, 1895–1992*; Dorothy Salem, "National Association of Colored Women's Clubs," in *Black Women in America: An Historical Encyclopedia*, ed. Darlene Clark Hine, Elsa Barkley Brown, and Rosalyn Terborg-Penn (Bloomington: Indiana University Press, 1994), 842–851; Mary Church Terrell, *A Colored Woman in a White World* (Salem, NH: Ayer, 1986); Deborah Gray White, *Too Heavy a Load: Black Women in Defense of Themselves, 1894–1994* (New York: Norton, 1999).

Julie Nelson Christoph

Woods, Paula L. (born 1953). Novelist and editor. Woods grew up as an only child in a middle-class section of **Los Angeles, California**. She was extremely close to her parents and loved reading, particularly books by **Zora Neale Hurston** and **Ann Lane Petry**. When Woods was a senior at the University of Southern California (USC), her mother died, and Woods lost interest in everything. In an effort to regroup, she took a job as a hospital telephone operator and, to her surprise, developed an interest in the workings of inner-city trauma centers. After graduating from USC with a B.A., Woods went to graduate school and earned a master's degree in hospital administration. Later, she and her husband, Felix Liddell, started their own hospital consulting firm; by 1992, they had also teamed up on their first book, *I, Too, Sing America*. Three years later they edited *Spooks, Spies and Private Eyes: Black Mystery, Crime, and Suspense Fiction of the 20th Century* and discovered, among other things, that Black people had been writing **crime and mystery fiction** since the turn of the century.

More important, Woods rediscovered her passion for crime and suspense novels. At the same time, she realized that the voice she heard least in the genre was that of the no-nonsense yet vulnerable Black woman. And so Woods's heroine, Charlotte Justice, was born. Justice is a homicide detective with the Los Angeles Police Department (LAPD) who, in addition to solving crimes, has to cope with the racial and sexual conflicts inherent in the LAPD. Woods's first Charlotte Justice mystery, *Inner City Blues*, was published in 1999. "When I started thinking about a surname for my character, I was struck by the irony of the name 'Justice' for a African American law enforcement officer," Woods says in an interview on her Web site. "It raised all kinds of interesting questions about whether African Americans get equal justice under the law and what responsibility does a cop in Charlotte's unique position carry along with that name." According to Woods, the character is motivated by a deep-rooted need to see the wrongs in her world made right. "I think most Black folks walk around with a strong sense of the injustice done to us individually and as a people," Woods continues. "Charlotte's in a position to see that rectified, which I hope makes for satisfying and thought-provoking reading." Evidently it has; in 2000, *Inner City Blues* received an Edgar Award nomination for best first novel by the Mystery Writers of America, and was cited among 1999's best novels of the year by the *Los Angeles Times*.

Resources: Paula L. Woods: *Dirty Laundry: A Charlotte Justice Novel* (New York: One World/Ballantine, 2003); *Inner City Blues: A Charlotte Justice Novel* (New York: Norton, 1999); *Stormy Weather: A Charlotte Justice Novel* (New York: One World/Ballantine, 2002); Paula L. Woods and Felix H. Liddell, *I, Too, Sing America: The African American Book of Days* (New York: Workman, 1992); Paula L. Woods and Felix H. Liddell, eds.: *I Hear a Symphony: African Americans Celebrate Love* (New York: Anchor, 1994); *Spooks, Spies, and Private Eyes: Black Mystery and Suspense Fiction* (New York: Doubleday, 1995).

Joy Duckett Cain

Woodson, Carter G. (1875–1950). Historian, educator, and editor. Known as the "Father of Black History," Carter G. Woodson dedicated his life to many works that helped lay the foundation for African American literature and inspire a change in the way African Americans perceived themselves and how others, particularly Whites, perceived African Americans. Born Carter Goodwin Woodson to parents who had been slaves, Woodson spent his early life sharecropping with his family and did not attend high school until age twenty. He went on to earn a Bachelor of Literature degree from Berea College in 1903. In the same year, he took a teaching position in the Philippines. He traveled throughout Asia, North Africa, and Europe before returning to the University of Chicago to earn a B.A. and M.A. in history, Romance languages, and literature. He then attended Harvard University and became the first descendant of African American slave parents to earn a Ph.D. in history (Smith). At this point, Woodson began his life's work: the preservation and teaching of African American history.

Woodson believed that "whites doubted the value of African American history, and that blacks were so afflicted by the specter of racial inferiority and the humiliation of **slavery** that they did not seek to know more about their past" (Smith). Often the educational system perpetuated this belief, either by misrepresenting Blacks or by ignoring them altogether. Given Woodson's personal interests and lifelong study, he believed that African Americans had a rich and fascinating history. He also thought that by teaching African American history to all people, of all ages and backgrounds, he could "not only build self-esteem among blacks, but [lessen] prejudice among whites" (LaBlanc).

In 1915, Woodson published *The Education of the Negro Prior to 1861*. In the same year, he and four scholars founded the Association for the Study of Negro Life and History, which exists today as the Association for the Study of African American History and Life. This organization was dedicated solely to the scholarly research of Black life, past and present. Its members collected and preserved material that had been overlooked by mainstream scholars and presented their work at scheduled meetings (LaBlanc). In 1916, Woodson founded the *Journal of Negro History*, in which scholars, both Black and White, published their works on a variety of topics about African Americans. The *Journal* often accepted articles that other periodicals would not, and continues to publish today. Some of the contributors include Charles H. Wesley and **W.E.B. Du Bois**. **Langston Hughes** worked for Woodson briefly in 1925 (Ostrom, 428).

In the 1920s, Woodson took teaching jobs to help fund the Association. While at Howard University, he introduced courses in African American history and "integrated the Negro's role in American history into all the courses he taught" (Goggin, 49). During this same period, he organized Associated Publishers, a publishing company that enabled writers often refused by White publishers to publish literature about African Americans. These books contributed greatly to the understanding and appreciation of African American culture, history, and achievement. One of his books, *The Negro in Our History* (1922), "was a central text of the Black [Arts] movement in the

1960s and is today a widely used textbook in universities" (LaBlanc). Another book, *The Mis-Education of the Negro* (1933), "condemns any educational institution for blacks that fails to make the education relevant to the needs of the students" (Smith). Woodson was also a regular contributor to **Marcus Garvey**'s newspaper, ***Negro World***.

By 1922, Woodson had retired from teaching and was working full-time for the Association. Four years later, he established Negro History Week, which celebrated the history and accomplishments of African Americans. Negro History Week took place during February between the birthdays of **Frederick Douglass** and Abraham Lincoln. By the 1970s, Negro History Week had become Negro History Month, and as such is still recognized in schools, businesses, churches, and communities across the country. In 1937, Woodson founded the *Negro History Bulletin* for laypersons rather than scholars. He also created a curriculum for teachers so that they could include African American history in their classrooms. Altogether, Woodson's work has helped to establish modern African American Studies, as well as to show the world the relevance and significance of African American history. (*See* **Franklin, John Hope**.)

Resources: Jacqueline Goggin: *Carter G. Woodson: A Life in Black History* (Baton Rouge: Louisiana State University Press, 1993); *Carter G. Woodson and the Movement to Promote Black History* (Rochester, NY: University of Rochester Press, 1984); Michael L. LaBlanc, "Carter G. Woodson," in *Contemporary Black Biography*, vol. 2 (Detroit: Gale, 1992), also *Biography Resource Center*, http://galenet.galegroup.com/ servlet/BioRC; Hans Ostrom, *A Langston Hughes Encyclopedia* (Westport, CT: Greenwood Press, 2002); M. Anthony Scally, *Walking Proud: The Story of Dr. Carter Godwin Woodson* (Washington, DC: Associated Publishers, 1983); Jessie Carney Smith, "Carter G. Woodson" in *Notable Black American Men*, ed. Jessie Carney (Detroit: Gale, 1998), also *Biography Resource Center*, http://galenet.galegroup.com/servlet/ BioRC; Carter G. Woodson: *African Heroes and Heroines* (Washington, DC: Associated Publishers, 1939); *African Myths* (Washington, DC: Associated Publishers, 1928); *A Century of Negro Migration* (New York: Russell & Russell, 1969); *The Education of the Negro Prior to 1861* (1915; repr. New York: Arno, 1968); *Free Negro Owners of Slaves in the United States in 1830, Together with Absentee Ownership of Slaves in the United States in 1830* (1924; repr. New York: Negro Universities Press, 1968); *The History of the Negro Church*, 2nd ed. (Washington, DC: Associated Publishers, 1945); *The Mis-education of the Negro* (1933; repr. Washington, DC: Associated Publishers, 1972); *The Negro in Our History* (Washington, DC: Associated Publishers, 1922); *Negro Makers of History* (Washington, DC: Associated Publishers, 1928); *The Rural Negro* (Washington, DC: Association for the Study of Negro Life and History, 1930).

Gladys L. Knight

Woodson, Jacqueline (born 1964). Children's writer and novelist. Woodson prides herself on writing about characters who exist outside of the mainstream society, such as African Americans, pregnant teens, gays, and abused individuals. Recognized as "one the foremost African American women writers of young adult books" (Paylor), Woodson provides a voice for her strong, vibrant characters. Her attraction to characters who feel out of place may be influenced by her own childhood. Moving back and forth between South Carolina and New York City, she found herself never feeling "quite . . . a part of either place" (Paylor). In addition, she was deeply affected by the politics of the day, especially President Nixon's resignation and the selection of his successor, Gerald Ford.

Writing has always been a part of Woodson's life. In fifth grade, she became the editor of her school's literary magazine. In seventh grade, at the encouragement of her English teacher, Woodson decided that she would be a writer and that she would write about what she knew. In particular, she decided to write about the things she felt were missing from the books she read, including communities of color, girls, and friendships.

Woodson's first novel was just such a book. *Last Summer with Maizon* (1990) is the story of a friendship between two girls, Margaret and Maizon. Margaret is dealing with the death of her father while Maizon is considering attending a private boarding school in Blue Hill, Connecticut. The book received praise for its sensitive portrayal of female friendship and was followed by two additional Maizon and Margaret books: *Maizon at Blue Hill* (1992) and *Between Madison and Palmetto* (1993).

Woodson also writes about families with problems; the parents don't have answers, and they are often distant or absent. The narrators are strong characters who manage to survive, although Woodson does not impose easy resolutions on the sometimes heartbreaking dilemmas her characters face. A noteworthy example is *I Hadn't Meant to Tell You This* (1994). Twelve-year-old Marie, who lives in an all-Black suburb of Athens, Ohio, with her father, befriends Lena, the "White trash" new girl at school. Their friendship blooms as the pair share their longing for their absent mothers. Marie is troubled to learn that Lena's father sexually abuses her; Lena is worried that her father will abuse her younger sister. Marie enlists her resistant father's help in the struggle to find a solution to Lena's problem, but there is no easy answer. Ultimately, Lena creates her own solution; she takes her sister and runs away, leaving friendship and home behind.

Woodson has said that her works can be classified into "good" books—including her trilogy about the schoolgirl friends Maizon and Margaret—and "controversial" books—including those that deal with such topics as teenage pregnancy, single parenthood, grief, homosexuality, race relations, and abuse (Brown). These books include *The Dear One* (1991), *I Hadn't Meant to Tell You This*, *From the Notebooks of Melanin Sun* (1995), *The House You Pass on the Way* (1997), and *Locomotion* (2003).

In addition to her young-adult novels, Woodson has written several picturebooks, including *Sweet, Sweet Memory* (2000), *Visiting Day* (2002), and *Our Gracie Aunt* (2002). In spite of their simple format, these books often deal with difficult issues: grieving the death of a grandparent, visiting a father in jail, dealing with foster care when a mother is unable to parent. Throughout them all is the theme of strength, survival, and family bonds.

Woodson also writes short stories and has edited two short story collections, including *A Way Out of No Way: Writing About Growing Up Black in America* (1996). To date, she has written one adult novel, *Autobiography of a Family Photo* (1995). In a series of vignettes, the book examines the impact of the **Vietnam War** on African American life.

Woodson continues to be recognized for her contributions to African American literature as well as children's and young-adult literature. In 2001, she received the Coretta Scott King Award for *Miracle's Boys*, a novel about three brothers in **Harlem, New York**, coping with the loss of their parents. Three of her books have been named Coretta Scott King Honor books: *Locomotion* (2004), *From the Notebooks of Melanin Sun* (1996), and *I Hadn't Meant to Tell You This* (1995). Woodson has also won the Lambda Literary Award for best fiction and best children's fiction (1996), and she has been a finalist for the National Book Award in Young People's Literature for *Hush* (2003). Woodson has twice won the Kenyon Review Award for Literary Excellence in Fiction (1992, 1995). (*See* **Children's Literature; Lesbian Literature**.)

Resources: Primary Sources: Jacqueline Woodson: *Autobiography of a Family Photo* (New York: Dutton, 1995); *The Dear One* (1991; repr. New York: Putnam, 2004); *From the Notebooks of Melanin Sun* (New York: Blue Sky, 1995); *The House You Pass on the Way* (1997; repr. New York: Putnam, 2003); *Hush* (2002; repr. New York: Speak, 2003); *I Hadn't Meant to Tell You This* (New York: Delacorte, 1994); *Last Summer with Maizon* (1990; repr. New York: Putnam, 2002); *Locomotion* (New York: Putnam, 2003); *Maizon at Blue Hill* (1992; repr. New York: Putnam, 2002); *Miracle's Boys* (New York: Putnam, 2000); *Our Gracie Aunt* (New York: Jump at the Sun, 2002); *Visiting Day* (New York: Scholastic, 2002). **Secondary Sources:** Rudine Sims Bishop, "Books from Parallel Cultures: New Voices," *Horn Book*, Sept. 1992, pp. 616–620; Jennifer M. Brown, "Jacqueline Woodson: From Outsider to Insider," *Publishers Weekly*, Feb. 11, 2002, pp. 1550–1557; Nicola Morris, "Jacqueline Woodson (1963–)," in *Contemporary African American Novelists: A Bio-Bibliographical Critical Sourcebook*, ed. Emmanuel S. Nelson (Westport, CT: Greenwood Press, 1999), 497–498; Diane R. Paylor, "Bold Type: Jacqueline Woodson's 'Girl Stories,'" *Ms.*, Nov.–Dec. 1994, 77; Catherine Saalfield, "Jacqueline Woodson (1963–)," in *Contemporary Lesbian Writers of the United States: A Bio-Bibliographical Critical Sourcebook*, ed. Sandra Pollack and Denise Knight (Westport, CT: Greenwood Press, 1993), 622–624.

Heidi Hauser Green

World War I (1914–1918). World War I had an enormous impact on African American culture and, indirectly, African American literature. The complexity of geographical, historical, and political circumstances leading to World War I is almost impossible to overestimate. The circumstances, in part, involved disputed territories resulting from the collapse of the Ottoman Empire in the nineteenth century, so that in the late 1800s and early 1900s, Austria-Hungry and Russia developed competing interests in controlling areas of southeastern Europe, including Bosnia and Serbia (Roberts; Tuchman).

Germany gradually aligned itself with Austria-Hungary, France with Russia, and England, ultimately, with France and Russia. All of these nations had imperial aspirations and holdings in one form or another, and the internal politics in several of the nations were volatile. Between the 1870s and August 1914, numerous political maneuverings occurred, and tensions among European nations multiplied and intensified. The situation was as explosive as it was complex.

As enormously complicated as the prelude to war was, however, the event that sparked the blaze of war was simple if shocking. Archduke Franz-Ferdinand, heir to the Austria-Hungary monarchy, was assassinated by a Bosnian terrorist on June 28, 1914, in Sarajevo. Austria-Hungary declared war on Serbia almost immediately, and less than ten days later, virtually all of Europe had committed itself to armed conflict. The devastation that followed over the next four years was unprecedented, partly because of protracted trench warfare, which led to carnage but little change in military positions, but also because of new military technology, including poison gas, more powerful artillery, and aircraft (Fussell). The United States did not enter the war until 1917, after Germany began attacking American merchant ships that held cargo helpful to England and France. However, U.S. participation proved crucial, first in preventing France from being overwhelmed by German forces, and second by helping to force a German surrender, which led to the end of the war in 1918 and the Treaty of Versailles in 1919.

African American participation in the war was significant. Franklin and Moss (360ff.) suggest that when registration for the military opened in July 1917, "more than 700,000 blacks registered. Before the end of the Selective Service enlistments, 2,290,525 black had registered, 367,000 of whom were called into the service" (360). The eagerness of African Americans to fight for the United States was, ironically, met with discrimination, and racist practices within the military were common. Ultimately over 50,000 African American soldiers served overseas in World War I. Many of these soldiers were stevedores and earned fame for moving cargo rapidly at European ports. Many others saw combat, especially in the 369th, 370th, 371st, and 372nd U.S. Infantry corps. African American soldiers often served under French command and earned military honors from the French, including the Croix de Guerre. African American units were especially helpful in driving German forces from France into Belgium (Franklin and Moss, 367ff.). The 369th Infantry fought so fiercely that the Germans dubbed them the "Hellfighters" (Cooper). In a novel, *Standing at the Scratch Line* (1998), **Guy Johnson** captures the experience of African American soldiers in World War I. African American women also served in Europe, chiefly as nurses for the Red Cross (Hunton).

The effect of World War I on African American culture and identity was multifaceted. Often Black soldiers were treated much better and enjoyed more freedom in France than in their own nation. Many French citizens were especially taken by the **jazz** that African American military bands played,

African American troops from the First Group, 165th Depot Brigade, at the movies, with their own musicians and performers. Photographs and Prints Division, Schomburg Center for Research in Black Culture, The New York Public Library, Astor, Lenox and Tilden Foundations.

including one led by a soldier named James Europe. African Americans' experience in France during the war led directly to **Paris, France**'s becoming a site for African American **expatriate writers** in subsequent years. Additionally, by participating so heavily and so well in the war, African Americans demonstrated loyalty and bravery as full American citizens, and yet, back home, genuine full citizenship eluded them, Jim Crow laws persisted, and the atrocity of **lynching** continued (Ellis).

One especially emblematic event occurred right after the war had ended, when the 369th Infantry participated in a parade in New York City (February 17, 1919). Nearly a million people witnessed the parade, which began on Fifth Avenue and ended in **Harlem, New York** (Franklin and Moss, 383). Many historians and scholars point to this heroes' welcome as one starting point for the **Harlem Renaissance**. However, as grand as the parade was, it did not reflect fundamental change in the way African Americans were treated in the United States. Therefore, **W.E.B. Du Bois**, among others, took pains to point out the enormous gap between what African Americans had done for the United States and what the United States continued to do to African Americans. He wrote, "We stand again to look America squarely in the face and call a spade a spade. We sing: This country of ours, despite all its better souls have done and dreamed, is yet a shameful land" ("Returning Soldiers," 4). In the essay, Du Bois goes on to indict the United States, pointing out that it "lynches," "disenfranchises," "encourages ignorance," "steals from us [African Americans]," and "insults us" (4).

Because African Americans continued to be treated badly after World War I, especially in **the South**, many streamed into northern cities as part of the **Great Migration**. This process had actually begun during the war, when many jobs opened up in the industrial North because so many White males had enlisted in the military. Large African American communities began to develop in northern cities, with Harlem and its cultural renaissance (c. 1920–1930) serving as only the most visible symbol for cultural activity that was occurring in many other cities, including **Chicago, Illinois, Detroit, Michigan, St. Louis, Missouri, Philadelphia** and **Pittsburgh, Pennsylvania**, and **Washington, D.C.** African Americans' participation in World War I raised expectations; demonstrated patriotism, capability, and valor; and helped to induce a demographic shift from the South to the North, all of which contributed to how African Americans, writers included, perceived themselves and their country.

Resources: Arthur E. Barbeau and Florette Henri, *The Unknown Soldiers: Black American Troops in World War I* (Philadelphia: Temple University Press, 1974); Michael L. Cooper, *Hell Fighters: African American Soldiers in World War I* (New York: Lodestar, 1997); W.E.B. Du Bois, "Returning Soldiers," in *The Portable Harlem Renaissance Reader*, ed. David Levering Lewis (New York: Viking, 1994), 3–5; Mark Ellis, *Race, War, and Surveillance: African Americans and the United States Government During World War I* (Bloomington: Indiana University Press, 2001); John Hope Franklin and Alfred A. Moss, Jr., *From Slavery to Freedom: A History of African Americans*, 8th ed. (Boston: McGraw-Hill, 2000); Paul Fussell, *The Great War and Modern Memory* (New York: Oxford University Press, 1975); Addie W. Hunton, *Two Colored Women with the Expeditionary Forces: Addie W. Hunton, Kathryn M. Johnson and William Alphaeus Hunton: A Pioneer Prohet of Young Men* (New York: G. K. Hall, 1997); Guy Johnson, *Standing at the Scratch Line* (New York: Random House, 1998); Arthur W. Little, *From Harlem to the Rhine: The Story of New York's Colored Volunteers* (New York: Covici and Friede, 1936); Samuel Eliot Morison, Henry Steele Commager, and Williams Leuchtenberg, *A Concise History of the American Republic*, rev. ed. (New York: Oxford University Press, 1977), 538–562; John Morris Roberts, *The Penguin History of Europe* (New York: Penguin, 1997), 831–851; Barbara Wertheim Tuchman, *The Guns of August* (New York: Macmillan, 1962); Tom Willard, *The Sable Doughboys: A Novel* (New York: Forge, 1997).

Hans Ostrom

World War II (1939–1945). Directly and indirectly, World War II had profound effects on African Americans. To some degree, the conflicts that led to World War II grew out of European political instability left unresolved by **World War I** and the Treaty of Versailles. The conflicts were intensified by the rise, in the late 1920s and early 1930s, of fascism in Germany, led by Adolf

Hitler, and in Italy, led by Benito Mussolini. Beginning after Germany's invasion of Poland on September 1, 1939, the war lasted six years; it pitted Germany, Italy, and Japan against England, the United States, France, and their allies. According to Garraty and Gay, the U.S. lost almost 300,000 soldiers and sailors in the war, and nearly 8 million Russian military personnel died; the Germans lost 3.5 million soldiers and sailors, France 200,000, and Japan well over a million, in addition to the civilians killed by two atomic bombs dropped by the United States (Garraty and Gay, 1136). Garraty and Gay go on to suggest that the "performance of Negro troops in the war inspired a new respect for their courage and patriotism, and the shortage of labor produced by the wartime boom enabled many Blacks both to improve themselves economically and to develop new self-respect" (1141). During World War II, Germany conducted a separate war against European Jews, Roma (gypsies), homosexuals, and political dissidents. Ultimately over 6 million Jews perished in what is now known as the Holocaust.

At the end of the war, not just the European but the global political map was radically redrawn. The United States, which did not enter the war until December 1941, went from being a relatively isolationist republic in the 1930s to an international superpower in the late 1940s, and the foundation of the **Cold War**, which shaped global politics for four decades, had been established. According to Franklin and Moss, "Approximately a half million African Americans saw service overseas during World War II" (483). However, as was the case in World War I, African American troops were segregated from White troops; not until January 1945 were some fighting units integrated. Once again, therefore, a brutal irony was highlighted: African Americans were asked to serve and volunteered to serve their country, while their country continued to practice segregation. And once again, as was the case in World War I, openings in the **labor** market, especially in Northern factories, meant more jobs for African Americans and an influx of African Americans from **the South** to the North.

The work of **Langston Hughes**, especially his poetry, reflects multiple attitudes of African Americans toward the war. In "The Southern Negro Speaks" (1941), Hughes highlights the hypocrisy of America's wanting to preserve democracy abroad while not allowing its Black citizens the complete privileges of democracy at home. Moreover, in the 1930s, Hughes had been extremely interested in socialism as one way that African Americans in particular and working people in general might overcome the damage inflicted by the **Great Depression**, and he was a supporter of Russian society. His socialist politics are reflected in such poems as "One More 'S' in the U.S.A." and "Let America Be American Again." As early as 1936, however, in the poem "Broadcast on Ethiopia," Hughes expressed outrage at Italy's invasion of that African nation. Ultimately, Hughes became a firm supporter of U.S. participation World War II, particularly when Hitler's racist views became clear and after Japan's attack on Pearl Harbor. In "Stalingrad: 1942," he pictures that city and the Soviet Union as victims of Germany's aggression while England and the United States let the aggression stand, thus not only supporting U.S. involvement but wanting the United States to participate on the war's eastern front.

Later, in "Dear Mr. President" (1943), a poem rhetorically addressed to President Franklin Roosevelt, Hughes points out that Black troops training in Alabama are segregated and must live under Jim Crow laws. Hughes takes a warmly humorous approach to the war in "Madam and the Army," in which the narrator, Madam, wonders how her boyfriend could be declared "1-A" for the military draft when he did so little to support her. In the poem "To Captain Mulzac" (1943) he celebrates the captain and crew of the merchant ship named after **Booker T. Washington**. In "Bonds for All" (1942), a poem circulated through the Associated Negro Press, Hughes urges people to buy war bonds to support the U.S. In "The Underground" (1943), a poem he dedicated "To the Anti-Fascists of the Occupied Countries of Europe and Asia," he predicts victory over the Nazis. In "Will V-Day Be Me-Day, Too?" (1945), he asks whether African Americans will finally enjoy the full citizenship in the United States for which they fought on behalf of others in Europe and Asia. Hughes's famous recurring character in his **short fiction**, Jesse B. Simple, works in a factory that produces military goods during the war. Overall, then, Hughes's work represents the variety of responses to the war that African Americans and others expressed.

In 1943, "the most serious **race riot** of the war period broke out in Detroit" (Franklin and Moss, 496), highlighting once again the unresolved racial tensions at home as the war was being fought abroad. In 1944, **Walter Francis White** wrote in support of U.S. involvement in the war: "In evaluating the merits of parties and candidates [in elections] we must include all issues—those touching the life of Negroes as a group as well as those affecting the entire country" (Franklin and Moss, 498). **Charles H. Fuller**'s play *A Soldier's Play* (1981) is set in the South in 1944 and involves the murder of a Black soldier and the racial tension faced by Blacks in the military. The play won the Pulitzer Prize for **drama** in 1982.

One of the most celebrated African American fighting units in World War II was "The Tuskegee Airmen," pilots trained at the Tuskegee Institute. After the U.S. Army Air Corps grudgingly allowed the unit to fly in support of American bombers, the Tuskegee Airmen not only succeeded but became one the most successful groups of fighter pilots in the war (Francis). Their story was turned into a feature film in 1995. African American women participated in the war, too, as factory workers in the United States and as military nurses overseas (Franklin and Moss, 492ff.).

During World War II, Benjamin O. Davis, Jr., became the first African America to rise to the rank of general, and he published an **autobiography**. The scholar Robin Lucy has studied allusions to World War II in the writings of **Ralph Ellison**, **Chester Himes**, and **Ann Lane Petry**. **Gail Lumet Buckley** has written a history of African Americans in the U.S. military. In 1968, the writer and independent film-maker **Melvin Van Peebles** created the feature film *The Story of a Three-Day Pass*, which concerns an African American soldier in France during World War II. (*See* **Walton, Anthony.**)

Resources: Gail Lumet Buckley, *American Patriots: The Story of Blacks in the Military from the Revolution to Desert Storm* (New York: Random House, 2001); Charles D. Chamberlain, *Victory at Home: Manpower and Race in the American South During World War II* (Athens: University of Georgia Press, 2003); Benjamin O. Davis, Jr., *Benjamin O. Davis, Jr., American: An Autobiography* (Washington, DC: Smithsonian Press, 1991); Charles Francis, *The Tuskegee Airmen: The Men Who Changed a Nation* (1955; repr. New York: Diane Books, 1998); John Hope Franklin and Alfred A. Moss, Jr., *From Slavery to Freedom: A History of African Americans*, 8th ed. (Boston: McGraw-Hill, 2000); Charles Fuller, *A Soldier's Play* (New York: Hill and Wang, 1982); John A. Garraty and Peter Gay, *The Columbia History of the World* (New York: Harper & Row, 1972); Langston Hughes: *The Best of Simple* (New York: Hill and Wang, 1990); *The Collected Poems*, ed. Arnold Rampersad (New York: Knopf, 1994); Robin Jane Lucy, "'Now Is the Time! Here Is the Place!': World War II and the Black Folk in the Writings of Ralph Ellison, Chester Himes and Ann Petry," *Dissertation Abstracts International, Section A: The Humanities and Social Sciences*, 63, no. 1 (2002), 188; Robert Markowitz, dir., *The Tuskegee Airmen* (Los Angeles: HBO Studios, 1995), DVD format, 2002; Alan M. Osur, *Separate and Unequal: Race Relations in the AAF During World War II* (Washington, DC: Air Force History and Museums Program, 2000); Melvin Van Peebles, dir., *The Story of a Three-Day Pass* (1968; repr. Los Angeles: Xenon 2, 1996), VHS format; Walter White et al., "A Declaration by Negro Voters," *The Crisis* 51 (Jan. 1944), 16–17, quoted in John Hope Franklin and Alfred A. Moss, Jr., *From Slavery to Freedom: A History of African Americans*, 8th ed. (Boston: McGraw-Hill, 2000), 498.

Hans Ostrom

Wright, Bil (born c. 1974). Novelist, poet, and playwright. Born in the Bronx, New York City, and a graduate of New York University, Wright has published poems in anthologies and collections and has had some dramatic pieces performed. But his most substantial works are his two **novels**, *Sunday You Learn to Box* (2000) and *One Foot in Love* (2004). The former, a much-acclaimed book, concentrates, with great sympathy and patience, on the experiences of a youth, Louis Bowman, growing up in the Stratfield Projects. Narrated in the first person, the novel appropriates traits from the bildungs-roman (**coming-of-age** novel), **historical fiction**, and **romance novel**. There is no explicit mention of Louis's homosexuality—an identity he is not aware of, partly because effeminacy is simply not tolerated in his tough-guy environment—until well into the book, when Louis says, "What I really wanted to do was ask Ray Anthony Robinson if he'd dance with me." Robinson is the local hoodlum, and much older, so a friendship with him is barely possible for Louis; much less realizable is the same-sex love that he can hardly define, let alone act on.

The novel is rarely uplifting; Louis sinks into an introverted isolation, even spending time in a psychiatric drop-in center. He is brutalized by an aggressive stepfather, bored into submission by the preponderance of housework which is foisted upon him, and ignored by his "sissy"-hating grandfather. Trapped, bereft of agency or choice, Louis is forced to learn to box, despite the fact that violence is anathema to him. The tragedy of Louis's circumstances is conveyed by Wright with a sensitivity that marks him out as a significant literary talent. Clearly, to the reader, Louis is a normal adolescent, but the homophobic milieu of Stratfield cannot countenance male effeminacy of any degree.

Wright's second novel, *One Foot in Love*, focuses on a recently widowed hospital worker, Rowtina Washington. Rowtina falls in with a group of women friends ("a whole little nigger army," as one racist drunk calls them) who, gradually, encourage a reinvigoration of her female vitality. Rowtina comes of age at the climax of the novel, not because she finds a new man but because she has the self-respect to dismiss the appeal of a hairdresser, Picasso Alegria, whose character she suspects. The novel is packaged and narrated much like a **romance novel**, so this ending is surprising. Readers may have expected Rowtina to waltz off into the sunset with this new man, but Wright's novels will not be so predictable. (*See* **Gay Literature**.)

Resources: D. W. Carbado, D. A. McBride, and D. Weise, eds., *Black like Us* (San Francisco: Cleis, 2002), 437–438; Bil Wright: *One Foot in Love* (New York: Simon and Schuster, 2004); *Sunday You Learn How to Box: A Novel* (New York: Touchstone, 2000); Web site, http://www.bilwright.com.

Kevin DeOrnellas

Wright, Charles H. (born 1918). Physician, museum founder, and writer. Wright was born in Dothan, Alabama, and grew up in impoverished circumstances, which did not, however, prevent him from becoming an obstetrician and gynecologist. He opened a medical practice in **Detroit, Michigan**, in 1948. In 1965, in the basement of the building serving as both his home and office, Wright founded the International Afro-American Museum (Web site). In 1987 it was moved to its own building and renamed the Museum of African American History. A new building was erected to house it in 1997, and in 1998 it became the Charles H. Wright Museum of African American History. It is located at 315 East Warren Avenue in Detroit. Wright is also an independent scholar with an interest in the life and work of the African American singer, actor, athlete, and activist **Paul Robeson**.

Resources: Charles H. Wright, *Robeson: Labor's Forgotten Champion* (Detroit: Balamp, 1975); Web site, Charles H. Wright Museum of African American History, http://www.maahdetroit.org.

Hans Ostrom

Wright, Charles S. (born 1932). Journalist and novelist. Wright was born in New Franklin, Missouri, and later studied at the James Jones & Lowney Turner Handy Writers' Colony in Marshall, Illinois. He served in the United States Army. In the 1960s he became a columnist for the *Village Voice*; he has also contributed to the *New York Times* and *Vogue*. He is the author of three novels: *Absolutely Nothing to Get Alarmed About*, *Messenger*, and *The Wig: A Mirror Image*. **Ishmael Reed** wrote an introduction to the reissue of *The Wig*. As a writer of fiction, Wright is known for his comic, satiric vision.

Resources: Frances S. Foster, "Charles Wright: Black Black Humorist," *College Language Association Journal* 15 (1971), 44–53; Eberhard Kreutzer, "Dark Ghetto Fantasy and the Great Society: Charles Wright's *The Wig* (1966)," in *The Afro-American Novel Since 1960*, ed. Peter Bruck and Wolfgand Karrer (Amsterdam: Grüner, 1982), 145–166; Robert P. Sedlack, "Jousting with Rats: Charles Wright's *The Wig*," *Satire Newsletter* 7 (1969), 37–39; Charles S. Wright: *Absolutely Nothing to Get Alarmed About* (New York: Farrar, Straus and Giroux, 1975); *Messenger* (New York: Farrar, Straus, 1963); *The Wig: A Mirror Image* (London: Souvenir Press, 1967; reiss. San Francisco: Mercury House, 2003).

Hans Ostrom

Wright, Courtni Crump (born 1950). Children's writer, romance novelist, businessperson, and teacher. Wright is best known for having written several picture books for children. Born in **Washington, D.C.**, she earned a B.A. at Trinity College in 1972 and a master's degree in education from Johns Hopkins University in 1980. In addition to writing, she has managed a telephone company and been a teacher. Wright has always known that she wanted to be a writer: "When I was six, I worked in the school library, shelving books. As an avid reader, I knew that one day I, too, would have books on the shelf" (Courtot).

Her plan was to write a best-seller, but when she began developing curriculum materials, Wright realized that discussion of African American history in textbooks was lacking. Wanting positive texts available for her son, she created her celebrated set of three picture books. *Jumping the Broom* (1994) discusses life on a plantation and preparations for a slave wedding. Despite their situation, the people do everything possible to make the wedding day a happy event, including preparing food, making household items as gifts, and crafting a wedding quilt. *Journey to Freedom* (1994) features **Harriet Tubman** leading a group of runaway slaves on a harrowing and exhausting journey to safety. Finally, *Wagon Train* (1995) follows a family of former slaves as they travel the Oregon Trail and settle in California. Currently, Wright is concentrating on writing African American **romance novel**s, "an old love" (Courtot). She has won an award from the National Endowment for the Humanities (1999) as well as an award from the Society of School Librarians International.

Resources: **Primary Sources:** Courtni C. Wright: *All that Matters* (Washington, DC: BET Books, 2000); *Blush* (New York: Kensington, 1997); *A Charmed Love* (Washington, DC: BET Books, 2002); *Espresso for Two* (Washington, DC: BET Books, 2004); *A Forgotten Love* (Washington, DC: BET Books, 2000); *It Had to Be You* (New York: Kensington, 1998); *Journey to Freedom: A Story of the Underground Railroad* (New York: Holiday House, 1994); *Jumping the Broom* (New York: Holiday House, 1994); *The Last Christmas Gift* (Washington, DC: BET Books, 2003);

"A Mother's Love," in *A Very Special Love*, with Janice Sims and Kayla Perrin (Washington, DC: BET Books, 2000); *The Music of Love* (Washington, DC: BET Books, 2003); *A New Beginning* (Washington, DC: BET Books, 2000); "New Year's Eve," in *Season's Greetings*, with Margie Walker and Roberta Gayle (New York: Kensington, 1998); *Paradise* (Washington, DC: BET Books, 1999); *Recipe for Love* (Washington, DC: BET Books, 2001); *Summer Breeze* (Washington, DC: BET Books, 2004); *A Sure Thing* (Washington, DC: BET Books, 1999); *Uncovered Passion* (Washington, DC: BET Books, 2002); *Wagon Train: A Family Goes West in 1865* (New York: Holiday House, 1995); *The Women of Shakespeare's Plays: Analysis of the Role of the Women in Selected Plays with Plot Synopses and Selected One-Act Plays* (Lanham, MD: University Press of America, 1993). **Secondary Sources:** Marilyn Courtot, "Meet Authors and Illustrators: Courtni C. Wright," http://www.childrenslit.com/f_wright.html; "Meet the Author: Courtni Wright," *Shades of Romance Magazine*, Mar./Apr. 2003, http://www.sormag.com/15wright.html.

Valerie Lynn Guyant

Wright, Jay (born 1935). Poet. Jay Wright was born in Albuquerque, New Mexico, and grew up there and in Southern California. The landscapes and cultures of the Southwest have been major influences on his work. After graduating from high school in 1954, he very briefly played semiprofessional baseball in the Arizona/**Texas** and California state leagues, then spent three years in the Army Medical Corps. Wright received his B.A. from the University of California at Berkeley in 1961 and his M.A. in comparative literature from Rutgers University in 1967. He first pursued a career as a playwright as well as a poet (two of his plays were produced in the late 1960s), but since the 1970s his creative work has focused on poetry. He has published nine collections of poetry since his first book, *The Homecoming Singer* (1971), including a volume of selected poems volume with an afterword by the literary critic Harold Bloom (1987) and a volume of collected poems titled *Transfigurations* (2000). He has received fellowships from the Guggenheim Foundation, the Academy of American Poets, the MacArthur Foundation, and the Lannan Foundation, among other awards and honors.

Wright's poetry invokes a rich mix of cultures and voices, incorporating high diction, African American **vernacular**, foreign languages (including Spanish and African languages), literary allusions, and quotes from texts ranging from personal letters to academic treatises. It is full of fascinating and unusual information, and brings together elements not often found together. This art of literary combination is part of Wright's project of making connections and creating new wholes out of the scattered pieces of our world. In this way, Wright is an heir of twentieth-century Modernist poets such as T. S. Eliot and Ezra Pound, who used montage, collage, and extensive literary allusions to produce poetry appropriate to the complexity of the modern world. Wright has also been influenced by the nineteenth century poet Walt Whitman and the twentieth-century Modernist poet Hart Crane. Both men tried to find a new poetic language that would be specifically American and suited to American topics, not an imitation of European models. Poems such as "Baptism in the Lead Avenue Ditch" and "Entering New Mexico" (both in *Soothsayers and Omens*) demonstrate the way that Wright maps out and gives voice to the landscapes of the Southwest.

Many commentators have called Wright's poetry philosophical and even scholarly. Some of his books, including *Dimensions of History* (1976) and *The Double Invention of Komo* (1980), include explanatory notes to guide readers through his many references. Many contemporary American poets are somewhat anti-intellectual, believing that thought and feeling are antagonistic to one another. But Wright is very much a poet for whom thinking is an integral part of writing. He is particularly gifted at combining intellectual exploration with emotional commitment, and at placing personal and historical experience in a larger context.

While his primary subject matter is African American experience and often autobiography, his treatment of personal and historical identity links it to larger themes of spiritual quest. His poems join African American cultural, historical, and personal material to African traditions and heritages, seeking the deeper roots of African American experience in African ritual and history. This aim has extended to anthropological research into African and other "primitive" religions and culture. Indeed, *Dimensions of History* and *The Double Invention of Komo* have been dedicated to anthropologists.

Wright's work also explores materials, forms, and language not normally associated with African American literature or experience, both to place that experience within a larger, universal context and to show the richness and complexity of that experience. His work shows the ways in which African American experience and literature are not defined by a single heritage, but are a meeting of many cultures and traditions. Thus Native American and Spanish American culture and history also play a large part in his work. For example, Wright has studied Navajo poetry and culture and incorporated it into his own poetry. This is in part due to Wright's having grown up in an area in which Anglo, Native American, and Spanish American cultures met and mingled. The connections between different cultures are a major part of his personal experience and of his work. Wright seeks in his poetry to synthesize his personal and cultural inheritances into a new and more inclusive value system and way of looking at the world. *The Double Invention of Komo* is made up of a series of poems that enact a West African initiation rite by means of which the speaker comes to a new and more complete identity: "I am reborn into a new life."

Much of Wright's poetry is written from the position of an outsider. This gives him a distinctive perspective on his society and his world, a larger view than that available to someone more comfortably placed in that world. However, this position as an outsider also produces a sense of isolation, and many of Wright's poems attempt to make connections by relating the experience of the American present not only to its own past but also to the African past. One commentator has spoken of Wright's quest to find "a new point of origin" for African American identity, one which could be a model for a new American identity that acknowledges and includes the many and diverse elements which have gone into it.

However, Wright's poems are not simply discussions of ideas. He embodies his ideas in rich, dense imagery and in beautiful, musical language, and frequently structures his poems about ritual patterns. Often the rhythms of his poems are influenced by African and Native American chants, which gives the poems a trancelike quality appropriate to the spiritual quest for wholeness of which they are a part. Poems such as "Desire's Persistence" (in *Elaine's Book*) or many of the poems in *The Double Invention of Komo* are examples of this chantlike aspect of Wright's work. For Wright, finding a new and living rhythm is a crucial part of finding a new identity and a new vision of the world. In this quest he draws on folk traditions of several cultures; on the work of such African American poets as **Langston Hughes**, who sought to write poetry in the patterns of African American speech; and on the work of such American experimental poets as Charles Olson, who in his theories of "Projective Verse" sought to emphasize the oral dimension of poetry. Wright's combination of formal care and exploration with African and African American **folklore** has affinities with the work of **Robert Hayden** and with that of more contemporary African American poets such as **Nathaniel Mackey** and **Clarence Major**.

Wright is a uniquely talented poet who, despite the honors and praise his work has received, is not as well known as he should be. While he has been acclaimed by figures ranging from the literary critic Harold Bloom and the poet-critic John Hollander to the African American poets **Langston Hughes** and **Amiri Baraka** (both of whom published his early work), his work has not been widely anthologized, and is even missing from some major anthologies of African American poetry. Wright's lack of greater reputation is in part due to the complexity and frequent difficulty of his work, which demands a great deal from the reader, and in part to his apparent preference for privacy over self-promotion. Though he has been a visiting writer at several universities and has given readings across the country, he does not occupy a permanent academic position.

Some critics have faulted Wright for the sometimes intimidating density and complexity of his work (Pinckney; Richard), and for what some have seen as a single-minded focus on personal development through spiritual or intellectual quest. However, many poets have a consistent set of material which they repeatedly address. Other commentators (Bloom; Hollander; Kutzinski) have praised Wright's intellectual and imaginative ambition and scope. The complexity of his work deepens and enriches his explorations of his chosen theme, and reminds readers of the complexity of African American experience.

Resources: Primary Sources: Jay Wright: *Balloons: A Comedy in One Act* (Boston: Baker's Plays, 1968); *Boleros* (Princeton, NJ: Princeton University Press, 1991); "Desire's Design, Vision's Resonance," *Callaloo* 30 (Winter 1987), 38–49; *Dimensions* *of History* (Santa Cruz, CA: Kayak, 1976); *The Double Invention of Komo* (Austin: University of Texas Press, 1980); *Elaine's Book* (Charlottesville: University Press of Virginia, 1988); *Explications/Interpretations* (Lexington: University Press of Kentucky, 1984); *The Homecoming Singer* (New York: Corinth, 1971); *Selected Poems of Jay Wright* (Princeton, NJ: Princeton University Press, 1987); *Soothsayers and Omens* (New York: Seven Woods, 1976); *Transfigurations: Collected Poems* (Baton Rouge: Louisiana State University Press, 2000). **Secondary Sources:** Harold Bloom, ed., *Jay Wright* (Broomall, PA: Chelsea House, 2004), collects most of the critical essays that have been written on Wright, many reprinted from the special issue of *Callaloo* devoted to Wright's work (vol. 19, no. 4 [Autumn 1983]); John Hollander, "Poetry in Review," *Times Literary Supplement*, Jan. 30, 1981, p. 115; Vera M. Kutzinski, *Against the American Grain: Myth and History in William Carlos Williams, Jay Wright, and Nicolás Guillén* (Baltimore, MD: Johns Hopkins University Press, 1987); Darryl Pinckney, "The May King," *Parnassus*, Spring/Summer 1981, 306–314; Philip M. Richard, "Jay Wright," in *Dictionary of Literary Biography*, vol. 41 (Detroit: Gale, 1985); Robert B. Stepto, "After Modernism, After Hibernation: Michael Harper, Robert Hayden, and Jay Wright," in *Chant of Saints: A Gathering of Afro-American Literature, Arts and Scholarship*, ed. Michael S. Harper and Robert B. Stepto (Urbana: University of Illinois Press, 1979).

Reginald Shepherd

Wright, Richard (1908–1960). Novelist, essayist, short story writer, and poet. Wright is best known for his novel *Native Son* (1940) and for being one of the most important, critically acclaimed, and popular American fiction writers active in the middle of the twentieth century. Although *Native Son* is considered his master work, he wrote a number of other important novels, essays, autobiographies, and short stories. Richard Nathaniel Wright was born on September 4, 1908, in Roxie, Mississippi, to Nathaniel Wright and Ella Wilson Wright. By 1912 his parents' marriage had dissolved, and he experienced great hunger and severe poverty. As a consequence, he and his younger brother, Leon, were shuffled among relatives. Although this situation caused his formal education to be disrupted, Wright was eventually able to immerse himself in the world of fiction. While he was staying with his grandparents, a lodger there introduced Wright to the story of Blue Beard. Wright would explain years later—in his best-selling **autobiography**, *Black Boy: A Record of Childhood and Youth* (1945)—that as she told him the story, "reality changed, the look of things altered, and the world became peopled with magical presences.... The sensations the story aroused in me were never to leave me" (39). Wright nurtured these passions well into his teen years, and in the spring of 1925 he published his first story in a Jackson, Mississippi, newspaper.

By November 1927 Wright had left **the South** to escape the brutalities of racism. Unfortunately, as he would explain in *Black Boy*, the North was hardly the utopia he envisioned: "My first glimpse of the flat black stretches of Chicago depressed and dismayed me, mocked all my fantasies"(261). Although the harsh realities of the **Great Depression** dimmed his hopes,

Chicago, Illinois, proved to be crucial to his development as a writer and an intellectual. He read literary periodicals and studied the techniques of such writers as Gertrude Stein, e. e. cummings, T. S. Eliot, and William Faulkner. By 1932 he had joined the John Reed Club, a literary society organized by the Communist Party. The club provided Wright with the opportunity to discuss fiction and share ideas. By 1933 he had joined the Communist Party and was excited by its promise to unite the working classes all over the world.

During this period Wright began writing poetry and first published it in the journals *New Masses* and *Left Front.* The poems that he produced were intended to inspire the proletariat to rise up against the bourgeois capitalist system. For example, "I Have Seen Black Hands" (1934) exalts the revolutionary potential of African Americans. Focusing on the spectrum of their experiences, he draws attention to their common economic and social oppression. By contrast, "Between the World and Me" (1935) is a far more personal work decrying the injustices of White racial terrorism. In this piece the narrator discovers a mutilated Black body, then in turn is victimized by a lynch mob.

Though Communist Party ideology had a profound effect on his development, Wright's first novel was devoid of these influences. In spite of his interest in revolutionary fiction, he did not intend *Lawd Today!* to serve as a symbolic representation of African American workers. Upon its completion in 1937 the novel was originally called *Cesspool,* a title reflecting its thematic content. *Lawd Today!/Cesspool* is replete with vain, ignorant braggarts who crave the approval of other men. Structurally, Wright relies upon tone more than the finer points of plot; it is a story full of moments of irony, sardonic humor, and poignancy. The experimental approaches to the narrative reflect the work of authors Wright read, including John Dos Passos and James Joyce. However, Wright's preoccupation with symbolic violence and his fascination with **gender** politics are his own.

Unfortunately for Wright, publishers were uninterested in his Chicago-based novel, which was released posthumously in 1967. Wright was undeterred, however, and he earned critical acclaim for his first published book, *Uncle Tom's Children* (1938). *Uncle Tom's Children* is a collection of five short stories focusing on African American manhood. Unlike *Lawd Today!* these stories were intended to be symbolic portraits of his race. All five stories—including the autobiographical essay "The Ethics of Living Jim Crow"—attempt to demystify the American South. To further this end, Wright explodes many conventional symbols of Southern life. The most sacred of these—hospitality, propriety, honor, and virtue—are ruined by the insecurities of White characters in his fiction. Wright even calls upon Mother Nature to heighten the reader's sense of urgency. Throughout the volume fire, flood, and drought eclipse the rural setting and make life inhospitable for both races.

The bleakest stories focus on African Americans who are politically disorganized and susceptible to White racial violence. "Down by the Riverside" is the prototype for this structural approach. Rather than compelling them to unite, floodwaters that threaten to engulf a rural community unleash the suppressed enmity between the two races. *Uncle Tom's Children* is not wholly cynical, however. The most inspiring stories concern group cohesion and political disobedience. For example, in "Fire and Cloud," Communists unite starving Black and White farmers against the state, which refuses to provide relief. Wright's central message in the volume is clear: alone, African Americans are vulnerable as a group, yet in coalition with the White working class they can secure a dignified way of life.

Rebellion and Black male survival are the subject of Wright's most successful novel, *Native Son* (1940), which is loosely based on the experiences of a convicted Chicago murderer, Robert Nixon. Wright tells the story of Bigger Thomas, whose profound instincts for survival enable him to recognize his own humanity. Bigger is a poor African American youth living in a single-parent home on Chicago's South Side. While employed as a chauffeur for a rich White family, he accidentally murders the daughter. What ensues is a wild scheme to dispose of the body and demand a ransom for her safe return. Eventually, Bigger is hunted down by the police and brought to trial. Just like his real life counterpart, Bigger Thomas is sentenced to death by an all-White jury.

One of themes of the novel concerns the American Dream. Wright constructs a narrative in which this established ideal is exposed as an empty **myth** maintained at the expense of African American lives. Bigger Thomas's victimization and tragic end are meant to establish this point. In this regard Bigger is intended to signify the revolutionary potential of the African American masses. At the same time, Wright constructs Bigger Thomas as a despicable figure. He is a morally ambivalent character whom readers often champion for his fierce survival instincts yet revile for his deviousness: he murders two women, betrays an acquaintance, and attempts to defraud the White family that employed him. Although his actions are depraved, the narration leads readers to find the United States culpable for creating its Bigger Thomases.

The 1940s was a decade of momentous adjustment for Wright. *Native Son* had established him as the most famous Black author in the world and the best-selling African American author in history. The almost universal recognition of his talents did not cause him to become idle, however. Troubled by his inability to complete another novel, Wright began a new project. In October 1941 he coauthored a photo documentary about the history of African American suffering. Titled *Twelve Million Black Voices: A Folk History of the Negro*, it was, according to Hazel Rowley, a work that inspired passion in Wright: "Wright's empathy for his own

Richard Wright, 1943. Courtesy of the Library of Congress.

people is more evident [in *12 Million Black Voices*] than in any of his fiction" (237). Even as Wright continued to work and travel, he found time to enrich his personal life. On March 12, 1941, he married fellow Communist Party member Ellen Poplowitz.

As Wright's career flourished, the political mood of the nation was shifting. The United States was growing less tolerant of political dissent and more apprehensive of communism. Wright, too, was finding his relationship with the Communist Party to be intolerable. The party began to dictate how he should address political issues in public. Also, its insistence that it could understand the plight of his race by applying White working-class theories frustrated him. Worse yet, the party did not share Wright's artistic vision and was dismayed by his unrelenting focus on African American political issues. They felt that he would better serve them as an author of nonracialized, proletarian-based fiction. By 1944 Wright regarded the Communist Party as a hindrance to Black liberation, and he publicly severed ties with them by penning the essay "I Tried to Be a Communist."

As the Communist Party fumed over his public disavowal of it, Wright redirected his energies into his work. His most renowned piece of nonfiction was released to the public in March 1955. *Black Boy* is an **autobiography** intended, arguably, to function as an allegorical biography of his race. It narrates Wright's life from his humble origins in Mississippi up to his abandonment of the South. The episodes address the symbolic and physical violence that intrude upon African American life—moments that parallel the events in *Uncle Tom's Children*. In particular, Wright focuses on the almost casual emasculations that African American men experience on a daily basis. But this work differed from his volume of short stories significantly in that he intended to juxtapose Southern racism and Northern racism. Unfortunately, Wright's publishers pressured him to lift this latter section from *Black Boy*. *American Hunger*, the second part of his autobiography, was not published until 1977, well after Wright's death.

In midcareer, Wright was in a unique position as an African American novelist. No longer beholden to anyone, he was able to serve as a spokesperson for his **race** and speak out against American racial injustice. And his considerable fame enabled him to serve as an advocate for aspiring authors. African American writers in particular—including **Gwendolyn Brooks**, **Chester Himes**, and **James Baldwin**—directly benefited from his generosity. Wright helped fledgling writers launch their careers by reading manuscripts, providing financial assistance, submitting books to reviewers, and bending the ears of publishers.

In spite of his fame, Wright was reconsidering his American citizenship—unwilling to raise his daughter in a society committed to segregation. In 1946 he and his family toured France, and by August 1947 they had become residents. Wright's expatriation produced a ripple affect in the lives of African American authors. For example, several of the major contributors to what is sometimes known as the Protest Era took up residence in Europe—**William**

Gardner Smith, Chester Himes, and, eventually, James Baldwin. (Baldwin and Wright quarreled one night in a **Paris, France**, café, and Baldwin was critical of *Native Son* in the opening essay of his book *Notes of a Native Son*, the title of which of course alludes to Wright's novel.) In fact, so many African American writers migrated to France that Tyler Stovall referred to the city as the "literary capital" of Black America (132). Wright was at the center of this African American French "colony," a celebrity in the eyes of tourists, intellectuals, and Parisians.

Transplanting himself from the United States to Europe provided Wright with renewed inspiration. The self-educated author of two best-sellers had long studied sociological theory, **Marxism**, Freudian theory, and the literary techniques of **Modernism** and naturalism. European residency introduced Wright to existentialism and the **Négritude** literary movement. From these experiences he published two novels: *The Outsider* (1953), an existential investigation of racial identity, and *Savage Holiday* (1954), a Freudian novel about a neurotic White businessman. Both works reflect Wright's interest in deviant behavior and criminal motivation. Neither work received positive reviews in the United States. Critics began to suggest that Wright's expatriation was handicapping his talents. Moreover, with the emergence of new writers, critics were asserting that Wright was out of touch with the African American experience. Nevertheless, these novels further the signature themes that reverberate in his body of work: psychological despair, interracial conflict, and Black American manhood.

Emerging as a true Renaissance man, Wright continued to broaden the scope of his intellectual interests. As African nations struggled for their independence, he became increasingly interested in the "Mother Land." He decided to visit the Gold Coast, now known as Ghana, in June 1953. In *Black Power: A Record of Reactions in a Land of Pathos* (1954) Wright observes **colonialism** as it affects the formally educated elite and the tradition-faithful masses. He was troubled by the clashing belief systems of these two groups. He questioned how a country could modernize while tied to tribal identity. Wright was befuddled by observance of ancient cultural rites, even among the Western-educated.

Considering the extent of Wright's international travels, his productivity during the 1950s was phenomenal. He followed *Black Power* with an analysis of the political aspirations of Third World nations in *The Color Curtain: A Report on the Bandung Conference* (1956) and social criticism of Spain, detailed in *Pagan Spain* (1957). With renewed vigor Wright recommitted himself to fiction. In 1957 he published a collection of essays on class, culture, and the construction of literary ideas: *White Man, Listen!*

Rather than revisit the theme of alienation, Wright returned in his final novel to a rural setting and the problematic relationship between American Whites and Blacks. Today *The Long Dream* (1958) is deemed by many scholars to be an exceptional effort, second only to his *Native Son*. *The Long Dream* focuses on the Tucker family and their identification with American capitalism. Once again, Wright constructs morally ambivalent figures to address a larger point about the economic system of the United States and the values that are sacrificed in order to maintain it. The Tucker father and son must reconcile their manipulation of the African American community with their victimization by the White power structure.

Wright's death from heart failure on November 28, 1960, marked the passing of one of the most important authors in American history and modern literary history. Toward the end of his life, he returned to poetry as a creative outlet. **Haiku** proved to be liberating for Wright, enabling him to focus on essences rather than structure and character motivation. Owing to his exposure to new peoples and ideas, many scholars are left with the impression that he was going through a transitional stage in his career. As his biographer Michel Fabre mused, "everything seems to indicate that Wright's fiction was ... headed in a new direction" (527). Wright introduced refreshing perspectives on criminal behavior and psychological neurosis into American fiction. He also compelled American novelists to reconceptualize the way that they dealt with Black characterization. Wright's legacy, and the impact of *Native Son*, was strongest during the **Chicago Renaissance**, the **Protest Literature** era, and the **Black Arts Movement**. Richard Wright's body of work contributes to the fields of sociology, political science, cultural studies, Whiteness Studies, **gender** studies, **queer theory**, and many other facets of American literature and criticism. (*See* **Expatriate Writers; Federal Writers' Project; Lynching; Marxism; Protest Literature**.)

Resources: Primary Sources: Richard Wright: *Black Boy (American Hunger): A Record of Childhood and Youth* (1945; repr. New York: HarperPerennial, 1998); *Black Power: A Record of Reactions in a Land of Pathos* (1954; repr. Westport, CT: Greenwood Press, 1974); *The Color Curtain: A Report on the Bandung Conference* (1956; repr. Jackson, MS: Banner Books, 1995); *Eight Men* (1961; repr. New York: HarperPerennial, 1996); *Haiku: This Other World* (New York: Arcade, 1998); "I Tried to Be a Communist," *Atlantic Monthly*, Aug.–Sept. 1944, repr. in *The God That Failed*, ed. Richard Crossman (Chicago: Regnery, 1983); *Lawd Today!* (1963; repr. Boston: Northeastern University Press, 1991); *The Long Dream* (1958; repr. Boston: Northeastern University Press, 1986); *Native Son* (1940; repr. New York: HarperPerennial, 1998); *The Outsider* (1953; repr. New York: HarperPerennial, 1993); *Pagan Spain* (1957; repr. Jackson, MS: Banner Books, 2002); *Savage Holiday* (1954; repr. Jackson, MS: Banner Books, 1994); *Uncle Tom's Children* (1938; repr. New York: HarperPerennial, 1993); *White Man, Listen!* (1957; repr. New York: HarperPerennial, 1995). **Secondary Sources:** James Baldwin, *Notes of a Native Son* (1963; repr. Boston: Beacon Press, 1984); Michel Fabre, *The Unfinished Quest of Richard Wright*, trans. Isabel Barzun, 2nd ed. (Urbana: University of Illinois Press, 1993); Henry Louis Gates, Jr., and K. A. Appiah, eds., *Richard Wright: Critical Perspectives Past and Present* (New York: Amistad, 1993); Addison Gayle, *Richard Wright: Ordeal of a Native Son* (Garden City, NY: Doubleday, 1980); Yoshinobu Hakutani, *Richard Wright and Racial Discourse* (Columbia: University of Missouri Press, 1996); Joyce Ann Joyce, *Richard Wright's Art of Tragedy* (Iowa City: University of Iowa Press, 1986); Hazel Rowley, *Richard Wright:*

The Life and Times (New York: Henry Holt, 2001); Virginia Whatley Smith, ed., Richard Wright's Travel Writings (Jackson: University Press of Mississippi, 2001); Tyler Stovall, Paris Noir: African Americans in the City of Light (Boston: Houghton Mifflin, 1996); Ellen Wright and Michel Fabre., eds., Richard Wright Reader (New York: Da Capo Press, 1997).

Lawrence A. Davis

Wright, Sarah Elizabeth (born 1928). Poet and novelist. Sarah Elizabeth Wright's work concerns Black men and women who must struggle to survive in an American society that makes life hard for poor people, Black people, and women. Wright was born in rural Maryland in 1928 to parents who worked hard to raise their nine children. During the late 1940s she attended Howard University, where she met **Langston Hughes**; during the mid-1950s she lived in **Philadelphia, Pennsylvania**, where she learned the trades of printing and typesetting; and in 1959 she moved to **Harlem, New York**, where she became an active member of the Harlem Writers Guild, which included **John Oliver Killens**, **Alice Childress**, and **Paule Marshall**. Her published writings include a book of poetry titled *Give Me a Child* (1955), which she wrote and designed with her friend Lucy Smith, and a novel titled *This Child's Gonna Live*, originally published in 1969 and kept in print ever since by the Feminist Press (Guilford, 293–295).

Wright's work is unique in the African American literary tradition because of the attention she pays to the ways that Black women and men must and do work together to fight the sometimes violent oppression of White America. While some of her contemporaries, such as **Richard Wright** and **Ann Lane Petry**, focused on the experiences of either Black men or Black women, Wright always sees both together, and sees, too, as John Oliver Killens writes of her work, that "the children are especially oppressed" (Killens, 279). Both Wright's poetry and her novel emphasize how difficult, yet vital, it is for parents to raise children who will help the community continue. That some children die from disease, starvation, and violence can make parts of Wright's novel very difficult to read.

Even though Wright has not published prolifically since the late 1960s, her work remains very important because of her beautiful rendering of Black **vernacular**. The language of her characters enables her readers to feel as though they are hearing the actual voices of people on Maryland's Eastern shore in the 1920s, and these voices are not controlled by a narrator who uses conventional middle-class grammar. Wright's use of language ensures that people who read her poems and novels will never forget the characters they meet.

Resources: Jennifer Campbell, "Afterword," in *This Child's Gonna Live*, by Sarah Elizabeth Wright (New York: Feminist Press, 2002); Virginia Guilford, "Sarah Elizabeth Wright," in *Dictionary of Literary Biography*, vol. 33, *Afro-American Fiction Writers after 1955*, ed. Thadious M. Davis and Trudier Harris (Detroit: Gale, 1984), 293–300; John Oliver Killens, "An Appreciation," in *This Child's Gonna Live*, by Sarah Elizabeth Wright (New York: Feminist Press, 2002), 277–286; Sarah E. Wright,

This Child's Gonna Live (1969; New York: Feminist Press, 2002); Sarah E. Wright and Lucy Smith, *Give Me a Child* (Philadelphia: Kraft, 1955).

Jennifer Campbell

Wright, Zara (flourished 1920s). Novelist. Biographical information on Zara Wright is scarce, but it is known she lived and published in **Chicago, Illinois**, in the 1920s. She is included in John Taitt's *Souvenir of Negro Progress* (1925) with ten other prominent members of the Chicago Black community. Wright is referred to as the author of *Black and White Tangled Threads* (1920) and is one of only two women mentioned in *Souvenir*. This suggests that her work was recognized and respected by the community. She was married to J. Edward Smith, to whom she dedicated her two novels, *Black and White Tangled Threads* and the sequel, *Kenneth*. The novels were privately published as one volume in 1920 and immediately went out of print. They were reissued in 1975. They are melodramatic and romantic novels whose plots center around interracial relations, race consciousness, and the **passing** of Black people as White. Wright wrote during the **Harlem Renaissance** and used many of the potentially volatile themes employed by the movement's male writers, yet critics have noted the absence of sex and violence in her books. Maggie Sale draws parallels between Wright and other "proper middle-class, almost Victorian, black women" writers such as **Angelina Weld Grimké**, **Alice Moore Dunbar-Nelson**, and **Jesse Redmond Fauset**, and suggests that Wright's inspiration came mainly from nineteenth-century women writers such as **Harriet Ann Jacobs** and **Frances Ellen Watkins Harper** (Sale, xvi).

Black and White Tangled Threads is set primarily in Louisville, Kentucky, and follows the fate of Zoleeta, the child of the son of a plantation owner and the daughter of a slave. The story focuses on Zoleeta's introduction into her White Southern family, the obstacles to her marriage to Lord Blankleigh, and her ignorance of her mixed-race heritage. Despite a fairy-tale plot, Wright realistically portrayed the prevailing racism in **the South** after **Reconstruction**. Through Zoleeta, Wright described the difficulties but also possibilities of a mixed-race marriage and the personal costs involved in passing as White. In *Kenneth*, Wright explored the relationship between a White woman and a Black man. Alice Bair, the daughter of a wealthy banker, falls in love with Dr. Philip Grayson, a handsome doctor who has saved her life. The depiction of Alice as the aggressive pursuer and Dr. Grayson as her unwilling love object is a departure from the stereotypical notion that Black men always desire White women. The book also hints at the danger in which Alice's advances put Dr. Grayson. Loretta G. Woodard points out that *Kenneth* indirectly addressed "the common southern practice of lynching black men for any attention or insults to white women" (Woodard, 284). Wright's novels have been described by critics as nineteenth-century melodramas "with a different twist" (Shockley, 280). According to Sale, they challenge assumptions of what is considered new and original, and urge readers to "discover the significance and originality in the older and familiar" (Sale, xxxi). (*See* **Lynching**.)

Resources: *Afro-American Women Writers 1746–1933: An Anthology and Critical Guide*, ed. Ann Allen Shockley (Boston: G. K. Hall, 1988); Maggie Sale, "Introduction," in *Black and White Tangled Threads and Kenneth*, by Zara Wright (New York: G. K. Hall, 1994); Loretta G. Woodard, "Wright, Zara," in *African American Authors, 1745–1945: A Bio-Bibliographical Critical Sourcebook*, ed. Emmanuel S. Nelson (Westport, CT: Greenwood Press, 2000); Zara Wright, *Black and White Tangled Threads and Kenneth* (New York: G. K. Hall, 1994).

Malin Lidström Brock

Y

Yarbrough, Camille (born 1934). Performance poet, children's writer, dancer, singer, actor, and teacher. Working in a variety of media, Yarbrough has spent the majority of her life illuminating and transmitting African American culture and literature. She was born and grew up on **Chicago, Illinois**'s South Side and found early artistic stimulation in the community. By the age of seventeen, she had begun studying variations of **Katherine Dunham**'s dance techniques and later toured with Dunham's dance company from 1955 to 1961. This experience exposed her to dances from throughout the African **diaspora**. Yarbrough later taught African dance at Southern Illinois University and City College New York during the 1980s.

After moving to New York City in 1961, Yarbrough began an acting and singing career, performing on and off Broadway in such shows as *Kwamina* (1961), *Trumpets of the Lord* (1969), *Sambo* (1969), and **Lorraine Hansberry**'s *To Be Young, Gifted and Black* (1970). She appeared in the 1971 film *Shaft*, and she had recurring roles on the daytime soap operas *Search for Tomorrow* and *Where the Heart Is*. In the 1970s, Yarbrough developed a one-woman show, titled *Tales and Tunes of an African American Griot*, that blended **drama**, dance, song, storytelling, and poetry into an Afrocentric performance, which she later recorded as the album *The Iron Pot Cooker* (1975).

In addition to her performance career, Yarbrough is recognized as the author of several books for children and young adults, such as *Cornrows* (1979), *Little Tree Growing in the Shade* (1985), *The Shimmershine Queens* (1989), and *Tamika and the Wisdom Rings* (1996). Each of her books explores aspects of African American identity, culture, community, and history. Yarbrough continues to perform for children and adults through her African American Traditions Workshop in New York City. (*See* **Performance Poetry.**)

Resources: Primary Sources: Camille Yarbrough: *Cornrows* (New York: Coward, McCann & Geoghegan, 1979); *The Iron Pot Cooker* (New York: Vanguard, 1975), audio CD; *Little Tree Growing in the Shade* (New York: Putnam, 1985); *The Shimmershine Queens* (New York: Putnam, 1989); *Tamika and the Wisdom Rings* (New York: Random House, 1994); *Watch Hour* (New York: Putnam, 2005). Secondary Sources: William L. Andrews, Frances Smith Foster, and Trudier Harris, eds., *The Oxford Companion to African American Literature* (New York: Oxford University Press, 1997); Bernice E. Cullinan and Diane G. Person, eds., *The Continuum Encyclopedia of Children's Literature* (New York: Continuum, 2001); Barbara Thrash Murphy, *Black Authors and Illustrators of Books for Children and Young Adults: A Biographical Dictionary*, 3rd ed. (New York: Garland, 1999); Barbara Rollock, *Black Authors and Illustrators of Children's Books*, 2nd ed. (New York: Garland, 1992).

Anthony J. Ratcliff

Yerby, Frank Garvin (1916–1991). Novelist, poet, and short story writer. Yerby published more than thirty books with sales of more than fifty-five million hardback and paperback copies over a forty-year span; his books were published in eighty-two countries and twenty-three languages (Draper, 2022). An early novel, *The Foxes of Harrow* (1946), was translated into twelve languages and made into a motion picture in 1947 (Draper, 2030). Also adapted to the cinema were *The Golden Hawk* (1948) and *The Saracen Blade* (1952).

Yerby was born in Augusta, Georgia, on September 5, 1916, to an interracial couple: Rufus Garvin Yerby and Wilhelmina Smythe Yerby. His mother was Scots-Irish, a grandparent was an Indian, and his father was African American (Draper, 2022). After attending a private school for Blacks during his primary and high school years, Yerby graduated from Paine College in Augusta, Georgia, with a B.A. in English. He earned an M.A. in English from Fisk University (**Nashville, Tennessee**) in 1938 (Goldsberry, 2985). In 1944 Yerby wrote his first award-winning short story, "Health Card." Yerby was twice married, in 1941 to Flora Helen Claire Williams, with whom he had two sons and two daughters, and in 1956 to Blanca Calle Perez. Yerby lived in Madrid, Spain, from the mid-1950s until his death on November 29, 1991.

Although Yerby's novels did not receive critical acclaim, he became very wealthy from sales of his books. Yerby defended his decision to create White rather than Black characters by stating, "The novelist hasn't any right to inflict on the public his private ideas on politics, religion, or race. If he wants to preach he should go on the pulpit" (Gunton and Stine, 487–491; Draper, 2022).

Yerby's novel *The Dahomean: An Historical Novel* (1971) is set in Africa during the nineteenth century. Yerby believed that this work vindicated him from his reputation of writing about Whites rather than Africans or African Americans. After the publication of this novel, he noted that African American readers seemed to bring him back into the fold while critics believed he had written a masterpiece (Draper, 2023). *The Dahomean* depicts the cruelty of **slavery** and is widely considered to be one of Yerby's finest works. In the *Massachusetts Review* (1968), critic **Darwin T. Turner** published a scathing assessment of Yerby's works and his personal character, stating that "Yerby did not prove effective as a symbol. He refused to plead for the race; he abandoned America without shrieking that bigotry had exiled him from his home; he earned a fortune writing his books and spent his time racing sports cars and lolling on beaches" (569).

Yerby's article "How and Why I Write the Costume Novel" (*Harper's Magazine*, October 1959) discusses three main ingredients of "the costume novel": a charming protagonist who is a dominant male, a heroine who must have a definable sexuality about her, and a strong, external conflict. (*See* **Expatriate Writers.**)

Resources: Primary Sources: Frank Yerby: *Benton's Row* (New York: Dial, 1954); *Bride of Liberty* (Garden City, NY: Doubleday, 1954); *Captain Rebel* (New York: Dial, 1956); *The Dahomean* (New York: Dial, 1971); *A Darkness at Ingraham's Crest: A Tale of the Slaveholding South* (New York: Dial, 1979); *Floodtide* (New York: Dial, 1950); *The Foxes of Harrow* (New York: Dial, 1946); *Golden Hawk* (New York: Dial, 1948); *The Man from Dahomey* (London: Heinemann, 1971); *An Odor of Sanctity: A Novel of Medieval Moorish Spain* (New York: Dial, 1965); *A Woman Called Fancy* (New York: Dial, 1951). **Secondary Sources:** James P. Draper, ed., *Black Literature Criticism*, vol. 3 (Detroit: Gale, 1992), 2022–2031; Dennis Goldsberry, "Frank Yerby," in *Critical Survey of Long Fiction: English Language Series*, ed. Frank N. Magill (Englewood Cliffs, NJ: Salem Press, 1983), 2985–2992; Sharon R. Gunton and Jean C. Stine, eds., *Contemporary Literary Criticism*, vol. 22 (Detroit: Gale, 1982), 487–491; Darwin T. Turner, "Frank Yerby as Debunker," *Massachusetts Review* 9 (1968), 569–577.

Deloice Holliday

Young, Al (born 1939). Poet, novelist, journalist, essayist, and screenwriter. Young is known a prolific, versatile, politically alert writer. He was born in Ocean Springs, Mississippi, and spent his formative years in **Detroit, Michigan**, where, because of his achievements as a writer, he was given the key to the city in 1982. Young describes his formative years as time spent acquiring his skills of listening and communicating. Young was very much aware of his love for the written word, even as he worked as a deejay at Detroit radio station WDET and at KJAZ in Berkeley. While growing up, he visited the exhibits at the Detroit Institute of Arts and Wayne State University. His interest in literature had begun while he listened to stories told in the rich Mississippi oral tradition of his family. His reading began in Detroit, where he discovered the poetry section of the Detroit Public Library when he was in the second grade.

Young attended the University of Michigan, where he majored in Spanish. A gifted musician, he played guitar at bars in Ann Arbor. Young's father, who retired from the Navy, was also a musician, but neither of them liked certain aspects of the **jazz** musician's lifestyle. Although Young was able to make a good living through performing while he was in college, and when he traveled to **San Francisco, California**, after leaving the University of Michigan, he returned to college in 1969 and graduated with honors from the University of California at Berkeley. His musical influences can be seen in his autobiographical novel *Kinds of Blue: Musical Memoirs* (1984), in which Young takes the reader through every phase of his life, using songs ranging from James Brown's "Cold Sweat" to Miles Davis's "All Blues." Young says of his style:

> The poetry influences I grew up with were such that, all my life, I have sought to communicate. Self-expression just doesn't cut it for me. From my southern upbringing—and all that oral storytelling and recitation you've heard about is no joke, it is unforgettably real—I formed the idea that a poem, a story, a statement of any kind was not complete until somebody got it. (Gonzales)

Young sought to communicate what he felt was a view of life that transcended racial and political issues, and he has been criticized because he did not always write in the style of the popular Black protest poets of his day. Interested in the **Beat Movement** poets of his generation and the global voice of poets such as Federico García Lorca, the early T. S. Eliot, Rabindranath Tagore, Vladimir Mayakovsky, Léopold Senghor, Blaise Cendrars, Nicolás Guillén, Nicanor Parra, LeRoi Jones (**Amiri Baraka**), Denise Levertov, Samuel Taylor Coleridge, John Keats, Percy Bysshe Shelley, Emily Dickinson, Walt Whitman, and Ezra Pound, Young created his own voice in the character of O. O. Gabugah. Gabugah was a comic alter ego, much like **Langston Hughes**'s character "Simple," who made humorous observations on issues within the Black community and the posturing that was taking place among artists. Young was not the first Black artist to struggle with such issues as what constituted true "Black art" and whether the primary concern of Black artists should be **racial uplift**. **Romare Bearden** and **Zora Neale Hurston**, who created in their art flawed images of Blacks, were criticized for not paying their "debt to the uplifting of the race." Young's poetry often begins with a single image and completes that image, while his novels usually have a universal idea that he explores throughout the novel.

Although Young thinks of himself as seeing what humans have in common, instead of exploring their differences, his writings sometimes suggest that the world does not always celebrate his view. His poem "Herrick Hospital, Fifth Floor" is dedicated to a musician friend who "overdosed on blackness" and now is "locked between Blue Cross nurse-padded walls" while the air outside is "shot up with softening Berkeley sunshine."

Young reminds the reader that he is keenly aware of who he is and what dangers his Blackness represents in America. His writings that can be found on his Web site include *A Piece of Cake*, which is a sequel to Young's celebrated novel *Sitting Pretty*. *Mad, Bad and Dangerous to Know: Or Opus de Funk* is an account in verse of Lord Byron and Lady Caroline Lamb's infamous romance of 1812. *The Literature of California, Volume Two*, edited with scholar-critic Jack Hicks and novelists James D. Houston and Maxine Hong Kingston and *CitiZen: Spirit & Democracy*, a collection of column-length conversations between O. O. Gabugah and Young on current events and democracy in America, are also included.

In the 1970s and 1980s, Young founded the journals *Yardbird Reader* and *Quilt* with the poet and novelist **Ishmael Reed**. His work has been widely anthologized and translated into many languages. Among Young's numerous honors are fellowships from the National Endowment for the Arts and the Guggenheim Foundation, a Wallace Stegner Fellowship, a Fulbright Fellowship, the Joseph Henry Jackson Award, the PEN/Library of Congress Award for Short Fiction, and an American Book Award. Young has also edited a number of books, including *African American Literature: A Brief Introduction and Anthology* (1996) and *Yardbird Lives!* with Ishmael Reed (1978).

Resources: Primary Sources: Jack Hicks, James D. Houston, Maxine Hong Kingston, and Al Young, eds., *The Literature of California*, vol. 1, *Native American Beginnings to 1945* (Berkeley: University of California Press, 2000); Al Young: *Ask Me Now* (New York: McGraw-Hill, 1980); *The Blues Don't Change: New and Selected Poems* (Berkeley, CA: Creative Arts, 1976); *Bodies and Soul: Musical Memoirs* (Berkeley, CA: Creative Arts, 1981); *Dancing: Poems* (New York: Corinth, 1969); *Drowning in the Sea of Love: Musical Memoirs* (Hopewell, NJ: Ecco, 1995); *Geography of the Near Past* (New York: Holt, Rinehart and Winston, 1976); *Heaven: Collected Poems, 1956–1990* (Berkeley, CA: Creative Arts, 1992); *Kinds of Blue: Musical Memoirs* (Berkeley, CA: Creative Arts, 1976); *Seduction by Light* (New York: Delta, 1988); *Sitting Pretty* (Berkeley, CA: Creative Arts, 1976); *Snakes: A Novel* (New York: Holt, Rinehart and Winston, 1970); *The Song Turning Back into Itself* (New York: Holt, Rinehart and Winston 1971); Web site, http://www.alyoung.org; *Who Is Angelina?* (Berkeley: University of California Press, 1975); Al Young and Janet Coleman, *Mingus/Mingus: Two Memoirs* (Berkeley, CA: Creative Arts, 1989). **Secondary Sources:** Douglass Bolling, "Artistry and Theme in Al Young's *Snakes*," *Negro American Literature Forum* 8, no. 2 (Summer 1974), 223–225; Ray González, "A Lyrical Legacy: An Interview with Poet, Essayist, Novelist and Memorist Al Young: Part 2," *Bloomsbury Review* 21, no. 6 (Nov.–Dec. 2001), 7–8; Nathaniel Mackey, "Interview with Al Young," *MELUS* 5, no. 4 (Winter 1978), 32–51.

Imelda Hunt

Young, Andrew (born 1932). Pastor, civil rights leader, ambassador, U.S. congressperson, mayor, and autobiographer. Young has succeeded in a remarkable array of endeavors. He was born in **New Orleans, Louisiana,** and attended segregated schools. Later he enrolled at Howard University in **Washington, D.C.,** intending to pursue premedical studies, but his interests turned toward theology; ultimately, he earned a degree from the Hartford Theological Seminary (Connecticut) in 1955. Young served as a pastor in several churches in **the South,** met **Martin Luther King, Jr.,** and became involved in the **Civil Rights Movement**. He worked with King and **Ralph David Abernathy** in the Southern Christian Leadership Conference, which was heavily involved in the movement, until he resigned from the organization in 1970. Young was elected to the U.S. House of Representatives three times, representing a district in Georgia (1972, 1974, and 1976). After his third term had begun, he was appointed by President Jimmy Carter to serve as U.S. Ambassador to the United Nations. Young served in that post until 1979, when a controversy erupted over his having met secretly with officials from the Palestine Liberation Organization, and he was forced to resign. He went on to be elected to two terms as Mayor of Atlanta (1981–1988). In 1994, Young published his autobiography, A Way Out of No Way, which he subtitled Spiritual Memoirs and which recounts his growing up during the **Great Depression**, his spiritual vocation and the development of his faith, and his multifaceted political career. (*See* **Theology, Black and Womanist.**)

Resources: "Andrew Young," EB.com, http://search.eb.com/blackhistory/micro/650/54.html; Andrew DeRoche, Andrew Young: Civil Rights Ambassador (Lanham, MD: SR Books, 2003); "Making of an Issue, and a New Black Leader," The Economist, Aug. 25, 1979, pp. 21–23; Arthur J. Moore, "Andy Young's Gamble," Christianity and Crisis 37 (June 27, 1977), 146–147; Andrew Young, A Way Out of No Way: The Spiritual Memoirs of Andrew Young (Chicago: Thomas Nelson, 1994).

Hans Ostrom

Young, Kevin (born 1970). Poet, essayist, and editor. Kevin Young, one of the new generation of African American poets, was born in Lincoln, Nebraska, and attended high school in Kansas. He studied poetry at Harvard University under the American poet Lucie Brock-Broido and the Irish poet Seamus Heaney. After earning his Bachelor of Arts degree from Harvard in 1992, Young went on to receive a Master of Fine Arts degree in creative writing from Brown University in 1996. Along with his three books of poetry, Young is a widely published essayist, with essays appearing in The New Yorker and The Paris Review, among other publications. His individual poems have appeared in numerous journals and papers, including Poetry, Virginia Quarterly Review, and the New York Times. Young has also edited two anthologies. Giant Steps: The New Generation of African American Writers, a volume of fiction, poetry, and essays, appeared in 2000, followed in 2003 by Blues Poems, a volume of collected poems paying tribute to the history, form, and power of African American **blues** music. Young's three collections of his own poetry, Most Way Home (1995, reprinted in 2000), To Repel Ghosts (2001), and Jelly Roll: A Blues (2003), received numerous awards. To Repel Ghosts was a finalist for the James Laughlin Award from the Academy of American Poets, and Most Way Home, Young's first collection of poetry, was selected by **Lucille Clifton** for the National Poetry Series and brought him the John C. Zacharis First Book Award from Ploughshares.

Young calls his second book, To Repel Ghosts, a "double album" that honors the paintings of the late artist Jean-Michel Basquiat, who died of a heroin overdose at the age of twenty-seven, and whom Young describes as "the best painter of the 1980s era" (Rowell, 52). Jelly Roll, Young's third book of poetry, was a finalist for the 2003 National Book Award in Poetry and the 2003 Los Angeles Times Book Prize in Poetry. *Jelly Roll* also received the 2004 Patterson Poetry Prize. Young's other awards include fellowships from the Guggenheim Foundation and the MacDowell Colony. Young says about his poetry, "I find . . . that people relate to what I have to say, whether it's preserving peaches or disappearing rural life or the Southern love of ruin or what have you. In fact, for me the symbolic act of preserving proved central to the processes of [*Most Way Home*] and its making" (Rowell, 48).

Along with his intention to preserve the heritage of African American poetry and art, the effect of American music on Young's work is undeniable. *Jelly Roll*, for example, combines African American idiom with the tragic and comic spirit and tradition of the **blues**. In an interview with the journal **Callaloo**, for which he served as an advisory and contributing editor, Young asserts that "jazz is crucial for black poetry, period" (Rowell, 51). The binding under the jacket of *Jelly Roll* displays dozens of blues and **jazz** sheet music covers from Young's extensive personal collection. Young is known for his engaging and entertaining reading style. To get the full effect of his poetry, his readers are often advised to listen to and to watch him read his words in person. Currently Young is Ruth Lilly Professor of Poetry at Indiana University in Bloomington. He has also been an assistant professor of English and African American Studies at the University of Georgia, and has served as a Stegner Fellow in Poetry at Stanford University.

Resources: Charles H. Rowell, "An Interview with Kevin Young," *Callaloo* 21 (1998), 43–54; Kevin Young: *Jelly Roll: A Blues* (New York: Knopf, 2003); *Most Way Home* (New York: Morrow, 1995); *To Repel Ghosts* (Cambridge, MA: Zoland, 2001); Kevin Young, ed.: *Blues Poems* (New York: Knopf, 2003); *Giant Steps: The New Generation of African American Writers* (New York: Perennial, 2000).

Stephen Roger Powers

Youngblood, Shay (born 1959). Novelist, playwright, short story writer, screenwriter, and professor. Youngblood is a remarkably versatile writer who has earned acclaim for her plays, short stories, and novels. She is considered one of the most important African American lesbian writers in the late twentieth and early twenty-first centuries (Waugh). Youngblood was born in Columbus, Georgia, and attended Clark-Atlanta University, earning a B.A. in mass communication in 1981. She worked for a television station in **Atlanta, Georgia**, and she also served in the Peace Corps before earning an M.F.A. in creative writing at Brown University in 1993. Youngblood received critical and popular recognition in 1989 with the publication of *The Big Mama Stories*, which are narrated by a young African American woman and concern her experiences and relationships with older African American women who mentor her. The play *Shakin' the Mess Outta Misery* concerns characters and conflicts related to those in the "Big Mama" stories (Jake-ann Jones), and it enjoyed a highly successful debut in Atlanta in 1988. Youngblood's play *Talking Bones* debuted in **San Francisco, California**, in 1992, and *Amazing*

Grace, a play for children, opened in Minneapolis in 1995. *Talking Bones* earned Youngblood the **Lorraine Hansberry** Award in 1993 ("Shay Youngblood").

In her first novel, *Soul Kiss* (1997), which is set in rural Georgia, Youngblood explores **coming-of-age** themes. *Black Girl in Paris* (2000), as the title suggests, concerns a young African American woman making her way abroad. Youngblood has written and directed two short videos, and she has adapted *Shakin' the Mess Outta Misery* for the screen. In an interview, she said, "I can't say that [writing] has always been easy. But the part that's been really easy is that I have—I'm really passionate about writing and about the work that I do. I think I plant a lot of seeds. There's like all these different elements to the writing life" (Jake-ann Jones). She has taught at Brown University and at the New School for Social Research in New York City. (*See* **Lesbian Literature**.)

Resources: Mary Hoffman and Shay Youngblood, *Amazing Grace* (New York: Dramatists Play Service, 1998); Jake-ann Jones, "Interview with Shay Youngblood 1996," Brown University, http://www.brown.edu/Departments/English/Writing/youngblood .html; Joni L. Jones, "Conjuring as Radical Re/Membering in the Works of Shay Youngblood," in *Black Theatre: Ritual Performance in the African Diaspora*, ed. Paul Carter Harrison, Victor Leo Walker II, and Gus Edwards (Philadelphia: Temple University Press, 2002), 227–235; "Shay Youngblood," *Women of Color, Women of Words*, http://www.scils.rutgers.edu/ ~cybers/youngblood2.html; Debra Riggins Waugh, "Delicious, Forbidden: An Interview with Shay Youngblood," *Lambda Book Report* 6, no. 2 (Sept. 1997), 1, 6–7; Paula L. Woods, "Writing, Activism, and Coming-of-Age Tales," *High Plains Literary Review* 12, no. 2 (Fall 1997), 119–124; Shay Youngblood: *The Big Mama Stories* (New York: Firebrand, 1989); *Black Girl in Paris* (New York: Riverhead, 2000); *Shakin' the Mess Outta Misery* (Woodstock, IL: Dramatic Publishing, 1994); *Soul Kiss* (New York: Riverhead, 1997); *Talking Bones: A Play* (Woodstock, IL: Dramatic Publishing, 1994).

Hans Ostrom

Z

Zane (born 1967). Novelist, short story writer, and publisher. Zane is the pseudonym of a best-selling writer of **erotica** who has never allowed herself to be photographed, revealed her true identity, or done television interviews. She remains a mystery and has always intrigued her audiences with erotic writing for the African American audience. She debuted in 1999, when she self-published her first book, a collection of forty short stories titled *The Sex Chronicles*. The impetus for the book can be traced to three years earlier, when Zane sent erotic stories via e-mail to friends, who soon demanded more. Zane created the Web site *Erotica Noir* (http://www.eroticanoir.com) and began distributing an electronic newsletter that included her erotic writing, both to promote her writing and to reach a wider audience within the African American community. Her writing began to reach editors at major publishing houses, but when she was approached with contracts from these publishers, they wanted her to censor her writing to make it less racy before they would publish her writing.

Zane refused to compromise her writing, and in 1999 she founded Strebor Books International, which published *The Sex Chronicles* in an initial printing of 3,000 copies. To date, her first book has sold more than 50,000 copies, and her following titles, *Addicted* and *Shame on It All*, were equally successful. From street vendors to Barnes & Noble and Borders Books, Zane's books have had brisk sales and have made the *Essence* and *Washington Post* best-seller lists. In 2001, at the age of thirty-four, Zane began writing and publishing full-time. She garnered a book deal with Pocket Books to publish her work as trade paperbacks and secured a contract for seven more titles. In addition to her own novels and short stories, Zane has edited or contributed to several anthologies, including *Chocolate Flava: The Eroticanoir.com Anthology*, *Best Black Women's Erotica*, *Brown Sugar 2*, and *Best American Erotica 2003*.

Despite the popularity of her books, Zane has met with criticism that her books aren't well written or are too **vernacular**—charges many popular Black writers have faced. And yet her titles remain best-sellers because of their popular appeal—a writing style that every Black woman or man can relate to. When Zane released *The Sisters of APF: The Indoctrination of Soror Ride Dick*, a novel that revisited characters introduced in *The Sex Chronicles* and follows the exploits of women in a sorority that believes in open sexuality, she received requests from women throughout the country who wanted to form chapters of their own.

Strebor Books has also met with success, and Zane has brought several authors onto the literary scene in a variety of genres including **science fiction**, **crime and mystery fiction**, urban dramas, and erotica. Strebor Books has a distribution deal with Simon and Schuster and a regular publishing schedule, and has provided unprecedented opportunities for Black writers. Strebor's author list, twenty-two strong, includes Lee Hayes, Michelle Valentine, Franklin White, and Jonathan Luckett.

Resources: Zane: *Addicted* (New York: Pocket Books, 2001); *Afterburn* (New York: Atria, 2005); *Gettin' Buck Wild: Sex Chronicles II* (New York: Atria, 2002); *Nervous* (New York: Atria, 2003); *The Sex Chronicles: Shattering the Myth* (New York: Pocket Books, 2002); *Shame on It All* (2001; New York: Atria, 2003); *The Sisters of APF: The Indoctrination of Soror Ride Dick* (New York: Atria, 2003); *Skyscraper* (New York: Atria, 2003); Zane, ed., *Chocolate Flava: The Eroticanoir.com Anthology* (New York: Atria, 2004).

Roxane Gay

Zu-Bolton, Ahmos, II (born 1935). Poet and playwright. Zu-Bolton is a veteran of the **Black Arts Movement**, and he is distinguished for his empathetic depiction of African Americans and his commitment to the preservation of African American culture. One example is Zu-Bolton's commitment to the Black oral tradition. According to Mona Lisa Saloy, in her essay "African American Oral Traditions in Louisiana," Zu-Bolton's "storytelling," which he learned from his family, "reflects his front porch introduction to the tradition. He has enjoyed a successful writing career while holding onto his oral roots." And, according to **Lorenzo Thomas**, Zu-Bolton's career exemplifies the Black Arts Movement idea that African American artists should be "cultural workers," responsive and responsible to their communities, affirming the belief Zu-Bolton expressed in his poem "Struggle-Road Dance" (from the book *A Niggered Amen*) that "this place/must be a workshop." Zu-Bolton's role as poet, according to Thomas, is complemented by his work as literary editor, small press publisher, teacher, and organizer of cultural events.

Zu-Bolton is the author of *A Niggered Amen*, a collection of poetry; editor with **E. Ethelbert Miller** of the *Synergy D.C. Anthology*; founder of *Hoo-Doo* magazine; and organizer of HooDoo Festivals that have featured writers and musicians performing their works in parts of Louisiana and **Texas**. Zu-Bolton's plays include *The Widow Paris: A Folklore of Marie Laveau*, *The Funeral*, and *Family Reunion*.

Ahmos Zu-Bolton II was born in Poplarville, Mississippi, on October 21, 1935. He grew up in the rural community of DeRidder, Louisiana, the oldest of thirteen children. His poems and plays are often portraits of people from his hometown. Zu-Bolton has received creative fellowships from the National Endowment for the Arts and the Louisiana Division on the Arts. He earned a bachelor's degree in English literature and journalism from California State Polytechnic University in 1971.

Resources: William L. Andrews, Francis Smith Foster, and Trudier Harris, eds., *The Oxford Companion to African American Literature* (New York: Oxford University Press, 1997), 800; John Oliver Killens and Jerry W. Ward, Jr., eds., *Black Southern Voices: An Anthology of Fiction, Poetry, Drama, Nonfiction, and Critical Essays* (New York: Meridian, 1992); Mona Lisa Saloy, "African American Oral Traditions in Louisiana," *Louisiana's Living Traditions* (May 1998), http://www.louisianafolklife.org/lt/articles%5Fessays/creole%5Fart%5Fafrican%5Fam%5Foral.html; Lorenzo Thomas, "Ahmos Zu-Bolton II," in *Dictionary of Literary Biography*, vol. 41, ed. Trudier Harris and Thadious M. Davis (Detroit: Gale, 1985), 360–364; Ahmos Zu-Bolton II, *A Niggered Amen: Poems* (San Luis Obispo, CA: Solo Press, 1975); Ahmos Zu-Bolton II and E. Ethelbert Miller, eds., *Synergy D.C. Anthology* (Washington, DC: Energy Blacksouth, 1975).

John Greer Hall

GENERAL BIBLIOGRAPHY AND RESOURCES

This section has four parts: Reference Sources; Anthologies; Criticism; and Selected Organizations, Museums, and Research Centers.

REFERENCE SOURCES (COMPILED BY LORI RICIGLIANO)

Aberjhani and Sandra L. West. *Encyclopedia of the Harlem Renaissance*. New York: Facts on File, 2003.

Andrews, William L., Frances Smith Foster, and Trudier Harris, eds. *The Oxford Companion to African American Literature*. New York: Oxford University Press, 1997.

Arata, Esther Spring, and Nicholas John Rotoli. *Black American Playwrights, 1800 to the Present: A Bibliography*. Metuchen, NJ: Scarecrow, 1976.

Arata, Esther Spring, et al. *More Black American Playwrights: A Bibliography*. Metuchen, NJ: Scarecrow, 1978.

Asante, Molefi K., and Mark T. Mattson. *The African-American Atlas: Black History and Culture. An Illustrated Reference*. New York: Macmillan, 1998.

Bassett, John Earl. *Harlem in Review: Critical Reactions to Black American Writers, 1917–1939*. Selinsgrove, PA: Susquehanna University Press, 1992.

Bruccoli, Matthew J., and Judith S. Baughman, eds. *Modern African American Writers*. New York: Facts on File, 1994.

Campbell, Dorothy W. *Index to Black American Writers in Collective Biographies*. Littleton, CO: Libraries Unlimited, 1983.

Chapman, Dorothy Hilton. *Index to Black Poetry*. Boston: G. K. Hall, 1974.

Chapman, Dorothy Hilton, comp. *Index to Poetry by Black American Women*. Westport, CT: Greenwood Press, 1986.

Davis, Thadious M., and Trudier Harris, eds. *Afro-American Fiction Writers after 1955.* *Dictionary of Literary Biography*, vol. 33. Detroit: Gale, 1984. Also *Literature Resource Center*, http://www.galegroup.com.

———. *Afro-American Writers after 1955: Dramatists and Prose Writers. Dictionary of Literary Biography*, vol. 38. Detroit: Gale, 1985. Also *Literature Resource Center*, http://www.galegroup.com.

Draper, James P., ed. *Black Literature Criticism: Excerpts from Criticism of the Most Significant Works of Black Authors over the Past 200 Years.* 3 vols. Detroit: Gale, 1992.

Elliot, Emory, ed. *Columbia Literary History of the United States.* New York: Columbia University Press, 1988.

Fairbanks, Carol, and Eugene A. Engeldinger. *Black American Fiction: A Bibliography.* Metuchen, NJ: Scarecrow, 1978.

Frankovich, Nicholas, and David Larzelere, eds. *The Columbia Granger's Index to African-American Poetry.* New York: Columbia University Press, 1999.

French, William P., and Geneviève Fabre. *Afro-American Poetry and Drama, 1760–1975: A Guide to Information Sources.* Detroit: Gale, 1979.

Gavin, Christy, ed. *African American Women Playwrights: A Research Guide.* New York: Garland, 1999.

Graham, Maryemma, ed. *The Cambridge Companion to the African American Novel.* New York: Cambridge University Press, 2004.

Harris, Trudier, ed. *Afro-American Writers, 1940–1955. Dictionary of Literary Biography*, vol. 76. Detroit: Gale, 1988. Also *Literature Resource Center*, http://www.galegroup.com.

Harris, Trudier, and Thadious M. Davis, eds. *Afro-American Poets Since 1955. Dictionary of Literary Biography*, vol. 41. Detroit: Gale, 1985. Also *Literature Resource Center*, http://www.galegroup.com.

———. *Afro-American Writers before the Harlem Renaissance. Dictionary of Literary Biography*, vol. 50. Detroit: Gale, 1986. Also *Literature Resource Center*, http://www.galegroup.com.

———. *Afro-American Writers from the Harlem Renaissance to 1940. Dictionary of Literary Biography*, vol. 51. Detroit: Gale, 1987. Also *Literature Resource Center*, http://www.galegroup.com.

Hatch, James V., and Omanii Abdullah, comps. and eds. *Black Playwrights, 1823–1977: An Annotated Bibliography of Plays.* New York: Bowker, 1977.

Hedgepeth, Chester M., Jr. *Twentieth-Century African-American Writers and Artists.* Chicago: American Library Association, 1991.

Hunter, Jeffrey W., and Jerry Moore, eds. *Black Literature Criticism: Excerpts from Criticism of the Most Significant Works of Black Authors over the Past 200 Years. Supplement.* Detroit: Gale, 1999.

Jordan, Casper LeRoy, comp. *A Bibliographical Guide to African-American Women Writers.* Westport, CT: Greenwood Press, 1993.

Kallenbach, Jessamine S., comp. *Index to Black American Literary Anthologies.* Boston: G. K. Hall, 1979.

Kutenplon, Deborah, and Ellen Olmstead. *Young Adult Fiction by African American Writers, 1968–1993: A Critical and Annotated Guide.* New York: Garland, 1996.

Magill, Frank N., ed. *Masterpieces of African-American Literature.* New York: HarperCollins, 1992.

———. *Masterplots II: African American Literature Series.* 3 vols. Pasadena, CA: Salem, 1994.

Margolies, Edward, and David Bakish. *Afro-American Fiction, 1853–1976: A Guide to Information Sources.* Detroit: Gale, 1979.

Metzger, Linda, et al., eds. *Black Writers: A Selection of Sketches from Contemporary Authors.* Detroit: Gale, 1989.

Miller, R. Baxter. *Langston Hughes and Gwendolyn Brooks: A Reference Guide.* Boston: G. K. Hall, 1978.

Murphy, Barbara Thrash. *Black Authors and Illustrators of Books for Children and Young Adults: A Biographical Dictionary.* 3rd ed. New York: Garland, 1999.

Nelson, Emmanuel S., ed. *African American Authors, 1745–1945: A Bio-Bibliographical Critical Sourcebook.* Westport, CT: Greenwood Press, 2000.

———. *African American Dramatists: An A to Z Guide.* Westport, CT: Greenwood Press, 2004.

———. *Contemporary African American Novelists: A Bio-Bibliographical Critical Sourcebook.* Westport, CT: Greenwood Press, 1999.

Ostrom, Hans. *A Langston Hughes Encyclopedia.* Westport, CT: Greenwood Press, 2002.

Peavy, Charles D. *Afro-American Literature and Culture Since World War II: A Guide to Information Sources.* Detroit: Gale, 1979.

Peterson, Bernard L., Jr. *Contemporary Black American Playwrights and Their Plays: A Biographical Directory and Dramatic Index.* Westport, CT: Greenwood Press, 1988.

———. *Early Black American Playwrights and Dramatic Writers: A Biographical Directory and Catalog of Plays, Films, and Broadcasting Scripts.* Westport, CT: Greenwood Press, 1990.

Pettis, Joyce Owens. *African American Poets: Lives, Works, and Sources.* Westport, CT: Greenwood Press, 2002.

Richards, Phillip M., and Neil Schlager. *Best Literature by and about Blacks.* Detroit: Gale, 2000.

Roses, Lorraine Elena, and Ruth Elizabeth Randolph. *Harlem Renaissance and Beyond: Literary Biographies of 100 Black Women Writers, 1900–1945.* Boston: G. K. Hall, 1990.

Rush, Theressa Gunnels, Carol Fairbanks Myers, and Esther Spring Arata. *Black American Writers Past and Present: A Biographical and Bibliographical Dictionary.* 2 vols. Metuchen, NJ: Scarecrow, 1975.

Shockley, Ann Allen, ed. *Afro-American Women Writers, 1746–1933: An Anthology and Critical Guide.* Boston: G. K. Hall, 1988.

Smith, Valerie, ed. *African American Writers.* 2nd ed. New York: Scribner's, 2001.

Southgate, Robert. *Black Plots & Black Characters: A Handbook for Afro-American Literature*. Syracuse, NY: Gaylord, 1979.

Valade, Roger M. *The Essential Black Literature Guide*. Detroit: Visible Ink, 1996.

Werner, Craig. *Black American Women Novelists: An Annotated Bibliography*. Pasadena, CA: Salem, 1989.

Williams, Dana A. *Contemporary African American Female Playwrights: An Annotated Bibliography*. Westport, CT: Greenwood Press, 1998.

Witalec, Janet, ed. *The Harlem Renaissance: A Gale Critical Companion*. 3 vols. Detroit: Gale, 2003.

Yancy, Preston M., comp. *The Afro-American Short Story: A Comprehensive, Annotated Index with Selected Commentaries*. Westport, CT: Greenwood Press, 1986.

Yellin, Jean Fagan, and Cynthia D. Bond, comps. *The Pen Is Ours: A Listing of Writings by and about African-American Women Before 1910 with Secondary Bibliography to the Present*. New York: Oxford University Press, 1991.

ANTHOLOGIES

Abrahams, Roger D. *African American Folktales: Stories from Black Traditions in the New World*. New York: Pantheon, 1999.

Branch, William B. *Black Thunder: An Anthology of Contemporary African American Drama*. New York: Signet, 1995.

Brown, Sterling Allen, Arthur P. Davis, and Ulysses Grant Lee, eds. *The Negro Caravan: Writings by American Negroes*. New York: Citadel, 1941.

Collier-Thomas, Bettye, comp. and ed. *A Treasury of African American Christmas Stories*. 2 vols. New York: Henry Holt, 1997–1999.

Courlander, Harold. *A Treasury of Afro-American Folklore: The Oral Literature, Traditions, Recollections, Legends, Tales, Songs, Religious Beliefs, Customs, Sayings, and Humor of Peoples of African American Descent in the Americas*. Repr. ed. New York: Marlowe, 2002.

Dance, Daryl Cumber, ed. *From My People: 400 Years of African American Folklore*. New York: Norton, 2002.

———. *Honey, Hush! An Anthology of African American Women's Humor*. New York: Norton, 1998.

Davis, Arthur P., and J. Saunders Redding, eds. *Cavalcade: Negro American Writing from 1760 to the Present*. Boston: Houghton Mifflin, 1971.

Donalson, Melvin Burke, ed. *Cornerstones: An Anthology of African American Literature*. New York: Bedford/St. Martin's, 1996.

Emanuel, James A., and Theodore L. Gross, eds. *Dark Symphony: Negro Literature in America*. New York: Free Press, 1968.

Gabbin, Joanne V., ed. *Furious Flower: African American Poetry from the Black Arts Movement to the Present*. Charlottesville: University Press of Virginia, 2004.

Gates, Henry Louis, Jr., ed. *The Classic Slave Narratives*. New York: Signet Classics, 2002.

Gates, Henry Louis, Jr., and Nellie Y. McKay, eds. *The Norton Anthology of African American Literature*. 2nd ed. New York: Norton, 2004.

Gilbert, Derrick I. M., ed. *Catch the Fire!! A Cross-Generational Anthology of Contemporary African-American Poetry*. New York: Riverhead, 1998.

Gilyard, Keith, ed. *Spirit & Flame: An Anthology of Contemporary African American Poetry*. Syracuse, NY: Syracuse University Press, 1997.

Hamilton, Virginia. *The People Could Fly: American Black Folktales*. New York: Knopf, 1985.

Harper, Michael, and Anthony Walton, eds. *The Vintage Book of African American Poetry*. New York: Vintage, 2000.

Harris, Juliette, and Pamela Johnson, eds. *Tenderheaded: A Comb-Bending Collection of Hair Stories*. New York: Atria, 2001.

Harrison, Paul Carter, ed. *Totem Voices: Plays from the Black World Repertory*. New York: Grove, 1989.

Hatch, James, and Ted Shine, eds. *Black Theatre USA: Plays by African Americans from 1847 to Today*. Rev. and enl. ed. New York: Free Press, 1996.

Hill, Patricia Liggins, Bernard W. Bell, Trudier Harris, William J. Harris, R. Baxter Miller, and Shondra A. O'Neale, eds. *Call and Response: The Riverside Anthology of the African American Literary Tradition*. Boston: Houghton Mifflin, 1998.

Hughes, Langston, ed. *The Best Short Stories by Negro Writers: An Anthology from 1899 to the Present*. Boston: Little, Brown, 1967.

Hughes, Langston, and Arna Bontemps, eds. *The Book of Negro Folklore*. New York: Dodd, Mead, 1958.

Johnson, James Weldon, ed. *The Book of American Negro Poetry*. New York: Harcourt, Brace, 1931.

Jones, LeRoi, and Larry Neal, eds. *Black Fire: An Anthology of Afro-American Writing*. New York: Morrow, 1968.

King, Woodie, Jr., ed. *The National Black Drama Anthology: Eleven Plays from America's Leading African-American Theaters*. New York: Applause, 1995.

King, Woodie, Jr., and Ron Milner, eds. *Black Drama Anthology*. New York: Columbia University Press, 1972.

Lewis, David Levering, ed. *The Portable Harlem Renaissance Reader*. New York: Viking, 1994.

Logan, Shirley Wilson, ed. *With Pen and Voice: A Critical Anthology of Nineteenth-Century African-American Women*. Carbondale: Southern Illinois University Press, 1995.

McMillan, Terry, ed. *Breaking Ice: An Anthology of Contemporary African American Fiction*. New York: Penguin, 1990.

Mitchell, Angelyn, ed. *Within the Circle: An Anthology of African American Literary Criticism from the Harlem Renaissance to the Present*. Durham, NC: Duke University Press, 1994.

Naylor, Gloria, ed. *Children of the Night: The Best Short Stories by Black Writers, 1967 to the Present*. Boston: Little, Brown, 1995.

Newman, Richard, Patrick Rael, and Philip Lapsansky. *Pamphlets of Protest: An Anthology of Early African American Protest Literature, 1790–1860*. New York: Routledge, 2001.

Oliver, Clinton, ed. *Contemporary Black Drama*. New York: Scribner's, 1971.

Patton, Venetia K., and Maureen Honey, eds. *Double-Take: A Revisionist Harlem Renaissance Anthology*. New Brunswick, NJ: Rutgers University Press, 2001.

Powell, Kevin, ed. *Step into a World: A Global Anthology of the New Black Literature*. New York: Wiley, 2000.

Ruff, Shawn Stewart, ed. *Go the Way Your Blood Beats: An Anthology of Lesbian and Gay Fiction by African American Writers*. New York: Henry Holt, 1996.

Sherman, Joan R. *African American Poetry: An Anthology, 1773–1927*. Mineola, NY: Dover, 1997.

Smith, Rochelle, and Sharon L. Jones, eds. *The Prentice Hall Anthology of African American Literature*. Upper Saddle River, NJ: Prentice Hall, 2000.

Watkins, Mel, ed. *African American Humor: The Best Black Comedy from Slavery to Today*. Chicago: Lawrence Hill, 2002.

Wilson, Sondra Kathryn, ed. *The* Crisis *Reader: Stories, Poetry, and Essays from the N.A.A.C.P.'s* Crisis *Magazine*. New York: Modern Library, 1999.

———. *The* Opportunity *Reader: Stories, Poetry, and Essays from the Urban League's* Opportunity *Magazine*. New York: Modern Library, 1999.

Worley, Demetrice A., and Jesse Perry, Jr., comps. *African American Literature: An Anthology*, 2nd ed. Lincolnwood, IL: NTC, 1998.

Yetman, Norman R., ed. *Voices from Slavery: 100 Authentic Slave Narratives*. Mineola, NY: Dover, 2000.

Young, Al. *African American Literature: A Brief Introduction and Anthology*. New York: HarperCollins, 1996.

CRITICISM

Andrews, William L. *To Tell a Free Story: The First Century of Afro-American Autobiography, 1760–1865*. Urbana: University of Illinois Press, 1986.

Asante, Molefi K. *The Afrocentric Idea*. Rev. and enl. ed. Philadelphia: Temple University Press, 1998.

Baker, Houston A., Jr. *Afro American Poetics: Revisions of Harlem and the Black Aesthetic*. Madison: University of Wisconsin Press, 1988.

———. *Blues, Ideology, and Afro-American Literature: A Vernacular Theory*. Chicago: University of Chicago Press, 1984.

———. *Modernism and the Harlem Renaissance*. Chicago: University of Chicago Press, 1987.

Baraka, Amiri. *Daggers and Javelins: Essays, 1974–1979*. New York: Morrow, 1984.

Birnbaum, Michele. *Race, Work, and Desire in American Literature, 1860–1930*. New York: Cambridge University Press, 2003.

Bolden, Tony. *Afro-Blue: Improvisations in African American Poetry and Culture*. Urbana: University of Illinois Press, 2004.

Bone, Robert. *The Negro Novel in America*. New Haven, CT: Yale University Press, 1958.

Brooks, Joanna. *American Lazarus: Religion and the Rise of African-American and Native American Literatures*. New York: Oxford University Press, 2003.

Brown, Fahamisha Patricia. *Performing the Word: African-American Poetry as Vernacular Culture*. New Brunswick, NJ: Rutgers University Press, 1999.

Carby, Hazel V. *Reconstructing Womanhood: The Emergence of the Afro-American Woman Novelist*. New York: Oxford University Press, 1987.

Christian, Barbara. *Black Feminist Criticism: Perspectives on Black Women Writers*. New York: Pergamon, 1985.

———. *Black Women Novelists: The Development of a Tradition, 1892–1976*. Westport, CT: Greenwood Press, 1980.

Collins, Patricia. *Black Feminist Thought: Knowledge, Consciousness, and the Politics of Empowerment*. Rev. ed. New York: Routledge, 2000.

Cook, Mercer, and Stephen E. Henderson. *The Militant Black Writer in Africa and the United States*. Madison: University of Wisconsin Press, 1969.

Davis, Arthur P. *From the Dark Tower: Afro-American Writers (1900 to 1960)*. Washington, DC: Howard University Press, 1974.

Elam, Harry J., Jr., and David Krasner, eds. *African-American Performance and Theater History: A Critical Reader*. New York: Oxford University Press, 2001.

Fabi, M. Giulia. *Passing and the Rise of the African American Novel*. Urbana: University of Illinois Press, 2001.

Feinstein, Sascha. *Jazz Poetry: From the 1920s to the Present*. Westport, CT: Greenwood Press, 1997.

Ferguson, Roderick A. *Aberrations in Black: Toward a Queer of Color Critique*. Minneapolis: University of Minnesota Press, 2004.

Gates, Henry Louis, Jr. *Loose Canons: Notes on the Culture Wars*. New York: Oxford University Press, 1992.

———. *The Signifying Monkey: A Theory of Afro-American Literary Criticism*. New York: Oxford University Press, 1988.

Gates, Henry Louis, Jr., ed. *Reading Black, Reading Feminist: A Critical Anthology*. New York: Merdian, 1990.

Gayle, Addison, Jr. *The Black Aesthetic*. Garden City, NY: Doubleday, 1971.

———. *The Way of the New World: The Black Novel in America*. Garden City, NY: Anchor, 1975.

Gibson, Donald B., ed. *Five Black Writers: Essays on Wright, Ellison, Baldwin, Hughes, and LeRoi Jones*. New York: New York University Press, 1970.

Gilroy, Paul. *The Black Atlantic: Modernity and Double Consciousness*. Cambridge, MA: Harvard University Press, 1993.

Gilyard, Keith. *Let's Flip the Script: An African American Discourse on Language, Literature, and Learning*. Detroit: Wayne State University Press, 1996.

Gordon, Lewis R., ed. *Existence in Black: An Anthology of Black Existential Philosophy*. New York: Routledge, 1997.

Harris-Lopez, Trudier. *The Power of the Porch: The Storyteller's Craft in Zora Neale Hurston, Gloria Naylor, and Randall Kenan*. Athens: University of Georgia Press, 1996.

———. *Saints, Sinners, Saviors: Strong Black Women in African American Litrerature*. New York: Palgrave, 2001.

hooks, bell. *Ain't I a Woman: Black Women and Feminism*. Boston: South End Press, 1981.

———. *Feminist Theory: From Margin to Center*. Boston: South End Press, 1984.

Hubbard, Dolan. *The Sermon and the African American Literary Imagination*. Columbia: University of Missouri Press, 1994.

Hubbard, Dolan, ed. *Recovered Writers/Recovered Texts: Race, Class, and Gender in Black Women's Literature*. Knoxville: University of Tennessee Press, 1997.

Hutchinson, George. *The Harlem Renaissance in Black and White*. Cambridge, MA: Belknap Press of Harvard University Press, 1995.

Jackson, Ronald L., II, and Elaine B. Richardson, eds. *Understanding African American Rhetoric: Classical Origins to Contemporary Innovations*. New York: Routledge, 2003.

McDowell, Deborah E., and Arnold Rampersad, eds. *Slavery and the Literary Imagination*. Baltimore: Johns Hopkins University Press, 1989.

McHenry, Elizabeth. *Forgotten Readers: Recovering the Lost History of African American Literary Societies*. Durham, NC: Duke University Press, 2002.

Miller, R. Baxter, ed. *Black American Poets Between Worlds, 1940–1960*. Knoxville: University of Tennessee Press, 1986.

Mills, Charles W. *Blackness Visible: Essays on Philosophy and Race*. Ithaca, NY: Cornell University Press, 1998.

Nelson, Emmanuel S., ed. *Critical Essays: Gay and Lesbian Writers of Color*. New York: Haworth Press, 1993.

Posnock, Ross. *Color & Culture: Black Writers and the Making of the Modern Intellectual*. Cambridge, MA: Harvard University Press, 1998.

Rampersad, Arnold. *The Art and Imagination of W.E.B. Du Bois*. Cambridge, MA: Harvard University Press, 1976.

Redmond, Eugene. *Drumvoices: The Mission of Afro-American Poetry. A Critical History*. Garden City, NY: Anchor, 1976.

Roth, Benita. *Separate Roads to Feminism: Black, Chicana, and White Feminist Movements in America's Second Wave*. New York: Cambridge University Press, 2004.

Royster, Jacqueline Jones. *Traces of a Stream: Literacy and Social Change Among African American Women*. Pittsburgh: University of Pittsburgh Press, 2000.

Schwarz, A. B. Christa. *Gay Voices of the Harlem Renaissance*. Bloomington: Indiana University Press, 2003.

Sherman, Joan R. *Invisible Poets: Afro-Americans of the Nineteenth Century*. 2nd ed. Urbana: University of Illinois Press, 1989.

Smethurst, James Edward. *The New Red Negro: The Literary Left and African American Poetry, 1930–1946*. New York: Oxford University Press, 1999.

Stepto, Robert B. *From Behind the Veil: A Study of Afro-American Narrative*. Urbana: University of Illinois Press, 1979.

Thompson, Robert Farris. *Flash of the Spirit: African and Afro-American Art and Philosophy*. New York: Random House, 1983.

Tracy, Steven C. *Langston Hughes and the Blues*. Urbana: University of Illinois Press, 1988.

Wallace, Maurice O. *Constructing the Black Masculine: Identity and Ideality in African American Men's Literature and Culture, 1775–1995*. Durham, NC: Duke University Press, 2002.

West, Cornel. *Race Matters*. New York: Vintage, 1994.

Williams, Roland Leander. *African American Autobiography and the Quest for Freedom*. Westport, CT: Greenwood Press, 2000.

Wintz, Cary D. *Black Culture and the Harlem Renaissance*. Houston, TX: Rice University Press, 1988.

SELECTED ORGANIZATIONS, MUSEUMS, AND RESEARCH CENTERS

African American Museum in Philadelphia
701 Arch Street
Philadelphia, PA 19106
(215) 574-0380
http://www.ushistory.org/tour/tour_afro.htm

Amistad Research Center
Tilton Hall
Tulane University
6823 St. Charles Avenue
New Orleans, LA 70118
(504) 865-5535
http://www.amistadresearchcenter.org

Anacostia Museum & Center for African American History & Culture
Smithsonian Institution
1901 Fort Place SE
Washington, DC 20020
(202) 287-3306
http://www.si.edu

Association for the Study of African American Life and History
CB Powell Building, Suite C142
Howard University
525 Bryant Street
Washington, DC 20059
(202) 865-0053; fax (202) 265-7920
http://www.asalh.com

Charles Wright Museum of African American History
315 E. Warren Ave.
Detroit, MI 48201-1443
(313) 494-5800; fax (313) 494-5855
http://www.maah-detroit.org

Delta Blues Museum
#1 Blues Alley
P.O. Box 459
Clarksdale, MS 38614
http://www.deltabluesmuseum.org

James Weldon Johnson Collection
Beinecke Rare Book and Manuscript Library
Yale University
130 Wall Street
New Haven, CT 06520-8240
(203) 432-1810
http://www.library.yale.edu/beinecke/ycaljwj.htm

Museum of Afro-American History
Administrative Office
14 Beacon St., Suite 719
Boston, MA 02108
(617) 725-0022
http://www.afroammuseum.org

National Association of African American Studies & Affiliates
P.O. Box 325
Biddeford, ME 04005-0325
(207) 839-8004
e-mail: naaasgrp@webcom.com
http://www.naaas.org

Schomburg Center for Research in Black Culture
515 Malcolm X Blvd.
New York, NY 10037-1801
(212) 491-2200
http://www.nypl.org/research/sc/sc.html

United States National Slavery Museum
1320 Central Park Boulevard
Fredericksburg, VA 22401
http://www.usnationalslaverymuseum.org/home.asp

INDEX

Note: Page numbers in **bold** indicate main entries.

Autobiographers (*continued*)
Thompson, Era Bell, 1590–1591; Toomer, Jean, 1603–1606; Wade-Gayles, Gloria Jean, 1671–1672; Washington, Booker T., 1691–1694; Waters, Ethel, 1700–1702; White, Walter Francis, 1728–1730; Wilkins, Roy, 1737–1738; Wilson, Harriet E., 1761–1763; Wright, Richard, 1787–1793; Young, Andrew, 1801–1802

Autobiography, **57–61**; Derricotte, Toi, use of, 416; Jacobs, Harriet Ann, and, 841; Seacole, Mary, use of, 1452; in slave narratives, 1487. *See also* Autobiographers

Autobiography (Smith), 1502

Autobiography of a Family Photo (Woodson), 1775

Autobiography of a Female Slave (Griffith), 839

The Autobiography of a Jukebox (Eady), 475

The Autobiography of an Ex-Colored Man (Johnson): as coming-of-age fiction, 321; detailed discussion of, 881; Great Migration and, 662; Harlem Renaissance and, 723; lynching in, 1004; mulatto in, 1135–1136; on passing, 1267–1268; as racial uplift literature, 1231–1232, 1350; on ragtime, 1356; realism in, 1374; on sermons, 1455; signifying in, 1478; as slave narrative, 1491; on swing, 1558

The Autobiography of an L.A. Gang Member (Shakur), 1322

The Autobiography of Malcolm X: Black Arts Movement and, 123; black nationalism and, 139; color of skin and, 313; detailed discussion of, 1031; Haley, Alex, and, 694–695; as literature of resistance, 1641; as prison literature, 1322; shifting race relations in Boston and, 170

The Autobiography of Miss Jane Pittman (Gaines): The Civil War and, 286; as coming-of-age fiction, 323; critque of racism in, 1236; detailed discussion of, 599, 601, 603; as folktale, 564; Henry, John as influence on, 759; as historical fiction, 779

Autobiography of My Mother (Kincaid), 928

Autographs for Freedom (Vashon), 1652

"Autumn" (Hayes), 745

Autumn Leaves (Harper), 80

An Autumn Love Cycle (Johnson), 872

Autumn Note (Hughes), 1265

Avalanche: Poems (Troupe), 97, 1617

Avenging the Maine (McGirt), 499

The Avenue, Clayton City (Lincoln), 978

Avi-Ram, Amitai F., 571

Awakening, and Other Poems (Davis), 398

The Awakening (Banks), 796

"The Awakening of the Afro-American Woman" (Matthews), 1050

"The Awakening of the Negro" (Washington), 507

"Award" (Durem), 468

Awooner, Kofi, 56

"Aye, and Gomorrah" (Delany), 411

Aye, Aye, Aye, I'm Integrated (Smith), 1503

Azalea, 974

Baba Chops (Gordone), 642

Babatunde, Don, 962

Babel-17 (Delany), 410, 1446

Baby Momma Drama (Weber), 1413

Baby of the Family (Ansa), 38

Baby Sweet's (Andrews), 33–34

Babylon Boyz (Mowry), 1133

Babylon Sisters (Cleage), 288

Bachelorette Blues (Amos), 28

Back-to-Africa Movement, **63–64**; expatriate writers and, 519; Garvey, Marcus, and, 607, 1154; Great Migration and, 659; protest literature and, 1329; travel writing and, 1608; Turner, Henry, and, 1626

Bacon, Francis, 505, 506, 1643

Bacon, Shonell, 1334

Bad Boy Brawly Brown (Mosley), 364, 995

Bad News Travels Fast (Haywood/Shannon), 749, 1466

Bad Night Is Falling (Phillips), 1294

Badges (Williams), 1749

"Bagel Shop Jazz" (Kaufman), 852

Bagneris, Vernel, 1149

Bahktin, Mikhail, 543, 544

Bailey, Peter, 934

Bailey's Café (Naylor), 1165, 1183, 1185–1186

Baisden, Michael, **65**

Baker, Anita, 850

Baker, Augusta, 81, 268

Baker, Chet, 850

Baker, Houston A., Jr., **65–66**; *African American Review* editor, 57; Black Nationalism, and, 300; Cain, George, and, 229–230; Davis, Arthur, and, 395; deconstruction and, 405; on formal verse, use of, 571; on Fuller, Hoyt, 593; Furious Flower Conference, 597; Jackson, Rebecca Cox, and, 835; jazz in literature, 854; on metaphors and race, 1087; *Obsidian: Black Literature in Review* contributor, 56; poetics and, 1308; poststructuralism and, 1319; rap and, 1368; Stepto, Robert Burns, and, 1540

Baker, Jean Claude, 66

Baker, Josephine, **66–68**, 450, 521, 660

Baker, Nikki, **68–69**, 365

"Bakin' an' Greens" (Davis), 397

Balancing Act (Bunkley), 215

Baldwin, James, **69–74**; African American folk sermon and its influence on, 800; African American women, positive portrayals in fiction, 764; Angelou, Maya, and, 37; assimilation and *Another Country*, 49; Atlanta child murders and, 53; autobiography, 58, 59; Black English and, 901; Black gay writers, and, 635, 1699; Black Power and, 146–147; blues and, 157; censorship of, 247; children's literature and, 271; civil rights movement and, 71, 284; on colonialism, 309; coming-of-age fiction and, 322, 324; cross-dressing and, 372; diasporic consciousness and, 430; Dixon, Melvin, influence on, 436; Douglass, Frederick, influence of, 444; dramatic works of, 452; Dumas, Henry, comparison with, 460; Early, Gerald Lyn, and, 476; Emanuel, James, and, 497; essay form, use of, 506, 508, 509, 510; Eugene Saxton fellowships and, 482; as expatriate writer, 519; folkloric elements, use of, 558; gay literature and, 613; gender and, 620; Glave, Thomas, and, 635, 636; Gomez, Jewelle, influenced by, 640; gospel music and, 644, 645; Great Migration and, 662; Harlem, New York, and, 717; Harrington, Oliver, living in Paris, France, 732; Heard, Nathan, identified with, 750; Hemphill, Essex, influenced by, 754; on homosexuality, 1458; influence of, 339; jazz and, 625, 850, 852; on Joans, Gayl, 892; Kelley, William Melvin, and, 917; Kenan, Randall Garrett, and, 921, 922, 923; on labor, 950; as literary influence, 1261, 1307; Malcolm X's influence, 290; McCarthyism and, 1056, 1057; McMillan, Terry, influence on, 1075; on misogyny, 1103; mythology in works, 1154; novels, author of, 1235; O. Henry Award and, 636; Paris, France and, 1257; prose poem and, 1325, 1326; on race, 1346; as romance writer, 1412; on Sambo and cultural clichés, 1426; satiric elements, use of, 1435; sexuality as theme of, 505; short fiction, use of, 1475; on skin color, 314; Smith, William Gardner, and, 1510; spirituals and, 1534; Thelwell, Michael, and, 1581; Till, Emmett, and, 1596, 1597; travel writing and, 1609; Troupe, Quincy, and, 1617; on *Uncle Tom's Cabin*, 1640; West, Cornel, and, 1717; Williams, John, and, 1746; Wilson, August, and, 1753; Wright, Richard, and, 1790, 1791; on Wright, Richard, 1640. *See also Another Country* (Baldwin); *Giovanni's Room* (Baldwin); *Go Tell It on the Mountain* (Baldwin)

Ballad, **74–78**

Ballad for Bimshire (Mitchell), 77

"Ballad of Birmingham" (Cullen), 1167

"Ballad of Birmingham" (Randall), 77, 180, 1361

"Ballad of Booker T." (Hughes), 77

"Ballad of Bullethead" (Hayes), 745

"The Ballad of Joe Meek" (Brown), 77

"The Ballad of Margie Polite" (Hughes), 77, 1349

"The Ballad of Nat Turner" (Hayden), 1014, 1628

"Ballad of Ozzie Powell" (Hughes), 77

A Ballad of Remembrance (Hayden), 743

"A Ballad of Remembrance" (Hayden), 1014

"Ballad of Roosevelt" (Hughes), 77

The Ballad of the Brown Girl (Cullen), 77, 377

"Ballad of the Fortune Teller" (Hughes), 77

"The Ballad of the Free" (Walker), 77

Ballad of the Free (Walker), 1679

"Ballad of the Landlord" (Hughes), 1167

Ballad of the Winter Soldiers (Mitchell & Killens), 78

"The Ballad of Walter White" (Hughes), 77

Ballads: folktales, difference between, 561; as formal verse, 568; free verse, use in, 590; Johnson, James Weldon, and, 880; narrative poetry and, 1167; as short fiction, form of, 1471; signifying and, 1477; sonnet versus, 1514

"Ballads [sic] of Lenin" (Hughes), 950

Ballard, Allen B., **78–79**

"The Ballot or the Bullet" (Malcolm X), 718

Balo (Toomer), 1604–1605, 1606

Baltimore, Maryland, **79–81**

Baltimore Afro-American, 80, **81–84**

Bambara, Toni Cade, **84–86**; Atlanta child murders and, 53; Black feminist literary criticism and, 318; children's literature and, 271; Combahee River Collective, 318; conjuring, and, 327; essay form, use of, 508, 509–510; feminism/Black feminism and, 535; Finney, Nikky, and, 549; folkloric elements, use of, 558, 559; name change, 1166; nature, use as theme element, 1182; *Sage: A Scholarly Journal on Black Women* and, 1421; short fiction, use of, 1475; Till, Emmett, and, 1597; Troupe, Quincy, and, 1617; Washington, Mary Helen, including in anthology, 1695

Bamboula, 1146

Banana Bottom (McKay), 430, 1068

The Band of Gideon and Other Lyrics (Cotter), 348

The Band Will Not Play Dixie: A Novel of Suspense (Browne), 209

Bandanna Land, 1146

Bandele, Asha, **86**

Bangers (Phillips), 1294

Index

Park, Robert, and, 264; Steward, Theophilus Gould, and, 1542; Washington, D.C. and, 1698; WPA projects, and, 257

Fred Hampton (Perkins), 1278

"Frederick Douglass" (Hayden), 1514

Frederick Douglass (Johnson), 872

Frederick Douglass' Paper, 1023

Free (Hunt), 817

A Free Black Girl Before the Civil War (Grimke), 1287

Free Enterprise (Cliff), 292

Free Lance, 50, 1024

The Free Negro Family (Franklin), 586

Free Southern Theater (FST), 416, **587–589**, 1025, 1225, 1423

Free Speech, 1708–1709

Free verse, **589–591**; Dandridge, Raymond Garfield, use of, 384; Davis, Frank Marshall, use of, 397–398; formal verse and, 568; Johnson, Fenton, and, 869; Johnson, Helene, and, 874; Johnson, James Weldon, and, 883

"Free Your Mind and Your Ass Will Follow" (Clinton), 295

Freedom and Citizenship (Langston), 954

Freedom Forum Fellows: Chambers, Veronica, 248

Freedom in the Dismal (Love), 1001

Freedom in the Family: A Mother–Daughter Memoir of the Fight for Civil Rights (Due), 458, 796

The Freedom Ship of Robert Smalls (Meriwether), 1080

Freedom's Children on the March (Miller), 1096

Freedom's Journal, 341, 984, 1216

The Free-lance Pallbearers (Reed), 1265, 1382, 1383

Freelance writers: Campbell, Bebe Moore, 233; Elam, Patricia, 484–485

Freeman (Dean), 401

French, Albert, 1662

Fresh Prince of Bel-Air (TV show), 1749

Freud, Sigmund, 515, 941, 1110

The Friends (Guy), 686

Friends (Williams), 1749

Friends and Lovers (Dickey), 1413

Friends of American Literature Fiction Award: Clair, Maxine, 287

The Friendship (Taylor), 1569

Frobenius, Leo, 515

Frolic Theater, 30

From a Broken Bottle Traces of Perfume Still Emanate (Mackey), 700, 1017

From a Land Where Other People Live (Lorde), 181, 991

From a Person Sitting in Darkness: New and Selected Poems (Barrax), 95

From Behind the Veil: A Study of Afro-American Narrative (Stepto), 1539

From Mammies to Militants (Harris), 737

From Memphis and Peking (Chase-Riboud), 251

From Newsboy to Bellhop to Playwright (Anderson), 30

"From Sea to Shining Sea" (Jordan), 901

From Slavery to Freedom (Franklin), 582

From the Book of Shine (Forbes), 566

"From the Dark Tower" (Cullen), 152, 378

From the Dark Tower: Afro-American Writers (1900 to 1960) (Davis), 395, 799

From the Darkness Cometh the Light; or, Struggles for Freedom (Delaney), 406

From the Land of Dreams (Still), 1547

From the Notebooks of Melanin Sun (Woodson), 1774, 1775

From the Pyramids to the Projects: Poems of Genocide and Resistance!, 1607

From the Virginia Plantation to the National Capitol (Langston), 803, 955

Front Page Award: Walker, Alice, 1675

Front Porch (Hughes), 451

Front Porch Stories at the One-Room School (Tate), 1565, 1566

Froula, Christine, 544

"The Frustration of Negro Art" (Lewis), 977

FST. *See* Free Southern Theater

Fucking A (Parks), 1262

The Fugitive Blacksmith; or, Events in the History of James W. C. Pennington, (Pennington), 1272, 1489

Fulbright Awards/Fellowships: Dove, Rita, 445; Glave, Thomas, 636; McElroy, Colleen, 1065; Nelson, Marilyn, 1203; Young, Al, 1801

Fulbright Scholars: Bryan, Ashley, 210; Chennault, Stephen D., 252–253; Ferrell, Carolyn, 548; Ladd, Florence, 951

Fulbright-Hays Fellowship: Mayfield, Julian, 1051

The Full Matilda (Haynes), 746

Fuller, Charles H., Jr., 452, **591–592**, 1689, 1780

Fuller, Hoyt, **592–593**; Atlanta, Georgia, and, 52; Black Arts Movement and, 120; Danner, Margaret, and, 385; dialect poetry, use of, 427; formal verse, use of, 571; Gayle, Roberta, and Black Arts Movement, 615; on the *Journal of Black Poetry*, 905; *Negro Digest*, and, 1024, 1196; on NOMMO, 1226; OBAC founder, 1243; Plumpp, Sterling D., and, 1307; Rodgers, Carolyn, and, 1410; travel writing and, 1611

Fullilove, Eric James, **593–594**

Fulton, David Bryant, **594–595**

Michele Faith, 1683–1684; Winbush, Raymond, 1763–1764

"Nonviolence and Social Change" (King), 934

Norris Wright Cuney: A Tribune of the Black People (Cuney-Hare), 382

"North American Slave Narratives, Beginnings to 1920," 41

North Carolina Arts Council Writing Fellowship: davenport, doris, 392

North Carolina Fiction Fellowship: Coleman, Evelyn, 303–304

North Carolina Governor's Award: Williams, Samm-Art, 1749

The North Star, 984; Delany, Martin R. as coeditor, 63, 1300; Frederick Douglass, founder of, 63, 1300

North Town (Graham), 269

Northrup's Odyssey (Williams), 1749

Northup, Solomon, 59, 1103, **1227–1228**

The Norton Anthology of African American Literature, 35, 592, 980, 982, 1015, 1069–1070, 1477, 1529, 1578

Norwood, Vera, 1175

Not a Day Goes By (Harris), 735

Not a Man, and Yet a Man (Whitman), 499, 1734

Not All Dogs (Robinson), 1405–1406

Not Guilty: Twelve Black Men Speak Out on Law, Justice and Life (Asim), 47

Not Long for This World (Haywood), 748, 995

Not Out of Africa (Lefkowitz), 128

Not We Many (Cooper), 335

Not Without Laughter (Hughes): assimilation and, 49; as coming-of-age novel, 321, 1233; detailed discussion of, 805; realism in, 657, 1374; use of humor in, 814

Notable Black American Women, 1306

Notable Book of the Year: McBride, James, 1052

Notable Book of the Year, *Washington Post*: Ballard, Allen B., 79

Notes from the Country Club (Wozencraft), 1323

Notes of a Native Son (Baldwin), 430, 508, 509, 1426, 1791

"Notes on Making: The Heroic Pattern Updated: 1997" (Harper), 729

Nothing but a Nigger (Perkins), 1278

Nothing But the Truth (Gayle), 616

"Nothing New" (Bonner), 164

Novel, **1229–1238**

"The Novel as a Function of American Democracy" (Ellison), 508

The Novel as Social Criticism (Petry), 1282

Novelists: Adams, Jenoyne, 5–6; Alers, Rochelle, 18–19; Anderson, Mignon Holland, 31; Andrews, Raymond, 33–34; Ansa, Tina McElroy, 38–39; Anthony, Sterling, 39; Armstrong, William, 46–47; Asim, Jabari, 47; Attaway, William, 54–55; Austin, Doris Jean, 56–57; Baisden, Michael, 65; Baker, Nikki, 68–69; Baldwin, James, 69–74; Ballard, Allen B., 78–79; Bambara, Toni Cade, 84–86; Bandele, Asha, 86; Banks, Leslie Esdaile, 86–87; Baraka, Amiri, 90–92; Barnes, Steven Emory, 93–94; Beadle, Samuel A., 99–100; Beatty, Paul, 105–106; Beckham, Barry, 106–107; Bennett, Hal, 112–113; Berry, Bertice, 115–116; Berry, Charlene A., 116; Bland, Eleanor Taylor, 149–150; Bontemps, Arna, 164–167; Bowen, Michele Andrea, 171–172; Bradley, David Henry, Jr., 174–176; Briscoe, Connie, 179–180; Brookhouse, Christopher, 170; Brown, Cecil, 191; Brown, Claude, 191–193; Brown, Frank London, 195–196; Brown, Linda Beatrice, 202; Brown, Lloyd, 203–204; Brown, Wesley, 205–206; Brown, William Wells, 58; Browne, Theodore, 208–209; Bullins, Ed, 213–214; Bunkley, Anita Richmond, 214–215; Burton, LeVar, 219; Busia, Akosua, 220–221; Bussey, Louré, 221–222; Butler, Tajuana, 225–226; Byrd, Adrianne, 226–227; Cain, George, 229–230; Campbell, Bebe Moore, 233; Carter, Charlotte, 239; Carter, Stephen L., 240–241; Cartiér, Xam Wilson, 241; Cary, Lorene, 242; Chancy, Myriam J. A., 249–250; Chase-Riboud, Barbara, 251–252; Chesnutt, Charles Waddell, 253–256; Childress, Alice, 272–274; Clair, Maxine, 287–288; Clarke, Breena, 288; Cleage, Pearl Michelle, 288–289; Cliff, Michelle, 291–292; Colter, Cyrus, 314–316; Cooper, Clarence, Jr., 334–335; Cooper, J. California, 335–337; Corbin, Steven, 338–339; Corrothers, James, 342–343; Cose, Ellis, 347; Crafts, Hannah, 355–356; Crouch, Stanley, 373–374; Cullen, Countee, 377–382; Danticat, Edwidge, 386–388; Darden, Christopher, 389; Dash, Julie, 390–391; Davis, Bridgett M., 396; Davis, Ossie, 398–400; Davis, Thulani N., 400–401; DeBerry, Virginia, 402–403; DeLoach, Nora, 413–414; Demby, William, 414–415; DeVeaux, Alexis, 423–424; Dickey, Eric Jerome, 433–434; Dixon, Melvin, 435–436; Dove, Rita, 445–448; Durham, David Anthony, 468–469; Edwards, Grace, 481; Edwards, Junius, 482–484; Edwards, Louis, 483–484; Elam, Patricia, 484–485; Ellis, Erika, 489–490; Ellis, Trey, 491–492; Ellison, Ralph, 492–497; Everett, Percival, 513–514; Fair, Ronald L., 526–527; Farmer, Nancy,

ABOUT THE EDITORS

HANS OSTROM is a professor of English at the University of Puget Sound in Tacoma, Washington, where he teaches literature, creative writing, and rhetoric. He is author of *Langston Hughes: A Study of the Short Fiction* (1993) and *A Langston Hughes Encyclopedia* (Greenwood Press, 2002). With Wendy Bishop and Katharine Haake, he wrote *Metro: Journeys in Writing Creatively* (2000). He has also published *Three to Get Ready* (1991), a novel, and *Subject Apprehended* (2000), a book of poems. Ostrom has taught at Johannes Gutenberg University in Mainz, Germany, and he was a Fulbright Senior Lecturer at Uppsala University in Sweden. He earned a Ph.D. in English from the University of California, Davis. He has also worked as a journalist and a carpenter.

J. DAVID MACEY, JR., is an assistant professor at the University of Central Oklahoma, where he currently serves as assistant chair of the Department of English. A former soup-kitchen cook, bank clerk, and seminarian, he holds degrees from Yale, Brown, and Vanderbilt universities and has taught at Vanderbilt, Central Oklahoma, and the University of Puget Sound. His academic interests range from contemporary African American literature to literary and critical theory, the history of the English language, and early modern British literature and culture.

ABOUT THE ADVISORY BOARD

HOUSTON A. BAKER, JR., is a native of Louisville, Kentucky. He received his B.A. (magna cum laude and Phi Beta Kappa) from Howard University, and his M.A. and Ph.D. from UCLA. He has taught at Yale, the University of Virginia, and the University of Pennsylvania. Currently, he is the Susan Fox and George D. Beischer Professor of English at Duke University. He is the editor of *American Literature*, the oldest and most prestigious journal in American literary studies. Professor Baker began his career as a scholar of British Victorian literature, but made a career shift to the study of Afro-American literature and culture. He has published or edited more than twenty books. He is the author of more than eighty articles, essays, and reviews. His most recent books include *Turning South Again: Re-Thinking Modernism, Re-Reading Booker T.* (2001) and *Critical Memory: Public Spheres, African American Writing, and Black Fathers and Sons in America* (2001). He is a published poet whose most recent title is *Passing Over*. He has served in a number of administrative and institutional posts, including the 1992 presidency of the Modern Language Association of America. His honors include Guggenheim, John Hay Whitney, and Rockefeller fellowships, as well as eleven honorary degrees from American colleges and universities.

EMILY BERNARD, a native of Nashville, Tennessee, is an assistant professor of English and ethnic studies at the University of Vermont in Burlington. She is the editor of *Remember Me to Harlem: The Letters of Langston Hughes and Carl Van Vechten* (2001), a New York Times Notable Book of the Year. Bernard is also the editor of *Some of My Best Friends: Writings on Interracial Friendships* (2004).

MICHELE ELAM, an associate professor in the English Department at Stanford University (2003–2005), was a Hewlett Fellow at Stanford's Research Institute of Comparative Studies in Race and Ethnicity (2002–2003), where she began her latest book, *Mixed Race in the New Millennium* (2005). She has also taught at the University of Puget Sound. Professor Elam is the author of *Race, Work, and Desire in American Literature, 1860–1930* (2003) and has published articles in *African American Review, American Literature,* and *Genre*. Her work also appears in collections on race and culture such as *Subjects and Citizens: Nation, Race, and Gender from Oroonoko to Anita Hill* (ed. Cathy Davidson and Michael Moon) and in *W.E.B. Du Bois and the Gender of the Color-Line* (ed. Susan Gillman and Alyce Weinbaum). The recipient of the St. Clair Drake Outstanding Teaching Award (2003) at Stanford, Professor Elam is currently teaching seminars on slave narratives; mixed race literature and theory; W.E.B. Du Bois and American culture; the Harlem and Chicago renaissances; and graduate seminars on African American literary history and theory.

DOLAN HUBBARD is professor and chair of the Department of English and Language Arts at Morgan State University, Baltimore, Maryland. He is author of *The Sermon and the African American Literary Imagination* (1994) and is a member of the editorial board of *The Collected Works of Langston Hughes*, with Arnold Rampersad, Leslie Sanders, and Steve Tracy. He is editor of *The Souls of Black Folk: One Hundred Years Later* (2003).

SHEILA SMITH McKOY is an associate professor of English at North Carolina State University. The second African American woman to earn tenure at Vanderbilt University, Smith McKoy has published works in the critically acclaimed Schomburg series *African American Women Writers 1910–1940, Callaloo, Contours,* and *Research for African Literatures*. Her book *When Whites Riot: Writing Race and Violence in American and South African Cultures* (2001) has received critical attention in the United States and in South Africa. Her current projects include a forthcoming study of African American literature of the 1930s.

ABOUT THE
CONTRIBUTORS

KATHLEEN ADAMS lives in Oklahoma and is a high school English teacher. She has a bachelor's degree in English education and additional degrees in reading and school administration. She is currently working toward a master's degree in composition and rhetoric at the University of Central Oklahoma.

ANTONY ADOLF received his B.A. from the University of Illinois at Chicago and his M.A. from the University of British Columbia, and is currently editor in chief of the c/art-el collective language group. His scholarly, critical, and creative works have appeared in journals in North America and Europe, and his current projects include a scholarly book titled *Modern Multilingualisms and Their Aftermaths: An Inquiry into Their Poetries, Philosophies and Politics.*

CORA AGATUCCI earned her Ph.D. at the University of California–San Diego, and is a professor of English at Central Oregon Community College in Bend. She has published on Chinua Achebe, Gish Jen, Michelle Cliff, Eric Walrond, and African American women writers. Her current projects focus on historical fiction and world cinema.

JESSICA ALLEN graduated magna cum laude from Vanderbilt University and earned a master's degree in English from the University of Washington. Currently she lives in New York City, where she works in publishing and writes freelance articles on everything from Rabindranath Tagore to production processes in documentary film.

HEATHER L. ALTHOFF is the assistant director of McEntegart Hall Library at St. Joseph's College in New York. She is in the process of creating an information literacy program at St. Joseph's College. She earned her M.S. in information and library science from Pratt Institute and her B.A. in history from Carleton College.

ALEX AMBROZIC teaches English literature at Memorial University of Newfoundland, Canada, where he received his doctorate in twentieth-century American fiction.

JEE HYUN AN is an assistant professor of English at Seoul National University in Seoul, South Korea. She earned her Ph.D. in English literature at the University of Chicago, where she completed her dissertation on the Black women writers Marita Bonner, Gwendolyn Brooks, Nella Larsen, Jessie Redmon Fauset, Ann Lane Petry, Paule Marshall, and Lorraine Hansberry.

JOEL ANDERSON is a graduate student at the University of Massachusetts, Amherst.

MICHAEL A. ANTONUCCI teaches in the Department of English at the University of Illinois at Chicago. His scholarly writing has appeared in *African American Review*, *Brilliant Corners*, *Obsidian III*, *Humanitas*, and *Cold Mountain Review*.

CATHERINE N. ANYASO is a graduate student in the liberal arts at the Johns Hopkins University. She plans to pursue a Ph.D. in cultural studies or cultural anthropology with an emphasis on West African culture.

MONIFA LOVE ASANTE is an award-winning writer and professor of creative writing and humanities at Morgan State University in Baltimore, Maryland.

JULIUS H. BAILEY is an assistant professor of religious studies at the University of Redlands. His area of research is African American religious history. His most recent publication is *Around the Family Altar: Domesticity in the African Methodist Episcopal Church, 1865–1900* (2005).

IVA BALIC is completing her doctoral dissertation in the Department of English at the University of North Texas, where she is writing on utopian fiction, with a particular focus on utopias by U.S. women at the turn of the twentieth century. She has presented papers at various conferences and translated a book on the director Quentin Tarantino from English to Czech.

SHARON L. BARNES is an assistant professor of interdisciplinary and special programs at the University of Toledo, where she teaches academic writing and women's studies. Her work on Audre Lorde's poetry and prose has appeared in

Things of the Spirit: Women Writers Constructing Spirituality (2004) and *Obsidian III.*

RACHAEL BARNETT earned her Ph.D. in literature from the University of Washington in 2001. She teaches American literature and writing with a comparative multiethnic focus. She is currently at work on a novel tentatively titled *Memories of a Counter-Culture Childhood.*

JAMES A. BECKMAN is an assistant professor of law at the University of Tampa, and holds degrees from the University of Tampa, the Ohio State University College of Law, and Georgetown University. He is the editor of a two-volume, 1,100-page book titled *Affirmative Action: An Encyclopedia* (Greenwood Press, 2004). Beckman served as an artist-in-residence for the National Park Service at Harpers Ferry in 2001, studying race relations issues during his park residency.

ANN BEEBE is an assistant professor of English at the University of Texas at Tyler. She is working on an article on counterfeiting in *Ormond* and *The Pioneers* as well as one on young women's Civil War diaries.

BRETT BEEMYN, Ph.D., is the coordinator of gay, lesbian, bisexual, and transgender student services at the Ohio State University and has edited or coedited a number of texts in LGBT studies, including *Bisexuality in the Lives of Men: Facts and Fictions* (2001), *Bisexual Men in Culture and Society* (2002), *Creating a Place for Ourselves: Lesbian, Gay, and Bisexual Community Histories* (1997), and *Queer Studies: A Lesbian, Gay, Bisexual, and Transgender Anthology* (1996). Beemyn's latest work is an anthology on transgender youth.

VALERIE BEGLEY has a Ph.D. in literary and cultural theory from Carnegie Mellon University. Her scholarship focuses on constructions of race and gender in the twentieth century. She has taught in the United States and in Turkey, and is currently residing in the Philippines, where she is an independent scholar at work on a study of foodways as a form of cultural transformation.

CHRIS BELL is a first-year Ph.D. candidate in disability studies at the University of Illinois at Chicago. His research interests include examining the intersections of race and disability.

ALLISON BENNETT is currently an undergraduate student of American literature and African American Studies at the University of Puget Sound in Tacoma, Washington. She plans to teach American Studies.

CELESTE-MARIE BERNIER is a lecturer in American literature at the University of Nottingham in England. Her Ph.D. dissertation was on dramatic representations of slave resistance in abolitionist literature of the nineteenth century. She has published in nineteenth-century American history and literature, African American literature, and African American visual culture. Her most recent publication is " 'Emblems of Barbarism': Black Masculinity and Representations of Toussaint L'Ouverture in Frederick Douglass's Unpublished Manuscripts," *Nineteenth-Century American History* (2004).

KIMBERLY BLACK-PARKER received her B.S. from Central State University, and her M.S. and Ph.D. from Florida State University. She is currently an assistant professor of library and information science at the University of Kentucky.

JACQUELINE A. BLACKWELL has a bachelor's degree in English arts from Hampton Institute (1983). After taking her master's degree in English language and literature at the University of Virginia at Charlottesville, she began her teaching career at Hampton University, where she was a professor for nearly twelve years. She is currently a professor of English at Thomas Nelson Community College in Hampton, Virginia.

ELLESIA ANN BLAQUE is a member of the English Department at Queensborough Community College of the City University of New York, where she teaches African American literature, hip-hop culture, and composition courses. She graduated from Temple University in 2001 after completing an English major and a minor in history. She earned her master's degree in African American literature at Wayne State University in 2003, and is completing her dissertation there.

ANITA BLEDSOE-GARDNER is an instructor at Central Piedmont Community College in the Division of Behavioral and Social Science. She has published in juvenile delinquency, community development, and religion, and is currently coauthoring a book on social diversity.

COLLEEN GLENNEY BOGGS is an assistant professor of English and Women and Gender Studies at Dartmouth College. She works in nineteenth-century literature, and her most recent article is "Margaret Fuller's American Translation" (*American Literature*, March 2004). She is currently completing a book, *American Translation and the Transatlantic Nation, 1773–1892*.

CHERYL D. BOHDE has completed a Ph.D. in nineteenth-century American literature at Texas A&M University. She has contributed to *American History Through Literature, 1820–1870, Contemporary American Women Fiction Writers: An A to Z Guide, American Women Writers 1900–1945*, and *Journal of the American Studies Association of Texas*.

B. J. BOLDEN is a retired professor of English from Chicago State University (2004). She is the author of *Urban Rage in Bronzeville: Social Commentary in the*

Poetry of Gwendolyn Brooks, 1945–1960 (1999). Her essay "The Rhetorical Power of Gwendolyn Brooks' *Maud Martha*" is included in *Gwendolyn Brooks' "Maud Martha": A Critical Collection* (2002), edited by Jacqueline Bryant. Her other scholarly publications include essays on Edgar Allan Poe, Sonia Sanchez, and Lucille Clifton.

MICHAEL BORSHUK is an assistant professor of African American literature at Texas Tech University. He is the author of the forthcoming book *Swinging the Vernacular: Jazz and African American Modernist Literature*, and of numerous articles on African American literature and culture. He also writes on jazz regularly for *Coda* magazine.

PATRICIA KENNEDY BOSTIAN is teaching at Central Piedmont Community College in North Carolina while she finishes a second degree in humanities. A freelance writer, she publishes poetry as well as articles on poetry and poets, especially on the work of lesser-known African American and Hispanic women.

JANAKA N. BOWMAN is a doctoral student in Northwestern University's Department of English. She earned bachelor of arts degrees in English and African American Studies from Duke University. She works with both nineteenth- and twentieth-century texts, and her current research interests are themes of Black subjectivity in African American literature of the Reconstruction period (1865–1877).

DAVID A. BOXWELL is an associate professor of English at the U.S. Naval Academy and has published articles on Zora Neale Hurston and the poet Essex Hemphill.

RON BRILEY teaches at Sandia Preparatory Academy in Albuquerque, New Mexico.

MALIN LIDSTRÖM BROCK is a doctoral candidate in English at Oxford University. She is completing a dissertation on women's biography and feminist theory, and teaches American literature.

DEBORAH BROWN is an assistant professor of English and the program coordinator for English education at the University of Central Oklahoma. She has published in journals including *Journal of Adolescent and Adult Literacy* and *Research in the Teaching of English*.

MARY HANFORD BRUCE, professor of English at Monmouth College, Monmouth, Illinois, was a Fulbright professor (1989–1990) at the University of Yaoundé in Cameroon, Africa. She directed a study-abroad program in Zimbabwe in 1995 and Monmouth College's program in England from 2001 to

2004. She has received Global Partners grants to Kenya (2000, 2002) and Tanzania (2004). *Holding to the Light*, a poetry collection, was published in 1991, followed by short stories and essays. Her novel, *Dr. Sally's Voodoo Man*, was published in 2003.

REGINALD BRUSTER teaches composition, literature, and professional communication at Greenville Technical College in Greenville, South Carolina.

DIANE TODD BUCCI is an assistant professor of communications skills and coordinator of the Communications Skills Program at Robert Morris University in Moon Township, Pennsylvania.

SCOTT BUNYAN, a faculty member in the Language Studies Department at Mohawk College in Ontario, received his Ph.D. from the University of Sussex, where he completed a dissertation on struggles for personal connections among characters, author, and audience in the works of John Edgar Wideman.

THERESA L. BURRISS is the director of the Learning Assistance and Resource Center at Radford University, as well as a member of the special-purpose faculty in English. She is a Ph.D. candidate at the Union Institute and University, where she is focusing on Appalachian studies and Women's Studies. Her latest essay, "Claiming a Literary Space: The Affrilachian Poets," was published in *An American Vein: Critical Readings in Appalachian Literature* (2005).

BRIAN BURTON recently completed his Ph.D. at the University of Durham. His dissertation examines influence and intertextuality in the poetry of Derek Mahon. He has had work published on Mahon, Samuel Beckett, and Michael Longley, and he is currently conducting research on regional identity in the poetry of Basil Bunting.

SUSAN HAYS BUSSEY is a visiting assistant professor at Wake Forest University. She has published an article on Pauline Hopkins in *African American Review*, and is currently working on an extensive project on Mark Twain's *Pudd'nhead Wilson* manuscript.

DARA N. BYRNE is an assistant professor in the Department of Speech, Theater, and Media Studies at John Jay College of Criminal Justice of the City University of New York. She holds a Ph.D. in rhetoric and intercultural communication from Howard University. She earned a B.A. honors degree in English and sociology, as well as an M.A. in English, from Carleton University in Ottawa, Canada. A specialist in critical language studies and intercultural communication, Byrne was the recipient of the 2002–2003 Rockefeller Residency Fellowship at the Institute for Research on the African Diaspora in the

Americas and the Caribbean at the City University of New York. She is the editor of the series Black Issues in Higher Education's Landmarks in Civil Rights History. Byrne edited *Brown v. Board of Education: Its Impact on Public Education 1954–2004*.

JOY DUCKETT CAIN has written book reviews and features for newspapers and many of the nation's top magazines. She is a graduate of Queens College.

KATRINA CALDWELL is completing her doctoral dissertation in the Department of English at the University of Illinois at Chicago. She is writing about the social activism of Black women fiction writers during the Cold War. She has an upcoming publication in *Footsteps* Magazine, "Black Women Writers and the Harlem Writers Guild." She has presented her work on urban Black films at the Midwest Modern Language Association and the Midwest Popular Culture Association conferences.

PATRICIA L T CAMP is an attorney, writer, teacher, and former juvenile court magistrate. A graduate of Rice University, the University of Houston, and the University of Chicago Law School, she practices law in North Carolina and Ohio. She has taught at Rice University, Sinclair College, and North Carolina Central University Law School, and is currently at work on a novel.

JENNIFER CAMPBELL is an assistant professor in the Writing Studies Department at Roger Williams University in Bristol, Rhode Island, where she teaches classes on race, gender, war, and class.

DAVID CARRELL (Ph.D., Purdue University, 1994) is an assistant professor of English at Langston University, where he teaches American literature, Victorian literature, and composition. His research interests include contemporary American poetry and early American literature.

WARREN J. CARSON is a Governor's Distinguished Professor and chair of the Department of Languages, Literature, and Composition at the University of South Carolina Upstate. He has published articles, essays, and reviews in *African American Review, Appalachian Heritage, Southern Literary Journal*, and *College Language Association Journal*. In addition, he is a contributor to the *Oxford Companion to African American Literature* and *The Gift of Story: 20th Century African American Writers*.

JAMES BUCKY CARTER is a Ph.D. candidate studying English education at the University of Virginia. He is focusing his research on connections among critical literacy, visual literacy, and popular culture. He holds B.S.Ed./B.A. degrees from Western Carolina University and an M.A. in English from the University of Tennessee, Knoxville. He has published in *International Journal of Comic Art* and has supplied entries for the *Encyclopedia of American Children's and Young Adult Literature.*

LINDA M. CARTER is an associate professor of English at Morgan State University and the executive associate editor of *Middle Atlantic Writers Review.* She has coedited four books and written more than forty articles on African American literature and culture.

TERRY CARTER is an assistant professor of English in the Humanities and Technical Communication Department at Southern Polytechnic State University in Marietta, Georgia. He completed his doctoral work in English with an emphasis in composition and rhetoric at the University of South Carolina in 2002; his dissertation is titled "Textual and Personal Representations of African Americans in Composition and Rhetoric." He teaches first-year composition and a writer's workshop course; he also teaches an online composition course through the University of Georgia's collaborative programs. He is currently a member of the Conference on College Composition and Communication's Language Policy Committee, and his research investigates representations of African Americans in composition and rhetoric, and how online composition courses impact student's writing and identity in virtual classrooms.

THOMAS J. CASSIDY received his Ph.D. in English from Binghamton University in 1991. Since then, he has taught at South Carolina State University, where he is a professor in the Department of English and Modern Languages. He has published widely on a broad array of topics relevant to American literature and African American literature in particular, with particular interest in the development of historical themes in early African American fiction.

JÉRÔME CECCON is a postdoctoral research fellow at the University of Antwerp. He holds a bachelor's degree in language sciences from the University of Caen in France and a master's degree in foreign languages and literatures from the Catholic University of Milan. In 2002 he obtained his Ph.D. from the University of Turin with a dissertation on migrant writing in Québec. From 1997 to 2000, he was a lecturer in French at the University of Turin, teaching French language and translation. He specializes in Francophone postcolonial literatures, in cross-cultural women's writing, and in comparative literature. He is currently working on a research project titled "Recolonizing the French Caribbean: The Postcoloniality of Female Haitian Writing in Diaspora." He is also preparing the publication of his Ph.D. dissertation, *Identità e cosmopolitismo nella letteratura quebecchese contemporanea.* As a member of the Faculty of Applied Economic Sciences at Antwerp, he also teaches business French.

JESSICA CHAPMAN teaches freshman composition at the University of Central Oklahoma. She received her undergraduate degree in English from

Oklahoma State University and her graduate degree from the University of Central Oklahoma.

RYAN CHAPMAN is currently working on a novel and learning Czech. He lives in Seattle.

DENISA CHATMAN-RILEY is a Ph.D. candidate at Claremont Graduate University. Her research interests include African American women writers, science fiction, and mythology. She currently teaches composition and African American literature in Southern California.

DENNIS CHESTER teaches African American literature at California State University at Hayward. He has published papers on Langston Hughes and other Harlem Renaissance figures and is currently coediting a critical volume on Claude McKay.

KATY L. CHILES is a Ph.D. candidate in the Department of English at Northwestern University, where her work focuses on critical race theory and American literature and culture. She is currently writing her dissertation on racial formation in the British North American colonies and U.S. nation-state during the period 1750–1800. A Jacob K. Javits fellow, Chiles has presented papers at the annual conferences of the Modern Language Association, the American Studies Association, and the American Culture Association. Her most recent publication is "Blackened Irish, Brown-Red Natives, and the Production of U.S. Whiteness in Dion Boucicault's *The Octoroon*" (*Nineteenth Century Theatre and Film*, Spring 2005).

PETER GLENN CHRISTENSEN is an assistant professor of English at Cardinal Stritch University in Milwaukee, Wisconsin. He received a Ph.D. in comparative literature from the State University of New York at Binghamton. He teaches courses in modern American literature, English literature to 1800, literary theory, and science fiction/fantasy.

JULIE NELSON CHRISTOPH is an assistant professor of English at the University of Puget Sound. She has published articles and delivered papers on topics including uses of "the personal" in academic writing, women's rhetoric and literacy in historical perspective, composition and writing center pedagogy, and the politics of adult literacy instruction. She is currently completing a book manuscript titled *Arguing with One's Life: Strategies of Placement in Pioneer Women's Writing on Westward Expansion*.

JULIE CLAGGETT received a B.A. in corporate communications from the University of Central Oklahoma in 2002. She is currently pursuing an M.A. in education, with an emphasis in English.

CAMERON CHRISTINE CLARK received her B.A. in English (creative writing) from Western Michigan University and earned her M.A. in English from the University of Florida, where she specialized in cultural studies. She wrote her thesis on the depictions of trauma and testimony in Toni Morrison's *Song of Solomon*. She is currently working on a collection of poetry.

PATRICIA E. CLARK is an assistant professor of English at the State University of New York at Oswego. She has made numerous presentations on modern African American literature and the literature of the Harlem Renaissance. Clark is currently working on a book that explores identity formation through representations of food rituals and practices in African American women's writing, focusing on the works of Ntozake Shange, Vertamae Grosvenor, and Harryette Mullen.

JEFF CLEEK is currently working on a master's degree in English at the University of Central Oklahoma, where he is an editor of *New Plains Review*.

BILL CLEM is a doctoral candidate in English, with emphases in multicultural American literatures and feminist theory, at Northern Illinois University. He is writing a dissertation on U.S. women writers of color and the discourses of power, sex, and sexuality. Clem is a tenured instructor of English at Waubonsee Community College.

JENNIFER R. COATES holds an M.A. in American civilization from Brown University and a B.A. from Amherst College. She currently teaches on the East Coast.

KEVIN L. COLE is an assistant professor of English at the University of Sioux Falls in Sioux Falls, South Dakota. He has published on a wide range of topics and authors, from medieval drama to Cormac McCarthy.

MICHAEL COOK is an independent scholar with degrees from the University of Washington who focuses on culture, literature, and human rights.

MELISSA COUCHON, a senior at the University of North Carolina at Chapel Hill, majors in English and philosophy. She plans to enter an English graduate program in the fall of 2006 and concentrate on modern American and British literature.

DAVID CUTHBERT is an instructor in the English Department at the University of Manitoba. He is completing his doctorate at Queen's University.

CAROL KLIMICK CYGANOWSKI is an associate professor of English at DePaul University in Chicago, where she has directed the American Studies program and the Women's Studies program. She holds a Ph.D. from the

University of Chicago. Her publications have focused mainly on women writers, though her current project is a complete history of Chicago drama, including its many African American firsts.

RITA B. DANDRIDGE is a professor in the English and Foreign Languages Department at Norfolk State University, where she teaches African American literature and Women's Studies. She received the TIAA-CREF Virginia Outstanding Faculty Award in 2004 from the Virginia State Council of Higher Education. Her articles have appeared in *College Language Association Journal*, *Black American Literature Forum*, *Virginia Quarterly*, and *The Oxford Companion to African American Literature*. Her books include *Ann Allen Shockley: An Annotated Primary and Secondary Bibliography* (Greenwood, 1987), *Black Women's Blues: A Literary Anthology, 1934–1988* (1992), and *Black Women's Activism: Reading African American Women's Historical Romances* (2004).

AMY L. DARNELL is a doctoral candidate in performance studies at Southern Illinois University. Her dissertation examines the ways in which photography and performance memorialize and construct specific sites of memory. She has presented her research in film adaptation, autoethnography, pedagogy, and performance at conferences including the annual meetings of the National Communication Association, the Popular Culture Association, and the Central States Communication Association.

ROBIN M. DASHER-ALSTON earned her Ph.D. in education at the University of Pennsylvania, where she specialized in higher education. She works for a higher education association, has written articles and reviews for several publications, and is at work on a book on William Still and the Underground Railroad.

AMANDA DAVIS is a Ph.D. candidate in the Department of English at the University of Florida, where she teaches courses through the Center for Women's Studies and Gender Research. Her dissertation centers on autobiographies written by incarcerated women, and her most recent publication on the topic is "On Teaching Women's Prison Narratives: A Feminist Approach to Women, Crime, and Incarceration" (*Women's Studies Quarterly*, Winter 2004). She also focuses on African American literature and literature and theory by women of color, and has presented several papers and published several reviews in these areas.

ELLA DAVIS is a professor of English and speech at Wayne County Community College in Detroit. She received a B.S. in speech from Jackson State University, an M.A. in speech and an M.A. in English from Wayne State University, and her D.A. in English language and literature from the University of Michigan. Davis has taught English, speech, and Africana Studies at several colleges and universities in metro Detroit. Her primary research interests are Black women's literary production, and the history and culture of Black Detroit. She coordinates a summer lecture series, "Renaissance in Detroit," at the Detroit Opera House. Davis has published articles in several popular and academic journals.

JAMES J. DAVIS, a past president of the College Language Association (1992–1994), is graduate professor of Spanish and foreign language education and is the chair of Modern Languages and Literature at Howard University.

LAWRENCE A. DAVIS earned his Ph.D. in American Studies at Purdue University, where he specialized in African American literature. Currently he is a postdoctoral fellow at the University of Michigan.

MATTHEW R. DAVIS is an assistant professor of English at the University of Wisconsin, River Falls. He teaches nineteenth-century and early-twentieth-century American and African American literature and culture, the freshman seminar in writing and rhetoric, and nonmajor courses in multiethnic American literature. He is completing revisions to his book manuscript "Who Are Our Brethren?" Brotherhood and Blood in Civil War–Era America.

CAROL MARGARET DAVISON is an assistant professor of English literature at the University of Windsor, Canada. The author of Anti-Semitism and British Gothic Literature (2004) and the editor of the award-winning study Bram Stoker's Dracula: Sucking Through the Century, 1897–1997 (1997), she has published numerous articles on women's writing and Victorian, postcolonial, and African American literature. She is at work on a monograph on the Scottish Gothic literary tradition.

MARY DE JONG is an associate professor of English and Women's Studies at Penn State University at Altoona. Besides publishing articles on nineteenth-century American hymn-writing and hymn-singing, she has researched nineteenth-century singing evangelists such as Mary D. James (a White hymnist from New Jersey) and Amanda Berry Smith (a former slave who distinguished herself as a temperance speaker and a preacher in the Holiness movement).

GERARDO DEL GUERCIO is a Montreal-born writer who plans to teach at the college level. He received his Bachelor of Arts degree from Concordia University (Montreal) and his Master of Arts degree from the Université de Montréal.

KEVIN DEORNELLAS teaches English at Queen's University, Belfast, Ireland. He is primarily a critic of early modern English literature. His book Bridled, Curbed, Tamed: The Horse in Early Modern English Culture was published in 2005. He also writes about twentieth-century literature, having published scholarly essays on such diverse writers as Robert Aickman, Jessie Redmon Fauset, and Arnold Wesker.

VANESSA HOLFORD DIANA is an assistant professor of English and co-ordinator of the Women's Studies program at Westfield State College in Westfield, Massachusetts, where she teaches courses in multicultural American literature and Women's Studies. Her research focuses on fiction by nineteenth- and twentieth-century women writers of color in the United States.

HEATH A. DIEHL is an instructor in the General Studies writing program at Bowling Green State University, where he teaches courses in composition, literature, and women's studies. He has published in *Studies in the Literary Imagination, M/MLA: The Journal of the Midwest Modern Language Association*, and in the forthcoming anthology *The Problem Body*.

CAROL ELIZABETH DIETRICH earned her Ph.D. in English at the Ohio State University. Professor of general education at DeVry University, she teaches communications and humanities courses. She has published articles on composition, twentieth-century poetry, Robert Frost, women and the media, the Progressive Era, and the Gilded Age, and is completing a master's degree in social sciences at the Ohio University.

KALENDA C. EATON DONALD is an assistant professor of English and Africana Studies at Barry University in Miami Shores, Florida. Her research interests include twentieth-century Africana literature, Black women's literature, and social movements. She is currently director of the Africana Studies program at Barry University.

STACEY LEE DONOHUE is chair of the Fine Arts Department and associate professor of English at Central Oregon Community College. She has published and presented on the writers Mary McCarthy, Dorothy Parker, and Mary Gordon, among others, and on subjects such as Whiteness in American literature, Native American literature, and teaching at a community college. She is editor of the quarterly newsletter of the Community College Humanities Association, *The Community College Humanist*, and chair of the Modern Language Association's Committee on Community Colleges.

KIMBERLY P. DRAGGOO is working on her M.A. in English at Boston College. A graduate of the University of Puget Sound (2001), she hopes to pursue a Ph.D. upon the completion of her M.A. degree. Over the past few years, she has worked at Sony Pictures Entertainment and was a freelance writer for ABC-CLIO online.

EVE DUNBAR is an assistant professor of English at Vassar College, where she specializes in African American literature and culture. Her current projects range from exploring issues surrounding the literary development of "passing" narratives to racial policing in the cityscape and African American–authored detective fiction.

BILL ENGEL (Ph.D., University of California, Berkeley) is an independent scholar and educational consultant. While engaged with the *Encyclopedia*, he was appointed visiting assistant professor of English at the University of the South, in Sewanee, Tennessee. He is the author of three books on cultural history and memory, most recently *Death and Drama* (2003), and is the Modern Language Association delegate for independent scholars and alternative careers.

KATE FALVEY teaches at the New York City College of Technology of the City University of New York. She received her Ph.D. in English and American literature from New York University, and has published work on nineteenth- and early twentieth-century women writers.

ALEX FEERST is a Ph.D. candidate in English at Duke University. He is writing a dissertation on the aesthetic history of urban poverty.

KEITH FELDMAN is a doctoral candidate in American literature and cultural studies at the University of Washington. His work focuses on issues of race, ethnicity, and diaspora in the twentieth century, particularly theories of liberalism and the American Empire in relation to the formation of Israel/Palestine. In particular, he considers resistant modes of transnational cultural production by an array of twentieth-century African American, Palestinian, and Jewish writers. Recent research projects have theorized the state-based racialization of migrants into and out of the United States across several periods of national emergency.

BEN FISLER is an assistant professor of theater at Otero College in La Junta, Colorado. His publications have appeared in *Theatre Journal*, *Theatre Studies*, *Theatron*, and *The Puppetry Yearbook*.

LAKISKA FLIPPIN is completing her M.A. at Brooklyn College of the City University of New York. She plans to pursue an M.F.A. in fiction writing upon completion of this degree.

GUY MARK FOSTER teaches literature in the English Department at the University of California, Santa Barbara. His current research explores the intersections of race and sexualities in African American literary texts as well as within U.S. popular culture.

ANNE MARIE FOWLER, a training instructor at Ramstein Air Base in Germany, holds an M.F.A. in writing and is currently a doctoral candidate at the Union Institute and University, where she is pursuing study of ethnic and women's literature. She is a poet, and her work has been published in national and international journals, and in *Coloring Book: An Eclectic Anthology of Fiction and Poetry by Multicultural Writers* (2003).

GREGORY W. FOWLER is an assistant professor of literature and American Studies at Penn State University at Erie. He was a Fulbright Scholar in Berlin, Germany, in 2002, and has published articles in Germany, India, Canada, and the United States.

JANICE E. FOWLER is Ronald McNair Scholar and a graduate student at Texas Woman's University. Her interests include writing and African American history. Currently she is working on a guide for nontraditional students in the university.

AISHA X. L. FRANCIS is a lecturer in the gender studies program at Vanderbilt University. She earned her Ph.D. in English literature from Vanderbilt, where she specialized in African American and late nineteenth-century American literature. She is currently revising her dissertation into a book that analyzes representations of etiquette and codes of conduct in African American literature and culture. The working title of this project is *Home Training and How to Be: Black Conduct Literature and Identity Politics in the United States*.

KIMBERLY A. FREEMAN is an assistant professor of English at Schenectady County Community College. She has contributed articles to *a/b: Autobiography Studies*, *American Literary Realism*, and various encyclopedias. Freeman is the author *Love American Style: Divorce and the American Novel, 1881–1976* (2003). She is currently working on depictions of marriage and divorce in African American literature.

MAR GALLEGO teaches American and African American literatures at the University of Huelva (Spain). Her major research interests are African American Studies and the African diaspora, with a special focus on the Harlem Renaissance and contemporary women writers. She has published a monograph titled *Passing Novels in the Harlem Renaissance* (2003) and has coedited *Myth and Ritual in African American and Native American Literatures* (2001) and *Razón de mujer: Género y discurso en el ensayo femenino* (2003).

ERIC GARDNER is an associate professor of English at Saginaw Valley State University and editor of the forthcoming anthology *Major Voices: The Drama of Slavery*. His articles and reference book entries on nineteenth-century African Americans have appeared in such resources as *New England Quarterly* and *African American Lives* (2004).

MARYBETH GASMAN is an assistant professor of higher education at the University of Pennsylvania. She has published extensively on the history of

African American higher education and philanthropy. Her most recent books include *Charles S. Johnson: Leadership Beyond the Veil in the Age of Jim Crow* (with Patrick J. Gilpin, 2003) and *Fund-raising from Black College Alumni: Successful Strategies for Supporting Alma Mater* (with Sibby Anderson-Thompkins). She is currently working on a history of the United Negro College Fund.

ROXANE GAY is a professional writer living in the Midwest. She holds an M.A. degree in English and creative writing from the University of Nebraska at Lincoln. Her work can be found in several anthologies, including *Far from Home: Father-Daughter Travel Adventures*.

THERESA L. GELLER is completing her doctoral dissertation in the Department of Literatures in English at Rutgers University, where she is writing on spectatorship and poststructuralist philosophy, with a particular focus on the role of the cinematic apparatus in theorizations of popular cinema and new media. She has essays in the journal *Frontiers* and in the collection *Gender After Lyotard*. Her work also appears in *Spectator* and *Senses of Cinema*.

APRIL GENTRY lives and writes in Savannah, Georgia.

CHRISTINE GERHARDT teaches American literature and culture at the University of Dortmund, Germany. Her main research interests include African American literature, regional literatures, and ecocriticism. She has published a monograph on representations of the Reconstruction era in American novels and is working on an ecocritical comparison of Walt Whitman's and Emily Dickinson's poetry.

D. SHANE GILLEY earned his M.A. at the University of Central Oklahoma, where he focused on twentieth-century literature. His most recent scholarship includes a study of the representation of American presidents in film.

TERESA GILLIAMS is an assistant professor of English at Albright College in Reading, Pennsylvania. She earned her Ph.D. in African American literature from Howard University, and her research and teaching focus broadly on the cultural and discursive practices that mark bodily differences, particularly the ways in which those practices establish selfhood and nationhood in twentieth-century African American literature and culture.

HEATHER TIRADO GILLIGAN is a visiting assistant professor of Black Studies at the University of California, Santa Barbara. Her research examines writings about race in late-nineteenth- and early-twentieth-century literary magazines.

ESTHER GODFREY is completing her doctoral dissertation in English at the University of Tennessee. Her dissertation concerns the January–May marriage in nineteenth-century British literature, and much of her writing addresses how such factors as age and race affect gendered identities. Her essay "From Governess to Girl-Bride in *Jane Eyre*" is forthcoming in *SEL* (Fall 2005).

CAROL GOODMAN is a teaching fellow in English literature at Memorial University of Newfoundland, Canada, where she is finishing her doctoral dissertation on African American autobiography.

STEPHANIE GORDON, Ph.D., teaches English at Auburn University. She has published work on Sherman Alexie, Elias Boudinot, and N. Scott Momaday, and her essay "Self-Made Ex-Slaves: Bass Reeves, Nat Love, and the Cultures of the American Frontier" is in *Post-Bellum, Pre-Harlem: African American Literature and Culture, 1877–1919*, edited by Barbara McCaskill and Caroline Gebhard (2005).

JOSH GOSCIAK is coeditor of the anthology *A Day in the Life: Tales from the Lower East* (1990). He teaches media studies and literature at City College of the City University of New York. His critical study, *The Shadowed Country: Claude McKay and the Romance of the Victorians*, is forthcoming.

HEIDI HAUSER GREEN reviews books for the Children's Literature Comprehensive Database. She has earned graduate degrees in English from Illinois State University and in library and information science from the University of Pittsburgh. Her interests include the role of family and the development of identity in children's books.

DELANO GREENIDGE-COPPRUE graduated from Columbia University with a Ph.D. in English and comparative literature. He teaches composition and literature on the Rose Hill campus of Fordham University, New York, and is at work on a study of jazz music and American literature.

SANTIAGO RODRÍGUEZ GUERRERO-STRACHAN lectures on American literature at the University of Valladolid (Spain). He has published extensively on the American short story and on the postcolonial essay. At present he is working on the reception of American literature in Spain and on literature and science.

VALERIE LYNN GUYANT is completing her doctoral dissertation in the Department of English at Northern Illinois University; its topic is speculative and fantastic fiction, with a particular focus on representations of female sexuality in vampire literature. Guyant has presented papers at the annual meetings of the Midwest Conference on Literature, Language and Media and at WisCon, a feminist science fiction and fantasy convention.

ERIC ASHLEY HAIRSTON earned his Ph.D. in English from the University of Virginia, where he specialized in American literature and classical backgrounds. Formerly the Honors Fellow at Sweet Briar College and a faculty member at North Carolina State University, he is currently working toward a J.D. from the University of North Carolina at Chapel Hill, expanding his dissertation into a book, and publishing in his areas of specialization.

ANGELENE J. HALL is a professor of literature and popular culture in the Department of African and African American Studies at the University of Cincinnati. She has published on African American women writers including Phyllis Wheatley, Carolyn Rodgers, and Alice Walker. In 2002, she won the Dolly Cohen Award, the University of Cincinnati's most prestigious teaching recognition.

JOHN GREER HALL received a bachelor's degree in African American Studies and American literature from the University of Massachusetts in Boston and a master's degree in education from Converse College in Spartanburg, South Carolina. He has contributed fiction, nonfiction, and poetry to *African Voices*, *Aim* magazine, *BackHome*, *Black Diaspora*, *Listen* magazine, and *The Sounds of Poetry*.

GEOFF HAMILTON is a graduate student in English literature at the University of Toronto. His research concerns the figure of the antisocial individualist in contemporary American novels. He has published essays in *University of Toronto Quarterly*, *Modern Drama*, *Essays on Canadian Writing*, and *Samuel Beckett Today/Aujourd'hui*.

JOHN J. HAN is a professor of English at Missouri Baptist University, where he teaches American, minority, and world literature. He has published journal articles on Flannery O'Connor, Andrew Marvell, John Steinbeck, and Christian issues within higher education, and is founding editor of *Intégrité: A Faith and Learning Journal*. Han has dozens of essays in such reference volumes as *An Encyclopedia of Catholic Literature*, *Writers of the American Renaissance* (2003), *Asian American Autobiographers* (2001), and *Asian American Novelists* (2000).

ROXANNE HARDE, a postdoctoral fellow at Cornell University, earned her doctorate in American literature at Queen's University. She works on American women's religious writing and writing for children, and has published her research in the journals *Legacy*, *Critique*, and *Mosaic*, and in several anthologies.

JENNIFER HARRIS is an assistant professor of English at Mount Allison University and managing editor of the Alphabet City book series. She has published in a number of journals, including *Canadian Review of American Studies* and *Journal of American Culture*.

STEVEN R. HARRIS is collection development librarian at Utah State University in Logan. Before that, for several years he was the English literature librarian at the University of Tennessee in Knoxville, where he helped to compile the online bibliography *Tennessee Authors Past & Present*. He is a graduate of Weber State College (B.A., 1982), the University of Utah (M.A., 1985), and the University of Arizona (M.L.S., 1991). He continues to do research on the impact of the Civil Rights Movement on libraries and librarians in the American South.

MELISSA HAMILTON HAYES lives Lincoln, Nebraska. She teaches at Doane College, and her research interests include twentieth-century American and women's literature.

KEVIN M. HICKEY is an assistant professor of English at Albany College of Pharmacy, New York. He has published on Africa, travel, and postcolonial theory (as well as his own travel articles). He is currently working on a book about his six-year bicycle trip through Europe and Africa.

CHRISTINE MARIE HILGER is a professor of developmental studies at Eastfield College. She is a Ph.D. student at the University of Texas at Dallas, and her research interests include electronic pedagogy, the documentary film as a rhetorical vehicle, and Holocaust studies.

MELVIN G. HILL is a Ph.D. student at Illinois State University, Normal. He is a member of the National English Honors Society and a Ronald E. McNair Scholar. His research interests include recovery and rhetorical analysis of representations of racial identity in historical documents such as runaway slave advertisements, and the mechanisms of passing and how passing may influence postmodern American thought about identity.

KAAVONIA HINTON-JOHNSON is an assistant professor at Old Dominion University in Norfolk, Virginia. Her specialization is English education, with an interest in multicultural literature, particularly African American literature for adults, young adults, and children. Her work has appeared in *Social Education*, *MultiCultural Review*, *VOYA*, *Kliatt*, and *English Journal*.

KURT HOCHENAUER is an English professor at the University of Central Oklahoma, where he teaches modern British and American literature.

SUSANNA HOENESS-KRUPSAW is an associate professor of English at the University of Southern Indiana in Evansville. She earned her doctorate at Southern Illinois University in Carbondale with a dissertation on the role of the family in the novels of E. L. Doctorow. She teaches contemporary American and Canadian literature and has recently published on Anne Devlin, Simone de Beauvoir, and Colette.

LAURA A. HOFFER has published book reviews, interviews, and fiction in journals such as *North Dakota Quarterly* and *Blue Mesa Review*. She is currently a Ph.D. candidate in creative writing at the University of Tennessee.

DELOICE HOLLIDAY graduated with two degrees from Indiana University, the B.A. in English and the M.L.S. from the School of Library and Information Science. She is multicultural outreach librarian at Indiana University at Bloomington.

DARRYL B. HOLLOMAN is associate dean/director of the Paul Robeson Campus Center at Rutgers University–Newark campus. In 2004 he received a Ph.D. from Rutgers University–Newark.

ANNA R. HOLLOWAY, a professor of English at Fort Valley State University, received her Ph.D. from Kent State University. Her current areas of interest are detective fiction (especially nineteenth-century), creative writing, and professional communication.

JANIS BUTLER HOLM is an associate professor of English at Ohio University, where she has served as associate editor for the film journal *Wide Angle*. She is the author of articles, poems, and essays, and the editor of a critical edition of *The Mirrhor of Modestie*, a sixteenth-century domestic conduct book.

AMANDA HOLT received her master's degree at the University of Central Oklahoma in 2005. She teaches freshman English composition, and plans to begin work on a Ph.D. in Victorian studies in the fall of 2006.

W. SCOTT HOWARD is an associate professor of English at the University of Denver, where he teaches courses in poetics and poetry. His publications have most recently appeared in the journals *Poetry Criticism* and *The Comparatist*, and the books *Studying Cultural Landscapes* (2003) and *The World in Time and Space* (2002).

MARY HRICKO is an associate professor of library and media services and library director at Kent State University, Geauga Campus. Although she holds a doctorate in American literature, she has published and presented numerous articles on topics related to distance education and instructional technology. She is coeditor of *Online Assessment and Measurement* (forthcoming).

MATTHEW W. HUGHEY is a Ph.D. candidate in sociology at the University of Virginia. His research interests include critical race theory, identity theory, sociology of culture and knowledge, cultural studies, critical and culturally centered pedagogy, the Black Panther Party, and the legacy of Huey P. Newton.

PIPER G. HUGULEY-RIGGINS is a Ph.D. candidate in twentieth-century American literature at Georgia State University. Her dissertation, "Living as Chisera," is about five female fiction writers and the way they illustrate their writing careers in their autobiographies. Huguley-Riggs has an M.F.A from the University of Pittsburgh in fiction writing and a B.A. in political science from UCLA. She is currently a technical communications fellow at the Georgia Institute of Technology.

IMELDA HUNT, Ph.D., is an instructor in the Department of Popular Culture at Bowling Green State University.

BRANDON L. A. HUTCHINSON is an assistant professor of English at Southern Connecticut State University. Her area of interest is Black women's drama, but she also teaches courses on historical fiction, bondage and freedom, and Black women in the arts.

CHARMAINE N. IJEOMA is an assistant professor of English and African and African American Studies at Abington College of Penn State University. Her area of expertise is the African American short story. She is currently working on a book-length project titled *The African American Short Story, 1900–1925: A Literary History*.

ROCHELL ISAAC, a graduate of Wesleyan University, is working on a second master's degree at Temple University. She is the editor of *Black Girls Who Eat Sushi: Life Stories* (2004). Currently Isaac is an adjunct professor of English at Long Island University and Borough of Manhattan Community College.

JAMES A. JAAP is currently the assistant director of Academic Affairs and an instructor in English at the Pennsylvania State University campus at McKeesport. He completed his doctorate in English from Duquesne University, with a particular focus on modern Irish autobiography. He is working on a book on Irish autobiography and postcolonial theory, and has a strong interest in Pittsburgh and western Pennsylvania history.

CANDICE LOVE JACKSON is an assistant professor of English at Tougaloo College in Tougaloo, Mississippi. She earned her doctorate in English from the University of North Carolina at Chapel Hill.

HOLLY A. JACKSON is a doctoral candidate in the Department of English and American Literature at Brandeis University. Her research on race and gender in nineteenth- and twentieth-century American literature focuses on reproduction, legal discourse, and the nation. She is a contributor to *African American National Biography* (forthcoming).

MONICA F. JACOBE is a lecturer in the Department of Literature at American University in Washington, D.C. She holds bachelor's degrees in English and journalism from Emory and Henry College (Virginia) and a Master of Fine Arts in creative writing from American University. Her research interests are in American literature, particularly Southern women writers and modernism, which has resulted in in-depth work on Gayl Jones, author of *Corregidora* and *Eva's Man*, among others. Jacobe has published both creative and scholarly works in small publications and has presented papers on modernist allegories, Gayl Jones and *Corregidora*, and postcolonial influences in literature.

RAYMOND E. JANIFER, SR., is an associate professor of English and director of the Ethnic Studies Program at Shippensburg University in Pennsylvania. He received his Ph.D. from the Ohio State University and an M.F.A. in professional writing from the University of Southern California. He has had scholarly articles published in *The Toni Morrison Encyclopedia* (2003) and *Contemporary Black Men's Fiction and Drama* (2001). He has also had a short story published about his experience as a California migrant worker, "Salinas Valley Fields."

YMITRI JAYASUNDERA is an assistant professor at Prairie View A&M University.

REGINA JENNINGS teaches African American literature, culture, and resistance in the Department of Africana Studies at Rutgers University. Her current books are *Race, Rage, and Roses* (2003) and *Malcolm X: The Muse in Haki Madhubuti's Poetics* (2005). She has published widely in journals and books, such as *International Journal of Africana Studies*, *Journal of Black Studies*, *Pennsylvania English*, *The Maud Martha Reader*, and *The Black Panther Party Reconsidered* (2005).

A. YEMISI JIMOH is an associate professor in the Department of English at the University of Arkansas, Fayetteville. She is a cultural analyst and critical race studies theorist who teaches African American literary and cultural studies. Jimoh is the author of the scholarly monograph *Spiritual, Blues, and Jazz People in African American Fiction: Living in Paradox* (2002). She also has published articles, reviews, and book chapters in various venues, and is currently working on a book-length manuscript which is focused on the political and cultural uses of group-name identifiers in African American fiction.

BRIAN L. JOHNSON is an assistant professor of English at Gordon College in Wenham, Massachusetts. He is the editor of a collection of W.E.B. Du Bois's writings, *Du Bois on Reform: Periodical-Based Leadership for African Americans* (2005).

SHERITA L. JOHNSON is completing her doctoral dissertation in the Department of English at the University of Illinois at Urbana–Champaign. She is writing about the representations of Black women in Southern literature and culture during the late nineteenth century, focusing on works by Frances Ellen Watkins Harper, Charles Waddell Chesnutt, and George Washington Cable. Her general research interests include early African American literature, nineteenth- and early-twentieth-century American literature, Black women writers (especially nineteenth century), Southern literature, and race, ethnicity, and gender studies.

ESTHER L. JONES is a Ph.D. candidate in the Department of English at the Ohio State University. Her area of specialization is women's literature of the African diaspora in the Americas, with an emphasis on speculative fiction and representations of folk religion.

REGINA V. JONES earned her Ph.D. in English from Michigan State University, concentrating on African American literature and comparative Black history. She is currently a visiting assistant professor at Indiana University Northwest, in the Minority Studies Department. Jones plans to publish a book about "Sass" and its use in nineteenth-century narratives by or about African American women.

HEE-JUNG JOO is a Ph.D. candidate in the comparative literature program at the University of Oregon. Her dissertation is titled "Speculative Fiction and the Spectacle of Race: African American and Asian American Visions of the Future."

RICHARD M. JUANG is an assistant professor of English at Susquehanna University. He writes about race and gender and is currently editing a collection of essays on transgender activism, politics, and legal issues, titled *Transgender Rights*.

NANCY KANG is completing a dissertation at the University of Toronto's Department of English that considers interracialism and masculinity in twentieth-century American literature. A Chancellor Jackman Scholar and Social Sciences and Humanities Research Council of Canada fellow, Kang most recently has published work that deals with African Canadian and African American slave migration.

JAMES B. KELLEY holds a Ph.D. in English from the University of Tulsa. As the recipient of a Fulbright Junior Lecturer award in 1999, he taught courses in American literature and cultural studies at the Otto-von-Guericke University in Magdeburg, Germany. He now teaches at Mississippi State University at Meridian, and has published on various topics in modern literature.

MAUREEN A. KELLY is an assistant professor of Library Science at Oregon State University. She is the librarian for the OSU Cascades branch campus in

Bend and the OSU Extended Campus. Her current research investigates using collaborative partnerships in multi-institutional settings to provide library services.

RENEE KEMP-ROTAN is Chief of Capital Projects for the Mayor of Birmingham, Alabama. She holds degrees in architecture and planning from Syracuse University, Columbia University, and the Architectural Association in London. Kemp-Rotan has lectured extensively on media design and cultural heritage at the Sorbonne, Cairo University, MIT, Cooper-Hewitt, Cornell, Howard University, and Parsons. She is the Smithsonian's expert on Josephine Baker, and worked on the Smithsonian's International Black Jazz in Paris exhibition.

ALICIA KESTER lives in Northern California and is currently working on a collection of poetry.

MARTIN KICH is a professor of English at Wright State University's Lake campus. He is the author of *Western American Novelists* (1995) and *An Encyclopedia of Emerging Writers* (2005). He has contributed articles and reviews to literary reference books, scholarly journals, and general periodicals. About 200 of his poems have been published in literary journals.

GLADYS L. KNIGHT is a former manager of the African American Museum in Tacoma, Washington. She is also a storyteller and an aspiring writer. Her work in progress includes short stories and novels based on the lives of African Americans in the fictional Southern town of Opportunity.

LIN KNUTSON is an assistant professor at Southeastern Louisiana University, where she teaches courses in African American literature, U.S. ethnic writers, immigrant literature, and women writers of color. She has published articles in *Journal of Caribbean Studies* and *Sagetrieb*, and has coedited *Journal of Commonwealth and Postcolonial Studies*.

AMOR KOHLI teaches in the African and Black Diaspora Studies Program at DePaul University. He has published on the Beat writer Bob Kaufman and is currently completing a dissertation on the poetry of Amiri Baraka, Kamau Brathwaite, and Linton Kwesi Johnson.

PHILIP J. KOWALSKI is a Ph.D. candidate in the Department of English at the University of North Carolina, Chapel Hill. His research interests lie primarily in late-nineteenth-century American literature and in American Studies. He is currently writing his dissertation on the relationship between domestic material culture and middle-class identity in the works of Harriet Beecher Stowe, William Dean Howells, Frank Norris, and Booker T. Washington.

SUSIE SCIFRES KUILAN is nearing completion of her dissertation on early American novels, which will complete her requirements for the Ph.D. at Louisiana State University. She has published articles on contemporary authors, composition pedagogy, and folklore. Her research interests include literary history, detective fiction and other popular literature, and early American and Southern writers. She is currently working on an edited volume of essays about John Kennedy Toole with Suzanne Disheroon-Green. She teaches American literature and first-year writing.

MICHELLE LaFRANCE is a graduate student in English at the University of Washington, Seattle. She studies representations of race and ethnicity in popular entertainment, particularly turn-of-the-century comedy, melodrama, and caricature. She has presented at the Futures of American Studies Institute at Dartmouth and the Society for Literature and Science annual conferences. She is a published poet and short story writer.

KIMBERLY LAMM, a Ph.D. candidate at the University of Washington, is completing a dissertation on literary and visual portraiture in turn-of-the-century American culture. She has published essays on Ralph Ellison's *Invisible Man* and contemporary American poetry.

TRUONG LE is a poet and writer who has published a memoir, a collection of short stories, a novel, and six books of poetry, including one in Vietnamese, English, and French. He is a member of the Vietnamese Writers Abroad PEN Centre and the Vietnamese International Poetry Society.

LEWIS T. LeNAIRE rceived his B.A. in English from the University of Central Oklahoma in 2001, and went on to earn a certificate of completion in French study from the Institut de Touraine in Tours, France, in the summer of the same year. Lewis is an M.A. candidate in the UCO English program and expects to complete his degree in 2006.

MARC LEVERETTE is a doctoral candidate in media studies at Rutgers University. His publications include *Professional Wrestling: The Myth, the Mat, and American Popular Culture* (2003) and *Understanding McLuhan* (2005), as well as several articles and book chapters in the areas of media and cultural studies.

RUDOLPH LEWIS is a writer and librarian at Baltimore City College. He is also one of the editors of *I Am New Orleans and Other Poems by Marcus B. Christian* (1999). His essays and poems appear in such journals as *New Laurel Review* and *African Renaissance*.

WENXIN LI is an assistant professor of English at the State University of New York at Old Westbury. His scholarly essays have appeared in *Paideuma*,

MELUS, and several critical anthologies. Currently he is at work on a book titled *Racial Maladies: Psychoanalysis, Diaspora, and the Asian American Literary Imagination*, which interrogates the processes of subjectivity formation and positioning in contemporary Asian American literary discourse in light of recent developments in gender and race theories. He has written many reviews and short essays on multiethnic American literature.

SAUNDRA K. LIGGINS is an assistant professor of English at the State University of New York at Fredonia. She is also coordinator of the African American Studies and Multiethnic Studies programs. She teaches courses in nineteenth- and twentieth-century African American literature and gothic literature.

JEEHYUN LIM is a Ph.D. candidate in English at the University of Pennsylvania. Her interests center on U.S. ethnic literatures and postcolonialism. She is a contributing editor to *North Carolina Roots of African American Literature* (forthcoming).

ELIZABETH BLAKESLEY LINDSAY earned an M.L.S. and an M.A. in comparative literature at Indiana University. She is the head of library instruction and the liaison librarian for English and American literature at Washington State University.

ELLINE LIPKIN received her Ph.D. in creative writing and literature from the University of Houston in 2003. She has published both critical work about contemporary American poetry and her own creative writing. Presently a Beatrice Bain Postdoctoral Scholar at the University of California at Berkeley, she is researching the impact of the visual within contemporary American women's poetry.

CRAIG LOOMIS is an associate professor of English at the new American University of Kuwait in Kuwait City. Since the 1980s he has spent much of his time working and living in Malaysia, Japan, South Korea, and now Kuwait. Much of his short fiction has been published in such literary journals as *The Iowa Review*, *The Colorado Review*, *The Prague Revue*, and *The Maryland Review*.

DEVONA MALLORY is a Ph.D. candidate in English Studies at Illinois State University. Her concentrations are magical realism and women's literature.

BRANDE NICOLE MARTIN is completing her Master of Arts degree in English at Northern Illinois University. She has been a medical editor for many years and has published in the *Journal of the American Medical Association*. She has presented papers at the Allerton Articulation Conference and at the 2005 Computers and Composition Conference.

CHARLES D. MARTIN is an assistant professor at Central Missouri State University. He has published *The White African American Body* (2002). His current project focuses on the idea of the mummy in American culture.

HEATHER MARTIN is arts and humanities librarian at Mervyn H. Sterne Library, University of Alabama at Birmingham. She earned an M.A. in English and an M.L.I.S. from the University of South Carolina.

SHELLEY MARTIN is a Ph.D. fellow in literary and cultural studies at the University of Louisiana at Lafayette, where she is focusing on women's studies and postcolonial theory. Her essay on the Canadian poet Bronwen Wallace will appear in a collection titled *Feminist Mothers* (forthcoming), and she is working on a dissertation that analyzes self-help and women's literature at the end of the nineteenth and in the twentieth centuries.

VARGHESE MATHAI is a professor of English at Bethel University in St. Paul, Minnesota. Focusing on literature and spirituality as a specialty, he publishes and presents papers frequently on George Herbert, Gerard Manley Hopkins, and several African American authors. Mathai is a fellow of the MacLaurin Institute at the University of Minnesota, a Christian Studies center for learning and research in integrating a theistic worldview into the academic world.

ALLIA A. MATTA is an adjunct lecturer and a Ph.D. candidate in Afro-American Studies at the University of Massachusetts, Amherst. Previously, she was associate director of the Writing Center at Long Island University's Brooklyn Campus and taught English composition and literature. She has published poetry in *Down Town Brooklyn*, LIU's journal, and an essay in *Black Girls Who Eat Sushi: Life Stories*.

SANDRA MAYFIELD is a professor of English and director of Women's Studies at the University of Central Oklahoma in Edmond. One of the professors who founded the Women's Studies program at UCO, she regularly teaches courses titled "Southern Women Writers," "Introduction to Women's Studies," and "Women in Literature" and codeveloped the course "African American Women Writers." Her interests include women and globalization and the inclusion of women of color in literary critical theory. Most recently, she read a paper titled "Women and Terrorism" at the Women's Leadership Conference at St. Antony's College, Oxford.

JAMES MAYNARD has an M.A. in creative writing from Temple University and is currently a Ph.D. candidate in English at the State University of New York at Buffalo, where he is assisting in the editing of *The Collected Works of Robert Duncan*.

MEREDITH McCARROLL is a doctoral student in English at the University of Tennessee. Interested in critical pedagogy, she writes about the uses of literature to engage students and encourage activism. With a focus on American literature, she looks through the lens offered by critical race theory, gender, and cultural studies.

JOAN F. McCARTY is a professional stage manager and an artistic associate at Jomandi Productions in Atlanta. She is an assistant professor in the Department of Drama and Dance at Spelman College.

BARBARA McCASKILL is an associate professor of English at the University of Georgia and a 2004–2005 fellow at the Radcliffe Institute, Harvard University. With Caroline Gebhard, she has written *Post-Bellum–Pre-Harlem: Rethinking African American Literature and Culture, 1877–1919* (2005). She has also published an edition of *Running 1,000 Miles for Freedom: The Narrative of William and Ellen Craft*.

PELLOM McDANIELS III is a student in the Graduate Institute of the Liberal Arts at Emory University in Atlanta. He is completing a dissertation on the impact of emancipatory representations of African American masculinity on twentieth-century America. His works include "We're American Too: The Negro Leagues and the Philosophy of Resistance," in *Baseball and Philosophy* (2004).

GRACE McENTEE is a professor at Appalachian State University, where she teaches nineteenth-century American literature and African American literature. Her areas of interest include neo-slave narratives and the works of Octavia Butler and Barbara Neely.

CANDIE McKEE is a full-time faculty member at the University of Central Oklahoma. Her research focuses on intercultural communications and cultural studies.

ADAM McKIBLE is an associate professor of American and African American literature at John Jay College of Criminal Justice in New York City. His areas of interest include little magazines and modernism, the Harlem Renaissance, and racial pseudoscience of the 1920s. He oversaw the publication of Edward Christopher Williams's previously lost novel, *When Washington Was in Vogue* (2003).

LAURIE McMILLAN is a Ph.D. student at Duquesne University. Her dissertation, "Practice, Practice, Practice: Innovative Feminist Literary Criticism," analyzes the work of Alice Walker, Susan Howe, Rachel Blau DuPlessis, and bell hooks.

1990

DANA MEDORO is an associate professor of English at the University of Manitoba, where she specializes in American literature. She is author of *The Bleeding of America* (Greenwood, 2002).

MICHELLE MELLON is a freelance writer and editor. She is currently expanding the fictional novella she wrote for her master's degree in liberal studies degree from Georgetown University into a full-length novel examining race and politics in the United States. In addition, she is writing a collection of short stories.

CHRISTINA MESA holds a Ph.D. in modern thought and literature from Stanford University, where she specialized in nineteenth-century literature. She is currently revising her dissertation manuscript, "White Guise and Dark White Women: Purity and Miscegenation in Nineteenth-Century American Culture."

CHRISTOPHER METRESS is a professor of English at Samford University. His essays on American and British literature have appeared in *Studies in the Novel, Southern Quarterly,* and *African American Review.* He is the editor of *The Lynching of Emmett Till: A Documentary Narrative* (2002), and is currently at work on a study of White Southern writers and the Civil Rights Movement.

DARREN J. N. MIDDLETON is an associate professor of religion and literature at Texas Christian University, Fort Worth. He is the author/editor of three books, and his most recent publications include studies of the Ghanaian poet Afua Kuma, John Updike, and Mel Gibson's controversial movie *The Passion of the Christ.*

D. QUENTIN MILLER, an associate professor of English at Suffolk University, is the author of *John Updike and the Cold War: Drawing the Iron Curtain* (2001) and the editor of *Re-Viewing James Baldwin: Things Not Seen* (2000) and *Prose and Cons: New Essays on Contemporary U.S. Prison Literature* (2005). He is also an editor of *The Heath Anthology of American Literature* (concise edition and fifth edition) and the author of the composition textbook *The Generation of Ideas* (2005). He has published a number of reference entries on Baldwin and Toni Morrison, among other authors, as well as articles in journals such as *American Literature, English Language Notes,* and *Legacy: A Journal of American Women Writers.*

DeMOND S. MILLER, Ph.D., is an associate professor of sociology and director of the Liberal Arts and Sciences Institute at Rowan University in Glassboro, New Jersey. He has worked as an evaluator for alcohol and tobacco social norms projects and as principal investigator to facilitate research projects involving environmental issues and community satisfaction. His primary area of specialization is environmental sociology, with concentrations in qualitative and quantitative evaluation research methods, community development, and social impact assessment. Miller has published professional papers in *The Researcher*, *The Qualitative Report*, *Journal of Emotional Abuse*, and *Southeastern Sociological Review*.

R. BAXTER MILLER is a professor of English and director of African American Studies at the University of Georgia. A doctoral graduate of Brown University in 1974, he has written or edited seven books, the best-known being *Black American Literature and Humanism* (1981) and *The Art and Imagination of Langston Hughes* (1989; American Book Award, 1991). As executive editor of *The Langston Hughes Review*, he has written nearly a hundred works, including numerous chapters, research articles, reviews, and critical essays on African American poetics and critical methodologies.

ROBERT H. MILLER earned his Ph.D. in African American literature and history at Temple University, where he specialized in African American history. He has published nine children's books in a series titled *Reflections of a Black Cowboy*. Two books from this series won the American Book Sellers "Pick of the Lists" Award. Miller is an assistant professor in the Department of Religion at Temple University.

SARAH ANTOINETTE MILLER received her M.A. in English from the Ohio University and is studying for an M.Phil. in classics at the University of Cambridge. She presented a paper at the 2005 Northeast Modern Language Association annual conference. Her current research focuses on the reception of Roman authors, particularly Virgil and Catullus, in contemporary women's poetry.

DEONNE N. MINTO is a Ph.D. candidate at the University of Maryland, College Park. Her areas of interest include twentieth-century African American, Afro-Latino, and Caribbean literature. Her dissertation will focus on the literary works of late-twentieth-century Black women authors of the Americas, paying particular attention to how authors such as Simone Schwartz-Bart, Toni Morrison, and Argentina Chiriboga construct diaspora through their fiction. She has presented papers at domestic and international conferences, and she has published essays in *The Explicator* and in *Sargasso*.

KEITH B. MITCHELL is a professor of English at Penn State University, New Kensington. In 2003, he received his Ph.D. in comparative literature from the University of North Carolina at Chapel Hill. His main areas of scholarship are French and English West Indian literature, African American literature, and world literature.

BILL MOHR is a poet, scholar, teacher, and editor who lived in Los Angeles from 1968 to 1996, mainly working as a blueprint machine operator and typesetter. He edited two major anthologies of Los Angeles poets, *The Streets Inside* (1978) and *Poetry Loves Poetry* (1985), both published under his own imprint, Momentum Press. He was a visiting scholar at the Getty Research Institute in 1996.

KARA L. MOLLIS is a Ph.D. candidate in the Department of English at Duquesne University, where she has taught composition and American literature courses. She is currently completing her dissertation, which examines the influences of the nineteenth-century sentimental novelistic tradition on contemporary American fiction by women.

CLAY MORTON is a Ph.D. candidate in English at the University of Georgia. His dissertation applies recent research in orality-literacy studies to the works of Black and White writers of the American South in order to read them as products of a residually oral culture. He has presented papers at numerous conferences, including meetings of the Philological Association of the Carolinas and the William Gilmore Simms Society, and the annual international conference Digital Arts and Culture.

SHONDRIKA L. MOSS earned her Ph.D. in performance studies at Northwestern University, where she specialized in African American performance and literature. She plans to expand her dissertation into a book and to explore Zora Neale Hurston's contributions to performance theory. She is currently teaching at Clayton College and State University in Atlanta, Georgia.

JUDITH MULCAHY is a doctoral candidate in English at the City University of New York Graduate Center. She specializes in nineteenth-century and early-twentieth-century American and African American literatures, as well as U.S. political history in the nineteenth century.

KAREN MUNRO is the literature librarian at the University of Oregon. She holds an M.F.A. in creative writing from the Iowa Writers' Workshop, and a B.A. in English literature from McGill University, Montreal, Canada.

KEAT E. MURRAY is a doctoral candidate at Lehigh University, where he works with literature representing Ohio Valley populations in the late eighteenth and early nineteenth centuries. He has contributed to several publications with writings on American literature and culture.

The Rev. STEPHEN BUTLER MURRAY is college chaplain, director of the Intercultural Center, and lecturer in religion and environmental studies at Skidmore College in Saratoga Springs, New York.

EMILY McTIGHE MUSIL is completing her doctoral dissertation in the Department of History at the University of California, Los Angeles. She is writing a social and intellectual history of the twentieth-century Black Atlantic world, with a particular focus on transnational journals, political involvement, and the networks of Black Francophone women.

JUDITH MUSSER is an assistant professor of English and American Studies at La Salle University. She has published on African American women writers of the Harlem Renaissance, in particular Marita Bonner and Zora Neale Hurston.

MYCHEL J. NAMPHY lectures on, teaches, and writes about African American literature, culture, and politics, in such diverse venues as churches and mosques, police academies, drug treatment centers, Ivy League colleges, graduate schools, high schools, elementary schools, and prisons. His B.A. is from Columbia University, and he completed his Ph.D. in English and African American literature at Princeton. He is currently working on a manuscript titled "Malcolm's Mood Indigo: A Theodicy of Literary Contests," a study of Malcolm X as an aspect of contemporary history and a close analysis of Malcolm's collaboration with Alex Haley that produced *The Autobiography of Malcolm X*. After holding teaching positions at Princeton and at Rutgers universities, Namphy is currently an assistant professor of English at York College of the City University of New York, where he teaches courses on African American and Native American literature, art, and music.

JULIE NEFF-LIPPMAN is a member of the English Department at the University of Puget Sound. She also directs the Center for Writing and Learning.

EMMANUEL S. NELSON is a professor of English at the State University of New York at Cortland. The author of over fifty scholarly articles on international literatures in English, he has edited a dozen reference volumes that include *Contemporary African American Novelists* (Greenwood, 1999), *African American Autobiographers* (Greenwood, 2002), and the five-volume *Encyclopedia of Multiethnic American Literature* (Greenwood, 2005).

TAMIKO NIMURA is an assistant professor of English at the University of Puget Sound, specializing in contemporary, comparative multicultural American literatures. She is currently revising a book manuscript, "Different Dark Colors: Comparing African American and Asian American Literatures Through Coalition Politics."

KINOHI NISHIKAWA is a Ph.D. candidate in the Graduate Program in Literature at Duke University.

TIMOTHY K. NIXON is a doctoral candidate in the English Department at the George Washington University. He is currently finishing the dissertation phase of his program and is writing about twentieth-century queer writers in exile. Nixon holds an M.A. in English from the College of William and Mary, has presented papers on nineteenth- and twentieth-century American literature, has written several entries for literary encyclopedias, and has published scholarly articles on Walker Percy, Eudora Welty, and Kate Chopin.

BRIAN J. NORMAN is an assistant professor of ethnic American literatures in the Department of English and Philosophy at Idaho State University. His research focuses on American protest literature, James Baldwin, other artist-spokespersons, and twentieth-century American social movements. His recent publications include articles in *African American Review*, *MAWA Review*, and *Michigan Feminist Studies*.

BETTY W. NYANGONI is an education consultant, former teacher, associate professor, and administrator at the K–12 and university levels. She earned a Ph.D. in education administration from American University, where her minor was African/African American Studies. More than forty of her articles, essays, reviews, and research papers have been published.

AARON PERON OGLETREE received a J. D. degree from the University of Minnesota Law School. He also holds a Bachelor of Arts degree with honors in political science and international studies from Wayne State University.

'BIODUN J. OGUNDAYO, Ph.D., is an assistant professor of French and comparative literature at the University of Pittsburgh, Bradford campus. His translation of a work on Berber ethnology and matriarchy is forthcoming. He is currently editing a volume on cross-cultural expressions of spirituality.

DEBBIE CLARE OLSON is a lecturer in the English Department at Central Washington University, Ellensburg. She teaches English and film, and has an M.A. in English/film studies from Central Washington. She plans to pursue her doctorate in English/film at Oklahoma State University.

KATHY HAWTHORNE OLSON teaches in the English Department at East Tennessee State University.

TED OLSON holds the Ph.D. in English (1997) from the University of Mississippi. Presently associate professor at East Tennessee State University in Johnson City, he is the author of *Blue Ridge Folklife* (1998); the editor of *CrossRoads: A Southern Culture Annual* and of James Still's *From the Mountain, from the Valley: New and Collected Poems* (2001); coeditor of *The Bristol Sessions: Writings About the Big Bang of Country Music* (2005); and the music section editor and associate editor for *The Encyclopedia of Appalachia*.

KEREN OMRY earned her Ph.D. in English literature at the University of London, where she focused on the relationship between jazz and African American literature of the twentieth century. She has presented numerous conference papers on her area of specialization and is working on a number of articles for publication. In addition, she is developing ideas introduced in her doctoral dissertation into a book, and is writing on race, gender, and genre in science fiction, with particular focus on Octavia E. Butler.

ELIZABETH A. OSBORNE is a doctoral candidate at the University of Maryland, College Park. Her work focuses on American theater and the Federal Theatre Project, particularly with respect to the dialectic between individual theaters and their surrounding communities. Her paper "Yankee Consternation in the Deep South: Worshipping at the *Altars of Steel*," was presented at the Theatre Symposium Conference in 2004.

IYABO F. OSIAPEM is a Ph.D. candidate at the University of Georgia. Her research interests are in languages of the African diaspora and qualitative methodologies. She is writing her dissertation on Black English in Bermuda.

DAVID M. OWENS is an assistant professor of English at Valparaiso University in Indiana. Following a twenty-one-year career as an Army officer, he earned a Ph.D. from Purdue University and is writing a book on Ambrose Bierce's Civil War fiction.

NANCY M. PADRON is a fiction writer and poet living in Los Angeles. Her most recent story, "The Day Chano Died," was published in *Proverbs for the People* (2003).

LOUIS J. PARASCANDOLA is an associate professor of English at Long Island University, Brooklyn, where he teaches nineteenth-century English literature and literatures of the African diaspora. His publications include *Winds Can Wake Up the Dead: An Eric Walrond Reader* (1998) and *"Look for Me All Around You": Anglophone Caribbean Immigrants in the Harlem Renaissance* (2005).

JOSHUA PARKER is a Ph.D. candidate in Anglophone literature at the University of Paris–Denis Diderot. His work on American expatriate writing has been published in England, and his writings on museology have appeared in journals and in the popular press. He has been a lecturer in English and critical theory at the Sorbonne.

LAURA GRACE PATTILLO received her Ph.D. from Louisiana State University and is assistant professor of English at St. Joseph's University in Philadelphia.

JEFFREY B. PERRY is editor of *A Hubert Harrison Reader* (2001) and author of *Hubert Harrison* (2005). He is Treasurer of Local 300, National Postal Mail Handlers Union, and serves as the union's newspaper and Web page editor.

WINDY COUNSELL PETRIE received her Ph.D. from the University of Delaware and is an assistant professor of English at Colorado Christian University. She has published and presented papers on the narrative techniques and rhetorical strategies of early twentieth-century American women literary autobiographers, focusing on a diverse group of authors ranging from Zora Neale Hurston to Edith Wharton.

SAMANTHA PINTO is working on her dissertation in English, titled "Postcolonial Blues," at the University of California, Los Angeles. Her work focuses on gender and sexuality in the Black diaspora, music, and formal innovation.

LAURA PIROTT-QUINTERO earned her Ph.D. in comparative literature at Brown University, where she specialized in twentieth-century Latin American narrative. She has published articles on hybrid identities in writings by selected contemporary Latin American authors. She is assistant professor of Spanish at the College of Staten Island, City University of New York.

DaNEAN POUND is completing her master's thesis in the Department of English at Northwestern Louisiana State University, where she is writing on the ex-slave narratives of the Louisiana Writers' Project. She has presented papers at the annual conference of the Society for the Study of Southern Literature and the "Conflict in Southern Writing" conference.

STEPHEN ROGER POWERS won an Academy of American Poets Prize while a Ph.D. candidate in the creative writing program at the University of Wisconsin–Milwaukee, and he has published his Dolly Parton poems in journals and anthologies, including *Margie/The American Journal of Poetry* and *Red, White, and Blues: Poets on the Promise of America* (2004). While working on his doctorate, he taught literature, composition, and creative writing at UW–Milwaukee.

LUCA PRONO holds a Ph.D. in American Studies from the University of Nottingham, where he taught courses in American culture and film studies. He has published articles on American ethnic literatures, proletarian literature, Italian neorealism, and gay and lesbian studies.

PAMELA RALSTON received her doctorate in comparative literature and critical theory at the University of Washington. Her areas of expertise are nineteenth-century African American autobiography, White temperance and abolitionist literature, and American Ethnic Studies pedagogy. She teaches English and American ethnic and gender studies at Tacoma Community College.

LAURI RAMEY is an associate professor of English at California State University, Los Angeles. She is coeditor of *Black British Writing* (2004) and *Every Goodbye Ain't Gone* (forthcoming). Her essays on creative writing, contemporary poetry and poetics, African American literature, and Black British literature have appeared in numerous journals. Ramey was the first curator of the African American Poetry Archive, housed at Hampton University.

KELLI RANDALL received her B.A. in English from Emory University and her M.A. in English from Penn State University. She is a Ph.D. candidate in English at Emory University. Her dissertation is titled "Black Women Writers in the Age of Realism." Her areas of expertise are eighteenth- and nineteenth-century American and African American literature, with a particular focus on the Black Atlantic writers and "race" and realism.

WILMA JEAN EMANUEL RANDLE is a writer-photographer who divides her time between the United States and Africa. For three years she was the director of the African Women's Media Center in Dakar, Senegal. She previously was a business writer for the *Chicago Tribune* and other U.S. newspapers. She holds a master's degree in international journalism from the University of Southern California and an undergraduate degree in history and communication arts and sciences from Rosary College (now Dominican University) in River Forest, Illinois.

ANTHONY J. RATCLIFF is a doctoral student in Afro-American Studies at the University of Massachusetts, Amherst, where he teaches the course "Cultural History of Hip-Hop." His scholarly interests include Afro-American cultural and literary history, Pan-African artistic performance, and Afro-diasporic movements, specifically among African Americans and Afro-Latinos. Ratcliff has written articles on the NAACP and Sarah Webster Fabio, and a comparative analysis of Toni Morrison's *Beloved* and John Edgar Wideman's *The Cattle Killing*.

DEIRDRE RAY received her Ph.D. from Arizona State University in 1998 and is an assistant professor in the Department of Communications and Modern Languages at Cheyney University of Pennsylvania, where she teaches African American literature, film, and advanced composition; she is also the assistant director of the Cheyney University Frederick Douglass Institute and its Frederick Douglass Fellowship program. Her book *Sex Theories and the Shaping of Two Moderns: Hemingway and H.D.*, was published in 2002, and she is currently working on her second book.

SHARON D. RAYNOR is an assistant professor in the Department of English and Foreign Languages at Johnson C. Smith University in Charlotte, North Carolina. She previously taught in the English Department at East Carolina University in Greenville, North Carolina. She completed her doctorate in literature and criticism at Indiana University of Pennsylvania. Raynor's most recent publications are "The World of Female Knowing According to Georgia Douglass Johnson," in *College Language Association Journal* and "Breaking the Silence: The Unspoken Brotherhood of Vietnam Veterans," in *NC Crossroads*.

LINDSEY RENUARD is an adjunct instructor in English at the University of Central Oklahoma, Oklahoma State University–Oklahoma City, Rose State College, and Oklahoma City Community College. Her poetry has appeared in *Moon Reader*, *Windmill*, and *New Plains Review*.

LORI RICIGLIANO earned her M.L.I.S. at the University of Washington Information School, where she specialized in information resources, services, and collections. She is the associate director for Information and Access Services at Collins Library, University of Puget Sound, where she serves as the library liaison and subject bibliographer for the African American Studies program.

CHAUNCEY RIDLEY, a graduate of Michigan State University, teaches a wide range of courses at California State University, Sacramento. He has published on Toni Morrison.

MELISSA A. RIGNEY graduated from the University of Nebraska with a Ph.D. in contemporary lesbian literature and film. She has published articles in *Film Criticism* and *Quarterly Review of Film*. She is currently working on her first book, a series of interviews with lesbian writers from around the world.

KYSHA BROWN ROBINSON is a poet and publisher. She is a founding member of Nommo Literary Society, now the Neo Griot Workshop. With Kalamu ya Salaam she edited *Fertile Ground: Memories and Visions* (1996). Her poems have been published in anthologies and journals such as *Beyond the Frontier* (2002), *Drum Voices*, *Role Call* (2002), and *Bum Rush the Page* (2001).

RAQUEL RODRIGUEZ is the librarian for the African American Collection in Hillman Library at the University of Pittsburgh.

TRACEY S. ROSENBERG's Ph.D. dissertation, written at the University of Edinburgh, is the first full-length work on the late Victorian writer Mona Caird. Previously, Rosenberg studied at Berkeley and Oxford, and held a Fulbright Scholarship to Romania. Her postdoctoral work will focus on the three-volume novel and Victorian morality.

REBECKA RYCHELLE RUTLEDGE is an assistant professor of literature at the Miami University of Ohio, where she teaches courses in literary theory and criticism, African American literature, and composition. She is the author of "Metaphoric Black Bodies in the Hinterlands of Race; or, Towards Deciphering the Du Boisian Concept of Race and Nation in 'The Conservation of Races,'" which appears in *Race and Ethnicity: Across Time, Space, and Discipline* (2004). Rutledge is currently at work on a book about the use of metaphor in racist and nationalist ideologies. It is tentatively titled *Metaphors of Mediation: Race and Nation in African American Literature.*

JOSHUNDA SANDERS is a reporter for the *San Francisco Chronicle*. She is working on her first book.

REBECCA R. SAULSBURY is an assistant professor of English at Florida Southern College, where she teaches American literature, African American literature, and Women's Studies, and directs the minor in African American Studies. She has published articles on nineteenth-century American women writers.

CATHY J. SCHLUND-VIALS is currently a doctoral candidate in the American Studies program in the Department of English at the University of Massachusetts—Amherst. Her research interests include immigration narratives at the turn of the twentieth century and post-1965 ethnic studies and Asian American studies. She has presented at the annual Asian American Studies Conference and the American Studies Association Conference. Since 2000, she has served as the literary manager/program curator at New World Theater, a multicultural theater company at the University of Massachusetts.

JUDITH M. SCHMITT is an instructor in the Humanities Division of Macon State College, where she teaches freshman composition and literature survey courses. She has also worked with the Macon Department of Continuing Education, teaching business writing courses in the community and at local businesses.

A. B. CHRISTA SCHWARZ is an independent lecturer in American literature at Freie Universität in Berlin, Germany. She specializes in African American literature and particularly in the Harlem Renaissance. Her monograph *Gay Voices of the Harlem Renaissance* was published in 2003.

SHAWNTAYE M. SCOTT resides in Pittsburgh, Pennsylvania, and is currently a research assistant. She has been writing for the last seven years and has published some of her poems in e-zines.

GLORIA A. SHEARIN is an associate professor in the Department of Liberal Arts at Savannah State University in Savannah, Georgia, and coordinator of the first-year composition program. She earned her Ph.D. at the University of South Carolina, where she specialized in eighteenth- and nineteenth-century rhetoric and composition.

MARY LAMB SHELDEN is an assistant editor for *The Writings of Henry D. Thoreau* at Northern Illinois University, where she is also a visiting assistant professor in English. She earned her Ph.D. in nineteenth-century American literature from Northern Illinois in 2003. She plans to revise her dissertation, "Novel Habits for a New World," for publication as a book surveying the use of cross-dressing in nineteenth-century American novels. She is currently at work on an article concerning gender and genre fluidity in Louisa May Alcott's *Little Women*.

REGINALD SHEPHERD is the author of four books of poetry: *Otherhood* (2003), *Wrong* (1999), *Angel, Interrupted* (1996), and *Some Are Drowning* (1994), which won the 1993 Associated Writing Programs Award in Poetry. He is also the editor of *The Iowa Anthology of New American Poetries* (2004).

MELISSA SHIELDS is pursuing a doctoral degree in the Department of English at Harvard University, where she specializes in nineteenth-century British and American literature. She is writing her dissertation on the Victorian father as represented in conduct literature and memoirs. She has presented papers on eighteenth- and nineteenth-century literature at annual conferences in New York, Massachusetts, Virginia, Missouri, and New Jersey, and has contributed to reference works about ethnic American literature.

DORSÍA SMITH SILVA is a doctoral student in the Department of English at the University of Puerto Rico in Río Piedras. She is studying Caribbean literature with a particular focus on the texts of Jamaica Kincaid and V. S. Naipaul. She has presented papers at annual conferences, including those of the Eastern Caribbean Island Cultures and the College English Association.

J'LYN SIMONSON is completing her Ph.D. in the Department of English at the University of Denver, where she is focusing on literary and cultural theory and particularly on representations of the body in eighteenth- and nineteenth-century medical documents and encyclopedias.

JOSEPH T. SKERRETT, JR., is a professor of English at the University of Massachusetts, Amherst, where he has taught American literature since 1973. He has published on African American writers, including essays on Ralph Ellison, James Weldon Johnson, Paule Marshall, and Richard Wright, in *American Quarterly*, *The Massachusetts Review*, *Callaloo*, *Studies in Short Fiction*, and elsewhere; essays on Richard Wright, Ralph Ellison, and Toni Morrison have been published or reprinted in volumes edited by Harold Bloom, Kimberly Benston, Arnold Rampersad, Valerie Smith, and Marjorie Pryse and Hortense Spillers. From 1987 to 1999 he was the editor of *MELUS, the Journal of the Society for the Study of the Multi-Ethnic Literature of the United States.* With Amritjit Singh and Robert E. Hogan, he edited *Memory, Narrative and Identity: New Essays in Ethnic American Literatures* (1994) and *Memory and Cultural Politics: New Approaches to Ethnic American Literatures* (1996). His textbook-anthology *Literature, Race, and Ethnicity: Contesting American Identities* was published in 2002.

KAREN SLOAN holds a Ph.D. in English from Texas A&M University. She is an assistant professor in the Department of Literature and Languages at the University of Texas at Tyler.

MARY J. SLOAT has taught English at the high school level for nine years. She obtained a B.A. in English, an M.Ed. in secondary education, and a Ph.D. in secondary education, and is currently working on an M.A. in English. She has presented on literary authors, poets, and pop culture at educational conferences.

LAURA SMITH is a Ph.D. candidate in English at the University of New Hampshire, where she is studying nineteenth-century American women's literature and its concern for domestic space and reform. She has presented papers at the annual conferences of the American Literature Association and the Pacific Ancient and Modern Language Association.

STEPHEN M. STECK is completing his doctoral dissertation in the Department of English Studies at the University of Montreal, where he is writing on American prison narratives and existential psychoanalysis. He has contributed to publications such as *Men and Masculinities* and has presented papers at the annual conferences of the Western Society of Criminology, the Northeast Modern Language Association, and the Central New York Conference for Language and Literature. He currently is the Prison Writing chair for the Popular Culture Association and the American Culture Association.

DANIEL T. STEIN is completing his doctoral dissertation in the American Studies program at the Georg-August-Universität, Göttingen (Germany), where he is writing on the autobiographies of American jazz musicians, with a particular focus on intermediality and music-text relations. His essay on the novelist Lee Smith was published in the *European Journal of American Culture* (2003); his article "The Performance of Jazz Autobiography" appeared in a special issue of *Genre* (2004).

DOUGLAS STEWARD has taught American literature and critical theory at Truman State University and Franklin & Marshall College. His writing has appeared in *Callaloo, African American Review, Literature and Psychology, Academe,* and *ADE Bulletin.* He is currently assistant director of English Programs and the Association of Departments of English at the Modern Language Association in New York City.

CLAUDIA MATHERLY STOLZ is an associate professor of humanities and director of the Honors College at Urbana University. In addition to her published articles on the works of John Dos Passos, she has written and directed a one-act play; has written materials for the educators' Web sites for use in conjunction with two PBS series, *ExxonMobil Masterpiece Theatre's American Collection* and *The Rise and Fall of Jim Crow*; and has presented papers at the NCTE National Convention and the West Virginia University Colloquium on Literature and Film. She is working on a book that explores the depiction of business ethics in literature and film.

JUDITH STRATHEARN earned a B.S. in professional and technical communications from Rochester Institute of Technology in 1993. She graduated as an English major specializing in ethnic literature from Metropolitan State College of Denver in 2005. Her career goal is to become a professor of African American Literature and a writer.

ROBERT STRONG holds a Ph.D. in poetry from the University of Denver and currently teaches at Saint Lawrence University. His essay "The Uncooperative Primary Source" will appear in *Building New Bridges: Sources, Methods and Interdisciplinarity* (forthcoming).

ROBERT D. STURR is an associate professor of English at Kent State University, Stark campus. His field is early American literature, but he has also published articles on the contemporary Chinese American writer Ha Jin. His most recent publication is "Civil Unrest and the Rhetoric of the American Revolution: Depiction of Shays' Rebellion in New England Magazines of the 1780s," in *Periodical Literature in Eighteenth-Century America* (2005).

MARCY L. TANTER is an assistant professor of English at Tarleton State University. Her primary area of scholarship is American literature before 1900. Her current work-in-progress examines portrayals of enslaved women in American and Caribbean narratives.

BETTY TAYLOR-THOMPSON received a B.A. in English from Fisk University, an M.S.L.S. in library science from Atlanta University, and an M.A. and Ph.D. in English from Howard University. Since her matriculation at Fisk University in Nashville, Tennessee, Taylor-Thompson has had a special interest in African and African American literature. She has continued her interest through scholarly research in the genres of African and African American literature. This research has led to publications, several National

Endowment for the Humanities grants, a Fulbright Award, and multiple scholarly presentations at conferences. Taylor-Thompson's master's thesis and dissertation concerned the writing and literary career of Arna Bontemps. In October 2004 she was a humanities scholar involved in a collaborative project of the Louisiana Endowment for the Humanities and the Arna Bontemps Museum in Alexandria, Louisiana. She is currently a professor of English at Texas Southern University.

PAUL TAYYAR is an English lecturer at Golden West College in Huntington Beach, California, and is working on his Ph.D. in American literature at the University of California, Riverside. His article on Bruce Springsteen was included in the collection *Men and Masculinity: A Social and Cultural History*, and his poetry has been published in various journals.

JENNIFER TERRY is a lecturer in English at the University of Durham in England. She earned her Ph.D. at the University of Warwick, where she specialized in African American fiction, with a particular focus on the works of Toni Morrison.

RHONDDA R. THOMAS is a Ph.D. candidate at the University of Maryland in College Park. She is a predoctoral fellow at the David C. Driskell Center for the Study of the African Diaspora. Her research interests are in eighteenth- and nineteenth-century African American literature.

ONDRA K. THOMAS-KROUSE is a doctoral student in the Department of English at the University of Georgia, where she teaches courses in multicultural American literature. Her research interests are in the representations and functions of African dance practices in African American women's novels. She holds a graduate certificate in Women's Studies.

PAMELA FELDER THOMPSON is a doctoral candidate in the Graduate School of Education at the University of Pennsylvania in the Policy, Management, and Evaluation Division, specializing in higher education. Her research interests are in graduate education, diversity in higher education, and recruitment and retention. Upon graduation she plans to secure a tenure-track faculty position in educational leadership or higher education.

STELLA THOMPSON teaches composition and literature courses at Prairie View A&M University, where she is an assistant professor of English, coordinator of English online, and a Writing Center tutor. Her research interests include multimodal learning and narrative identity.

STACY TORIAN is a poet and freelance journalist. Her work has appeared in *Voices, Prometheus Black, Transformations, Real Change, San Diego Writer's Monthly, Stanford Black Arts Quarterly*, and other publications. She is the author of the poetry collection *Soul Speak* (2000) and a recipient of the Gender and Race Research Award from the Duke University Council on Women's Studies. Torian holds a Master of Arts in liberal studies and a graduate certificate in African and African American Studies from Duke University.

STEVEN C. TRACY is a professor of Afro-American literature at the University of Massachusetts, Amherst. He is author of *Langston Hughes and the Blues* (1988), *Going to Cincinnati: A History of the Blues in the Queen City* (1993), and *A Brush with the Blues* (1997); editor of *Write Me a Few of Your Lines: A Blues Reader* (1999), *A Historical Guide to Langston Hughes* (2004), *A Historical Guide to Ralph Ellison* (2004), *Langston Hughes, Works for Children and Young Adults: Biographies*, and the forthcoming *African American Writers of the Chicago Renaissance* volume in the *Dictionary of Literary Biography*; and general coeditor of the *Collected Works of Langston Hughes*. Author of numerous articles, chapters, interviews, reviews, and CD liner notes, Tracy is also a singer and harmonica player who has recorded with his own band.

eboni treco earned her bachelor's degree in psychology at the University of Puget Sound, where she performed in such plays as *Angels in America, Part One: Millennium Approaches, Big Love, Fefu and Her Friends*, and *for colored girls who have considered suicide/when the rainbow is enuf*. She plans to continue her education in the field of industrial/organizational psychology, and she currently works as a human resources administrator in Colorado.

ZOE TRODD is writing her Ph.D. dissertation in the American Civilization program at Harvard, where she teaches a course on American protest literature. She also has a first-class B.A. with honors in English literature from Cambridge University. She has published articles on photography, literature, and history, most recently in Henry Louis Gates's volume *In Search of Hannah Crafts* (2004). Her book *Meteor of War: The John Brown Story* (with John Stauffer), was published in 2004.

MARK TURSI is an instructor in creative writing, literature, and rhetoric at the University of Denver. He is also one of the founders and editors of the online literary magazine *Double Room: A Journal of Prose Poetry and Flash Fiction.*

AIMABLE TWAGILIMANA is a professor of English at the State University of New York, Buffalo State College. He teaches African American literature, world literature, postcolonial theory, literature of Continental Europe, and comparative literature. Some of his publications are *The Debris of Ham: Ethnicity, Regionalism, and the 1994 Rwandan Genocide* (2003), *Race and Gender in the Making of an African American Literary Tradition* (1997), *Hutu and Tutsi* (1998), *Teenage Refugees from Rwanda Speak Out* (1997), and *Manifold Annihilation: A Novel* (1996). He is currently working on two book manuscripts,

"A Historical Dictionary of Rwanda" and "The Poetics of Liberation in African American Literature."

GAIL L. UPCHURCH is an assistant professor in the Department of English and Speech at Olive-Harvey Community College in Chicago. She is pursuing an M.F.A. in creative writing at Chicago State University, where her emphasis is fiction. Among her interests are African diasporic literature, particularly Black female writing of the twentieth century, and feminist literary theory.

ROBIN GOLDMAN VANDER has a doctorate in comparative literature from the University of North Carolina at Chapel Hill and has held an appointment as a postdoctoral fellow in the Department of African and Afro-American Studies, also at UNC. Her primary research is centered on Black diaspora literary studies, with particular emphasis on performance studies and critical ethnography in African American and Caribbean literature.

ELIZABETE VASCONCELOS is an adjunct in the Department of English at the University of Georgia in Athens. She has presented at numerous conferences on the work of Afro-Caribbean and Afro-Brazilian writers, and is interested in the conceptual work of Toni Morrison—using the idea of (re)memory as a tool to uncover the possibilites of narrative in creating a space for women of color in the diaspora. She is at work on the *New Georgia Encyclopedia*, the first state encyclopedia conceived and published online, and hopes to developa similar online project focused on the diaspora.

MARTHA MODENA VERTREACE-DOODY, a National Endowment for the Arts fellow, is Distinguished Professor of English and poet-in-residence at Kennedy-King College, Chicago. Her most recent book is *Glacier Fire* (2004).

PAUL VON BLUM is a senior lecturer in African American Studies and communication studies at UCLA. He has published extensively about African American art. His most recent book is *Resistance, Dignity, and Pride: African American Art in Los Angeles* (2004).

MARK WADMAN is a Ph.D. candidate in English at York University in Toronto, Canada. His research interests include autobiography, postcolonial literature and theory, and race.

WENDY WAGNER teaches at Johnson and Wales University and wrote her dissertation on motherhood and racial identity in late-nineteenth- and early-twentieth-century African American women's writing. Her article on Amelia Johnson appeared in *The Black Press: New Literary and Historical Essays* (2001).

YVONNE WALKER is an adjunct instructor of creative writing and African American literature at Empire State College of the State University of New York. She is a poet, and under the nom de plume of Kenya Blue, she writes poetry and edits the journal *Opened Eyes Poetry and Prose*.

EARNEST M. WALLACE is completing his master's thesis in the Department of English at DePaul University, where he is writing on contemporary African-American fiction, with an emphasis on the Harlem Renaissance, the Black theater, and the works of Amiri Baraka. He is a Ronald McNair Scholar and a member of Sigma Tau Delta, an English honor society. Wallace enrolled at Howard University as a doctoral candidate in 2005.

MZENGA AGGREY WANYAMA is an assistant professor of English at St. Cloud State University in Minnesota. His areas of specialization are African American literary history and theory and modern African literature. Dr. Wanyama also teaches general introduction to literature and writing courses.

AMA S. WATTLEY is an assistant professor of English at Pace University in New York. She has written several essays on Black women's literature and African American drama. Her most recent essay, " 'Beating Unavailing Palms Against the Stone': Spatiality, Sexuality, Stereotyping, and the American Dream in Ann Petry's *The Street*," was published in *The Critical Response to Ann Petry* (2005).

LINDA S. WATTS is a professor of interdisciplinary arts and sciences at the University of Washington, Bothell. Watts is the author of *Rapture Untold: Gender, Mysticism, and the "Moment of Recognition" in Writings by Gertrude Stein* (1996) and *Gertrude Stein: A Study of the Short Fiction* (1999).

SEAN HARRINGTON WELLS is a Ph.D. candidate at Auburn University, where he studies American literature, with a particular focus on Southern literature. He has presented papers at the Society for the Study of Southern Literature annual conference.

DERA R. WILLIAMS is a member of the instructional support staff in the Peralta Community College District in Oakland, California. She has published creative nonfiction in anthologies, and most recently in *Peralta Press: A West Coast Journal*. Currently she is writing a coming-of-age novel set in the South.

JEFFREY R. WILLIAMS is an assistant professor of English at the University of Missouri. He is currently completing an intellectual biography that examines Benjamin Brawley's achievements as educator, historian, and literary critic.

KIMBERLEY BUSTER WILLIAMS is the Director of Admissions at the University of Michigan–Flint. She was previously senior assistant director of admissions at Old Dominion University. After receiving an undergraduate degree in English with emphasis in journalism from Old Dominion, Williams commenced her professional career in admissions at Johnson and Wales University in Norfolk, Virginia. She received a Master of Science in educational administration in 1999 from Old Dominion University in Norfolk, Virginia.

SARAH LYNSEY WILLIAMS has a master's degree in American and Canadian literature and is currently writing her doctoral dissertation at the University of Cardiff in South Wales. She is researching the representation of mental illness and physical disability in contemporary Welsh and Canadian literature, with particular focus on the works of Niall Griffiths and Patrick Jones.

SERETHA D. WILLIAMS is an associate professor of English at Augusta State University and the coordinator of the Minority Advising Program. She earned her Ph.D. in comparative literature at the University of Georgia, where she specialized in African diaspora and women's literatures. She is completing a manuscript on the role of mothers in the novels of Leon Forrest.

YVONNE C. WILLIAMS is the Hampton and Esther Boswell Distinguished University Professor of Black Studies at DePauw University in Greencastle, Indiana. She is also professor emerita of political science and Black Studies at the College of Wooster, Ohio, where she was the founding director of the Black Studies program and, subsequently, the Black Studies Department. She received her Ph.D. in political science from Case Western Reserve University. Her primary research interests have been in public policy implications of female criminality and currently are focused on Black women's role in education and politics.

ALICIA D. WILLIAMSON is a senior English major and Spanish minor at the University of Puget Sound. She is strongly interested in contemporary American literature and is active in the university's literary community as the events coordinator for the Writers' Guild, the organizer of the *Finnegans Wake* Reading Group, and as a member of the layout crew for *Crosscurrents*, the student arts magazine. She plans to pursue graduate studies in English.

SHARESE TERRELL WILLIS is pursuing a Ph.D. in English with a concentration in professional writing at the University of Memphis. Her research interests include the fiction of Gloria Naylor and the rhetoric of science.

IAN W. WILSON is completing his doctoral dissertation in the curriculum of comparative literature at the University of North Carolina at Chapel Hill, where he is writing on literary strategies in the contemporary novel of the undead, with a particular focus on the works of Marie Darrieussecq, John Edgar Wideman, and Elfriede Jelinek. He has presented papers at the annual conferences of the American Comparative Literature Association, the Southern Comparative Literature Association, and the Midwest Modern Language Association; has published an article on the bilingual text of Samuel Beckett's *Company/Compagnie*; and was a junior fellow at the International Research Center for Cultural Studies in Vienna, Austria in 2000–2001. He is visiting instructor in German and humanities and chair of German Studies at Centre College in Danville, Kentucky.

MARIANNE WILSON has been teaching music in the Woodbridge Township school district since 1979. She is writing her dissertation on Irving Berlin and George Gershwin. Wilson has published articles in the *Biographical Dictionary of Literary Influences: The Nineteenth Century, 1800–1914* and the *Biographical Dictionary of Literary Influences: The Twentieth Century, 1914–2000* (both published by Greenwood Press).

SULE GREGORY C. WILSON received his M.A. in history and a certificate in archives management from New York University. An archivist, folklorist, and musician, he prepared the Melville and Frances Herskovits Papers and the Larry Neal Papers for the Schomburg Center for Research in Black Culture at the New York Public Library. He has written three books on African American culture and numerous articles on music and culture, and has produced two music CDs. He teaches history and poetry at the Tempe Preparatory Academy in Tempe, Arizona.

DAVID WOODARD holds a Ph.D. in literature from Duke University. He is currently a lecturer at the Ontario School of Art & Design in Toronto, Canada.

LORETTA G. WOODARD is an associate professor of English at Marygrove College and the president of the African American Literature and Culture Society. She has published extensively on twentieth-century African American women writers.

DANA C. WRIGHT is a librarian and an assistant professor of library administration at the University of Illinois at Urbana–Champaign, where she coordinates outreach services to undergraduate students and assists in developing the Diversity Studies collections.

STEPHANIE M. YARBOUGH is a doctoral student in the Department of African American Studies at Temple University. She received a Master of Arts in African American Studies as well as a Bachelor of Arts in radio/television/film from the university. Her research focus is in Afrocentric film analysis and literary criticism. She has contributed entries to the *Encyclopedia of Black Studies* (2005).

VERONICA ADAMS YON, Ph.D., is an assistant professor of English at Florida Agricultural and Mechanical University, where she teaches courses in composition and American literature. She also directs the FAMU Writing Resource Center.

DAVID YOST is pursuing an M.A. in English at the University of Louisiana at Lafayette.

HARVEY YOUNG is an assistant professor of theater at Northwestern University. He has published articles on the playwright Suzan-Lori Parks and the performer Robbie MacCauley. He is currently revising the manuscript for his first book, which studies how contemporary African American artists record their personal, racialized experiences in their work.

CHRISTY J. ZINK is an assistant professor of writing at the George Washington University in Washington, D.C., where she teaches courses on cities and the imagination, with a particular focus on artists' connections to urban centers. Her published work centers on the intersections of place and character in contemporary fiction and on teaching critical research through models from creative nonfiction. She is the former director of PEN/Faulkner's Writers in Schools program, a national initiative to bring professional authors into urban public schools.